Japanese Foreign Policy Today

Japanese Foreign Policy Today
A Reader

Edited by Inoguchi Takashi and Purnendra Jain

palgrave

JAPANESE FOREIGN POLICY TODAY
Copyright © Inoguchi Takashi and Purnendra Jain, 2000.
All rights reserved. No part of this book may be used or reproduced in any manner whatsoever without written permission except in the case of brief quotations embodied in critical articles or reviews.

First published 2000 by
PALGRAVE™
175 Fifth Avenue, New York, N.Y. 10010 and
Houndmills, Basingstoke, Hampshire, England RG21 6XS.
Companies and representatives throughout the world.

PALGRAVE™ is the new global publishing imprint of St. Martin's Press LLC Scholarly and Reference Division and Palgrave Publishers Ltd (formerly Macmillan Press Ltd).

ISBN 0-312-22707-8 hardback

Library of Congress Cataloging-in-Publication Data

Japanese foreign policy today / edited by Inoguchi Takashi and Purnendra Jain.
    p. cm.
  Includes bibliographical references and index.
  ISBN 0-312-22707-8 (cloth)
    1. Japan—Foreign relations—1989- I. Inoguchi, Takashi. II. Jain, Purnendra.

  DS891.2 .J36 2000
  327.52—dc21   99-462010

A catalogue record for this book is available from the British Library.

Design by Westchester Book Composition

First edition: November 2000

10 9 8 7 6 5 4 3 2 1

Printed in the United States of America.

The transcription of personal names in this book follows country practice, with exceptions made for the name order adopted in publications originally published in English.

CONTENTS

About the Authors vii
Introduction: Beyond Karaoke Diplomacy? Inoguchi Takashi and *Pumendra Jain* xi

PART I: THE ACTORS

1. Domestic Politics and Foreign Policy, *Tanaka Akihiko* 3
2. Emerging Foreign Policy Actors: Subnational Governments and Nongovernmental Organizations, *Purnendra Jain* 18

PART II: THE ISSUES

3. Japan and International Organizations, *Edward Newman* 43
4. Globalization and Regionalization, *Moon Chung-in* and *Park Han-kyu* 65
5. Japanese Foreign Policy and Human Rights, *Ian Neary* 83
6. Japanese Environmental Foreign Policy, *Ohta Hiroshi* 96
7. Japanese Role in PKO and Humanitarian Assistance, *Caroline Rose* 122
8. Ironies of Japanese Defense and Disarmament Policy, *Tsuchiyama Jitsuo* 136
9. Official Development Assistance (ODA) As a Japanese Foreign Policy Tool, *Fukushima Akiko* 152

PART III: THE RELATIONSHIPS

10. U.S.-Japan Relations in the Post–Cold War Era: Ambiguous Adjustment to a Changing Strategic Environment, *Akaha Tsuneo* 177
11. Japan and the European Union, *Reinhard Drifte* 194
12. The Waiting Game: Japan-Russia Relations, *C.W. Braddick* 209

13. Japanese Foreign Policy Toward Northeast Asia, *Kamiya Matake*   226
14. Japanese Relations with Southeast Asia in an Era of Turbulence, *Lam Peng Er*   251
15. Japan and South Asia: Between Cooperation and Confrontation, *Purnendra Jain*   266
16. Japan and Australia, *Rikki Kersten*   283

Bibliography   297

Index   312

ABOUT THE AUTHORS

AKAHA Tsuneo is director of the Center for East Asian Studies at the Monteray Institute of International Studies, California. He received his Ph.D. in international relations from the University of Southern California. He is author of *Japan in Global Ocean Politics* (University of Hawaii Press and the Law of the Sea Institute, 1985), editor of *Politics and Economics in the Russian Far East: Changing Ties with Asia-Pacific* (Routledge, 1997), and *Politics and Economics in Northeast Asia: Nationalism and Regionalism in Contention* (St. Martin's Press, 1999); coeditor of *International Political Economy: A Reader* (Harper Collins, 1991), and *Japan in the Posthegemonic World* (Lynne Rienner, 1993). He is currently spearheading a multinational collaborative research project on international cooperation in establishing regional order Northeast Asia.

C. W. BRADDICK is Professor of International Relations at Musashi University, Tokyo. He is a graduate of the University of Wales and the University of London and received his D. Phil. from Oxford University for a thesis entitled: *Japan and the Sino-Soviet Alliance, 1950–1964* (forthcoming from St. Antony's/Macmillan). He is also the author of numerous articles on Japan's postwar foreign relations, including most recently, "In the Shadow of the Monolith: Japan's China Policy During the Early Cold War, 1949–1954," in Harold Fuess ed., *The Japanese Empire in East Asia and Its Postwar Legacy*, Munich: Iudicium Verlag, 1998, and "Distant Friends: Britain and Japan in the Age of Globalization, 1958–1995," in Ian Nish and Yoichi Kibata, eds., *The History of Anglo-Japanese Relations, 1600–2000: The Political Diplomatic Dimension*, Volume II 1931–2000. (Forthcoming from Tokyo: University of Tokyo Press [in Japanese] and Macmillan [in English], 1999).

Reinhard DRIFTE is Professor of Japanese Studies and in the Department of Politics at the University of Newcastle upon Tyne and former Director of the Newcastle East Asia Centre (1989–96). Author of many books, book chapters, and articles on issues of Japan's defense, security, foreign policy, and Japan-

Europe relations, his latest book is *Japan's Quest for a Permanent Security Council Seat: A Matter of Pride or Justice* (Macmillan/St. Antony's Series; St. Martin's Press, 2000; Japanese edition Iwanami Shoten, 2000).

FUKUSHIMA Akiko is a Senior Researcher at the National Institute for Research Advancement, a government-affiliated policy research organization based in Tokyo. She has served as a member of the Committee on International Economy of the Prime Minister's Office since 1995. She received her master's degree in international politics from Johns Hopkins University and her Ph.D. in international public policy from Osaka University. She is the author of *Japanese Foreign Policy: The Emerging Logic of Multilateralilsm* (London: Macmillan, 1999).

INOGUCHI Takashi is Professor of International Relations at the University of Tokyo. In addition to more than two dozen books in Japanese on international relations and politics, he is the author in English of *Japan's International Relations* (Pinter Publishers, 1991), *Japan's Foreign Policy in an Era of Global Change* (Pinter Publishers, 1993), and *Global Change: A Japanese Perspective* (Macmillan, forthcoming), has edited and co-edited, among others, the *Political Economy of Japan: The International Context* (Stanford University Press, 1989), *United States–Japan Relations and International Institutions After the Cold War* (Graduate School of International Relations and Pacific Studies, University of California, San Diego, 1995), *Northeast Asian Regional Security* (United Nations University Press, 1997), *The Changing Nature of Democracy* (United Nations University Press, 1999), *Cities and the Environment* (United Nations University Press, 1999), and *American Democracy Promotion* (Oxford: Oxford University Press, 2000).

Purnendra JAIN is Professor of Japanese Studies and Head of the Centre for Asian Studies at the University of Adelaide in Australia. He is the author of *Local Politics and Policymaking in Japan* (Commonwealth Publishers, 1989), coauthor of *Japan's Internationalisation at the Grassroots Level* (in Japanese, Habetosha, 1996), editor of *Distant Asian Neighbours: Japan and South Asia* (Sterling Publishers, 1996), and *Australasian Studies of Japan: Essays and Annotated Bibliography* (Central Queensland University Press, 1998), and co-editor of *Japanese Politics Today: Beyond Karaoke Democracy?* (Macmillan, 1997).

KAMIYA Matake is Associate Professor of International Relations at the National Defense Academy of Japan. He is also a member of the editorial board of the Australian Journal of International Affairs. He served as Distinguished Research Fellow at the Centre for Strategic Studies, New Zealans, during 1994–95. He is the author of over fifty articles, book chapters, and other works in Japanese and English in the areas of international relations and international security. His recent publications in English include: "The U.S.-Japan Alliance and Regional Security Cooperation: Toward a Double-layered Security System," in *Restructuring the U.S.-Japan Alliance,* Ralph Cossa, ed. (CSIS Press: 1997) and "Will Japan Go Nuclear? Myth and Reality" (*Asia-Pacific Review*, 1995).

About the Authors

Rikki KERSTEN obtained her Ph.D. in modern history from Oxford University. She is currently Senior Lecturer in Modern Japanese History, University of Sydney, Australia. She is the author of *Democracy in Postwar Japan: Maruyama Masao and the Search for Autonomy* (Routledge, 1996).

LAM Peng Er obtained his Ph.D. from Columbia University and is Research Fellow at the East Asian Institute, University of Singapore. He has published several research papers in such journals as *Japan Forum, Pacific Affairs,* and *Asian Survey.* He is the co-editor of *Managing Political Change in Singapore* (Routledge, 1997), *Lee's Lieutenants: Singapore's Old Guard* (Allen & Unwin, 1999), and author of *Green Politics in Japan* (Routledge, 1999).

MOON Chung-in is Professor of Political Science and Director of Yonsei University's Institute for Korean Unification Studies in Seoul. Author of many books, book chapters, and articles, both in English and in Korean, his latest books are: *Post–Cold War, Democratization and National Intelligence* (Yonsei University Press, 1996), *Democracy and the Korean Economy* (Hoover Institution Press, 1999), *Air Power Dynamics and Korean Security* (Yonsei University Press, 1999), and *Democratization and Globalization in Korea* (Yonsei University Press, 1999).

Ian NEARY has taught at Huddersfield and Newcastle Universities, and has been professor of government, Essex University, since 1989. He has been visiting professor at the Department of Law, Kyushu University on several occasions, most recently in the summer of 2000. He has published books and articles on human rights in Japan and East Asia and the pharmaceutical industry in the United Kingdom and Japan. His current projects include a textbook on Japanese politics and a biography of Matsumoto Jiichiro.

Edward NEWMAN is Academic Programme Associate at the Peace and Governance Programme of the United Nations University. He was educated at the University of Keele and the University of Kent, where he received a Ph.D. in international relations. He has taught at Shumei University, Japan (1996–98), the University of Kent (1993–95), and Aoyama Gakuin University (1999). His publications include *UN Secretary-General from the Cold War to the New Era* (Macmillan, 1998), *The Changing Nature of Democracy* (co-edited, United Nations University Press, 1998), *Cities and the Environment* (co-edited, UNU Press, 1999). He is currently working on a project on *The United Nations and Human Security: Mediating post-Westphalian International Relations,* which will be published by Macmillan.

OHTA Hiroshi obtained his MA in international affairs from the School of International Service, the American University, and his Ph.D. from the Department of Political Science of Columbia University. His doctoral dissertation is "Japan's Politics and Diplomacy of Climate Change" (Columbia University, 1995). He is currently Professor in the School of International Politics, Economics, and Business at Aoyama Gakuin University in Tokyo.

PARK Han-kyu is Assistant Professor of International Relations at Kyung Hee University in Seoul. He received his Ph.D. in political science from Columbia University. His research interests encompass such subjects as international security, nuclear nonproliferation, Japanese foreign policy, and the Japan–South Korean Relationship. His recent articles include: "Between Caution and Cooperation: The ROK–Japan Security Relationship in the Post–Cold War Period (1998), "Post–Cold War Era and Nuclear Nonproliferation in East Asia (1998), and "Emerging Patterns of Force Structure in East Asia and the Implications for South Korea" (1999).

Caroline ROSE is lecturer in Japanese studies in the Department of East Asian Studies at the University of Leeds. Her book *Interpreting History in Sino-Japanese Relations* was published by Routledge in 1998. She is currently researching issues in contemporary Sino-Japanese relations and the rise of nationalism in China and Japan in the 1980s and 1990s.

TANAKA Akihiko obtained his Ph.D. from MIT in Political Science and is now Professor of International Relations at the University of Tokyo. He has authored many books in Japanese and has contributed numerous book chapters and articles in English. His latest works include *Atarashii chusei* [A New Medieval Age] (Nihon Keizai Shinbunsha, 1996) and *Anzen hosho* [National Security] (Yomiuri Shinbunsha, 1997).

TSUCHIYAMA Jitsuo is Professor of Security Studies and International Politics in the School of International Politics, Economics, and Business at Aoyama Gakuin University, Tokyo. He holds a Ph.D. from the University of Maryland. His latest publications include *Reisengo no Nichi-Bei kankei* [U.S.-Japan Relations After the Cold War] (co-authored, NTT Press, 1997), *Nichi-Bei domei: Q ando A 100* [U.S.-Japan Alliance: 100 Questions and Answers] (co-edited, Aki Shobo, 1998), and *Gurobaru gabanansu* [Global Governance] (co-edited, University of Tokyo Press, forthcoming).

INTRODUCTION

Beyond Karaoke Diplomacy?

Inoguchi Takashi and Purnendra Jain

In Japan, as elsewhere, the constant rub between domestic and international politics prefigures the landscape in which national foreign policy is planned and played out. In the chapters that follow, we survey this landscape to broaden understanding of Japan's foreign policy at the approach of a new millennium. We find that internationally and domestically, this landscape has been subject to significant change in the past decade. This presents a policy picture that is rather different from those of earlier years, with new actors, interests, imperatives, strategies, and technologies inextricably shaping the policy scene. At the start of a new millennium, Japan confronts demanding challenges as an important player—a leader and a follower—in a global environment whose norms of international diplomacy are transforming swiftly. The nation's foreign policy cannot but respond.

Internationally, the powerful, ubiquitous commercial forces that many recognize as "globalization" are eroding the legitimacy of national borders and the ability of national governments to regulate international flows. The end of the Cold War sees new alliances and cleavages still forming, as international and local power plays continue in its wake almost a decade on. Domestically, the capacity of national bureaucrats to maintain their traditional hold over policy is also weakening. The domestic actors, the policy tools, and the overriding goal of national economic development that had been the steady staples of Japan's postwar foreign policy for roughly four decades no longer have their earlier predictive capabilities. New international actors, new policy instruments, and more comprehensive strategic goals now also take their place on the policy landscape. The scope of policy interest has been forced out beyond national economic well-being and security to embrace global and other strategic concerns that we can expect to invoke the powerful national actor that Japan is today.

For all the change, however, there are still constants in Japanese foreign policy. Some key policy pillars have held their place as defining features: powerful domestic actors, Japan's principal international alliance with the United States, the compelling economic imperative to sustain essential commercial relations, and a "peace" constitution that severely constrains Japan's overseas military engagement. Inevitably, recurrent throughout the chapters of this book is discussion of all four of these features, and particularly of the two most influential of these policy determinants. One is the preeminence of the United States among all nations as Japan's principal ally, trade partner, and defender. The other is the preeminence of Japan's bureaucrats, particularly those in the foreign ministry, among all of Japan's domestic international actors who are involved in policy decision making. Thus, change and continuity are central to this foreign policy picture.

In this introduction to our volume on Japan's foreign policy at the start of a new millennium, we explain the central concerns of this book and our motivations for preparing it. We spell out the content, its separations (into three subheadings and 16 chapters) and the linkages between these chapters, highlighting areas of shared opinion between authors as well as their divergent assessments of this dynamic picture. Finally, we offer overall assessment of Japan's foreign policy on the basis of findings presented in these chapters.

Earlier Explanations

Ineluctably, Japan's foreign policy at the end of the twentieth century presents a picture that is rather different from those put forward by observers in earlier years, when the pace and nature of change were less portentous. Over time, Japanese observers have delivered mixed assessments of Japanese foreign policy. Three assessments have been offered by Japanese observers. The first notes the broadening landscape of Japanese foreign policy, both in its global aspirations and its limitations.[1] The second marks the Asianization of Japan, suggesting a parting of the ways with the United States.[2] The third, as advanced and debated over by Hosokawa Morihiro, Yamazaki Taku, Hatoyama Yukio, and other lawmakers, calls for abrogation of the U.S.-Japan security treaty. It may be worth noting that Japanese scholarship on Japanese foreign policy offers a more global and regional outlook than its English-language counterpart, which tends to be written by Japan specialists and to focus on bilateral relations.

English-language scholarship from outside Japan has tended to focus on specific bilateral relationships (particularly with the United States) or relationships with important regions across Asia and elsewhere. Some studies have taken up specific policy areas such as aid, trade and security, or the politics of policy making. This report card, too, is mixed. Calder has described Japan's postwar foreign policy as "reactive"[3]—an influential political assessment presenting Japan as a nation where foreign pressure (*gaiatsu*) holds greater sway over national policy than domestic pressure (*naiatsu*) and political initiatives.[4] Some observers have found Japan lacking political leadership in specific and general matters of foreign policy.[5] Others have explored more comprehensively, finding signs of increasingly assertive policy orientation in many areas, to portray Japan as "a new kind of superpower."[6]

Purposes and Motivations of This Book

This book seeks to present a comprehensive picture of Japan's foreign policy that draws on, and where necessary critiques, earlier assessments, and expands analysis with attention to policy developments particularly through the 1990s. Overall it seeks to discuss the who, what, how, and why of these developments. We have aimed to set out key policy issues and identify and explain relationships (and disparities) between them. We have asked individual authors to survey recent developments in specific areas of the policy landscape, indicating both the pushes and pulls on policy. As well as issues, we include analysis of specific regional and bilateral relationships that we recognize as essential for a comprehensive picture of the policy landscape. The insights offered here also include constructive assessment of where Japan's international relations are headed in the first decade of the next millennium.

The book was conceived as a companion volume to our 1997 collected work, *Japanese Politics Today: Beyond Karaoke Democracy?*, which surveyed recent developments on the domestic political landscape. We decided to prepare this companion volume on foreign policy recognizing the absence of a comprehensive work in the English language that offers wide-ranging perspective on the most important concerns of Japan's foreign policy, particularly the actors, issues, and relationships around which policy is built. We recognize that individual authors have individual perspectives that are shaped by their personal and professional experiences as well as their ideological persuasion. The contributors to this volume come from countries across the Pacific and the Atlantic. We believe their wide-ranging perspectives and specialized insights into Japan's foreign engagements make it richly informative.

Arrangement of Chapters

The chapters in this volume are organized around three themes: actors, issues, and relationships. The first two chapters look respectively at the domestic politics of the principal policy actors in Japan (Tanaka), and at two new types of actors emerging on this scene, subnational governments and nongovernmental organizations (Jain). We then shift our spotlight to the broad issues that are at the forefront of Japan's foreign policy today, most of which have come into this position only in the course of the 1990s. Here we consider Japan's expanding role in international institutions (Newman), in the propelling trends of globalization and (Moon and Park), in the controversial issues of international human rights (Neary), protecting the global environment (Ohta), and peacekeeping and humanitarian assistance (Rose). From these newer areas of policy we turn to two of the major long-standing policy concerns, looking at defense and disarmament (Tsuchiyama) and Japan's burgeoning Official Development Assistance (ODA) (Fukushima).

The final theme addressed in this collection is relationships, focusing on the most important bilateral and regional relationships that Japan is careful to maintain. We begin with the relationship with the United States (Akaha), since this is still the most important of all Japan's bilateral relationships. Not deliberately to privilege Western nations but to continue consistent treatment of Western partners, the next chapters treat relationships with the European Union (Drifte) and Russia (Braddick). We then turn to Japan's relations inside Asia—with East Asia (Kamiya), Southeast Asia (Lam), and South Asia (Purnendra Jain), and finally with its ally at the southern edge of the Pacific, Australia (Kersten).

Overall Assessment: Japan's Foreign Policy at the Turn of the Millennium

It is useful here to make some overall observations on policy development on the basis of this strong, comprehensive collection of chapters, especially given the breadth of expertise and perspective provided by our diverse collection of authors.

Overall, a mixed picture emerges. In some policy areas such as ODA, humanitarian assistance, and global environmental policy, Japan has demonstrated innovation, political leadership, and the genuine desire to assist regional and international communities. In other areas of policy, however, planners appear to remain bogged down in Cold War thinking that immobilizes policy, such as seen in relation to the disputed sovereignty of the "northern territories" currently occupied by Russia. In other areas such as involvement in international peacekeeping operations and defense and disarmament, only incremental change has been effected.

Of the changes sweeping Japan's foreign policy landscape in the past decade, the end of the Cold War at the start of the decade had a profound impact on Japan's international relations. Historical benchmark that it was, rendering many of the international strategic structures of the Cold War era no longer strategically meaningful, it did little to alter Japan's regional security concerns, for East Asia remained volatile through the 1990s, as noted below. More significantly for Japan, the end of the Cold War propelled its principal ally, the United States, into preeminence as the sole superpower; that assertive weight inevitably affects Japan's most important bilateral relationship. This power dimension has considerable policy implications for Japan in the global arena, both as a would-be independent actor and as a U.S. ally in an East Asian context sensitive about U.S. interference. Within the region, and of far greater strategic significance to Japan, China's economic resurgence is altering the power balance across the Asian–Pacific region and beyond, and the expanded military capacities of regional wild-card neighbor North Korea add extra spark to the regional picture. The region is now at least as volatile as during the Cold War—perhaps more so—and there are no effective regional institutions that could be compared with Europe's NATO to manage Northeast Asian conflict resolution.

In the post–Cold War period, as the world's second largest economy and with great economic clout internationally, Japan has been urged to play a more constructive role in international and regional affairs. Japanese leaders have sought these moves as well, to some extent. The United States in particular has pressured Japan to share the burden of global governance at least through practical contributions, but clearly this does not constitute in any way an invitation to Japan for shared leadership with the United States. The chapters in the second section of this book that explore key policy issues demonstrate how Japan has responded with more active involvement in a range of global and regional issues, through means other than the earlier financial contributions that were criticized outside Japan as "checkbook diplomacy." Yet despite these initiatives, we recognize that overall, Japan's foreign policy directions are still overshadowed by its relationship with its most important commercial partner and security ally, the United States, on whom nuclear-free Japan depends for protection under the American nuclear umbrella.

Several chapters in this volume reveal how, on a range of issues, the United States has lobbied or coerced Japan to toe its policy line. In most cases, for whatever mix of pragmatic reasons, Japan has complied. A noteworthy exception when Japan said "No" to the United States was in response to the war in the Middle East in the mid-1970s, when Japan did not follow the U.S. lead in siding with Israel. Even so, it is a constant in their bilateral relationship that the United States at times puts forward major policy agendas with which Japan complies, as exemplified in Japan's huge financial "contribution" to the cost of the 1991 Gulf War, and more recently in the late 1990s with its tacit approval of the policy position of the United States and NATO forces in Serbia.

We have dwelt on this issue of Japan's policy compliance with U.S. directives for two reasons. First, it is central to explaining much of Japan's foreign policy behavior. Second, it leads to the concept presented in the title of this chapter: karaoke diplomacy.[7] Karaoke (literally meaning "empty orchestra") is a music system first devised in Japan before spreading beyond its shores to become a virtually global form of entertainment. Here a singer chooses a song from a set menu and sings along with lyrics shown on the screen and accompaniment provided by the equipment. The choice of songs is limited and the singer can vary the performance only through choice of specific songs and manner of delivery. So while the person singing at the microphone might change, the songs from which to choose and the background served up by the karaoke are both clearly circumscribed. What is the parallel here with Japan's foreign policy?

It could be argued that Japan's choice of foreign policy directions is also circumscribed in a "set menu" of alternatives provided by the United States. Japan has very little room to choose from options other than those offered by Washington on its foreign policy menu. Depending on circumstances, Japan may have some limited leeway in deciding who, when, where, what, or how it will engage internationally. But the essential choices are often predetermined by Washington with little scope for initiative, or innovation, from Tokyo. This portrayal highlights the degree of Japan's compliance with, and dependence on, the U.S. lead. As with karaoke, the background music (the U.S. policy line) remains the same and the choice of songs (policy options) is predetermined; the only scope for singer input is the style of delivery (policy implementation).

Still, the beauty of karaoke is that the choice of songs can be incrementally increased to suit one's convenience. One can boast of a choice of as many as

6,000 songs in a number of languages in a full-scale karaoke set. In a similar sense, karaoke diplomacy need not necessarily be considered a straitjacket. The style of delivery can change over time, as the changing environment compels one to do. This is another thrust of the present volume: just as karaoke is adaptive and can be gradually enriched, depending on the demands of the singers-cum-audience, karaoke diplomacy harbors a dimension of the adaptive and mutational.

As we see in this volume, within the broad parameters set by this U.S. "karaoke" menu, Japan has taken multiple new initiatives in recent years. These are concentrated especially in official development assistance (ODA), environmental management, and through personnel and monetary contributions to regional and international institutions. New actors (local governments and NGOs, for example) have been drawn onto the foreign policy landscape as their interests reach beyond Japan's national borders. Japan has also taken a tougher stance on some bilateral matters than its key partners, including the United States (e.g., it has maintained strict economic sanctions on both India and Pakistan since both conducted nuclear tests in May 1998). However much these actions may appear to indicate Japan's initiative, policy maturity, and diplomatic independence, all have nevertheless taken place within the broad scope of the core U.S.-Japan bilateral framework.

Where Japan's policy actions move beyond this framework, U.S.-initiated pressure is brought to bear until Japanese leaders acquiesce and policy is appropriately compromised (or abandoned). A recent case demonstrates this well. In the wake of the Asian currency crisis in 1997, the Japanese government presented a proposal to establish an Asian Monetary Fund (AMF). Because this Japanese initiative was perceived by U.S. interests as a major challenge to U.S. hegemony in the region and likely to undermine the status of the International Monetary Fund, a postwar U.S. government creation, the proposal was scotched in its early stages under U.S. pressure, without serious regard for the remedial potential of an AMF.[8]

The karaoke analogy can be drawn in yet another context, namely, domestic policy. Japanese bureaucrats retain a strong hold in determining national and foreign policy, largely at the hands of the foreign ministry. In fact, many in Japan recognize a bifurcation of power in which bureaucrats shape public policy in Kasumigaseki (the political heartland of inner Tokyo where most government ministries are located) while politicians protect their electorate's interests inside the district, which is usually geographically distant from this political inner sanctum. In the 1990s, politicians were taking a stronger hand in shaping public policy, as we see in these pages, but it is still largely the bureaucrats who put forward their menu of legislation from which politicians will choose and then attempt passage through the Diet. Because this is a distinctive feature of Japan's political system, the title of our companion volume on domestic politics similarly questions Japan's reach beyond "karaoke democracy." Foreign policy is especially suited to the karaoke menu style of Japanese bureaucrats, since politicians who are concerned with cultivating votes in their electorate are primarily concerned with pork barrel and social policy issues and have much less interest in foreign policy. This means they are more susceptible to the legislative "karaoke" menu offered by bureaucrats in foreign policy than for most other public policy areas.

Even so, inside Japan, the players in Japan's political system are diversifying and the capacity of any of them to maintain rigid sway over national policy is weakening. Legislative initiatives come much more from Diet members these days than from bureaucrats. Interaction between Diet members and bureaucrats prior to drafting of bills for legislation appear to enhance the chances of success in getting it passed. Such interaction was a feature of three major items of legislation in 1998-99 (the economic stimulus package, the administrative and fiscal reform package, and the defense cooperation guidelines legislation). The Democratic Party, currently the largest opposition party, was able to draft an original bill quite forcefully; Prime Minister Hashimoto Ryutaro and the Diet members of the Liberal Democratic Party (LDP) worked tenaciously to draft the sweeping administrative reform package; the Liberal Party, another smaller opposition force, gave the defense cooperation guidelines legislation a strong push along with some revisions to the original bill. This is not just a move toward decentralization of power away from the central government and the national bureaucrats; concomitantly the system of political parties remains in flux after the once dominant LDP briefly lost its mandate over the national government, and lasting alliances are yet to be proven. International affairs play into, and are sometimes pulled into, this domestic political fluidity. This is testimony to the thesis presented in this volume that karaoke diplomacy can be a self-transforming, adaptive diplomacy in a changing environment. As we see in the following chapters, foreign policy is usually the product of compromise between competing domestic and international interests.

Moves Toward Greater Policy Independence

For several decades there have been moves by some domestic forces, especially among right-of-center politicians within the LDP, to have Japan take a more assertive, independent policy line rather than constantly buckling to cooption and coercion by powerful U.S. interests. Even those who still prefer to maintain the alliance with the United States have advocated a stronger role for the Japanese military in international affairs.

Prime Minister Nakasone Yasuhiro's call in the mid-1980s to change Japan from a "peace-oriented country" (*heiwa kokka*) to an "ordinary nation" (*zairaigata kokka*) underscored the idea of a greater role for Japan's Self-Defense Force, reduced dependence on the United States for national security, and by implication, revision of the Japanese Constitution that currently forbids this possibility. The early 1990s notion, advocated by powerful political string-puller Ozawa Ichiro, of making Japan a "normal country" (*futsu no kuni*), is also embedded in the idea of a more independent foreign policy for Japan, through a larger role for the Japanese military. Both aspirations, for Japan to become an "ordinary nation" and a "normal country," also suggest understandings that Japan's present position in international life is somehow "abnormal" and therefore "unsettling" in a changing environment.

Some right-wing nationalists and others have been vocal in supporting a more independent foreign policy for Japan, as these examples suggest. Nevertheless, they are a small minority. Most mainstream politicians and officials in the foreign ministry and the Defense Agency still see the U.S.-Japan security treaty as the cornerstone of Japan's foreign policy. One could argue that passage of the new Defense Guidelines in 1999 has reinforced the security treaty.[9] Debate as to how Japan might achieve balance in political as well as economic roles in the global arena is well and truly on in Japan.[10] But apart from the above examples, there is very little debate about freeing Japan from the United States or from the bureaucrats who together generally hold sway over it.

Conflicting Tugs on Japan's Foreign Policy

The discussions above and in the 16 chapters that follow point to how Japan's foreign policy is caught at times between virtually antithetical tugs. We see a quest for independence to act as a nation on the international stage free of U.S. intervention in policy. Yet as we have also seen, Japan's national security arrangements lock Japan into this bilateral relationship and to accepting its benefits on terms dictated by powerful U.S. interests that erode Japan's capacity for policy autonomy. A second tug concerns the constraints of Japan's "peace" constitution, vis-à-vis a yearning by some policy makers for a more active overseas military engagement for Japanese forces. A third tug behind much of policy interaction is that of money. For much of the 1990s, Japan's economy has been in recession, which severely undermines Japan's capacity for expensive "international contributions" through ODA and programs that involve large and direct injection of funds. A final tug that is worthy of note here is that surrounding Japan's national identity. Japan is in some international forums (such as G7) a "Western" industrialized nation one moment and others (such as APEC or ASEAN regional forum meetings) an "Asian" regional nation the next. Mediating between these two standpoints is Japan's unavoidable task from now on.

Summary

Overall we see that Japan's foreign policy is complex, sometimes contradictory and certainly subject to considerable change beyond the year 2000. The pace of these changes is likely to maintain its momentum as technological developments enable new forms of communication, as globalization moves forward apace, and as ever more people are engaging in private international relationships without leaving their homes. Japan's foreign policy in the 1990s tells a story of expansion virtually across the board, and it is for this reason, especially given Japan's important position in regional and global affairs, that we have compiled the present collection of studies.

We are grateful to all the contributors for their cooperation in preparing work for this volume. Most presented draft papers at a workshop in Tokyo in October 1998, which was held especially for this project. We are grateful to Ishii Motofumi, head of policy planning of the Japanese Ministry of Foreign Affairs,

Introduction

for sharing with us his rich experiences in his luncheon speech on the first ~~~ of the workshop. We would like to thank Doi Sakiko for her assistance in holding the workshop and the staff of the Institute of Oriental Culture, University of Tokyo, for making available the conference venue and other facilities and providing backup support for the workshop.

Comments, suggestions, and feedback from the workshop have been useful to authors in revising for publication these papers piecing together a comprehensive picture of Japan's foreign policy landscape at the end of the twentieth century. We thank Ellen Dowling, Karen Wolny, Ruth Mannes, and the editorial staff of Palgrave, and Lynne Riggs and Takechi Manabu for their support at every stage of publishing this book.

October 1999

Notes

1. Takashi Inoguchi, *Japan's International Relations* (London: Pinter Publishers; Boulder: Westview Press, 1991); Akiko Fukushima, *Japanese Foreign Policy: The Emerging Logic of Multilateralism* (London: Macmillan, 1999).
2. Yoichi Funabashi, "Japan and the New World Order," *Foreign Affairs* 70:5 (1991): 58–74.
3. Kent Calder, "Japanese Foreign Economic Policy Formation: Explaining the Reactive State," *World Politics*, XL:4 (1988): 517–41.
4. Most who have advocated this view are scholars examining Japan's relations with the United States. See, for example, Leonard Schoppa, *Bargaining With Japan: What American Pressure Can and Cannot Do* (NY: Columbia University Press, 1997).
5. For example, Alan Rix, *Japan's Foreign Aid Challenge: Policy Reform and Aid Leadership* (London and NY: Routledge, 1993).
6. Craig C. Garby and Mary Brown Bullock, eds., *Japan: A New Kind of Superpower?* (Baltimore and London: The Johns Hopkins University Press, 1994).
7. Purnendra Jain would like to thank Chris Braddick for suggesting the term and for his input regarding the concept of karaoke diplomacy.
8. This example is explained in further detail in the chapters by Lam Peng Er and by Moon Chung-in and Park Han-kyu in this volume.
9. Both Tsuchiyama in his chapter on defense and disarmament and Akaha in his analysis of U.S.-Japan relations look at this issue in greater detail.
10. Tokyo's desire to be a permanent member of the United Nations Security Council is one such means. Others have advocated that Japan's true contribution lies in its role as a global civilian power. See Yoichi Funabashi, "Tokyo's Depression Diplomacy," *Foreign Affairs* 77:6 (1998): 35–36.

PART I
The Actors

CHAPTER 1

Domestic Politics and Foreign Policy

Tanaka Akihiko

As in many other countries, so also in Japan domestic politics provides an important context within which foreign policy is formulated. In many respects, constraints imposed by domestic politics on foreign policy can be stronger in Japan than in many other countries. In recollecting the process involved in the normalization of relations with China, the late Prime Minister Tanaka Kakuei once said, "Issues of Japan-China relations have been domestic issues rather than diplomatic issues."[1] Some of the critical foreign policy areas such as Sino-Japanese relations have long been dominant themes of maneuvering among domestic actors in the Diet, in the interagency bureaucracy, and in the media. In these cases, changes in the international environment can affect Japan's foreign policy via the complex intervening mechanism of domestic politics. Foreign policy issues that have an immediate impact on domestic politics include the U.S.-Japan alliance, policy toward the Korean Peninsula, and trade liberalization, especially of agricultural products.

Domestic politics also offers critical clues to the reactive, rather than proactive, nature of Japan's foreign policy. Why Japan tends to act only after international changes have occurred and seems hesitant to take the initiative cannot be understood without a proper examination of the domestic Japanese setting. While the conventional view that Japan can act only under heavy "external pressure" (*gaiatsu*) is misleading, it is nevertheless the case that *gaiatsu* does sometimes play a critical role in bringing about Japanese foreign policy initiatives. But since *gaiatsu* does not always work, it is necessary to examine domestic conditions, if only to understand the efficacy of external pressures.[2]

The following does not treat Japanese domestic politics as a whole; for that purpose, the reader should consult introductory texts on Japanese politics.[3] Instead, this chapter focuses on the characteristics of those domestic actors who affect foreign policy in important ways, so that the constraints of their actions and the dynamics of their interaction may be understood.[4]

Prime Ministers[5]

The prime minister is the head of Japan's government. There is no question about his importance in the areas of foreign and domestic policy, but he is not as independent as the U.S. president. As the Japanese Constitution stipulates, "Executive power shall be vested in the Cabinet," not in the prime minister. Contrast this with the U.S. Constitution, which says, "The executive power shall be vested in the President of the United States." Thus, it is the Cabinet, not the prime minister, that is tasked to "conduct affairs of state," "manage foreign affairs," "conclude treaties," and perform other functions; "The Cabinet, in the exercise of executive power, shall be collectively responsible to the Diet." Because of this stipulation, the general legal interpretation indicates that the decisions of the Cabinet should be made on the basis of unanimity. Thus, if one Cabinet member does not agree, he or she could stop measures that the prime minister wants to adopt.[6]

According to the current Constitution, however, the prime minister is more powerful than his counterpart under the Meiji Constitution, for he has the power to appoint and dismiss the ministers of state who constitute the Cabinet. Theoretically, this makes the prime minister all-powerful, because anybody in the Cabinet who does not agree with his opinions can be dismissed. While unanimous Cabinet decisions can always be achieved legally as long as the prime minister is willing to dismiss those Cabinet members who disagree with him, the power to do so is not easy to apply.[7] First, the Constitution stipulates that the majority of Cabinet members should be selected from the Diet; in practice, almost all are Diet members. In the case of the Cabinet of Prime Minister Obuchi Keizo, established in early August 1998, of the 21 members of the Cabinet, all except Sakaiya Taichi, director general of the Economic Planning Agency, were either representatives or councilors. Moreover, even if they were dismissed as ministers of state, they retain their positions as representatives or councilors, yet their dismissal could have immediate political repercussions in the Diet, on which the Cabinet depends for the passage of various bills. They are not like U.S. Cabinet members, whom the president can appoint and dismiss on the basis of merit.

The prime minister could dismiss Cabinet members more easily if he were in practice, as he is in theory, the most powerful leader in the ruling party. But although there is nothing legal preventing him from assuming such power, Liberal Democratic Party (LDP) presidents have never achieved such power over individual Diet members. The support of the president, though useful, has never been crucial for the election campaigns of rank-and-file LDP Diet members. In Britain, for example, which has a parliamentary system, the British prime minister has more power over ruling party members of Parliament than has his Japanese counterpart.[8]

These limitations—which are even more significant in a coalition government—sometimes give the impression that the prime minister is not particularly important. The plight of Murayama Tomiichi is a case in point. A left-wing leader of the Social Democratic Party of Japan (SDPJ), he was forced to declare immediately after his most unexpected assumption of the prime minister's position in July 1994, that he considered the Self-Defense Forces (SDF) constitutional and strongly supported the maintenance of the U.S.-Japan security treaty. Surely, if a prime minister from the SDPJ—which had been insisting on the unconstitutionality of the SDF and had strongly opposed the U.S.-Japan security treaty, changes his position merely in order to keep his Cabinet, one cannot be blamed for believing that the role of prime minister is terribly limited.[9]

In addition to the legal and political constraints, the prime minister faces organizational constraints. The size of the support staff (179 in total) has long been regarded as small. The most important figure in his support staff is the chief Cabinet secretary, one of the Cabinet members mostly selected (under an LDP government) from the same faction as that to which the prime minister belongs. The chief Cabinet secretary is given the task of coordinating mainly domestic policies and politics between the government and the ruling and opposition parties. Some of the previous chief Cabinet secretaries, such as Gotoda Masaharu,[10] have, however, been influential in the area of foreign policy. There are three deputy chief Cabinet secretaries: one selected from among experienced career civil servants, and the other two from among fairly young and promising ruling party politicians. The post of deputy chief Cabinet secretary for administrative affairs is regarded as the highest-ranking position in the entire Japanese bureaucracy and often represents the continuity in government. For example, in the 1990s, during which time Japan had seven prime ministers, it had only two administrative deputy chief Cabinet secretaries: Ishihara Nobuo and Furukawa Teijiro. Ishihara served seven prime ministers as deputy chief Cabinet secretary from November 1987 to February 1995.[11] Like the chief Cabinet secretaries, deputy chief Cabinet secretaries for administrative affairs are essentially specialists in domestic affairs, most of them having been bureaucrats in the home affairs, labor, and health and welfare ministries, or in the National Police Agency—ministries and agencies that have developed from the prewar Naimusho (Ministry of Internal Affairs). But, as the most senior and experienced civil servant, the deputy chief Cabinet secretary for administrative affairs can be critical in coordinating policies related to the management of important international affairs such as the U.S.-Japan alliance.

The post of deputy chief Cabinet secretary for political affairs, selected from among members of the Diet, has traditionally been important for promising, fairly young politicians. The deputy chief Cabinet secretary for political affairs does not generally play an important role in foreign affairs; he is often expected to manage relations with the Diet in cooperation with the chief Cabinet secretary. Sometimes, a politician in this post may play an important coordinating role, as was the case with Ozawa Ichiro, who, as deputy chief Cabinet secretary for political affairs, managed trade disputes with the United States in 1988.[12] But Ozawa's case was considered exceptional. Recently, appointees to this post have been familiar with international affairs, and have acted as general advisors to the prime minister in matters related to international affairs; they include Yosano Kaoru and Nukaga Fukushiro in the Hashimoto Cabinet, and Suzuki Muneo in the Obuchi Cabinet. In the Obuchi administration, two deputy chief Cabinet secretaries were appointed and their statuses were raised, appointees having already served as ministers of state (as were Suzuki Muneo and Uesugi Mitsujiro).

In terms of day-to-day affairs, prime ministers are supported by political secretaries—who are in charge of their activities as politicians, that is, the management of their contacts with other politicians and their constituencies—and four policy-related secretaries seconded from the four important ministries: finance, international trade and industry, National Police Agency, and foreign affairs. The secretaries are generally bureaucrats between the rank of division head (*kacho*) and deputy bureau director-general (*shingikan*). Prime Minister Hashimoto Ryutaro appointed a political secretary seconded from MITI, Eda Kenji, who acted more as an immediate policy adviser to Hashimoto than as an intermediary with other politicians. Prime Minister Obuchi appointed Furukawa Toshitaka, his long-term Diet member secretary, as his political secretary.[13] In 1996, when it was decided to create up to three posts of advisor to the prime minister, Okamoto Yukio, a prominent diplomat-turned-consultant, was appointed and specially tasked with dealing with the Okinawa military base issues.

The Cabinet secretariat (*naikaku kanbo*) is the organization that supports prime ministers' general activities. In 1986, as a result of criticism that the Cabinet secretariat is weak in terms of coordinating policies—especially foreign and security policies—new offices were created: the Councilor's Office for External Affairs (Gaisei Shingi Shitsu) and Office of Security Affairs (Anzen Hosho Shitsu). The head of the former has always been selected from among senior Ministry of Foreign Affairs (MOFA) officials, roughly of the rank of bureau director-general; the latter has been selected from the Defense Agency, and is of about the same rank as the former. The Councilor's Office for External Affairs has often been tasked to carry out foreign policy-related measures that involve other ministries, such as issues related to the "comfort women," Okinawa bases, ODA, and economic friction arising from government procurement. The Office of Security Affairs is the secretariat of the Security Council, which makes basic decisions on Japan's security policy such as the revision of the National Defense Program Outline and the Guidelines for U.S.-Japan Defense Cooperation. In addition to the function of secretariat of the Security Council, the Office of Security Affairs—now called the Office of Security Affairs and Crisis Management (Naikaku Anzen Hosho Kiki Kanri Shitsu) is charged with fulfilling crisis-management functions under the leadership of the Cabinet Crisis Management Officer (Naikaku Kiki Kanrikan), a post created after the Peru hostage crisis.[14] The Cabinet Intelligence and Investigation Office has existed since 1952, under various names. It is obligated to provide prime ministers with information, and its head is usually selected from among senior police officials. A Cabinet Information Integration Center was created within the office in 1996, mainly to facilitate information collection at times of crisis. The Councilor's Office for External Affairs is essentially a MOFA branch in the Cabinet, and the Office of Security Affairs is a Defense Agency branch there. In this sense, it is doubtful that prime ministers utilize these offices for their own policy initiatives and coordination independent of the respective ministries.

Despite these constraints, the prime minister is the single most important player in the game that is Japan's domestic politics, and particularly in the games of complex domestic/foreign policy interaction. First, there are no political actors other than the prime minister who can mobilize the resources of multiple ministries for common objectives. To the extent that a foreign policy item requires the involvement of various ministries, the prime minister's leadership is essential. Second, when there is opposition or reluctance on the part of important ministries and agencies, the prime minister is the only person who can make a decision. Thus, for instance, Prime Minister Nakasone Yasuhiro decided to increase Japan's defense budget, despite the reluctance of the finance ministry. According to Nakasone's diary on 30 December 1982, "The defense budget was troubled. I ordered Mr. Yamaguchi, director general of the Budget Bureau, to make a 6.5 percent increase. He showed reluctance but I ordered a revision of [their plan]. He looked stiff and pale but I pushed him."[15] Third, in a negative fashion, the prime minister's passive attitude toward a foreign policy issue could confuse the policy arena. In the spring of 1982, when Prime Minister Suzuki Zenko virtually retracted his statement concerning "alliance relations" (*domei kankei*) by saying that the "alliance relations" did not have "military implications," he caused tremendous confusion in U.S.-Japan relations. But the person who resigned to take responsibility for the "confusion" was then Foreign Minister Ito Masayoshi, rather than the prime minister, who revealed his ignorance concerning, or lack of interest in, the alliance. Prime ministers can make a difference both positively and negatively.[16]

Various incidents in the mid-1990s, including the Korean Peninsula crisis of 1994, the Great Hanshin earthquake, Aum Shinrikyo's urban terrorism, and the Peru hostage crisis, led to criticism of the Cabinet's decision-making skills. Based on the recommendation of the Administrative Reform Council, issued in late 1997, the Diet in March 1998 passed the Basic Law for the Reform of Central Government Ministries and Agencies, which calls for the strengthening of the powers of the prime minister and the functions of the Cabinet secretariat in addition to the reduction of the number of ministries and agencies. As all the implementing bills were passed in the Diet in 1999, the prime minister now holds the explicit legal authority to propose basic policies at Cabinet meetings, and the Cabinet Secretariat will be managed more flexibly by the prime minister in terms of staff appointments. The new system is scheduled to become effective 1 January 2001.

Bureaucracy[17]

The reverse side of the relative weakness of the prime minister is the relative strength and independence of the bureaucracy. The bureaucracy in Japan does not act in chorus; because of the relative weakness of the central coordination of the prime minister, each ministry acts as if it were a sovereign state, especially where jurisdictional demarcation is clear. This tendency, called *tatewari gyosei* (vertically divided administration) in Japanese, is blurred in international affairs because the Ministry of Foreign Affairs is generally in charge of any policy issues that have international implications. As in many other countries, bureaucrats from ministries seconded to embassies abroad are, in theory, under the direction of ambassadors. Theoretically, in other words, the foreign ministry is supposed to have the power to coordinate all international interactions of the Japanese government. In practice, however, the foreign ministry does not have such power and capability.

As the issue becomes more technical and closely connected to domestic policies, the relevant ministries are increasingly more dominant in the formation of Japan's foreign policy. International finance is the typical area, where the Ministry of Finance (MOF) plays an almost exclusive role in it's policy formulation. The Ministry of Agriculture, Forestry, and Fisheries (MAFF) is also dominant in the areas of market opening of agricultural products and international agreements related to agriculture, forestry, and fishery. The foreign ministry has an Economic Policy Bureau but it does not seem to have much power in the areas of international finance or agriculture.

Although MITI is generally most important, the Ministry of Foreign Affairs and the Ministry of Finance play important roles when it comes to the more general issues of trade liberalization and preparations for important trade-related international gatherings. The Japanese negotiating team in the controversial Strategic Impediment Initiatives (SII) talks between Japan and the United States was headed by the deputy vice minister for foreign affairs (*gaimu shingikan*), deputy vice minister for international trade (*tsusan shingikan*) and the vice minister of international finance (*zaimukan*). As the issue became more specific to a certain industrial sector—for example as in the final phase of the Japan-U.S. framework talks that dealt almost exclusively with automobiles and automobile parts—MITI played a dominant role.

Economic assistance is an area where responsibility is shared widely by various ministries. Generally, the formation of the basic policy of official development assistance (ODA) is made by the coordinated efforts of MOFA, MOF, MITI, and the Economic Planning Agency (EPA). The power of MITI is most pronounced in yen loans, and the foreign ministry plays an important role in determining grant aid. An interesting issue of ODA policy is its political use. Since the Tiananmen Square incident of 1989, Japan has increasingly used ODA as a political tool to influence recipient countries. The Official Development Charter of 1992 stipulates some principles of such political use. It is generally believed that the foreign ministry is critical when making disbursement decisions, but the precise decision-making process has not yet been studied very carefully. Contrary to the general tendency of the bureaucratic dominance of economic assistance policy to decline, the influence of the Diet and the media seems to be on the rise.

More traditional areas of foreign and security policy are generally managed by MOFA and the Defense Agency. In the past, it used to be the case that the U.S.-Japan alliance was virtually dominated by the Security Division of the North American Affairs Bureau of MOFA. Not just alliance management but security policy in general was made by this one division, a foreign ministry official once told this author. Thus, the Defense Agency was simply regarded as the implementing agency taking care of the Self-Defense Forces. The decline of the

Security Division started in the mid-1970s, when the first National Defense Program Outline and the U.S.-Japan Guidelines were compiled.[18] Serious thinking about defense planning, within the context of changing international relations, was beginning to take place within the Defense Agency roughly at the time of Defense Vice Ministers Kubo Takuya and Maruyama Ko.

In the 1990s, the bureaucratic decision making within the foreign ministry expanded. In 1993, there was partial reorganization of the Ministry of Foreign Affairs and a Foreign Policy Bureau (Sogo Gaiko Seisaku Kyoku) was created. It "takes charge of the planning of basic and middle- or long-term foreign policy from wider points of view and the coordination of policies formulated by other bureaus. Special emphasis will be put on national security issues and issues related to the United Nations."[19] The center of the alliance policy remains in the North American Bureau and its Japan-U.S. Security Treaty Division. But the emergence of the Foreign Policy Bureau seems to have created an environment within the ministry that will allow the alliance issues to be discussed in a wider perspective.

In the Defense Agency, some significant changes have been taking place, including an increase in the number of bureaucrats and SDF officials who have long overseas experience. An increasing number of these officials have undertaken graduate studies in the United States and created a basis on which the agency can communicate more directly not only with the Pentagon, but with a wide audience in the United States.[20]

When Japan's security policy is analyzed, an agency that should not be overlooked is the Cabinet Legislation Bureau.[21] Its responsibilities are to give legal opinions on a variety of matters to government agencies, and to judge the legal consistency and constitutionality of laws and treaties that the Cabinet proposes to the Diet. This office creates practically the most authoritative interpretation of the Constitution. Obviously, the Supreme Court is the final arbiter of any constitutional dispute, but in many instances that involve security issues, the Supreme Court is reluctant to produce its own judgment because of the "highly political nature" of an issue. As a result, the Cabinet Legislation Bureau is virtually the single most important legal actor in any decision making in Japan. Particularly relevant to the U.S.-Japan alliance is its interpretation of the constitutionality of the right of collective self-defense.

Part of the reason that external pressure often plays an important role in Japan's decision making is the *tatewari gyosei* system. When the jurisdictional demarcation is clear, no one, not even the prime minister, finds it easy to interfere into the "internal affairs" of the ministry in charge. When other ministries or political actors, including the prime minister, feel it necessary to bring about change, it is sometimes useful to attract foreign attention and let foreigners criticize the ministry. So it is that, when the jurisdiction is not clear, as in the case of newly emerging industries such as telecommunications, and turf battles among ministries attract foreign pressures, each ministry will try to entice foreign governments and business to support its case and oppose its adversaries.

Finally, a few words on the role of politicians—ministers (*daijin*) and *seimu jikan* (the foreign ministry now translates this post as state secretary and other ministries translate it as administrative vice minister). The posts of foreign minister, finance minister, and MITI minister are regarded as the most important in the Cabinet. The post of director general of the Defense Agency (defense minister) has long been considered a rather minor post for a fairly inexperienced middle-level politician. Although there appear some signs that more importance is being attached to the office of defense minister, no clear indication is evident.

One of the more important developments over the last few years is the elevation of the position of the state secretaries for foreign affairs. *Seimu jikan* was translated as "parliamentary vice minister" in contrast to *jimu jikan* (administrative vice minister). *Jimu jikan,* as those familiar with Japan's bureaucracy know, is the highest-ranking position among the career civil servants in a ministry and, hence, its holder is regarded as the substantively most powerful figure in the ministry, more powerful in many instances than the minister. In contrast with the *jimu jikan,* the *seimu jikan* is often likened to an appendix, which is present but performs no particular function. Until quite recently, most *seimu jikan* posts were filled by fairly junior politicians. But the appointment of Komura Masahiko as *seimu jikan* for foreign affairs during the Hashimoto Cabinet was quite a departure from previous custom. Komura had served as a director general of the Science and Technology Agency. In order to accommodate such a senior official (*omono*), the foreign ministry changed the English translation of the *seimu jikan* and refer to the post as "state secretary for foreign affairs," to indicate that the person in this post is almost equivalent to a member of the Cabinet. The same pattern has been followed in the Obuchi Cabinet. Machimura Nobutaka, former education minister and a future prime minister hopeful, was appointed state secretary for foreign affairs. And for that matter, as Obuchi became prime minister, Komura took Obuchi's position to become foreign minister. Furthermore, a second state minister for foreign affairs was added, another new tendency. In the past, each ministry had only one *seimu jikan;* under the Obuchi administration, MOFA and MOF had two *seimu jikan.* The second state secretary, Takemi Keizo, seemed to follow the previous pattern, because he was a first-term councilor. But Takemi is well known for his foreign policy expertise, as he was previously a professor of international politics at Tokai University. These new developments in the position of *seimu jikan* clearly show that at least people like Komura, Machimura, and Takemi are no longer dismissed as simple appendices. How much influence they wield remains to be seen, however.

The proposed reforms, under the auspices of the Basic Law for the Reform of Central Government Ministries and Agencies, are in line with strengthening the political appointees in the bureaucracy. Instead of *seimu jikan,* the current government bill proposes to create three posts of *fuku-daijin* (deputy minister) and three posts of *seimukan* (political officer) in the foreign ministry. How the names of these posts are translated into English is yet to be finalized (deputy ministers and political officers are my direct translation). But *fuku-daijin* are conceived of as posts comparable to British ministers without portfolio, while *seimukan,* posts comparable to previous *seimu jikan,* are posts for junior politicians. In any case, once this plan is realized, seven political appointees will be sent to all ministries, which could have significant decision-making implications. With seven political appointees at the higher echelon of a ministry (in the case of the foreign ministry), it would become more difficult for career bureaucrats to dominate decision making. However, how the new system will work remains to be seen.

Diet and Political Parties

The Diet consists of two houses, the House of Representatives (lower house) and the House of Councilors (upper house), and is defined by the Constitution as "the highest organ of state power" (see Table 1.1). A bill becomes law when it passes both houses, but the House of Representatives takes precedence over the budget, treaty ratification, and the appointment of the prime minister. The term of representatives is four years but, since the House of Representatives can be dissolved by the prime minister, the average tenure of representatives is much shorter. The House of Councilors cannot be dissolved and a councilor's term is six years.

Because the Japanese system is essentially a parliamentary system where the prime minister is supported by the majority in the Diet, the Diet's role is generally passive. It deliberates what the Cabinet is proposing and has done, but rarely is it responsible for new initiatives. Both houses have committees corresponding to various ministries, including foreign affairs and security. In recent years there has been active deliberation on international affairs in committee meetings, but their purpose is generally to review the international situation and increase the understanding of Diet members as well as the public.

When the LDP had a solid majority in both Houses before the 1990s, its internal decision-making system counted more than the Diet in many areas, including foreign policy. Most important foreign policy initiatives, drawn up by the foreign ministry and other areas of the bureaucracy, had to be cleared by the LDP Foreign Affairs Committee (Gaiko Bukai) and finally the General Affairs Council (Somukai), the highest decision-making organ of the LDP. The same process is still valid within the LDP in the late 1990s. But under the conditions of the new coalition politics, where the LDP does not have a majority in both houses, the more complicated process of interparty negotiations has to be taken into account. In general, given the current political fragmentation, the voices of a very small number of vocal politicians are having an impact on foreign policy, something that was previously rather rare. Their voices were raised against French and Chinese nuclear tests in 1995, and North Korea's launch of Taepodong missiles in 1998.

Since the collapse of the so-called "1955 year system" in 1993, Japan's politics have been in flux. The only political parties that have so far survived the last five years and maintained their party identity are the Liberal Democratic Party and the Japan Communist Party (JCP). The Social Democratic Party of Japan is no longer the previous Socialist Party (JSP). Hosokawa Morihiro's New Party of Japan no longer exists. Nor does the grand coalition of Ozawa Ichiro: the New Frontier Party. Currently, the largest opposition party is the Democratic Party of Japan (DPJ), which was formed hastily in March 1998 as an amalgam of the previous Democratic Party of Kan Naoto and Hatoyama Yukio with various splinter groups of the former New Frontier Party. In the House of Councilors' election in July 1998, the DPJ gained the most while the LDP lost some of its seats.

Table 1.1 Strength of Political Parties in the Diet

	Lower House (as of 28 July 1998)	Upper House (as of 27 July 1998)
Liberal Democratic Party	263	106
Democratic Party of Japan	92	55
Peace and Reform Network	47	—
Liberal Party	40	12
Japan Communist Party	26	23
Social Democratic Party	14	14
Komei	—	24
Other	16	18
Vacancies	2	0
Membership	500	252

Traditionally, what divided political parties in foreign policy was their attitude toward the U.S.-Japan security relationship. The Japan Communist Party had the clearest policy; it declared that it wished the U.S.-Japan security treaty abolished. What is unclear in the JCP policy, as in the case of the policy of the past JSP, which insisted on an "unarmed neutrality," is the kind of security policy it envisages for Japan after the abolition of the U.S. alliance. The party documents released before the July 1998 upper house election promised that "along with the abolition of the U.S.-Japan security treaty," the JCP "will require a fundamental reduction in SDF arms and put an end to the SDF dependence on the United States. SDF staff will be required to follow the constitutional principle that sovereignty resides in the people and adhere to political neutrality as civil servants. After national consensus has been achieved, Article 9 of the Constitution will be implemented and the SDF dissolved."[22] What is unclear, of course, is what the Communists would do after the dissolution of the SDF.

Virtually all other important parties support the U.S.-Japan security treaty. Now that the SDPJ has split with the LDP as a coalition partner, it is beginning to show characteristics similar to those evident before the Murayama Cabinet. Still, its Basic Principles and Policy Agenda, released before the upper house election, declares that the SDPJ will "contribute to building confidence among countries of the Asia-Pacific region and develop a mutually interdependent framework for Asia, while maintaining the Security Treaty with the USA."[23] The DPJ, the largest winner of the upper house election, is more straightforward; its "Basic Policy" indicates that "We will continue to place the Japan-U.S. Treaty of Mutual Cooperation and Security at the center of our national security policy."[24] The Komei party, a descendant of the previous Komeito party, may hold a swing position in the upper house because of the defeat of the LDP in the July election. Its exact security policy is not clear but its "Priority Policies" released in December 1994 admit that "the Japan-U.S. Security Treaty is contributing to peace and stability of Japan and in the Asia-Pacific region and that it should be maintained in the future."[25] In late 1998, it renamed itself again to become Komeito and joined with the lower house's Peace and Reform Network, another descendant of the previous Komeito. (The political arm of Soka Gakkai, a Buddhist sect, the Komeito was disbanded in 1994 for political convenience and again regrouped in a party of the same name.) The small Liberal Party headed by Ozawa Ichiro is clearly in support of the U.S.-Japan alliance; its basic policy stresses the necessity to improve "the operations of the U.S.-Japan alliance based on the U.S.-Japan security treaty."[26]

The LDP support of the U.S.-Japan alliance is obvious, as it is the party that led Japan's foreign and security policy for most of the time since the formation of the pact. In March 1996, the Security Research Council of the LDP produced a detailed report on the significance of the alliance in the post–Cold War era, entitled "The Current Importance of the Japan-U.S. Security Arrangements." It lists three reasons that justify the importance of the alliance: first, the alliance is "indispensable to Japan's security" because of the "unpredictable and uncertain" situation surrounding Japan since the end of the Cold War. "The Japan-U.S. security arrangement has become more indispensable to Japan than to the United States as the danger of all-out confrontation with the former Soviet Union has drastically decreased since the end of the U.S.-Soviet conflict."[27] Second, the report argues that the alliance is "indispensable for peace and stability in the Far East and the Asia-Pacific region." Third, the report points out the "indispensable" nature of the alliance for "Japanese diplomacy" because it forms the "basis" of sound U.S.-Japan relations.

Besides security policy, the most conspicuous involvement of Diet members in international affairs is in the areas of agricultural and fishery protection. Diet members with strong ties to interests in these areas played an active role in concluding fishery agreements with South Korea in 1998 and China in 1999. They were a vocal force arguing against the early voluntary sectoral liberalization (EVSL) in APEC. In terms of international affairs, the iron triangle made up of politicians, bureaucrats, and sectoral interests is most pronounced in the agricultural sector.

Business

It was believed in the past that business interests in Japan were mediated through two types of business grouping; *gyokai* (the sectoral world) and *zaikai* (the business world). The *gyokai* represents the industrial sector and lobbies relevant ministries directly as well as through *zoku* LDP Diet members whom it supports.[28] In terms of political function, this grouping is similar to other special-interest bodies, such as agricultural interests.[29]

The *zaikai* is represented by four organizations, Keidanren (Federation of Economic Organizations), Nissho (Japan Chamber of Commerce and Industry), Nikkeiren (Japan Federation of Employers' Associations), and Keizai Doyukai (Japan Committee for Economic Development). Keidanren, because it acts as a conduit for the distribution of funds to political parties, has long been very influential, especially in support of the LDP during the Cold War era. Furthermore, business leaders representing these organizations have close formal and informal relations with political leaders. With the end of the Cold War and the radically reduced ideological confrontation in domestic politics, however, the role of the *zaikai* seems to be undergoing changes and has become more reluctant to side with political parties. Moreover, as globalization proceeds rapidly, it has become difficult to aggregate Japan's business interests. Among the four *zaikai* organizations, Doyukai, an organization made up of individual businessmen rather than companies, has been the most flexible and vocal in recent years under the leadership of Ushio Jiro (1995–99) and Kobayashi Yotaro (1999–). Its general thrust is deregulation and further liberalization. However, it is hard to measure its impact as an organization separate from the influence of Ushio or Kobayashi as individuals.

Media

The media participate in domestic and international politics in at least two ways: one as opinion distributors and as reporters of significant events. In terms of opinion, like political parties, national newspapers are characterized by their attitudes toward security policy. Currently, while no major newspapers have stated outright opposition to U.S.-Japan security relations, they represent different shades of opinion. Generally speaking, the *Yomiuri, Nikkei (Nihon keizai shimbun)*, and *Sankei* are more supportive of strengthening and widening the scope of U.S.-Japan defense cooperation, while the *Mainichi* and *Asahi* are more reserved.[30] Most noteworthy is the *Yomiuri*'s campaign to revise the Constitution; in 1994 it published a proposal to revise the current Constitution, including Article 9. Its proposed revision did not change the first paragraph of Article 9, which renounces "the threat, or use of force as a means of settling international disputes," but it explicitly states that Japan can have the means of self-defense. Then, in 1995, it proposed an Outline of a Comprehensive Security Policy, which declares that Japan, as a sovereign nation, "has and can resort to the individual and collective self defense."[31]

The *Asahi*, on the other hand, has consistently opposed revision of Article 9. It argues that the article has contributed to "the postwar framework in which the nation does not attach privileged values to the military," and that its revision "runs against the trend of the times, doing more harm than good." The *Asahi* also states that despite Article 9, Japan has the right of self defense, but it argues that the Constitution prohibits the exercise of the right of "collective self defense." In this respect, the *Asahi*, which is generally the most critical of the LDP government, has interpreted the Constitution in virtually the same way as the LDP government. However, it calls for a reduction of the SDF forces as well as review of U.S.-Japan security arrangements.

Television seems to have a more immediate impact on domestic politics than the print media when it comes to the reporting of potentially significant events. The role of news features for nighttime viewing was quite clear after the Okinawa rape incident of September 1995. Since such influential anchor persons as

Kume Hiroshi and Chikushi Tetsuya revealed opinions quite similar to those of the *Asahi,* sympathy for the Okinawans grew quite strong.

Conclusion

The basic characteristics of Japan's domestic politics change only slowly. Japan's prime ministers cannot emulate U.S. presidents unless the constitutional framework changes, and even a change in the legal framework may not prompt much change in actual behavior. Relatively weak prime ministers and a vertically divided administration continue to be the major tenets of Japan's decision-making process. Nevertheless, as the above discussion indicates, several moves are being made both to strengthen the role of the central decision-making power of the prime minister, and to increase the direct involvement of Diet members in the executive branch. Furthermore, there are signs that the Diet is becoming more assertive even in foreign policy issues. While such changes may not bring about any fundamental change, the dominance of the bureaucracy is being challenged and Japan's domestic politics is becoming more complex as it comes to involve more and different types of actors.

Notes

1. Yanagida Kunio, *Nihon wa moeteiruka* [Is Japan in Flames?] (Tokyo: Kodansha, 1983), p. 266.
2. Recent studies on the "reactiveness" of Japan's international behavior and the efficacy of "external pressure" include: Kent E. Calder, "Japanese Foreign Economic Policy Formation: Explaining the Reactive State," *World Politics* 40:4 (1988); Leonard J. Schoppa, *Bargaining with Japan: What American Pressure Can and Cannot Do* (NY: Columbia University Press, 1997); and Taniguchi Masaki, *Nihon no taibei boeki kosho* [Japan's Trade Negotiations with the United States] (Tokyo: University of Tokyo Press, 1997).
3. See, for example, Gerald L. Curtis, *The Japanese Way of Politics* (NY: Columbia University Press, 1988); and Muramatsu Michio, Ito Mitsutoshi, and Tsujinaka Yutaka, *Nihon no seiji* [Japanese Politics] (Tokyo: Yuhikaku, 1992).
4. For a comparable treatment of this subject in English, see Kent Calder, "The Institutions of Japanese Foreign Policy," in *The Process of Japanese Foreign Policy,* ed. Richard L. Grant (London: The Royal Institute of International Affairs, 1997), pp.1–24. Useful studies can be found in chapters of Robert A. Scalapino, ed., *The Foreign Policy of Modern Japan* (Berkeley: University of California Press, 1977); Hosoya Chihiro and Watanuki Joji, eds., *Taigai seisaku kettei katei no Nichi-Bei hikaku* [Japan-U.S. Comparison of Foreign Policy-Making Process] (Tokyo: University of Tokyo Press, 1977); Aruga Tadashi, et al., eds., *Koza kokusai seiji, 4, Nihon no gaiko* [Studies of International Politics, vol. 4., Japan's Diplomacy] (University of Tokyo Press, 1989).
5. For a general discussion of the role and power of prime ministers, see Shinoda Tomohito, *Soridaijin no kenryoku to shidoryoku* [The Power and Leadership of Prime Ministers] (Tokyo: Toyo Keizai Shimposha, 1994).
6. In practice, this type of revelation of dissent rarely takes place in Cabinet meetings because, in practice, the Cabinet meetings are a ritual in which all members of the Cabinet sign documents already agreed upon by the vice ministers' meeting that has taken place on a previous day. There is little discussion during Cabinet meetings. According to Kan Naoto, leader of the Democratic Party and minister of health and welfare under the Hashimoto Cabinet, the average length of the Cabinet meetings is 10 to 15 minutes. Since the Hosokawa Cabinet, formal Cabinet meetings have generally been followed by *kakuryo kondankai* (chat meetings of Cabinet members), which allows "free discussion." But such chat meetings also end within 10 to 15 minutes, according to Kan. Kan Naoto, *Daijin* [Ministers] (Tokyo: Iwanami Shoten, 1998), pp. 25–30. Vice ministers' meetings, in turn, are virtually rituals at which unanimous consent is given to decisions already

worked out by relevant ministries, according to Ishihara Nobao. See Mikuriya Takashi and Watanabe Akio, eds., *Shusho kantei no ketsudan: Naikaku fukukanbochokan Ishihara Nobuo no 2600 nichi* [Decisions at the Prime Minister's Residence: 2,600 Days of Deputy Chief Cabinet Secretary Ishihara Nobuo] (Tokyo: Chuo Koron Sha, 1997), pp. 230–31.

7. A concise explanation is given by Ishihara Nobuo, "Naikaku no shikumi to shusho no kengen" [The Mechanisms of the Cabinet and the Powers of Prime Ministers] in *Naikaku gyosei kiko: Kaikaku e no teigen* [The Yomiuri Proposal for Restructuring the Cabinet and the Government Administration], ed. Yomiuri Shinbunsha (Tokyo: Yomiuri Shimbunsha, 1996), pp. 103–107.

8. For a concise comparison between British and Japanese politics, see Yamaguchi Jiro, *Igirisu no seiji Nihon no seiji* [British and Japanese Politics] (Tokyo: Chikuma Shobo, 1998).

9. Murayama gives a candid recollection of his tenure as prime minister in Murayama Tomiichi, *So ja no* [Well, Let's See] (Tokyo: Dai-san Shokan, 1998).

10. For Gotoda's career and experiences as chief Cabinet secretary, see Gotoda Masaharu, *Seiji to wa nanika* [The Nature of Politics] (Tokyo: Kodansha, 1988); Gotoda Masaharu, *Naikaku kanbo chokan* [Chief Cabinet Secretary] (Tokyo: Kodansha, 1989); Gotoda Masaharu, *Jo to ri: Gotoda Masaharu kaikoroku* [Sentiment and Reason: Memoirs of Gotoda Masaharu], 2 vols. (Tokyo: Kodansha, 1998).

11. Murayama Tomiichi describes Ishihara as a "permanent presence in the prime minister's residence" (*kantei no nushi*) (Murayama, 1998, p. 81). However, Ishihara's long tenure is exceptional; tenure of previous deputy chief Cabinet secretaries was much shorter. But since late 1970s, their tenure is longer than most prime ministers. For Ishihara's career and experiences, see Ishihara Nobuo, *Kantei 2668 nichi: Seisaku kettei no butaiura* [2668 Days in the Prime Minister's Residence: The Backstage of Decision-making] (Tokyo: NHK Shuppan, 1995); and Mikuriya and Watanabe, 1997.

12. Shinoda Tomohito, "Taigai seisaku kettei akuta toshite no Ozawa Ichiro" [Ozawa Ichiro as a Foreign Policy Decision-maker] in *Nihon no gaiko seisaku kettei yoin* [Domestic Determinants of Japanese Foreign Policy], ed. Gaiko Seisaku Kettei Yoin Kenkyukai (Tokyo: PHP Kenkyujo, 1999), pp. 25–69.

13. "Shusho hishokan" [Prime Ministers' Secretaries], *Nihon keizai shimbun*, 17 August 1998.

14. *Yomiuri shimbun* (evening edition), 7 April 1998; *Yomiuri shimbun* (morning edition), 9 April 1998.

15. Sekai Heiwa Kenkyujo, ed. *Nakasone naikakushi: Shiryo-hen* [History of the Nakasone Cabinet: Documents and Materials] (Tokyo: Sekai Heiwa Kenkyujo, 1995).

16. For a more detailed description of this episode, see Tanaka Akihiko, *Anzen hosho: Sengo 50 nen no mosaku* [National Security: Postwar Japan's Fifty Years of Groping] (Tokyo: Yomiuri Shimbunsha, 1997), pp. 289–91.

17. The most up-to-date study on the decision-making processes of various ministries can be found in Shiroyama Hideaki, Suzuki Hiroshi, and Hosono Sukehiro, eds., *Chuo shocho no seisaku kettei katei—Nihon kanryosei no kaibo* [The Decision-making Processes of Central Ministries and Agencies: The Anatomy of the Japanese Bureaucracy] (Tokyo: Chuo University Shuppankai, 1999).

18. Murata Koji's study reveals that the foreign ministry was not particularly positive when the Defense Agency attempted to start negotiations that led, eventually, to the original Guidelines of 1978. Murata Koji, "Boei seisaku no tenkai" [Development of Defense Policy] in *Nihon seiji gakkai nenpo* (1997), pp. 79–95.

19. http://www2.nttca.com:8010/infomofa/about/hq/org.htm.

20. Shikata Toshiyuki, retired general and professor at Teikyo University, points out that because internationally minded bureaucrats and SDF officials have similar experiences abroad, often attending the same universities and research institutes, the "psychological barriers" that had long existed among the bureaucrats of the foreign ministry and the Defense Agency and officials in the SDF have "virtually disappeared." Shikata Toshiyuki, "Nichibei boei kyoryoku no tame no shishin (gaidorain) kaitei no keii" [The Process of Revising the "Guidelines of U.S.-Japan Defense Cooperation"] in Gaiko Seisaku Kettei Yoin Kenkyukai, 1999, p. 207.

21. Not much has been studied about the Cabinet Legislation Bureau. The exception is Nakamura Akira, *Sengo seiji ni yureta kenpo 9 jo* [The Ups and Downs of Article 9 of the Constitution in Postwar Politics] (Tokyo: Chuo Keizai Sha, 1996).

22. http://www.jcp.or.jp/Kenkai/Seisaku/98san-pol.html. The Communist Party's official "program" as amended in 1994 stipulates as follows: "The party fights for abrogation of the Japan-U.S. Security Treaty and all other treaties and agreements which undermine national sovereignty, and for the withdrawal of all U.S. troops from Japan and the complete removal of

U.S. military bases. The party demands and fights for a policy to ensure a peaceful and neutral Japan, which will abrogate Japan's military alliance with the United States and take part in no military alliances but establish friendly relations with all countries. The party fights for the genuine independence of Japan, including abrogation of the articles of the San Francisco peace treaty, which undermine Japan's sovereignty. The party makes peaceful diplomatic efforts to get the reversion of Habomai, Shikotan and all the Chishima Islands to Japan." http://www.jcp.or.jp/Jcpdata/Koryo/e-koryo.html.

23. http://www.omnics.co.jp/politics/SDPJ/cong64/basicprinE.html.
24. http://www.dpj.or.jp/english/policies.html.
25. http://www.komei.or.jp/tou/sei7.htm.
26. http://www.jiyuto.or.jp/s4/s4_2e.htm#c4.
27. http://www.jimin.or.jp/jimin/saisin96/saisin-07.html. The quoted sentence was not translated in the LDP's English translation of this report as found in the same Internet address.
28. *Zoku* simply means "tribe," but in the context of Japanese domestic politics it means a group of Diet members who are closely connected with certain special interests such as agriculture, construction, and transportation. See Inoguchi Takashi and Iwai Tomoaki, *"Zoku" giin no kenkyu* [A Study of *Zoku* Diet Members] (Tokyo: Nihon Keizai Shimbunsha, 1987).
29. Somewhat dated but still useful studies on the relations between the business community and foreign policy are Sadako Ogata, "The Business Community and Japanese Foreign Policy: Normalization of Relations with the People's Republic of China," in Scalapino, 1977, pp. 175–203; and Otake Hideo, *Zoho kaiteiban gendai Nihon no seiji kenryoku keizai kenryoku* [Political and Economic Powers in Contemporary Japan, Expanded and Revised] (Tokyo: San-ichi Shobo, 1996). Though not exclusively focusing on international relations, the following provides more updated analysis of Japan's interest groups including business organization: Tsujinaka Yutaka, *Rieki shudan* [Interest Groups] (Tokyo: Tokyo Daigaku Shuppankai, 1988).
30. The circulation of the five national newspapers, as of November 1997, is: *Yomiuri*, 10.216 million; *Asahi*, 8.342 million; *Mainichi*, 3.958 million; *Nihon keizai*, 2.998 million; and *Sankei*, 1.941 million. *Yomiuri nenkan [Yomiuri Yearbook] 1999 Data File* (Tokyo: Yomiuri Shimbunsha, 1999), p. 83.
31. *This is Yomiuri: Nihonkoku kenpo no subete* [Everything You Need to Know about the Japanese Constitution] (Tokyo: Yomiuri Shimbun, May 1997), p. 419.

CHAPTER 2

*Emerging Foreign Policy Actors:
Subnational Governments and
Nongovernmental Organizations*

Purnendra Jain

In recent decades, significant changes in both the international and domestic contexts of Japan's external relations have wrought a rather different ball game among the players on Japan's foreign policy field. Today, as "globalization" sees national borders losing some of their authority as defining mechanisms that regulate international flows, inside Japan the traditional capacity of the national government to regulate international flows is also weakening. It is not just the nature, the extent, the style, and the goals of Japan's international relations that are transforming. Inevitably, who conducts these relationships is also changing. At the end of the twentieth century, foreign policy is no longer the sole preserve of Japan's central government and its representative, the Ministry of Foreign Affairs (MOFA) based in Tokyo. Other actors are involved in conducting Japan's international relations. The two most significant of these are subnational governments (SNGs) and nongovernmental organizations (NGOs).

This chapter looks at these two types of actors emerging in Japan's international relations. SNGs and NGOs are by no means new to Japan. Yet their involvement in international affairs has begun to flourish, particularly in the 1990s. In this chapter, we examine what they are doing as international actors. We consider the forces that have pushed the reach of both these domestic actors beyond Japan's national borders, drawing them into the foreign policy domain, and we assess the consequences of their involvement for management of Japan's international relations.

We see here how SNGs and NGOs are gaining recognition as legitimate actors in Japan's foreign policy. Initial tensions over bureaucratic turf are easing, as institutional arrangements are put in place, allowing these relatively new actors some independence from the central government, while still within its regulatory power. The interests and priorities of noncentral government bodies across the nation do not always coincide with those of the foreign ministry in Tokyo. Yet their contributions to the national interest are usually beneficial, and sometimes irreplaceable. The signs are clear that both are forging a significant place in Japan's foreign relations and national policy has begun to respond accordingly.

Explaining Japanese SNGs and NGOs

Let us begin by clarifying the ambiguous concepts of SNGs and NGOs that are central to this analysis. We will turn first to SNGs: subnational governments. Japan has a unitary political system as do the United Kingdom, Italy, and France. This system is more centralized than the federal systems of the United States, Canada, Germany, and Australia, where subnational units enjoy more freedom from the center to administer their own laws and policies. And it has a convoluted structure because of this.

Subnational governments in Japan number over 3,000 and operate at two levels under the national government. The prefectural level (*to-do-fu-ken*) is the second tier of government covering Japan's 47 prefectures. The third tier includes all other local entities known as municipalities (*shi-cho-son*) and covers thousands of cities, towns/townships, and villages. Among them are 12 special or designated cities (*seirei shitei toshi*), so designated because of their large size and functional jurisdiction.[1] Collectively, SNGs in Japan form a mammoth and influential public body, both in terms of the multitude of their elected and other public officials and the magnitude of their annual aggregated budgets (far exceeding the national government budget).[2] Individually, SNGs are political actors with varying degrees of clout, beholden to the central government but usually seeking to increase their autonomy from it. We see this in their push to become international actors that are independent of the central administration, with their own interests and priorities. Usually their goals are reasonably consistent with those of the central government (whose priorities are not always coordinated, in any case, from one ministry to another), but certainly not always.

NGOs are less easily identified—in Japan as elsewhere—with the ambiguity sometimes offering political opportunity. The Japanese NGO Center for International Cooperation (NGO Katsudo Suishin Senta, or JANIC), a Japanese NGO umbrella organization based in Tokyo, treats as NGOs only those non-government, nonprofit, citizens' groups that are involved in global issues such as human rights, education, environmental protection, and world peace.[3] Citizens' organizations that are purely domestic in their activities are included under NPOs (nonprofit organizations). This distinction is generally accepted in the Japanese mass media[4] and is the one we will use here. The 1998 JANIC directory listed 368 Japanese NGOs.[5]

Pluralism in International Actors:
A Contemporary Global Development

Analyses of who or what are the actors in international relations have noted how technological advancement and the complex forces of globalization are eroding the relevance of the traditional units in international diplomacy: nation states and the foreign offices of central governments.[6] These powerful developments have propelled the involvement of many other governmental, semigovernmental, and nongovernmental bodies as informal but legitimate actors in an increasingly pluralized international community. As Mike Clough has put it, at the turn of the millennium "consulates belong to yesterday's diplomacy."[7] Beyond general and theoretical analyses, case studies have examined the role of nonstate actors—the business community, local governments, nongovernmental organizations, and private individuals—in the international affairs of specific countries (both industrialized[8] and developing[9]) and around specific issues, particularly environmental protection.[10] These studies make it clear that the flourishing of international actors beyond the traditional bastions of nation-state diplomacy is a global trend.

Japan's International Actors

Japan is no exception to the pluralist trend. Postwar Japan has been recognized by many as primarily an "economic state," with the focus of its international diplomacy on pursuing economic benefit for Japanese interests through international trade, investment, and other commercial arrangements. Nonstate international actors are mostly business groups, transnational corporations, and other private actors promoting Japan's commercial interests abroad through "private economic diplomacy."[11] A tight network linking government and business enabled the central government to incorporate the overseas pursuits of these nonstate actors within the national foreign policy to some extent. This picture may be fairly true of postwar Japan into the 1980s. However, particularly from the late 1980s, other actors with other motivations and interests have begun to take a more prominent role in Japan's international relations. Our spotlight is on the most important two of these "other" actors.

SNGs and NGOs in Japan's International Relations

Absence from Analytical Discussion
Japanese SNGs and NGOs have become increasingly active outside Japan. Perhaps because their involvement is still limited when compared with the extent of their overseas counterparts in Europe and North America, these actors have barely registered in most analyses of Japan's international relations. Accounts of their activities have come mostly from practitioners—governors, mayors, other local officials, and leaders and other workers in Japan's NGOs.[12] Ignorance is also at work here. In 1997, a senior Japanese newspaper journalist suggested dismissively that I was wasting time treating this as an expanding area of Japan's international relations.

Another reason for the epistemic absence of these new international actors is that much of the analysis of Japan's political system has argued consistently that Japan is a centralized state. This failure to recognize slow systemic change blocks proper recognition of newly emerging actors that operate largely outside the center. In this perspective, because local governments in Japan are severely limited in both legal authority and financial autonomy, they have almost no actual power to make policy or act independently; their status is nothing more than subsidiary agencies (*desaki/shitauke kikan*) of the central government. Some observers posit a similar argument about the impotence of Japan's NGOs and other nonprofit organizations (NPOs) in the policy arena. One foreign observer has classified Japan in the ranks of China and the Middle East on the lowly status of its NGOs.[13] This observation may have had stronger currency a decade back, but by the end of the 1990s it is clearly a misjudgment. As we see in this analysis of SNGs and NGOs as international actors, although institutional change comes slowly and with resistance, Tokyo's ability to drive foreign policy in a unitary fashion is weakening. SNGs and NGOs are now making valuable contributions to Japan's international diplomacy.

International Initiatives

Japanese SNGs and NGOs have taken some productive initiatives in developing international relationships. Depending on the type and location of the activity, the central government may be involved to some extent—as coordinator, financier, partner, or advisor—via the new institutional infrastructure established for this purpose. In exceptional cases it will stand back completely. Usually the central government seeks some degree of involvement, and usually this is through the foreign ministry (and possibly other ministries as well; for SNGs, it is often the Ministry of Home Affairs). SNGs are involved directly in a range of international activities, from establishing sister-city relations, cultural agreements, technology transfers, and training programs to promoting economic cooperation with overseas partners. Many of these overseas links are with counterpart bodies abroad. Most relationships have remained bilateral, although some have begun to take a multilateral form, with Japanese SNGs and their overseas counterparts setting up forums to consider issues that unify their interest at the local level.

Japanese NGOs are involved ever more deeply than before in what the Japanese government calls Japan's "international contributions" (*kokusai koken*) in Asia, Africa, and elsewhere. Many participate in international programs of development, peace-making, and postcrisis reconstruction. After years of effort, Japanese NGOs now have access to the corridors of Tokyo's policy-making circles. Increasingly, these NGOs are present in key international forums, keen for involvement in issues such as environmental protection, human rights, and sustainable economic development. Some also participate in lobbying activities nationally and internationally.

Japan's internationally active SNGs and NGOs rank poorly in domestic and international influence, when compared with some very active counterparts in North America and Europe. SNGs and NGOs in Japan have developed in a historical, cultural, political, and socioeconomic context that differs from circumstances that have propelled their North American and European counterparts earlier into international affairs. Nevertheless, the move by Japanese bodies into the global arena is gaining momentum. It appears set to take SNGs and NGOs further into the heartland of Japan's international diplomacy. Before we examine the international involvement of Japanese SNGs and NGOs, let us review developments elsewhere to enable a comparative perspective.

SNGs and NGOs in Comparative Perspective

SNGs

Many SNGs in industrialized states play a vital, self-sustaining role by pursuing their own interests abroad, largely through promoting trade and attracting foreign investment to their local area. As Clough has argued, the inability of national institutions to fully serve local and regional needs is a key reason why cities and states are developing their own foreign economic policies and creating institutional structures to carry them out. In the U.S. example, by the mid-1990s, there were more than 150 American state offices in foreign countries,[14] almost all 50 of the American states had trade offices abroad, and all have official standing in the World Trade Organisation.[15]

Overseas activities of SNGs are not exclusively to satisfy economic goals. They may involve pursuit of cultural, educational, and other grassroots programs such as technological cooperation. The sister-city program began in the United States in the 1950s to promote international goodwill and world peace through exchange at the grassroots level. It has been expanded into sister relationships between a multitude of SNG bodies such as states, islands, and districts that have shared interests such as climate, geophysical location, language, leading industry (e.g., grape or rice growing) and so forth. Today these programs foster direct formal and informal links between counterparts around the world.[16]

European cities and other subnational administrative units are also exploring greater international involvement. German *Lander* and British local governments maintain offices at EU headquarters in Brussels. A number of regions in Europe have opened "embassies" abroad and negotiate their own trade agreements. France's Rhone-Alpes region, centered in Lyon, maintains overseas embassies on behalf of the regional economy that includes Geneva in Switzerland and Turin in Italy.[17] European cities have linked themselves in state-of-the-art transportation networks and have attracted foreign business using this to appeal. Citing developments in Germany's *Lander,* northern Italy, the Rhone-Alpes, and Spain's Catalonia, Newhouse argues that regionalism involving local actors is the coming dynamic, especially in Europe.[18] In similar vein, Bomberg and Peterson have outlined the growing role of European local governments in EU decision making.[19]

NGOs

The increasing international involvement of NGOs post–Cold War has been extraordinary. Salamon sees in organizations like these that, "we are in the midst of a global 'associational revolution' that may prove to be as significant to the latter twentieth century as the rise of the nation-state was to the latter nineteenth."[20] The international influence of NGOs is lubricated by their specialized approach. Their commitment, human and technical resources, and capacity to access grassroots energies leave them unmatched by other organizations, including central governments, in their global contributions. The influence of NGOs is also growing in the UN system, where their status has transformed from observer to partner in policy direction and agenda setting.[21]

When we consider how the international involvement of SNGs and NGOs has begun to flourish in the last decade or two, it is clear that national borders are losing significance as markers of identity and sources of community. National governments are losing their hold on the flow of traffic across national borders. Other actors are becoming involved in conducting and deciding foreign policy. Developments in Japan do not fully parallel those in North America and Europe, but the trends are clearly incipient, as the following examination reveals.

Japanese SNGs as International Actors

With this basis for comparison, let us turn to consider what Japanese SNGs are doing as international actors. SNGs in Japan, like elsewhere, are primarily responsible for providing essential services to local residents. Many are now following the lead of their overseas counterparts into the international arena to enhance the services that they provide, pursuing economic linkages, technical cooperation, cultural exchange, and other programs of mutual interest with SNGs abroad. The range of programs has certainly expanded in recent years, with varying degrees of diplomatic import. Some Japanese SNGs are involved in developmental assistance with SNGs in developing nations. A few have been drawn to the edge of "hard" diplomacy on the sensitive antinuclear issue, which impinges directly on Japan's crucial relations with the United States and has profound implications for national security. *Jichitai gaiko* (local-level diplomacy) has become a common term. It registers clearly the diplomatic significance of what SNGs are doing internationally and their place as consequential actors in Japan's international affairs.[22]

One indicator of the extent of Japanese SNG activities in the international arena is the amount of money SNGs spend on these activities. The aggregate SNG budget for international activities increased steadily from ¥86.5 billion in 1992 to ¥130.1 billion in 1995 (by just over 50 percent in three years). As part of this, their aggregate budget for international cooperation (technical assistance, training, and dispatch of technical staff to developing countries, termed "local official development assistance, ODA") virtually doubled from ¥3.8 billion in 1992 to more than 7.5 billion in 1995.[23]

The international activities of SNGs can be divided loosely into two categories. One includes those in cooperation with, and/or under the guidelines of, the central government and its agencies. The other includes those that originate primarily at the local level and are carried out by SNGs with relative independence from the national government. However, as we see below, in some cases the mix of initiative, effort, funding, and responsibility is unclear, making it difficult to assess the degree of noncentral government initiative and central government intervention or involvement. To increase their independence, SNGs are establishing their own institutional supports for their international efforts. These include international divisions (*kokusai koryuka*) in SNG offices to serve as a window for international activities, and international exchange associations (*kokusai koryu kyokai* or IEA) that serve as separate, third-sector organizations to assist foreign residents in their local areas and promote activities overseas. In mid-1997 there were 793 IEA.[24]

One of the first forms of local-level diplomacy in Japan was the sister-city program that began in the mid-1950s based on the American model. Most sister linkages have been with SNGs in developed countries. Nowadays, however, Japanese cities have begun to embrace some partners from developing countries, with a particular concentration in China. By April 1998, Japanese sister-city affiliations numbered 1,304 with 58 countries.[25] A few of the older official sister linkages between cities, states, and other administrative units have moved little beyond the traditional, symbolic connections. Others, however, have generated considerable flows of people and commerce, with reciprocal flows of ideas, culture, friendship, technology, and economic benefit in their wake.[26]

A major initiative begun in 1988 between SNGs, the Ministry of Home Affairs (MOHA), which is nationally responsible for them, and the MOHA's liason body CLAIR, is the JET (Japan Exchange Teaching) program. Under the JET program, young women and men from various countries with different language backgrounds are invited for a minimum one-year period to work as language teachers in Japanese schools or with administration in local government. In 1997, the JET program invited 5,351 participants, with SNGs sharing the cost with MOHA and other ministries. The financial costs of this program to SNGs are significant, but if we consider the unmeasurable diplomatic and other gains to be generated from these "exchanges," the benefits for SNGs are considerable too.

In recent years, Japan's SNGs have taken on a new role in international diplomacy: delivery of "local" ODA (official development assistance) that was until recent years the sole jurisdiction of the national government. Here local governments accept trainees from developing countries: some under the national ODA program run by the foreign ministry agency JICA (Japan International Cooperation Agency), others invited by local governments themselves through sister-city programs or as part of local ODA activities.[27] In this way SNGs help national government to implement the national ODA program, and initiate, fund, and administer their own developmental activities.

SNGs are now turning their attention from international exchange (*kokusai koryu*) to international cooperation (*kokusai kyoryoku*)—from ritualistic or symbolic programs to a range of cooperative activities with mutual concrete benefits. In the past, sister-city exchanges were mostly symbolic; official visits, but with very little solid benefit for the local communities on either side. Now the emphasis is on cooperation, with opportunities for learning from each other's experience through the sharing of ideas and information, joint research, developing trade, investment potential, and "local" aid. For example, in 1995 the city of Takasaki in Gunma established a multinational study group to explore global environmental problems, in association with its partner cities in the United States, Brazil, China, and the Czech Republic. Project results were posted on the Internet for wide accessibility. The Takasaki initiative led to several cooperative multilateral research programs, and many other Japanese cities have followed this initiative to organize their own international forums and conferences on pressing global issues.[28]

With SNGs' international programs emphasizing cooperation and practical outcomes, the trend toward multilateralism gains strength. Sapporo offers another telling example. The Sapporo City Office in Hokkaido has served as the secretariat for the International Association of Mayors of Northern Cities whose main objective is to forge cooperation among member cities on shared problems arising from their geographical locations. Issues addressed include city planning, housing, winter transportation, snow-clearing, and tackling the pollution thus created. The genesis of the association is a network formed in 1981 by then mayor of Sapporo, Itagaki Takeshi. Having the opportunity to find solutions to local problems through overseas contacts has helped to increase the local autonomy of the city of Sapporo. In similar circumstances elsewhere in Japan, international cooperation programs have enabled Japanese SNGs to rely less on the national government for solutions to their specific problems, which in any case may not be relevant to other Japanese localities and can best be addressed through a transnational coalitions of local governments that share concerns.[29]

Thus the forms of SNGs' international cooperation vary across bilateral and multilateral arrangements. An interesting addition in the 1990s has been region-based activities that have introduced a new type of actor, geographic regions, onto the international cooperation scene. Specific regions in Japan are targeting neighboring countries for economic and other cooperation, in moves similar to those of counterpart geographic units in Europe. Kyushu island, for example, has targeted East Asia for local-level exchanges and economic initiatives. The city of Fukuoka in Kyushu projects itself as the "hub city for Asia." The Kansai area in western Japan focuses on Southeast Asia. Hiroshima Prefecture has proclaimed itself as the center for international exchanges with Asia. Hokkaido's emphasis has been on the Russian Far East. A number of prefectures and cities bordering the Japan Sea actively promote economic cooperation with nearby countries like North Korea and South Korea. Clearly, geographic proximity and potential for developing economic links are the principal motivating factors. We can see, here, too how competition between Japan's regional and other subnational actors has translated into new patterns of regional identification, with interesting consequences for national and subnational diplomatic maneuvering.[30]

Shared involvement in international affairs in some ways unifies the interests of the central government and those of SNGs. Both are government actors, with responsibility to the citizens who elected them. But the extent of their electoral domains, and by extension the sphere of their responsibilities and primary concerns, clearly differs, irrespective of Japanese nationhood as the core of these intragovernment relations. One issue on which the two diverge sharply concerns an appropriate antinuclear stance. Japan's SNGs have taken a leading role in peace and antinuclear movements and at times their actions have embarrassed the national government. Japan has a "peace" constitution, it is committed under international treaty to a nonnuclear regime, and in 1971 adopted a resolution on the three nonnuclear principles of not possessing or manufacturing nuclear bombs, and not permitting entry of nuclear armaments into Japan. Over time many SNGs have taken independent steps to affirm their antinuclear stance; by 1995 about two-thirds of SNGs in Japan had declared themselves nuclear-free.[31] Kobe upped the ante for the nuclear-free movement in 1975 when its assembly passed a resolution requiring foreign warships to produce a certificate that no nuclear facilities are carried on board. According to one Kobe city official, no American warship has visited Kobe port since the city adopted this resolution.

Support for the move to demand these certificates gained momentum among SNGs in mid-1999, just before parliament passed the revised Guidelines for U.S.-Japan Defense Cooperation, stipulating that local governments must provide their port facilities to U.S. warships during a crisis situation around Japan. Calls pushing for the "no-nuclear" certificates based on the Kobe model have come from SNGs nationwide. In Kochi Prefecture, the local chief executive went further, asking for a prefectural ordinance rather than just an assembly resolution on the matter. The Ministry of Foreign Affairs claims that local governments do not have authority to ask for these certificates, as the core of the dilemma concerns national diplomacy on which the central government is legally the final arbiter.[32] So far the issue has not created major discord between the three levels of government, and foreign ministry officials have held meetings with SNGs and local residents in an effort to contain the political fallout by winning their acceptance of the new defense guidelines.[33]

Thus SNGs do not need international contact, nor even to leave port, in order to have an impact on Japan's international relations. They can become diplomatic actors by challenging the central government on its international diplomacy—through actions and through words. In one recent exceptional case, criticism made by the nation's highest-profile chief executive have had front-page punch. Tokyo's new governor Ishihara Shintaro stridently criticized the national government's huge aid package to China, claiming that since China is producing hydrogen bombs it does not deserve Japan's aid bounty. Even while still on the campaign trail in April 1999, Ishihara criticized China's violation of human rights in Tibet and its belligerence toward Taiwan.[34] The national government was deeply embarrassed by these public outbursts. In attempts to engage China for diplomatic expediency, it had long ago swept these issues under the carpet. Ishihara has also spoken out on the U.S. military presence within the Tokyo metropolis and his voice is not alone. SNG officials on Japan's southernmost prefecture of Okinawa have been at the forefront of opposing large numbers of U.S. troops stationed in the prefecture.

Japanese NGOs as International Actors

Worldwide, NGOs are gaining new ground in international affairs and Japanese NGOs are no exception. Volunteerism has begun to surge in Japan. Responses to the 1995 Great Hanshin earthquake centered around Kobe were a meaningful trigger to popularize, legitimize, and promote voluntary work by exposing its importance to the national livelihood. This has had significant consequences for citizens' organizations working on international as well as domestic causes.[35] NGOs are now gaining the public and official support essential to sustaining their work, and the media are helping to push this trend. The *Asahi Newspaper's* 1995 "Earth Project 21" exploring the problems Japan is likely to confront early in the twenty-first century, urged that because NGOs would become central in delivering a range of services abroad, government should pay greater attention to these organizations.[36] Media coverage of NGO activities has also grown conspicuously.[37]

Japanese NGOs have a short, unremarkable history. Most have their origins in religious organizations. As one typical example, the Japan Overseas Christian Medical Cooperative Service (Nihon Kurisutokyo Kaigai Iryo Kyoryoku Kai) was established in 1960 to provide medical services in Nepal and elsewhere in Asia. Until the mid-1970s, Japanese NGOs were extremely few, and their overseas presence was very limited. When resettlement of Indo-Chinese refugees who arrived in Japan became an international issue in the late 1970s, this was a turning point in the evolution of NGOs in Japan. Partly because in the relative brevity of NGO history there is no Japanese indigenous equivalent of OXFAM, Medecins Sans Frontiers, or Amnesty International, which have built up long and venerable histories based on their humanitarian work abroad. Today, Japanese NGOs work closely with other international NGOs, and naturally use these international connections for added clout in lobbying the Japanese government to influence policy outcomes.

The 1992 UN Earth Summit in Rio de Janeiro was an important forum for the international activities of Japanese NGOs. Yet it was not until the UN Conference on Population and Development in Cairo in September 1994 that NGO members were included in the Japanese official delegation. Gradually Japanese NGOs have begun to assert their influence in international organizations, and within Japan's political and policy circles. Establishment of the NPO Law in March 1998, which set new guidelines on establishment and control of Japan's nonprofit community organizations including NGOs, marked a historic victory for Japan's voluntary community groups, including NGOs, when the law was passed unanimously by all political parties. NGO leaders had lobbied hard and passionately, and the success of this effort itself suggests the stronger sway of these nongovernment bodies in the political processes that shape Japan's international involvements.

Politicians and government officials now recognize unique value in NGO contributions to Japan's international diplomacy. This signals a recent shift in attitude. Most who are involved in national political life have long held a scathing view of NGOs; *hi-seifu soshiki* to many meant "antigovernment" organizations, rather than the literal meaning of "nongovernment" organizations. Japan's political establishment saw NGOs as radical, anti-establishment organizations with the sole purpose of criticizing government action. NGOs were stamped ideologically as pro-U.S. or pro-Soviet during the Cold War, a tag that by the end of the 1990s has largely been dropped. It is thus not surprising that, as one senior Liberal Democratic Party (LDP) politician explained, even in the early 1990s it was difficult to discuss NGOs at LDP headquarters and many LDP politicians would defer discussion to a private context. This same politician recognizes a qualitative change in the attitude of many politicians, even inside the LDP, although most do not see a large space yet for NGOs in Japanese policy making.[38]

One particular benefit that Japanese policy makers see in the international involvement of Japanese NGOs is their ability to "humanize" Japan's international relations. NGO workers bring human faces into the arena of Japanese diplomacy. This is now recognized by the foreign ministry as an important contribution, in the face of years of international criticism for the "facelessness" of its ODA program, its international contributions, and indeed its international image.

The most instrumental way in which NGOs show Japan's human face internationally is through their involvement in overseas development projects, particularly with delivery of humanitarian aid. These are one of the most important rallying points for Japanese NGOs, and many are involved on the ground and overseas in a wide range of programs. These NGOs operate either directly through their own efforts or in cooperation with local and other international NGOs. Like SNGs, NGOs have become involved in delivery of Japanese ODA, with some receiving financial support from the Japanese government for their on-site work with aid recipients. Again like SNGs, NGOs have gained the official recognition that they are legitimate international actors making valuable contributions to effective delivery of Japanese official aid. The role of NGOs in global environmental policy is also officially recognized and generally endorsed.[39]

Not all Japanese NGOs are active outside Japan, and not all are concerned with humanitarian or environmental issues. Some serve as effective pressure groups inside Japan, pursuing their own policy agenda for worthy international causes. One of these causes is global banning of use of landmines. Japanese NGOs lobbied strenuously throughout the mid-1990s to have a divided Japanese government sign a global treaty banning antipersonnel landmines.[40] The NGOs pressured government directly, and lobbied hard through the media, signature campaigns, and international NGOs such as the International Campaign to Ban Landmines (ICBL), a winner of the Nobel peace prize.

Behind government foot-dragging was powerful opposition from another source outside Japan, whose impact on Japan's international diplomacy had almost nothing to do with a humanitarian assessment of the danger of landmines: Japan's most important ally, the United States, remained opposed to this treaty and lobbied Japan not to sign it. Japanese foreign ministry and defense officials rallied to resist the mounting domestic and external pressure to sign the treaty. Under this pressure's heavy weight, and with then Foreign Minister Obuchi Keizo's personal commitment to the cause, the government eventually signed the treaty in December 1997. Foreign ministry officials again stalled on ratifying the treaty, and again NGO actions helped seal the process.[41] Japan ratified the antipersonnel landmines treaty in September 1998. Japanese NGOs were crucial to this outcome, which had given them useful political experience, a welcome precedent for NGOs within Japan, and an indication of diplomatic praxis on a specific issue between the foreign actor that is treated as most crucial to Japanese international diplomacy (the U.S. government) and the Japanese actor that ultimately controls foreign policy (the foreign ministry).

The standing of Japanese NGOs in the international community is still relatively low. For example, some NGOs in Asia have made clear their concerns that Japanese NGOs are unable to stand up to their own government and are therefore weak in the important areas of advocacy and agenda setting. These outside organizations hold that until Japanese NGOs are able to engage their own government in constructive dialogue on domestic issues, their contributions to issues of regional or global advocacy is likely to remain weak.[42] Japan's NGOs are generally not as assertive as some of their Western counterparts. But they have begun to make some impact on Japan's international diplomacy as is clear in the landmine banning and in their growing "contributions" to "Japan's international contributions." If the current momentum continues, their role in setting policy agenda will also strengthen markedly.

The State of Diplomatic Play Among SNGs, NGOs, and the National Government

Establishing Legitimacy

We see from the above discussion that SNGs and NGOs are now emerging as significant actors in Japan's foreign policy. The rise has involved struggle to gain recognition from the central government (particularly from the foreign ministry) that they are indeed legitimate actors on this landscape. Initially, the ministry found the involvement of these new and unfamiliar actors in international relations something of a threat to its own jurisdiction—not to be trusted and perhaps to be dismissed as intrusive or irrelevant players—in the ministry's attempts to manage international relations exclusively. The foreign ministry, which is structurally responsible for international relations, has battled to retain its responsibilities. It has guarded diplomatic turf even from other government ministries, and certainly from more distant actors such as SNGs at different levels of government and NGOs that are not government.

For NGOs (by their very nature nongovernmental), the struggle for official recognition has been hard. As a classic early example of central government abnegation, in 1989 the Japanese government barred NGOs from participating in the international conference on global environmental protection that it organized in Tokyo.[43] Again considerable ignorance has been a problem. Even in 1998, a Japanese academic claimed in a posting to the Internet discussion group on Japanese politics moderated by the University of Tokyo's Institute of Social Science:

> There are virtually no NGOs in Japan. With a few, very courageous and strong exceptions, most in Japan are classified as SGOs or Subcontracted Government Organizations or in Japanese, "*Shitauke* Government Organi-

zations," thinly disguised "amakudari" sites for the same government officials that [sic] dole out their SGO funds.[44]

There are shreds of truth in this comment. Yet dismissing NGOs as nothing more than subsidiaries or subcontracted organizations of the national government is a gross misjudgment of the degree of their independence from government intervention, their current status inside and outside Japan, and their expanding contributions to Japan's international diplomacy. Japanese NGOs may not yet be as vigorous and influential in foreign policy making as their counterparts in other industrialized nations, but they are emerging as important international actors with growing influence on Japan's foreign policy.

In a nation with a long tradition of the public accepting central government and national bureaucrats as sole or ultimate policy makers and as custodians of national interest, SNGs and NGOs have first had to overcome a wall of bureaucratic resistance to their international activities.[45] Part of the problem concerns their identity as international actors. Although they do not claim to represent the Japanese nation, because of their official status as Japanese SNGs and NGOs rather than as private actors, their actions abroad may be taken as representing or indicating a "Japanese" position, whatever their intentions. The central government recognizes the possible consequences for Japan's foreign policy, which is why the foreign ministry in particular is keen to regulate the involvement of these noncentral government actors in Japan's international relations.

For SNGs, another reason explaining moves for regulation by the central government is embedded in domestic politics: the center wants to maintain SNG dependency upon it to staunch the weakening hold of the central government on policy at the subnational level. Some SNG international activities serve to distance subnational bodies from the hold of the national government. Economic benefits gained independently through local-level programs enable SNGs to bolster their own income, which reduces their financial dependence on the central government. And as we saw in the example of the city of Sapporo, multilateral forums with like-placed counterparts that are addressing similar problems abroad reduce the fealty of SNGs to the advice and policy direction of their national government. Further, engagements with their SNG counterparts abroad (especially those in more liberal federal systems) can present precedents for Japanese SNGs to observe and strive to achieve in their own relations, as they struggle for greater autonomy at the subnational level.

Institutional Framework for Coordination
For the reasons discussed above, relevant parts of the central government have moved to establish the institutional framework that they consider necessary to work with these potentially valuable international actors—to guide, coordinate, and collaborate with them as national policy needs demand. We will begin with institutions for SNGs. One that we noted earlier for coordinating the JET program is CLAIR (Council of Local Authorities for International Relations), which serves as the liaison body between Japanese SNGs and SNGs overseas, as

well as between SNGs and the Ministry of Home Affairs (MOHA). When it was established in 1988, CLAIR was the only major *gaikaku dantai* (external organization) of the home affairs ministry. The JET program is an important international activity for SNGs and in CLAIR we see how the central government, through the ministry, has established infrastructure to regulate, as well as coordinate, SNG involvement. In 1989 the home affairs ministry took a more comprehensive approach by establishing formal guidelines and further support structures for SNG international activities. This was intended to encourage them but was also, patently, a way to keep the reins on these potentially liberating activities of SNGs as international actors.

To coordinate with NGOs, the Ministry of Foreign Affairs established the NGO Assistance Division (Minkan Enjo Shienshitsu) within the ministry's Economic Cooperation Bureau after legislation was passed in 1994. This move was significant since at the time the government's tight program of administrative reform made it almost impossible for any ministry to establish a new division. The new institutional framework was one indication that the government had recognized the importance of NGOs in international affairs and had taken steps to ensure that it could steer these emerging international actors. After all, NGOs have the potential to make valuable contributions to Japanese diplomacy, especially in delivery of humanitarian programs of development and postwar reconstruction. But they are also, potentially, loose and threatening cannons that the ministry is keen to guide through funding, consultation, and cooperation.

The foreign ministry's NGO division provides subsidies to NGOs for their developmental work in developing countries. The subsidy system was set up in 1989 with a modest budget of ¥110 million. This was increased more than tenfold to ¥1,200 million in 1997. NGO projects also receive financial support from the national government through the 1991 government-initiated International Volunteer Savings Plan administered by the Ministry of Posts and Telecommunications. Depositors nationwide voluntarily contribute 20 percent of their after-tax interest earned on deposits in post office savings accounts. As of March 1997, some 21 million investors had joined the volunteer plan and a total of 12.2 billion yen had been collected in the six years since the program was begun.[46]

The NGO/MOFA *teiki kyogikai* (periodic conference) was established in 1996 as a forum for regular consultation. The conference group is made up of seven representatives of NGOs and eight representatives of the foreign ministry. It meets four times annually to discuss ways in which the ministry can support NGOs and identify new areas for cooperation. It aims to build a relationship of mutual trust while coordinating the interests and capacities of both sides.[47] Other government ministries have begun to court NGOs for their ideas and policy advice. The Division of Economic Cooperation in MITI (Ministry of International Trade and Industry), for example, in mid-1999 sent a letter to 18 Japanese NGOs, seeking new ideas for effective delivery of Japan's ODA in which MITI is involved. Some senior officials of MITI have even joined the national Association of NPO Studies hoping to garner new policy ideas as well as contacts from the group.[48]

Cooperation Between SNGs and NGOs

It is not just the central government bodies that have moved to engage SNGs and NGOs. The two have also moved to engage each other. On many issues they share concerns and priorities, and recognize mutual benefit from cooperation between them. This is especially so on overseas development programs. The NGO-Municipality Network of International Cooperation (NGO Jichitai Kyoryoku Suishin Kaigi) was established in April 1997 to facilitate these connections. The network aims to unify SNGs' technical expertise with the capacity of NGOs in aid delivery. It is one of a number of national-level and subnational-level organizations that promote cooperation between the two. Many SNGs also provide subsidies to NGOs to carry out developmental activities in their partner cities abroad.

There are many strong examples of local-level cooperation. In 1997 Hiroshima Prefecture established the Hiroshima International Cooperation Center (Hiroshima Kokusai Kyoryoku Senta), which in turn established an NGO college whose main aim is to train volunteers with the help of a Hiroshima-based NGO, AMDA (Association of Medical Doctors of Asia). In Kyushu, a local NGO, the Kagoshima Karaimo Koryu Dantai (KKD), receives financial support from Kagoshima Prefecture for promoting cooperation with farmers in Asia. KKD has initiated various kinds of exchange programs with rural communities in Asian countries, for teaching, learning, and recognizing shared problems confronting their rural communities.

Pluralism in Foreign Policy

As I demonstrate in this chapter, slowly but surely both SNGs and NGOs are taking their place as legitimate actors in Japan's foreign affairs. This is not to suggest erosion in the primary place held by national government, via the foreign ministry, in Japan's foreign policy. These actors do not play a zero sum game in international diplomacy. Rather, I argue that in conducting and managing Japan's increasingly complex international relations, the contribution of these newer actors continues to expand, at a time when the central government to some extent needs their input. In some ways, it appears that the central government—especially through the foreign ministry—is attempting to harness their involvement in international affairs to mutual advantage. This is producing a more pluralist approach to foreign policy in Japan.

Earlier tensions are gradually easing between the central government and these emerging international actors. Both sides increasingly emphasize partnership rather than confrontation, cooperation rather than isolation. The central government has come to recognize that Japan's interests abroad can best be served by allowing these nonnational actors to carry out some of Japan's international responsibilities and where appropriate, national government can work in tandem with these actors to deliver services overseas. With this has also come recognition by many in the central government that SNGs are no longer simply subsidiaries that carry out functions dictated by the national government.

Despite the closer engagement, SNGs, NGOs and the national government do not share visions on all issues. A few, usually strategic, issues have been the source of disagreement, division, or at least acknowledged differences in priority, as we see in the antinuclear policies of SNGs and landmine-banning work of NGOs. Furthermore, none of the three types of actors—central government, SNGs, and NGOs—are themselves internally unified as political monoliths. Having the same legal status as members of these categories on the one hand helps to unify their interests in policy outcomes. But it also inherently sets up competition between them, for money, power, kudos, and other achievement, with the potential for alliance building and division that this presents to all the actors involved in Japan's international diplomacy.

Nevertheless, most significant is recognition by the national government and politicians that these organizations are genuine actors in Japan's international affairs and the former are prepared to cooperate with these organizations in the interests of international diplomacy. The foreign ministry retains control over the crucial elements of Japan's foreign policy agenda but it cannot drive its own agenda in unitary fashion. The range of issues and actors is now too complex and inextricable. The growing involvement of Japanese SNGs and NGOs in international affairs gives us glimpses of some new trends in managing foreign policy in Japan across diverse domestic actors, from isolation toward cooperation, from dependence toward interdependence, from a unitary toward a more pluralist approach, and with some small and guarded inevitable steps toward decentralization. These trends are still directions, not destinations yet achieved. Yet they are beginning to influence profoundly how foreign policy is conducted in Japan.

Exemplifying the New Partnerships: A Tripartite Response to Yugoslavia

One strong example of the relationship developing between the three players can be seen in the Japanese response to the tragedy of Yugoslavia in mid-1999. Japan learned the hard way how to respond to international crisis, when its U.S. $13 billion contribution to the 1991 Gulf War efforts was dismissed outside Japan as checkbook diplomacy without human contribution. After the NATO bombings ended in Yugoslavia in mid-1999, Japan was eager to help rehabilitate people suffering losses from the war, this time with a show of Japanese faces, as well as dollars. Here the national government, SNGs, and NGOs acted in unison. The government arranged to contribute to relief programs in Kosovo by providing funds to a Japanese NGO, Peace Winds Japan, to carry out relief work on the ground. Part of these funds have come from the Human Security Foundation, which was set up in the United Nations at Prime Minister Obuchi's suggestion. The Hyogo prefectural government responded with an offer of prefabricated housing that it had used a few years earlier for victims of the Kobe earthquake, and this was shipped to Yugoslavia for the homeless. Costs of shipment and construction will be borne by the national government, but supervision and allocation of houses will be conducted by NGOs.[49]

Many Japanese politicians held the view that Japan's contribution to bringing peace and restoration in Kosovo would be recognized outside Japan only if Japanese NGOs took the lead role in relief efforts. This was a sea change in their attitude of just five years earlier.[50] Here was recognition that NGOs could be the sorely needed "human contribution" from Japan. Thus, NGOs were also making an important contribution to Japan's international diplomacy, since constitutional restrictions and public backlash prevent Japan from sending personnel in a military capacity to contribute to overseas peacekeeping efforts. So strongly have some politicians felt about this issue that parliamentarians have established a suprapartisan group called the Kokusai Kyoryoku NGO Katsudo Suishin Giin Renmei (Federation of Parliamentarians to Promote NGO International Cooperation Activities) to consider effective cooperation with NGOs. Hence, Japan's delivery of *heiwa enjo* (aid for peace) to Yugoslavia offers useful insights into the new thinking inside Japan on its international contributions, effective cooperation between domestic international actors, and pragmatic, innovative strategies for foreign policy implementation.

Explaining the Rise of Japanese SNGs and NGOs in International Activities

A complex mix of domestic and international factors explains the rise of SNGs and NGOs in Japan's foreign policy, and why the foreign ministry has come to recognize that careful promotion and guidance of their involvement, rather than its discouragement, usually also serve the ministry's interests. First, these bodies have the will and the interest to make useful international connections. Both have the commitment to pursue relations abroad because of their vested interest in the outcome; for NGOs, such is their raison d'être, from environmental protection to delivery of postcrisis medical assistance. Second, these bodies have the wherewithal. They have financial and other resources at a time when government resources are diminishing. Increasingly, they have gained experience in the domestic and international contexts and have become better able to work, and reshape, the political systems in which they operate. The experience has also enabled them to build the close links with counterparts outside Japan—SNGs and NGOs in other parts of the world—that can offer valuable connections in diplomacy.

Third, these bodies are at times able to act where the central government cannot, precisely because they are not recognized abroad as central government actors with the political and other stigma that this status can carry in international diplomacy. Politically contentious matters, such as human rights activities and implementation of sensitive cultural programs, are two of numerous examples. Fourth, again because they are not recognized as national government actors, SNGs and NGOs help to popularize Japan's international relations. This is a valuable contribution given that overseas criticisms of Japan's checkbook diplomacy left the foreign ministry claiming the need to introduce the "human face" in Japan's international relations, as we noted earlier. Their contribution to Japanese diplomacy comes as the foreign ministry has sought to develop Japan's international profile with contributions to the global community, by involvement in international issues that goes beyond straight injections of Japanese money.

A fifth reason concerns the nature of the global context in which Japan conducts international relations. In summary, since the Cold War structures on which postwar Japanese diplomacy relied crumbled, the Japanese government has confronted new imperatives to engage with other international actors in securing cooperation and support. Also significant among many factors here are that technological advancements have enabled all international actors to work together with greater ease and efficiency, and that the flourishing of SNGs and NGOs in other parts of the world has set a useful precedent from which counterparts in Japan can take lessons and inspiration.

SNGs and NGOs in Japan's Foreign Policy: Significant Parallels

This examination of SNGs and NGOs as international actors points to a number of interesting parallels between them, in the context of their involvement in Japan's foreign policy. We may expect this to some extent, since both operate within the same domestic and international contexts and have been basically contemporaries in their emergence on the foreign-policy landscape.

First, both have extended considerably the range of their actions outside Japan and their status in national policy matters has risen as a result. We have seen in this discussion how official explanations of their involvement in foreign policy have been recast accordingly to accommodate the new status of these bodies through their "international cooperation" and "international contribution" that implies the perceived value of what they accomplish abroad. Both have been drawn by default, and on rare occasion, into hard diplomacy on matters that concern national security. Both have been relegated outside this domain at the hand of a dominant, cautious foreign ministry for whom national security is taken as its sole preserve.

Second, in tandem with their greater international activity, both SNGs and NGOs have gained confidence in their own abilities to act independently of the central government to the extent that they are able. They have sought, and to a limited extent have gained, some scope for independent action in their international activities. The process has served to strengthen their profiles in domestic affairs and their place as legitimate international actors, with due recognition by politicians, central government, and other policy actors that these international actors cannot, and should not, be sidelined from policy matters.

Third, both comprise quite disparate "members" under their respective labels. SNGs include small rural villages with populations of a few hundred and minimal political pull, through to huge, thriving metropolises such as Tokyo, islands such as Kyushu, and entire regions such as Kansai, all with populations of many million and enough clout in Tokyo to sway national policy. NGOs are similarly not uniform in size, purpose, and outlook. In both cases, the label applied confers status (or lack of it), implies purpose, and helps to forge connection between disparate members whose interests may not otherwise align.

Fourth, both have developed new relations with other international actors. Many of these actors are their counterparts abroad. International forums and work on-location in overseas developmental programs have been valuable opportunities for building these relationships, mostly bilaterally, but with some multilateral linkages. These newly forged relationships have helped to bolster the position of Japanese SNGs and NGOs domestically (and internationally) through opportunities for alliance-building and other strategies that have sharpened both their political savvy and their voice inside the Tokyo policy forums.

Fifth, both have relatively short histories as international actors. SNGs began with small, almost invisible steps abroad through sister-city relationships in the mid-1950s. NGOs undertook small-scale international forays from around the 1960s. Both have begun to figure more prominently on the scene in the 1990s, when their quest for further involvement in activities outside Japan met with international and domestic environments more conducive to their involvement. As we have seen, though, this has not been plain sailing into the foreign policy domain for either of them, and the central government has tried to steer, partner, and coopt both of them through various regulatory mechanisms.

Sixth, through one of these regulatory mechanisms—law—SNGs and NGOs are both subject to legislation set in place by the national government in the late 1990s that directly and indirectly limits their international involvement. The Decentralization Law passed by the Diet in June 1999 is one step forward in giving a small degree of legal autonomy to Japanese SNGs, but their financial status is still tied firmly to the national government. For NGOs, the NPO Law passed in 1998 makes it much easier to establish legally, but this law also puts severe restrictions on NGOs through requiring their supervision by an appropriate ministry and formal accounting of their funds.[51]

A mix of reasons helps explain these parallels between SNGs and NGOs as international actors. Both are subject to similar forces shaping the domestic and international contexts in which they operate. Significantly, however, a key source of these parallels can also be found in their status vis-à-vis central government actors. In the foreign policy domain, both have had to struggle with central actors to assert identity and legitimacy, a shared struggle that has helped to forge empathy and shared political turf between them.

Conclusion

Comparative literature on international relations informs us that international diplomacy and global governance are no longer the sole preserve of nation-states. Global problems such as the management of the environment, human rights, demographic change, and basic human needs can be managed most effectively only when a range of actors bring ideas, advice, personnel, and technical and other resources to address these issues. SNGs and NGOs are two of these types of actors who are bringing their strengths to the domain of international relations.

In the 1990s, this trend has helped to kick start the emergence of Japanese international actors that are not part of the central government. Both SNGs and NGOs in Japan will continue to confront domestic and international challenges to their status as international actors. Both are now seen in a favorable light domestically and are making efforts to improve their profiles as international actors both at home, and in the international arena. But they are still beholden to some extent to a foreign ministry that is used to unitary action in foreign policy.

Japan is part of the international trend toward pluralism in international relations. Inevitably, the new international actors have encroached on the more specific, formerly protected, domain of foreign policy. That is why SNGs and NGOs have begun to take their place within Japan's foreign policy. If present trends continue, this place will gain further ground, though the central government, particularly via the foreign ministry, will surely aim to keep its hand firmly on the reins.

Notes

1. Osaka, Kyoto, Nagoya, Yokohama, Kobe, Kitakyushu, Sapporo, Kawasaki, Fukuoka, Hiroshima, Sendai, and Chiba are designated cities. There is a move to amalgamate Omiya and Urawa cities in Saitama Prefecture so that the newly created city will be able to seek designated city status and the benefits this confers.
2. There are over 65,000 elected local assembly members and about 3,300 elected heads in Japan . In 1996, SNGs employed around 2.8 million people as against 1.5 million employed by the national government. Asahi Shimbunsha, ed., *Japan Almanac 1999* (Tokyo: Asahi Shimbunsha, 1997).
3. NGO Katsudo Suishin Senta [JANIC], *NGOtte nanda* [What Are NGOs?] (Tokyo: JANIC, 1996).
4. See the third of a three-part series on NPOs in *Asahi shimbun*, 29 June 1999. The writers of this series define NGOs as those NPOs that are engaged in overseas activities.
5. JANIC, *NGO Dairekutori-98: Directory of Japanese NGOs Concerned with International Cooperation* (Tokyo, 1998).
6. See, for example, Michael H. Shuman, "Dateline Main Street: Local Foreign Policies," *Foreign Policy* 65 (Winter 1986–87): 154–74; Hans J. Michelmann and Panayotis Soldatos, eds., *Federalism and International Relations: The Role of Subnational Units* (Oxford: Clarendon Press, 1990); Heidi H. Hobbs, *City Hall Goes Abroad: The Foreign Policy of Local Politics* (Thousand Oaks: Sage Publications, 1994); Jessica T. Matthews, "Power Shift," *Foreign Affairs* 76:1 (January–February 1997): 50–66.
7. Mike Clough, "Consulates Belong to Yesterday's Diplomacy," *Los Angeles Times*, reprinted in *Daily Yomiuri*, 17 August 1998.
8. These include Earl H. Fry, *The Expanding Role of State and Local Governments in U.S. Foreign Affairs* (New York: Council on Foreign Relations Press, 1998); Lawrence T. Woods, *Asia-Pacific Diplomacy, Non Governmental Organisations and International Relations* (Vancouver: University of British Columbia Press, 1993).
9. These include G. Silliman and Lela Garner Noble, eds., *Organizing for Democracy, NGOs, Civil Society and the Philippine State* (Honolulu: University of Hawaii Press, 1998); Gerard Clarke, "Non-Governmental Organizations (NGOs) and Politics in the Developing World," *Political Studies* 46:1 (1998): 36–52.
10. See Thomas Princen, "NGOs: Creating a Niche in Environmental Diplomacy," in *Environmental NGOs in World Politics: Linking the Local and the Global*, eds. Thomas Princen and Matthias Finger (London and New York: Routledge, 1994).
11. This has been recognized widely and critiqued by various scholars. See, for example, William E. Bryant, *Japanese Private Economic Diplomacy: An Analysis of Business-Government Linkages* (New York: Praeger, 1975); also see Sadako Ogata, "The Business Community and Japanese Foreign Policy: Normalization of Relations with the People's Republic of China," in *The Foreign Policy of Modern Japan*, ed. Robert A. Scalapino (Berkeley: University of California Press, 1977), pp. 175–203.
12. Among the few exceptions in this literature are Tadashi Yamamoto and Yoichi Funabashi, *The Role of Non-State Actors in International Affairs: A Japanese Perspective* (Tokyo: Japan Center for International Exchange, 1995); Purnendra Jain and Mizukami Tetsuo, *Gurasurutsu no kokusai koryu* [Japan's Internationalization at the Grassroots Level] (Tokyo: Habesutosha, 1996); David Arase, "Shifting Patterns in Japan's Economic Cooperation in East Asia: A Growing Role for Local Actors?" *Asian Perspective* (Seoul) 21:1 (Spring–Summer 1997): 37–53; Gilbert Rozman, "Backdoor Japan: The Search for a Way out via Regionalism and Decentralization," *Journal of Japanese Studies* 25:1 (1999): 3–31.

13. Matthews, 1997, p. 52.
14. Clough, 1998. Also, see his "Grass-roots Policymaking," *Foreign Affairs* 73:1 (January–February 1994): 2–7.
15. Matthews, 1997, pp. 61–62.
16. Clough, 1994, p. 4.
17. Matthews, 1997, p. 62.
18. John Newhouse, "Europe's Rising Regionalism," *Foreign Affairs* 76:1 (January–February 1997): 67–84.
19. Elizabeth Bomberg and John Peterson, "European Union Decision Making: The Role of Subnational Authorities," *Political Studies* 2 (June 1998): 219–35.
20. Lester M. Salamon, "The Rise of the Nonprofit Sector," *Foreign Affairs* 73:4 (July–August 1994): 109.
21. See Ann Marie Clark, "Non-governmental Organizations and Their Influence on International Society," *Journal of International Affairs* 48:2 (Winter 1995): 507–27; Jonathan A. Fox and L. David Brown, eds., *The Struggle for Accountability: The World Bank, NGOs, and Grassroots Movements* (Cambridge: The MIT Press, 1998); Peter Willetts, ed., *"The Conscience of the World": The Influence of Non-governmental Organisations in the UN System* (London: Hurst & Company, 1996); Megan Park, "The Growing Role of Non-Governmental Organizations in Global Politics," *Swords and Poughshares: A Journal of International Affairs* 7:1 (Fall 1997): 47–62.
22. Menju Toshihiro, "Jichitai gaiko no susume" [Local Diplomacy], *Chuo Koron* (October 1998): 204–14; Abe Hitoshi and Shindo Muneyuki, *Gaisetsu Nihon no chihojichi* [An Outline of Japan's Local Government] (Tokyo: University of Tokyo Press, 1997), see chapter on *jichitai gaiko*, pp. 189–99.
23. Nihon Kokusai Koryu Senta [Japan Center for International Exchange] and Jichitai Kokusaika Kyokai [Council of Local Authorities for International Relations], *Chiho jichitai no kokusai kyoryoku katsudo no genjo to kadai* [The Status and Problems of International Exchange and Activities of Local Governments] (Tokyo, 1997).
24. Menju, 1998, pp. 208–209.
25. Council of Local Authorities for International Relations, *1998 Japanese Local Government International Affiliation Directory* (Tokyo, 1998), p. 2.
26. See Purnendra Jain, "Chiho jichitai no kokusaiteki yakuwari" [The International Role of Local Governments], in Jain and Mizukami, 1996, pp. 61–96.
27. In 1996, SNGs received 573 trainees through the JICA program and through their own programs received 390 trainees and dispatched 470 technical staff to Asian and other countries. See Menju, 1998, p. 210. For more details, see Jichiro Jichiken Chuo Suishin Iinkai [National Prefectural and Municipal Workers Union, Central Committee for the Promotion of Local Authority], *Jichitai no kokusai kyoryoku to jichitai ODA* [International Exchange and Local ODA] (Tokyo, 1995).
28. Menju, 1998, p. 209.
29. Information based on the author's interview with officials of the city of Sapporo on 2 July 1999.
30. See Arase, 1997, pp. 37–53.
31. Abe and Shindo, 1997, p. 195.
32. See *Asahi Evening News*, 25 February 1999; 3 March 1999.
33. See "Gaiko, kokumin to katarimasu: Gaimuseimujikan chiho de taiwa no tsudoi [Explaining Foreign Policy to the People: Foreign Secretary Holds Dialogue Meetings with Localities], *Asahi shimbun*, 24 April 1999.
34. See Purnendra Jain, "Japan's 1999 Unified Local Elections: Electing Tokyo's Governor," *Japanese Studies* 19:2 (1999): 117–32.
35. Nakata Toyokazu, "Budding Volunteerism," *Japan Quarterly* (January-March 1996); Umahashi Norio, "Gendai kokusai kankei ni okeru NGO: Kokuren o chushin ni" [NGOs in Contemporary International Relations: Focusing on the UN] *Kokusai mondai* (December 1996): 2–16.
36. Details of these recommendations are available in Asahi Shimbun, *Priorities for the Coming Century: Proposals by the Asahi Shimbun* (Tokyo, 1997). For further details and analysis, see Asahi Shimbun Chikyu Purojekuto 21, *Shimin sanka de sekai o kaeru* [Citizen Participation as a Vehicle for Changing the World] (Tokyo: Asahi Shimbunsha, 1998).
37. Yamauchi Naoto, ed., *NPO detabukku* (Yuhikaku, 1999), p. 15; also, see, Menju Toshihiro, "Nihon" [Japan], in *Ajia Taiheiyo no NGO* [NGOs in Asia Pacific] ed., Nihon Kokusai Koryu Senta (Tokyo: Aruku, 1998), p. 202.

38. Author's interview with former education minister Kosugi Takashi at Daiichi Gikai Kaikan in Tokyo, 12 July 1999.
39. See Alan Rix, *Japan's Foreign Aid Challenge: Policy Reform and Aid Leadership* (London and New York: Routledge, 1993), pp. 64–70; Kurosawa Miwako, "Accepting the Role of NGOs: Examples from the Environmental and Developmental Community," *Social Science Japan* (August 1999): 39–43.
40. Two NGOs particularly active in this process were the Japan Campaign to Ban Landmines (JCBL) and the Association to Aid Refugees (AAR), which is involved in mine-clearing activities and projects for landmine victims.
41. A newspaper column published in the influential *Asahi shimbun* on 4 August 1998 triggered a positive response from Obuchi, who by this time was serving as prime minister. The prime minister brought together the author (an international relations researcher and NGO activist) and officials from the foreign ministry, and it was agreed that Japan would ratify this treaty without delay. See Mekata Motoko, "Jirai shomei no Obuchi-san, tsugi wa hijun desu" [Mr. Obuchi, after the Signature, the Next Step Is Its Ratification], Rondan, *Asahi shimbun*, 4 August 1998.
42. Andra L. Corrothers and Estie W. Suryatna, "Indonesia: Review of the NGO Sector in Indonesia and Evolution of the Asia Pacific Regional Community Concept among Indonesian NGOs," in *Emerging Civil Society in the Asia Pacific Community* ed., Tadashi Yamamoto (Singapore: Institute of Southeast Asian Studies and the Japan Center for International Exchange, 1996), pp. 135–37.
43. This was the International Conference on Global Environmental Protection Towards Sustainable Development. See Princen and Finger, 1994, p. 22.
44. SSJ Forum Moderator, ssjmod@iss.u-tokyo.ac.jp (1 August 1998).
45. Mekata Motoko, an activist with the Japan Campaign to Ban Landmines (JCBL), explained a viewpoint well understood by her NGO counterparts: that the traditional Japanese concept of power relations between *okami* (national government and bureaucrats) and *shimojimo* (ordinary people) still resonates in the minds of Japan's government officials and policy makers. Personal interview with the author in Tokyo, 1 June 1999.
46. *Nikkei Weekly*, 17 March 1997.
47. Author's interview with Saotome Mitsuhiro, director of the foreign ministry's NGO Assistance Division, 2 September 1998.
48. See "Henkaku no sapota: NPO 1" [Supporter of Change: NPO 1], *Asahi shimbun*, 29 June 1999.
49. *Asahi shimbun* (evening), 8 July 1998.
50. Interview with Kosugi Takashi, 12 July 1999. Also, see his interview "Ima Nihon no hatasubeki yakuwari towa: Yugosurabia de mitekita koto" [What Role Should Japan Play Now? My Experience in Yugoslavia], *Sekai* (August 1999), pp. 63–64.
51. The 1998 law was a significant milestone in the development of civil society in Japan. But because it offers very little incentive for individuals or corporations to donate funds to these organizations, it retains potential for external control through dependence on the nonprivate source of funding, i.e., government. NGOs are still lobbying vigorously for changes in the taxation system so that NGOs are able to seek donations from a range of sources to enhance their financial status and by extension, their independence from government.

PART II
The Issues

CHAPTER 3

Japan and International Organizations

Edward Newman

International institutions have clear relevance for the perennial debates concerning Japan's engagement with the rest of the world. Many of the challenges that Japanese foreign policy elites have faced since the World War II have embraced international institutions, to various degrees and for various motives. The same holds true as the twenty-first century begins, and Japan's leaders consider how best to manage a rapidly evolving security and economic environment and changing expectations for Japanese foreign policy from inside and outside Japan. In addition to the dilemmas and challenges inherent in the changing international environment, Japan's internal economic and political restructuring is steadily planting Japan more deeply in international commitments and networks.

Themes and Dimensions

For a number of reasons, international organizations have been important to Japan's foreign policy. Moreover, the directions in which political evolution takes the country will embrace international organizations to a greater or lesser degree. This can be approached in the context of Japan's history, its political structure, and its social tenets, in addition to external environmental factors. A number of themes and dimensions, both historical and current, are involved in this foreign policy area.

First, given the historical, political, and perhaps social factors that condition Japanese foreign policy, and the constraints—constitutional and political—upon the exercise of military "hard" power, multilateralism has figured prominently in Japan's diplomacy and its pursuance of national interest in the broadest sense. Multilateralism, and in particular the United Nations, provided a vehicle for the reintegration of Japan into the international community in the 1950s and 1960s, and an opportunity to exercise some diplomatic independence from the United States. The continuing wariness of countries—and especially Japan's neighbors—toward overt Japanese foreign policy initiatives has similarly encouraged

Japan to seek a circumscribed, low-profile approach to its objectives within the legitimizing functional framework of multilateralism. This low profile has often conditioned its behavior; policy initiatives have often been made behind the scenes.

Related to this, Japan was something of a "latecomer" to international society, emerging from a long period of isolation in the latter half of the nineteenth century, and then experiencing a period of recalcitrance and aggression in the 1930s and 1940s. Thus, multilateral organizations have provided frameworks within which to exert leverage and make its voice heard as a country not among the traditional great powers.

Second, in later years a number of adjustments have been forced upon Japan that have pointed to an increased importance of international institutions for Japan's foreign policy. The "Yoshida doctrine" has been, by necessity, superceded: Japan can no longer conceive of national interest and national security in terms of production and export, and nor can it rely indefinitely upon U.S. security guarantees. Greater burden-sharing responsibilities are necessary in Japan's relationship both with the United States and with the wider international community, yet sensitivities toward a greater Japanese military role remain, within and without the country. In this context Japan has been attempting to play a more creative and substantive role in international institutions, involving a variety of issue areas. While the concept of a "UN-centered" foreign policy had a somewhat hollow ring to it in the past, Japan's efforts to forge a foreign policy embedded in new internationalist thinking *has* been centered on the United Nations to some extent.

Third, the role of the United States—and more specifically, the evolving postwar relationship between Japan and the United States—has conditioned and in part characterized Japan's multilateral diplomacy. Historically, the United States has directly or indirectly constrained Japan's multilateral diplomacy in areas such as arms control and the environment. Yet this role has acted also to encourage Japan's participation, as a counterbalance to U.S. influence on Japanese foreign policy, but also making Japan more committed to UN reform in order to in turn keep the United States committed.

Fourth, in addition, the global movement toward interdependence and transnational institutionalization—and a shift toward "soft" forms of power—has further encouraged Japan to consider many of its interests in a multilateral framework. In general, power is becoming increasingly diffuse; globalizing forces in international economics, information and culture, and various fragmentary forces are imposing pressures upon the state from above and below and putting the utility of traditional power political tools into doubt. Two decades ago Keohane and Nye popularized the concept of "complex interdependence," which argued that the nature of international politics was changing: states were increasingly entrenched in transnational economic interdependencies that were altering the nature of national interest and national security and reducing the utility of military power.[1] This process has since accelerated, and the state enclosure is being further challenged as national economic tools are less and less effective in the face of a globalizing finance and commodity market, and leaps in information technology. The evolving basis of the global economy and the information revolution are changing the meaning of power and raising questions regarding the state.[2] Pressure for deregulation of financial and commodity markets, the internationalization of production through investment, and the primacy of multinational corporations have undermined the traditional realist conception of international politics as a state-centric contestation for power based upon military superiority and military conquest. The Ricardian model of states trading on the basis of "national" factor endowments is barely recognizable.

Fifth, the growing importance of international organizations and regional economic arrangements has contributed to the trends of interdependence and perhaps globalization, and vice versa. Within this environment, the agenda of multilateralism is also rapidly evolving and broadening. Voting rights and influence in the leading international economic and aid institutions carry enormous influence for millions of people worldwide. The prominence of multilateralism in foreign policy is similarly underscoring the ethos of the collective management of common issues. Most governments would accept—although in varying degrees—that the environment, international economic and trade rules, the spread of disease, narcotics, terrorism, underdevelopment, and civil conflict are issues that demand collective management. The age of international hegemony appears to be past, which also means by necessity a greater reliance upon multilateral arrangements. The logic of this has not been lost on Japan's foreign policy elites.

The increasing prominence of international institutions following the end of the Cold War—including the rather ill-conceived "new phase in the history of the [UN] Organization"[3]—similarly encouraged Japan's political leaders and policy elites to consider Japan's burgeoning engagement with international politics within international institutions. The logic is simple: if the future is to embrace deeper international integration and institutional networks, the country's decision makers desire to be strategically placed within this, although this is not to say that any Japanese foreign policy analyst would vest Japan's foreign policy fundamentally within international organizations.

Sixth, in terms of regional security, Japan faces the challenge of balancing international demands for a greater share of the security burden with the reservations of many groups in Japan to an expanded military role and the wariness of a number of Japan's regional neighbors. Satisfying the expectations of allies, and fulfilling the needs of national security in a sensitive neighborhood, have thus been complicated. Thus, in a more general sense the Japanese government is attempting to reconcile the country's constitutional and sociopolitical makeup with the responsibilities of collective security and collective self-defense. Regional security challenges involve the cultivation of confidence and trust in relations with various states, while simultaneously addressing the probable need for a more viable independent Japanese military deterrence in the long term. Japan also confronts the challenge of remaining economically competitive in the face of international pressures for deregulation and liberalization, and of maintaining a stable supply of primary commodities. International institutions offer a framework to address these challenges, although foreign policy elites are far from convinced of the utility of security institutions.

Seventh, a further dimension to Japan's engagement with international institutions concerns the domestic political evolution of the country. Japan's role in international institutions reflects political dynamics within the country as different actors pull in different directions. Until recently, the dominant assumption was that international organizations provided a framework for Japan to contribute to "international public goods" and pursue national interests in the context of constraints upon military power. In effect, multilateralism provided some substitutes for "hard power," and in particular, traditional military power political tools. (Although, of course, the greatest substitute for Japan's "hard power" has been the U.S. security umbrella.) In the 1990s, however, largely as a result of the Gulf War and various pressures upon Japan to "contribute more," political groups within Japan have been attempting to use international organizations as a means to facilitate an expansion of Japan's international presence—including military—in a legitimate context. According to one observer, the pacifism of the Constitution faces its greatest threat as great power strategists seek to project Japanese military power under the "pretext of contributing to international society."[4] This is somewhat hysterical. Nevertheless, policy groups inside and outside the Liberal Democratic Party actively support greater Japanese participation in UN peacekeeping, advocating an interpretation or revision of the Constitution to allow Japan to militarily support collective security and collective self-defense.[5]

The formation of a new ruling coalition based on a conservative alliance between the Liberal Democratic Party and the newly formed Liberal Party in the autumn of 1998 brought such a scenario closer. The reformist leader of the Liberal Party, Ozawa Ichiro, is well-known for his view that Japan should participate fully in international peace and security activities as a "normal country."[6] His support of the coalition was widely believed to be premised upon the government's willingness to submit legislation that would allow greater participation of Japanese forces in peacekeeping and widen the area of responsibility within peacekeeping operations. To the extent that conservatives have often promoted rigorous support of the UN, and the Left has resisted it on pacifist grounds, it is indeed a paradox of Japanese politics.[7]

Eighth, regional international organizations have been, and continue to be, an important instrument in Japan's approach to regional issues. In particular, regional economic institutions have facilitated Japan's investment and market interests and allowed a circumscribed, legitimized form of leadership in a form that might otherwise have been politically difficult. Indeed, the Asian Development Bank has seen commitment and initiative by Japan within a region where Japan has natural leadership qualities that are tainted by past events.

For most Japanese elites—although to varying levels of commitment—these issues require a more forthright engagement with the outside world in pursuance of Japan's interests and also to fulfil the responsibilities expected as an integrated member of the "international community." International institutions have represented an important vehicle for this. Thus Japan has been projecting itself as a major actor in international politics and committing itself—in material and diplomatic terms—to a greater burden of responsibilities within this international context. The campaign for a permanent seat on the UN Security Council, the articulation of an agenda for peace, development and "global issues," and a number of diplomatic overtures are all a part of this. The official thrust has been an attempt to articulate a creative, progressive vision of international politics and to outline the modalities through which the international community can prosper and address common challenges. International institutions are a major vehicle for the pursuance of these objectives, although one has the impression that while the country has committed much of its foreign efforts in a multilateral setting, doubts remain in the minds of much of the decision-making elite. A major question is thus the extent to which a supposed "global role" is being pursued in a multilateral setting. Undoubtedly, behind the liberal internationalism of the official statements, a more national interest-orientation exists and is likely to strengthen.

Some commentators have been critical of Japan's multilateral efforts, arguing that the country does not have firm ideas to match its substantial financial input, that it is concerned mostly with the prestige of a prominent multilateral profile, and that it has employed dubious methods in the exercise of its influence.[8] Moreover, a number of—often revisionist—critics claim that Japan's use of international institutions is an extension of its domestic political structure, which invariably results in an unreformed pursuit of self-interest in international institutions, rather than a genuine support of the "international society" ethos or "international public goods." This is often argued to be a result of Japan's diffuse but rigid political structure, its insular culture, its historical experiences, and its pacifist Constitution. According to some observers, these conditions form an obstacle to forthright and creative leadership qualities, an obstacle to prompt decision making, and an obstacle to the communication of a convincing "global vision." Expressed most bluntly, the image some analysts still hold—largely incorrectly—is that Japan represents a passive-reactive actor mired in a insular and bureaucratic culture, governed by largely unseen interests preoccupied by trade and investment superiority, while shying away from international political involvement and gaining a "free-ride" on security.

It may be possible to question the extent to which Japan genuinely supports the "international society" ethos of international institutions and the UN, which are based upon a Grotian conception of international rules and order. According to the liberal view, an "International organization is not so much a contrived deviation from the natural course of international relations as a modern expression of some of the perennial tendencies and requirements of states operating in a multistate system . . . a part of the political and administrative apparatus of human society."[9] The pragmatic nature of Japanese foreign policy—in addition to the history of isolation and the prewar challenge to international society—tends to reflect a lack of commitment, perhaps an alienation or distance, from this ethos. Perhaps this may be reflected in the bureaucratic culture more than the general public. Generally, educated Japanese people are quite supportive of the UN—and even idealistic—but the establishment appears not to always reflect this. The relatively low proportion of Japanese nationals in international organizations is often said to reflect the low rating attached to international service in most career paths in government and administration.

A further negative theme is more closely related to Japan's post-bubble recession and the implications this holds for Japan's engagement with international organizations. If these economic woes are to be long term, then the domestic pressure upon Japan's financial contribution (which had always been the most notable contribution to international organizations) will increase. In addition, criticism of Japan's handling of its own economic problems, and its response to the regional economic challenges, which are widely believed to be inextricably linked to Japan's economic policies, may have implications for its authority in international organizations. Indeed, while Japan supports a bedrock of economic standards and institutions, its role in crisis situations has been criticized; during the Asian currency crisis between 1997 and 1998, many commentators bemoaned a supposed lack of leadership on Japan's part.[10] Conceivably, these points could lead one to consider *declining* Japanese role and authority in multilateralism, contrary to what most people have anticipated in recent decades.

Perceptions of Japan

To make sense of these divergent viewpoints and directions it is necessary to consider the wider and deeper political trends occurring in Japan that clearly condition Japan's engagement with international institutions. Many of the perceptions of Japan are based upon various misunderstandings. In particular, much analysis is unable to free itself from outdated images, models, and evidence, and much is distorted as a result of approaching Japan with a biased framework of reference. The study of Japan is itself very politicized—dominated by "convergence theorists" and "revisionists"—which heightens the element of bias in this subject. The result is often a polarization of arguments and grand observations, which are a world away from Japan's everyday interaction with international politics.

Nevertheless, some images exist—and have existed—and it is useful to consider them as a starting point. A common belief is that the country has been "unable to convey clearly how it conceives its own interests [and] unable to demonstrate a "world vision" that it is supposedly beginning to realize."[11] Inoguchi has presented the historical models or perceptions of Japan as free rider (in economic and security terms), challenger (in trade terms), and as a supporter of international economic and political structures.[12] It is the coexistence of these models that presents an enigma to the world. In recent years perceptions have varied from the expectation of Japan's search for international "role, recognition and respect"[13] to warnings of the "coming war with Japan,"[14] and everything in between.[15] The uncomfortable juxtaposition of perceptions continues, although the image of Japan as a benign—if competitive—and supportive member of the international community is becoming ascendant.

A prominent debate in scholarship on Japan concerns the extent to which its "internationalization" is progressing, and Japan is converging with international norms and standards in economics and politics. The official Japanese position is that this convergence is progressing inexorably and that the friction over trade imbalances and protectionism are merely the residue of historical legacies, which are now being ironed out. Efforts toward deregulation and administrative reform are argued to be further promoting this convergence. According to this view, Japan is a capitalist representative democracy along the lines of the liberal Western model. Those in Japan and elsewhere who support and expect a deeper engagement of the country with international politics and in support of the structures and values of the international community generally support this convergence view. A progressively deeper engagement with international organizations and institutions is an integral part of this theory.

At variance with this approach is the "revisionist" school. This argues that Japan's society, political system, and economic arrangements do not conform to the Western model of capitalism or notions of democracy, transparency, representation, and the separation of powers.[16] Fundamental structures of society and public life are argued to be peculiar, hiding behind a façade of superficial political and economic organizations. During the Cold War, this was obscured in the context of bipolar ideological and strategic confrontation, within which Japan was obviously firmly in the Western camp. This similarly allowed Japan a favorable trading and security relationship with the rest of the world, and particularly the United States. With the end of the Cold War, the revisionists argue, the trade imbalances between Japan and its trading partners appeared increasingly incongruous, and there have been growing demands that Japan open up and deregulate. However, these demands are premised upon a misunderstanding in believing that Japan can readily adjust its political and economic arrangements in line with the West. The failure of this adjustment, and the failure of outside analysts to understand the reasons why, inevitably leads to friction.[17] Hence the growing realization in the United States since the late 1980s that the Japanese system is dominated by a bureaucratic drive to "carve out niches of power in foreign markets without reciprocity."[18] This debate is central to the evolution of Japan's foreign policy—including its role in international organizations—although these arguments are somewhat polarized and politicized.

International Institutions and Japan's Agenda

The remainder of this chapter will present the development of Japan's participation in international organizations in the context of these themes, pressures, and incentives. This participation generally reflects a deepening material and human commitment and a steadily increasing diplomatic profile, within a broad range of international organizations. However, these trends are not consistent in all the organizations that Japan is involved in, or the types of activities within each organization. The level of financial, human, and diplomatic commitment tends to vary from institution to institution, as a result of domestic and international factors. The evolution of these political dynamics is the key to the direction of Japan's policy toward international organizations. This participation has been within three broad and overlapping types of organizations, and it has taken a variety of forms.

First, economic and aid organizations such as Asia-Pacific Economic Cooperation (APEC), Bank for International Settlements, Columbo Plan for Economic and Social Development in Asia and the Pacific, Group of Ten, Organization for Economic Cooperation and Development (OECD), African Development Bank (AfDB), Asia Development Bank (ADB), European Bank for Reconstruction and Development (EBDRD), Inter-American Development Bank (IADB), and organizations that come under the UN umbrella, such as World Bank, International Monetary Fund, World Trade Organization, UN Industrial Development Organization, the International Development Association, the International Finance Corporation, International Fund for Agricultural Development, and the Economic and Social Council.

Second, functional and scientific organizations such as the Customs Co-operation Council, the International Criminal Police Organization, the International Energy Agency, International Mobile Satellite Organization, International Telecommunications Satellite Organization, and those under the UN umbrella: Food and Agriculture Organization, International Civil Aviation Authority, International Labor Organization, International Maritime Organization, International Telecommunications Union, UN Industrial Development Organization, Universal Postal Union, World Health Organization (WHO), World Meteorological Organization, and World Intellectual Property Organization.

Third, political and security organizations such as the UN Security Council, General Assembly, International Court of Justice, and the International Atomic Energy Agency.

These are the chief international institutions through which Japan pursues its multilateral interests, contributes to international public goods, and maintains certain alliance commitments. Within the confines of this chapter it will not be possible to conduct a thorough analysis. Rather, certain themes will be addressed through Japan's activities in some of these organizations.

The Formative Years

After Japan's uncomfortable relationship with the League of Nations finally became estranged in the 1930s,[19] international institutions played a significant role in Japan's reintegration into international society. The country's aggression before and during World War II, and its total defeat in that war, formed an important historical background to this process. It is commonly observed that Japan's membership of the United Nations in 1956 signified its reentry into the international community of states after two decades of recalcitrance.[20] Membership of the United Nations also offered great promise for Japan's security in the context of Japan's new "Peace Constitution," Article 9 of which states that:

> Aspiring sincerely to an international peace based on justice and order, the Japanese people forever renounce war as a sovereign right of the nation and the threat or use of force as a means of settling international disputes.
> In order to accomplish the aim of the preceding paragraph, land, sea,

and air forces, as well as other war potential, will never be maintained. The right of belligerency of the state will not be recognized.

Some historians have argued that the article—indeed the constitution—was "imposed" upon Japan by the United States. Nevertheless, the article reflected a widely and strongly felt desire among the people of Japan that a strong military establishment had led the country into disaster and international ostracism and that war could not be considered an option in Japan's future.[21] Thus there was an element of idealism in Japan's "UN-centered" foreign policy as Prime Minister Yoshida Shigeru, among many others, had faith in the new organization. Moreover, there was a widespread belief that a demilitarized Japan in a UN context was the only form in which the rest of the world would accept Japan's development and reemergence. Japan's security would be guaranteed by the UN; it would not be a threat to any country because it had demilitarized, and thus it could concentrate on economic growth and development; the military obligations attached to membership of a collective security organization were conveniently put aside. In conformity with this ethos, in the early years of its UN membership Japan kept a low profile, paying its dues and generally following U.S. voting patterns, without making forthright or diplomatic overtures. The eventual realization that Japan's security would be firmly under the U.S. umbrella, rather than UN-centered, did change the perceptions of Japan's elites toward the UN. However, it remained an organization that offered many functional and diplomatic opportunities, and it continued to be in tune with the pacifist mentality that was so deep within the Japanese psyche.

Since the formative years of Japan's participation in the United Nations, its political engagement, its diplomatic independence, its human support, and especially its financial input have gradually increased. By 1973, Japan was assessed the third largest financial contributor and Kissinger and Nixon expressed support for a Japanese permanent seat on the Security Council.[22] Japan itself had already been thinking in such terms since the late 1960s.[23] The country was exercising more independence from the United States following the first oil crisis, and its growing economic confidence was producing a sense of strength partly channeled into the UN. Still, the small diplomatic overtures at the UN were largely in pursuance of narrow national interests: given Japan's dependence on the import of raw materials, it sought to use international institutions in its policy toward Arab oil-exporting states and Third World countries with which it had trade ties. It was not really until the 1980s that Japan could reasonably be said to be contributing something to the organization other than its financial support.

During that decade, Japanese efforts were directed into a number of areas. First, there were administrative and reform proposals, with the objective of overhauling the UN and addressing the rift that existed between the organization and the United States. In the 1980s a number of trends culminated: the "nefarious influence" of the Cold War,[24] East–West and North–South bloc maneuvering, a reversion to unilateralism, the seeming inability of the Security Council to address a number of key threats to international peace and security, the de facto abstention of key UN members from certain programs and agencies, and severe financial problems. In the words of Taylor and Groom, the organization "was on the sidelines and penniless.... The United Nations framework itself had become dilapidated and in gross need of reform. In short, a great experiment was in danger of failure."[25] It was in this context, which Secretary-General Pérez de Cuéllar described as the "crisis in the multilateral approach," that Japan initiated the Group of High Level Intergovernmental Experts (G18) on UN reform, seeking to reduce interbloc tensions and politicization of the organization that was undermining the organization. The approach was one of conciliatory even-handedness, recommending a rationalization of processes, bridge-building, and consensus-forging between estranged political groups. Japan's position as an industrialized country with an affinity with the "non-Western world" was, and is, an important dimension to this approach.

Second, in terms of peace and security the 1980s was a decade when Japan gradually became more prepared to break out of its passivity. It encouraged fact-finding by the secretary-general and aired ideas for the improvement of peace and security mechanisms. For example, Japan contributed to the General Assembly Declaration on the Prevention and Removal of Disputes and Situations Which May Threaten International Peace and Security. According to one view, Japan was displaying a forward-looking, broad view of security that embraced preventive measures.[26] This included an increasingly proactive engagement with conflict situations with the intention of promoting peaceful settlement. Japan was increasingly seen as the de facto "representative of Asia" on the Security Council, in addition to being a contender for permanent membership. Indeed, Japan has served as a nonpermanent member more than any other nonpermanent state: in the years 1958-59, 1966-67, 1971-72, 1975-76, 1981-82, 1987-88, 1992-93, and 1997-98.

The New Era

In the decades following World War II, Japan experienced a deepening—although still retarded—engagement with the structures and processes of international politics in parallel with, and in some senses as a consequence of, its meteoric economic rise. In the 1980s and 1990s, this engagement went beyond supporting structures and norms, and it went beyond projecting and protecting Japanese national interests narrowly conceived. Groups throughout Japanese society became increasingly willing, even eager, to address political issues and embrace a broader conception of national interests, to do more in Japan's relationship with its allies, and consider Japan's image and status in the international community as a part of this agenda.

The end of the Cold War and the relative decline of the United States (economic power) also encouraged Japan to consider a variety of future contingencies, most of which indicated the need for greater diplomatic independence and a more proactive and activist foreign policy. This recognition has been underscored by the exigencies of Japan's domestic political and economic reform agenda, with the effect that, in an increasingly deregulated and globalizing world, policy makers must be sensitive to the causes and effects of international trends and processes. This ethos has underscored Japan's desire to increase its authority, influence, and perhaps power in international organizations, and to play a more independent role. The motivations are multifaceted: simultaneously serving Japan's broadening international agenda, raising its status internationally, while also attempting to fulfill the normative/ethical agenda that has growing significance internationally and at home. Indeed, Japan has demonstrated recognition of its responsibility to commit more to the structures and norms of "international public goods" (although the outcome of this recognition is open to question).

The growing salience of international organizations is another motivation. International institutionalization is thickening; international organizations play a more pervasive role in international life, and some even approach supranational authority in the case of financial/trade organizations. Moreover, during the post–Cold War "honeymoon," there was a resurgence of the liberal international ethic: that international organizations should be the underpinnings of an "international society" based upon rules, justice, and collective approaches to common problems. The failure of the UN—or rather the international community—to fulfill this hope dashed the expectations of many observers and undoubtedly tempered the expectations and faith of Japanese foreign policy elites via-à-vis UN security capability. Nevertheless, even the more "realist" foreign policy analysts in Japan have recognized the importance of international organizations—especially in economic and diplomatic spheres—and thus the need for Japan to have some controlling influence.

The themes of Japan's approach to international organizations are multiple: a growing desire to set the agenda, to increase Japan's profiles and authority, even at the risk of courting controversy; a desire to strengthen, facilitate, and in some cases legitimize Japan's economic needs; and to complement Japan's security in East Asia in the face of future uncertainties. The approach has continued to be characteristic of Japan's wider foreign policy—still somewhat circumspect and tentative. According to a journalist with long experience in Japan and East Asia, the country is "far more passive than anyone would expect the world's second largest economic power to be."[27]

Over the last decade an interesting dimension of Japan's foreign policy has been its purported commitment to "international public goods": norms, structures, and institutions of "international society." Naturally, the motivations and substance may be somewhat different from the liberal internationalism that is embraced in the Ministry of Foreign Affair's policy statements. Yet there is a certain frankness and logic in putting Japan's deeper engagement in international politics—and the humanitarian dimensions of this—into a broader conception of "national interest": as the foreign ministry observes, "resource-poor Japan cannot survive today unless the world is stable and prosperous."[28] The national interest—as opposed to the liberal internationalist—orientation is gaining ground.

In the wider context Japan has addressed this agenda through a number of approaches. In conflict settlement, the country has been promoting itself as a third party, for example between India and Pakistan and among Afghanistan's combatants. In development, Japan has been taking an increasingly vocal line in support of the New Development Strategy in official development assistance (ODA) and through conferences, such as the Tokyo International Conference on African Development. In disarmament through its support of an antipersonnel landmine ban, the Tokyo Conference on Nuclear Safety in Asia (October 1996), the concept of an Emergency Action Forum on nuclear disarmament/ proliferation, in an attempt at diplomatic leadership by cosponsoring UN resolutions on Iraq, India, and Pakistan's nuclear tests, and in unilateral diplomatic initiatives, it has displayed a new assertiveness. Participation in peacekeeping and continuance of its fledgling regional leadership also reflect a commitment to engage in international politics. A number of issue areas serve to demonstrate this emboldened approach to "international public goods," especially within international organizations.

Disarmament and Nuclear Non-proliferation
For the obvious reason that Japan is the only country to have suffered nuclear assault, nuclear disarmament has been close to the heart of Japanese foreign policy. In addition, the historical experience gives Japan a moral superiority in the nuclear debate that can be manipulated for diplomatic purposes; a means of leverage for purposes of leadership. In 1995, Japan submitted to the General Assembly a resolution on nuclear weapons with the objective of disarmament. The resolution was adopted by a majority of 154 in favor, 0 opposed, and 10 abstentions. In the 1998 session of the General Assembly, Japan prepared the a draft resolution on phasing out nuclear tests with the objective of a complete ban on nuclear weapons, which would certainly signal a more forthright approach. Japan has also been officially making efforts to promote compliance with the Non-Proliferation Treaty and the Comprehensive Test-Ban Treaty through UN organs. The planned Emergency Action Forum on nuclear disarmament/proliferation would be a further demonstration of Japan's multilateral leadership in this area. Following from hosting the Tokyo Conference on Nuclear Safety in Asia in 1996, the UN Conference in Disarmament Issues has been held in Japan every year since 1989. This conference represents government officials, diplomats, and nongovernmental organizations from Japan and abroad. Japan is also involved in eliminating weapons of mass destruction in cooperation with international institutions. For example, it has provided approximately US$100 million to support the destruction of nuclear weapons in the former Soviet Union.

Diplomatically, a further demonstration of Japan's desire to make this issue area a niche of its foreign policy was provided by its cosponsorship (with Sweden, Costa Rica, and Slovenia) on 6 June 1998 of a Security Council resolution that "condemns the nuclear tests" conducted by India and then Pakistan in May 1998, and "demands" that these countries refrain from further tests (Resolution 1172). Japan has not had a record of sponsoring such resolutions and so—alongside its cosponsorship of the Iraq resolution—this was highly significant and obviously a platform for Japan's renewed interest in the banning of weapons of mass destruction. This was mirrored by Japan's early support of a total ban on the use of landmines, in opposition to the U.S. reservation. Japan also is able to boast that it does not export military arms, despite a significant export potential.

However, Japan's multilateral approach does not fit comfortably with the reality outside the UN. For example, Japan has not taken such a strong line with the preeminent nuclear state—the United States—and indeed benefits from the U.S. nuclear umbrella (some observers predict that, in the absence of U.S. security guarantees, Japan could conceivably go nuclear). The substantial—albeit latent—military might of Japan, including the nuclear potential, is well known.[29] Even if Japan's own military capabilities are apparently purely defensive, the tacit acceptance of the U.S. nuclear shield casts doubt upon Japan's multilateral stance.

Peace and Security

Some of Japan's policy elites have promoted the country's role in a broad conception of security based upon multilateral security instruments. They have also sought to acknowledge, and balance, the constitutional and political limitations that exist in Japan with the need to shoulder some of the burdens of international peace and security. It is therefore clear that Japan's role—or emphasis—lies in supporting the socioeconomic foundations of peace and security and in postconflict reconstruction, rather than combative participation in collective security. While some adjustments may be necessary, the country's contribution to the foundations of international peace are already in place: in ODA, as the largest contributor to the UN Population Fund since 1986;[30] sponsoring research on human rights and participating in the UN Commission on Human Rights since 1982; taking an advocacy role on women's issues, including an initiative on Women in Development and the successful sponsorship of the Resolution on the Role of the UN Development Fund for Women in Eliminating Violence Against Women; and in injecting human and material resources into social development and the fight against narcotics, international crime, and terrorism. Japan helped to sponsor a General Assembly Declaration in 1988 that encouraged proactive approaches to conflict prevention and settlement, and coordinated the drawing-up of the Declaration on the Critical Economic Situation in Africa, 1984.[31] Japan has also been active in promoting reform and encouraging fact-finding and preventive diplomacy by the UN Secretariat. A further area of substantial commitment—partly motivated by its geographical vulnerability—is in the care and resettlement of refugees. Indeed, in 1995 Japan was the top donor to UN High Commissioner for Refugees (UNHCR) (at US$121 million) and the UN Relief and Works Agency for Palestinian Refugees (US$28 million) and also made substantial material contributions to the World Food Program (about US$106 million) and the International Committee for the Red Cross (about US$15 million).[32]

Peacekeeping is a contentious issue in Japan, and one which projects the domestic political and constitutional constraints upon military activities into the international realm. The issue of peacekeeping also reflects the attitudes of foreign countries, especially in Asia, toward a Japanese military role. In Japan, debate revolves around three standpoints: those who believe that the Constitution must be rigorously adhered to and Japan's participation in multilateral operations must be limited to civilian assistance; those who believe that the Constitution should be reinterpreted or revised to allow Japan to take a greater responsibility in peacekeeping and in supporting collective security; and those who adhere to the argument that the Constitution already allows Japan to play a substantial role if the political will and leadership exist. Since the Gulf War shocked the Japanese into the reality that the international community expects their country to shoulder part of the burden of peace and security, this latter school of thought is gaining ground. Yet a deep wariness prevails among Japanese toward overseas commitments—however apparently innocuous and limited—that might escalate into military confrontation, as well as anything that might allow the Japanese military establishment to gain strength. However, the changing political landscape has made a more substantial role in peacekeeping more likely. Indeed, this formed one of the conditions upon which the Liberal Party leader, Ozawa Ichiro, joined the Liberal Democratic Party in a ruling coalition in 1998. The expectation was that legislation would be passed that would reduce the constraints on peacekeeping activities (under the 1992 law) and widen the scenarios in which Japan could send forces to contribute to peacekeeping.

Japan has participated in a number of peacekeeping operations under guidelines that are aimed at accommodating these pressures and sensitivities. Before Japan will become involved, certain conditions must obtain and be maintained: agreement on a cease-fire shall exist; the parties to the conflict must give their consent to the deployment of peacekeepers and to Japan's participation; the peacekeeping force must be impartial; the use of weapons must be limited to the minimum necessary to protect the lives of personnel; and Japan reserves the right to withdraw if these guidelines cease to be satisfied.[33] Under these principles and through the International Peace Cooperation Law passed in 1992, Japanese nationals have participated in UN operations in Angola, Cambodia, Mozambique, El Salvador, Rwanda, and the Golan Heights in Syria. Smaller civilian contributions have been made to Tajikistan, where an officer was tragically killed in 1998, and Bosnia. Although the Japanese contingents have started at a relatively modest level, the amount of goodwill created has been invaluable. In terms of Asia, a region of obvious importance to Japan, the effects have been especially useful given the history of Japan and the region. For example, all the Association of South East Asian Nations, with the exception of Brunei, participated in the Cambodia operation alongside Japan, and this was a valuable confidence-building exercise. In the 1950s Japan appeared to use the United Nations in the context of its insular, minimalist outlook upon foreign policy. Conversely, in the 1990s the UN was integral to Japan's efforts to protect itself beyond its earlier constraints and into prominence in the international scene.[34]

The government has made progress in raising public consciousness in the support of peacekeeping. The swing of public opinion in 1990 from caution and wariness for any such international involvement to much greater support for participation in peacekeeping with the second UN cooperation bill, was notable. There is acceptance of the argument that, in addition to the substantial financial contribution of Japan to the UN—which comprises more than those of most of the permanent Security Council members—more is necessary. Credible participation in the processes of multilateral security—the substance of which will be the outcome of debate involving various elites and the public—is an essential prerequisite for taking on permanent membership of the UN Security Council. Even if the practical—and especially military—contribution may be somewhat modest, the symbolism of the "blue helmet" confirms Japan's challenge remains to combine "new internationalism" with a form of pacifism.[35] A significant section of the educated public believe that this could be a central part of Japan's "global mission," grounded not in idealism but a realistic belief that such a voice can make a positive impact internationally. This must be a departure from the insular, isolationist pacifism that dominated Japan's ethos of *ikkoku heiwa shugi* (the doctrine of peace in one country). There has already been criticism that Japan's willingness to contribute to international peace and security stops short of risking Japanese lives and that the Constitution is exploited to shirk international responsibilities.

Japan has likewise been attempting to play an active role in the ongoing policy debates on the peace and security apparatus of the UN. In the wake of the landmark *Agenda for Peace* report of 1992—that sought to guide UN peace and security activities after the Cold War—the UN has experienced mixed fortunes in its peace and security activities. A working group was established to discuss areas—such as preventive diplomacy, peacekeeping, postconflict peace-building, sanctions—and Japan has been participating in the discussions. Diplomatically, Japan has been increasingly willing to take the initiative and in some cases court controversy. An interesting case was that of the Iraq resolution in early 1998. Cosponsored with Britain, this warned of "very severe" consequences if Iraq prevented UN inspectors from searching for weapons of mass destruction. Although this was in some ways a compromise resolution—an earlier draft had threatened "the severest consequences"—the resolution continued to be controversial because many countries, including France and Russia, did not support the coercion of Iraq for a number of reasons. France and Russia openly desire to see the sanctions lifted and the non-Western world is increasingly wary of the U.S. agenda. In the past Japan studiously avoided involvement in such controversies, preferring to observe from the sidelines. Given Japan's dependence upon Middle Eastern oil and its desire to avoid antagonizing Arab countries since the oil price shocks in the 1970s, this direct involvement is somewhat uncharacteristic (despite its obvious role of serving the United States as a major ally).

UN Reform
With the end of the Cold War, there was much discussion on the reform of the United Nations. A number of stimuli have fueled the debate: the structure and ethos of the organization are not wholly suited to the demands imposed upon it; the apportionment of financial costs among members is increasingly untenable; and the practices of the UN Secretariat have been the target of criticism. In fact, the expectations for a renewed UN have not been met, and partly because the UN did not have the resources—both material and conceptual—with which to

face the burgeoning agenda. The reform debate has clearly become very politicized, through competing conceptions of the UN's future, and the dashed hopes of the peace and security mandate. The rising significance of NGOs, able to work less bureaucratically and often with greater effectiveness in the field, has also put the structure and credibility of the UN into some doubt.

Japan's purported activism in the reform debate is motivated by a number of factors: its foreign policy elites recognize that aims can be accommodated in a multilateral context to some extent, and it follows that there is an incentive to improve the effectiveness of international organizations; UN reform is seen as a relatively "safe" issue in which to raise Japan's diplomatic profile; and UN reform is an issue directly connected to the projection of Tokyo's influence because the reform of the structure of the UN offers opportunities for greater institutional leverage, most obviously in the case of permanent membership of the Security Council. The sense of entitlement to greater authority that comes from the substantial financial contribution is clear. As a corollary, the inertia of Security Council reform will increasingly cause ill will among Japanese policy elites toward the UN. This tension between entitlement and organizational stagnation will heighten if Japan's economy continues to suffer and the financial contribution comes under greater political scrutiny.

Japan's official position on the reform of the Security Council argues that steps should be taken to enhance its legitimacy and effectiveness, as well as ensure the balance between the representative character of the Security Council and its efficiency:

- a limited number of permanent seats should be added in addition to the current permanent members to reflect the emergence of new global powers. Japan supports the suggestions that the number of seats on the reformed Security Council should be kept in the low twenties;
- the number of nonpermanent seats should be increased appropriately in order to improve the representativeness of the Security Council;
- special consideration should be given to those regions that are now underrepresented, namely Asia, Africa, and Latin America in increasing the number of nonpermanent seats; and
- measures should be considered and implemented to further the improvement of working methods and procedures of the Security Council, including the enhancement of the transparency of its work.[36]

It is interesting that the foreign minister urged that the debate for reforming the UN should be pursued "not from the viewpoint of pursuing its own parochial interests but from the genuinely broad perspective of maximizing benefits to the international community as a whole."[37] A number of observers would question the extent to which Japan truly commits itself to UN reform according to this spirit. Certainly, Japan's desire to be a permanent member with veto does not appear to be very imaginative while other countries are proposing more progressive reform agendas aimed at widening the representation and transparency of the Security Council. Moreover, some still argue that Japan's campaign for a permanent seat on the Security Council is surprisingly reticent. There are still reservations in some quarters regarding Japan's bid: that the country looks upon the position as an opportunity to enhance its diplomatic status rather than to substantively contribute to peace and security issues.

Japan's institutional tactics have also drawn criticism and raised some doubts about the country's motivations for participating in, and extending influence in, international organizations. This criticism strengthens the revisionist claim that Japan's participation in international organizations is an extension of its quest to dominate economic markets, especially regionally, rather than a genuine commitment to collective internationalism. The nature of Japan's bid to win a nonpermanent Security Council seat and the efforts expended to have Dr. Nakajima Hiroshi reelected as WHO chief in 1993 despite widespread opposition, were damaging to Japan's image.[38] Japan reportedly threatened to withhold substantial support to WHO if Nakajima was not reelected, and threatened to cut imports from several developing countries if they did not support his candidature.[39] Japan's diplomatic efforts aimed at swaying the International Whaling Commission against continuing the ban on whaling and reports of Japanese citizens being "imposed" upon positions in international organizations have also been somewhat unbecoming.

Japan has held nonpermanent membership more than any other country, but most analysts would agree that the country has not shown great leadership during these periods, until the 1990s. Moreover, there is clearly still some reluctance among countries, especially in Asia, to encourage political leadership on the part of Japan, and this sensitivity has no doubt conditioned the tentative approach of Japan. The methods employed in lobbying also cast doubt upon the attitude of Japanese elites toward the UN. There obviously also still remains doubt regarding the capability of Japan to fulfill the responsibility of permanent membership as the organ entrusted with maintenance of peace and security. For political, historical, and constitutional reasons, there are constraints upon Japan's use of military force. Therefore, there are constraints upon Japan's support of, and participation in, collective security and collective self-defense. There are even constraints upon Japan's self-defense capabilities: the U.S. security umbrella is a pervasive issue in Japan's foreign policy that does raise implications for Japan's sovereignty.

In the realist conception of international politics, this is a weakness—demonstrated most explicitly before and during the Gulf War—which questions the credibility of Japan's bid for permanent membership. Japan appears to be suffering from the persistence of a "heroic" conception of leadership that continues to pervade international politics. Indeed, even though the country commits a great deal to multilateralism and development—albeit for reasons that are partly and justifiably self-centered—the country's perceived lack of "leadership" is often derided at home and abroad because it does not live up to the dominant images and symbols of "leadership." Japan cannot readily mobilize a substantial military force with global reach and is not gifted at dramatic military displays.

The innate problems of Security Council reform are also complicating Japan's bid. Indeed, by the General Assembly of 1998, the reform debate was beginning to lose momentum as a result of the balance of geographical, social, and political interests defying reconciliation. The inherent inertia of the organization also frustrates reform even though Japan has support for its bid. Indeed, it is not a positive reflection that two of the most supportive members of the UN—Japan and Germany—are still referred to as "enemy states" in the UN Charter.

Proponents of reform—in particular Security Council reform—often observe that the world has changed since the UN was established, and that the structure should be adjusted in line with these changes. While this may be a logical argument for reform of the Security Council, it is not necessarily a realistic one. The world has indeed changed, and so those countries that are privileged by the existing structure are wary of change that might hold implications for their privileges.

It will be interesting to observe Japan's attitudes toward the UN should the Security Council reform process continue to remain stalled. Generally, the people of Japan are not preoccupied with this issue and support for the ideals of the UN is fairly strong irrespective of Japan's diplomatic influence. However, foreign policy elites have invested much, materially and diplomatically, in this campaign and expect to see some returns. In the absence of progress, pressures to be more conditional in Japan's support for the UN could arise.

Interesting developments external to Japan have altered the equation. India, with a long history of activism and nonaligned leadership at the organization, has recently been a rival to Japan as "representative" of Asia in the UN. Indeed, Japan and India fought a competitive campaign for Asia's seat in the 1997–78 Security Council. In debates on permanent membership, it is often also observed that, although Japan has a strong case for membership, in the context of the geographical/social balance of the Security Council, there was equally a case for a candidate not in the Western "camp." India was an obvious contender. However, the nuclear tests by India in 1998 have altered the equation, damaging the credibility of India's UN status and directly and indirectly enhancing that of Japan (although a realist interpretation of events might be that, after the controversy has died down, India's credibility as a great power will have increased: after all, the existing permanent members are nuclear powers).

Functional and Financial Organizations

Japan's role in commercial, functional, and financial organizations, on a regional and global basis, has also been steadily deepening in terms of political engagement, financial commitment, and diplomatic profile. Japan ranks second to the United States in terms of subscriptions to the World Bank organizations; is leading donor to the Special Program of Assistance for Low Income Debt-Distressed Countries in sub-Saharan Africa, under the auspices of the World Bank structural adjustment policies; Japan is the largest contributor to the Asian Development Bank (ADB) with a subscription of 19.1 percent; the largest contributor to the Asian Development Fund (55.41 percent at the end of 1995); largest contributor from outside the region to the Inter-American Development Bank; the second largest contributor from outside the region to the European Bank for Reconstruction and Development and the African Development Bank, and the largest contributor to the African Development Fund.[40]

Clearly, this is a charitable lens through which to view Japan's economic position. Critical voices have argued that Japan's participation is basically motivated by a desire to facilitate a domination of the process of economic globalization that is serving the interests of rich states like itself. Moreover, while Japan supports a bedrock of economic standards and institutions, its role in crisis situations has been criticized; during the Asian currency crisis between 1997 and 1998, many commentators claimed to observe a lack of leadership on Japan's part.[41]

Aside from this issue, a number of themes are reflected in Japan's work in these organizations: promoting and protecting national economic and security interests, achieving a foothold in regional economic units, bolstering extended national interests—the thesis of a "stable, prosperous world benefiting Japan"—and pursuing a humanitarian agenda for pragmatic and ethical reasons. Japan's involvement in the ADB demonstrates some of these issues at work and also illustrates a context in which Japan has been increasingly keen to take the initiative and have a substantive input.

The ADB was the first international institution that Japan had a role in creating. It thus provides a demonstration of Japan as the leading actor in an international organization with a leading economic and diplomatic stake and close institutional links to Japanese economic and bureaucratic actors. Since the ADB was established in 1966, to facilitate economic development of Asian countries, Japan has been active behind the scenes but wary of playing the overt leader. It is thus the ideal demonstration of Japan using multilateralism to facilitate and legitimize a regional economic agenda while also repairing damaged relationships with neighboring countries. Moreover, with the U.S. domination in the World Bank—despite the burgeoning Japanese financial input—the ADB has provided the framework for an institution closer to Japanese interests and concerns, and with greater independence from the United States.[42] All the presidents have been Japanese, and Japanese money is the bedrock of the bank, at a 16.054 percent shareholding (which represents the largest regional shareholding and is equal to the U.S. nonregional shareholding). Generally, Japan has been reserved in its policy initiatives and often preferred to take a back seat, or work behind the scenes. Clearly, Japan's somewhat tentative approach in the early years reflected its sensitivity to regional concerns toward Japanese hegemony. Indeed, it was partly such an environment that led to the ADB's establishment in Manila rather than Tokyo.

Generally, the ADBs lending policies have tended to conform to the wider economic trends behind Japan's bilateral and multilateral ODA. Loans correlated to commercial interests, and most significantly to countries that have strong trade and investment ties to Japan, and to the procurement of Japanese goods and services. Nevertheless, there have been some "internationalist" ADB presidents who sought to promote a responsible ethos toward the region, beyond Japan's narrow interests.[43] Indeed, there have been periods when loans have not correlated to the procurement of Japanese services or investment and there appeared to be a genuine effort toward improving Japan's image in the region. This coincided with an acceptance among a growing number of Japan's foreign policy analysts that a broader definition of national interests involves supporting public goods that bring indirect returns in the longer term and include the promotion of Japan as a responsible regional actor. With this, Japan has been increasingly assertive at the ADB, and, in the context of its wider ODA philosophy, has sought to use the forum as a vehicle for some of its development ideas, such as the New Development Strategy.

Despite this work, it is unfortunate, and perhaps ironic, that other countries are using international organizations as a forum to criticize Japan's *negative* effects upon economic liberalization. Indeed, at the Asian Pacific Economic Cooperation (APEC) forum the United States complained that Japan's alleged reluctance to open its economy was slowing down an APEC liberalization plan. A senior official at the OECD noted that Asia's economic outlook has deteriorated noticeably in recent months, and that the situation in Japan remains "very worrying."[44]

Japan can undoubtedly play a constructive role internationally in support of certain multilateral "public goods," but only within the framework of its political culture, its Constitution, and its relationship with the United States. It has been widely observed that this will represent practical and perhaps modest contributions, rather than a major leadership role, and maintaining rules rather than forging them.[45] This is wholly consistent with the ethos of pragmatism that is strong throughout the Japanese foreign policy elites and that is likely to remain pronounced in light of the uncertainty that underlies international politics. If pragmatism is the guiding light of Japan, and its political culture does not envision a singular "world vision," then an overt and pervasive international agenda is unlikely. International organizations will therefore continue to provide a pivotal framework for Japanese foreign policy to exercise itself discreetly yet effectively.

Notes

1. Robert O. Keohane and Joseph S. Nye, Jr., *Power and Interdependence* (Boston: Little Brown, 1977).
2. For the globalization debate see, for example, Wolfgang H. Reinicke, "Global Public Policy," *Foreign Affairs* 76:6 (1997); Peter F. Drucker, "The Global Economy and the Nation-State," *Foreign Affairs* 76:5 (1997); Walter B. Winston, "Bits, Bytes, and Diplomacy," *Foreign Affairs* 76:5 (1997); Jessica T. Matthews, "Power Shift," *Foreign Affairs* 76:1 (1997); Joseph S. Nye, Jr. and William A. Owens, "America's Information Edge," *Foreign Affairs* 75:2 (1996); Mark Z. Taylor, "Dominance through Technology," *Foreign Affairs* 74:6 (1995); Peter Drucker, "Trade Lessons from the World Economy," *Foreign Affairs* 73:1 (1994).
3. B. Boutros-Ghali, "Report on the Work of the Organization" (NY: United Nations, September 1992). The end of the bipolar era represents a "new chapter in history. . . . Clearly, it is in our power to bring about a renaissance—to create a new United Nations for a new international era," pp. 1–2; also B. Boutros-Ghali, "Empowering the United Nations," *Foreign Affairs* 72:5 (Winter 1992–93): 89; B. Boutros-Ghali, *Building Peace and Development*, Report on the Work of the Organization (NY: United Nations, 1995); and B. Boutros-Ghali's "UN Peace-keeping in a New Era: A New Chance for Peace," *The World Today* (April 1993): 66–69.
4. Sasaki Yoshitaka, "Japan's Undue International Contribution," *Japan Quarterly* XXXX:3 (July-September 1993).
5. Nakasone Yasuhiro, "Rethinking the Constitution—Make It a Japanese Document," *Japan Quarterly* 44:3 (July-September 1997): 7; Yomiuri Shimbun Constitutional Studies Group, "A Proposal for a Sweeping Revision of the Constitution," *Japan Echo* 22:1 (1995).
6. Ichiro Ozawa, *Blueprint for a New Japan: The Rethinking of a Nation* (Tokyo: Kodansha International, 1994).
7. Ronald Dore, *Japan, Internationalism and the UN* (London: Routledge, 1997): xv.

8. Edward J. Lincoln, *Japan's New Global Role* (Washington, DC: Brookings Institute, 1993), pp. 141–47 and p. 134; "the Japanese do not bring any well-defined sense of purpose to their higher financial and voting power" (Lincoln, 1993, p.134); Robert M. Immerman, "Japan and the United Nations," in *Japan: A New Kind of Superpower?* eds. Craig C. Garby and Mary Brown Bullock (Washington, DC: The Woodrow Wilson Center Press, 1994).
9. I. L. Claude, Jr., *Swords Into Plowshares: The Problems and Progress of International Organization*, 4th ed. (NY: Random House, 1984), p. viii and p. 5. S. Bailey supports this, *The Secretariat of the United Nations* (London: Pall Mall Press, 1964). See also P. Taylor and A. J. R. Groom, eds., *International Organization: A Conceptual Approach* (London: Frances Pinter Ltd., 1978), p. 11.
10. For example, Edward Neilan, "Blame Japan for much of the Asian crisis," *Japan Times*, 18 January 1998; Kagami Mitsuhiro, "The Asian Currency Crisis: A Bigger Role for Japan," *Japan Echo* 24:5 (1997); Robert A. Manning and James Przystup, "From Model to Millstone," *Japan Times*, 7 February 1998; Donald C. Hellmann, "Will Japan Rise to Connect East and West?," *Japan Times*, 16 January 1998.
11. Takashi Inoguchi, introduction to *Japan's Foreign Policy in an Era of Global Change* (NY: St. Martin's Press, 1993). See also Yoichi Funabashi, "Japan's International Agenda for the 1990s," in *Japan's International Agenda*, ed. Yoichi Funabashi (NY: New York University Press, 1994). Richard D. Leitch Jr., Akira Kato, and Martin E. Weinstein observed that Japan is turning its back on insularity, but is not clear on its future: "although Japan is being pressured to take part in shaping the post–Cold-War international order' it will do so cautiously and reluctantly because of the uncertainty of what that order will look like." *Japan's Role in the Post Cold War World* (Westport, Connecticut: Greenwood Press, 1995), p. xv.
12. Leitch, Kato, and Weinstein, 1995.
13. Warren S. Hunsberger, ed., *Japan's Quest: The Search for International Role, Recognition and Respect* (Armonk, NY: M. E. Sharpe, 1997).
14. George Friedman and Meredith Lebard, *The Coming War with Japan* (NY: St. Martin's Press, 1991).
15. Reinhard Drifte, *Japan's Foreign Policy in the 1990s: From Economic Superpower to What Power?* (London: Macmillan, 1996); Dennis T. Yasutomo, *The New Multilateralism in Japan's Foreign Policy* (London: Macmillan, 1995); Roger C. Altman, "Why Pressure Tokyo?" *Foreign Affairs* 73:3 (1994); Jagdish Bhagwati, "Samurais No More," *Foreign Affairs* 73:3 (1994); Clyde V. Prestowitz, Jr., *Trading Places: How We Allowed Japan to Take the Lead* (NY: Basic Books, 1988); Ronald Morse, "Japan's Drive to Pre-Eminence," *Foreign Policy* 69 (Winter 1987-88); Ezra F. Vogel, *Japan as Number 1: Lessons for America* (NY: Harper Colophon Books, 1979); Ezra F. Vogel, "Pax Nipponica," *Foreign Affairs* 64:4 (1986).
16. For example, Chalmers Johnson, *MITI and the Japanese Miracle* (Stanford: Stanford University Press, 1982); and Chalmers Johnson, *Japan: Who Governs? The Rise of the Developmental State* (NY: W.W. Norton and Company, 1995); Karel van Wolferen, *The Enigma of Japanese Power* (Tokyo: Charles E. Tuttle Company, 1993), chapter 16; Eamonn Fingleton, "Japan's Invisible Leviathan," *Foreign Affairs* 74:2 (1995); Eamonn Fingleton, *Blindside: Why Japan Is Still on Track to Overtake the U.S. by the Year 2000* (Boston: Houghton Mifflin, 1995); Michael Crichton, *Rising Sun* (NY: Knopf, 1992); Masao Miyamoto, *Straitjacket Society: An Insider's Irreverent View of Bureaucratic Japan* (Tokyo: Kodansha International, 1994); Donald C. Hellmann, "Will Japan Rise to Connect East and West?" *Japan Times*, 16 January 1995.
17. B. Stokes, "Divergent Paths—U.S.-Japan Relations Towards the 21st Century," *International Affairs* 72:2 (1996).
18. van Wolferen, 1993, p. 29; and Johnson, 1995, p. 71.
19. F. P. Walters, *A History of the League of Nations* (London: Oxford University Press, 1960); E. F. Ranshofen-Wertheimer, *The International Secretariat: A Great Experiment in International Administration* (Washington, DC: Carnegie Endowment for International Peace, 1945); David Armstrong, Lorna Lloyd, and John Redmond, *From Versailles to Maastricht: International Organizations in the Twentieth Century* (London: Macmillan, 1996), pp. 40–42.
20. Sadako Ogata, "Japan's Policy Towards the United Nations," in Chadwick F. Alger, Gene M. Lyons, John E. Trent, *The United Nations System: The Policies of Member States* (Tokyo: United Nations University Press, 1995), p. 251.
21. Ronald Dore, *Japan, Internationalism and the UN* (London: Routledge, 1997), chapter 5, particularly pp. 53–57.
22. Ogata, 1995, p. 241.

23. Reinhard Drifte, "Looking Forward: Prospects for Multilateralism: Implications for Japan" (paper written in 1998 and given to the author).
24. J. Pérez de Cuéllar, "Reflecting on the Past and Contemplating the Future," in *Global Governance* 1:2 (1995): 153.
25. P. Taylor and A. J. R. Groom, *The United Nations and the Gulf War, 1990-91: Back to the Future?* The Royal Institute of International Affairs Discussion Paper 38 (London, 1992), p. 2.
26. Ogata, 1995, p. 247.
27. Private correspondence the author dated 8 September 1998.
28. ODA Summary 1997, Ministry of Foreign Affairs Internet Web site, September 1998.
29. See, for example, Selig S. Harrison, ed., *Japan's Nuclear Future: The Debate and East Asian Security* (Washington, DC: Carnegie Endowment for International Peace, 1996), p.40; Richard Halloran, *Chrysanthemum and the Sword Revisited: Is Japanese Militarism Resurgent?* (Honolulu: The East-West Center, 1991); "Japan Rising," *Asiaweek,* 20 June 1997; Saburo Ienaga, "The Glorification of War in Japanese Education," in *East Asian Security,* eds. M. E. Brown, S. M. Jones, S. E. Miller (Cambridge, MA: MIT Press, 1996). In contrast, Peter J. Katzenstein and Nobuo Okawara, argue that "[t]he structure of the Japanese state has made it virtually impossible, short of a domestic political revolution, for an autonomous and powerful military establishment to emerge in Japan." See "Japan's National Security: Structures, Norms, and Policies," in Brown, Lynn-Jones, and Miller, 1996, p. 267.
30. Ministry of Foreign Affairs, *Gaiko seisho* [Diplomatic Blue Book] (Tokyo: Ministry of Finance Printing Bureau, 1998, p. 93.
31. Ogata, 1995, pp. 231-32.
32. *Japan's ODA Annual Report 1997,* Association for Promotion of International Cooperation, February 1997, p. 168.
33. *Peacekeeping: Japan's Policy and Statements* (Ministry of Foreign Affairs, 1997), pp. 15-16. See also Fujita Hiroshi, "UN Reform and Japan's Permanent Security Council Seat," *Japan Quarterly* XLII:4 (October-December 1995); and Ogata, 1995; Robert M. Immerman, "Japan and the United Nations," in *Japan: A New Kind of Superpower?,* eds. C. Garby and Mary Brown Bullock (Washington, DC: The Woodrow Wilson Center Press, 1994); and "Nani ga Nihon no kokueki nano ka," [Symposium: What Is the Japanese National Interest?], *Chuo Koron* (February 1996).
34. For an interesting discussion of these themes, see Ronald Dore, *Japan, Internationalism and the UN* (London: Routledge, 1997).
35. See Charles Overby, "A Quest for Peace with Article 9," *Japan Quarterly* XLI:2 (April-June 1994); Yasumasa Kuroda, *Japan in a New World Order: Contributing to the Arab-Israeli Peace Process* (NY: Nova Science Publishers, 1994); Leitch, Kato, and Weinstein 1995, p. 206; Warren S. Hunsberger, "Japan's International Role, Past Present, and Prospective," in *Japan's Quest: The Search for International Role, Recognition and Respect,* ed. Warren S. Hunsberger (NY: M. E. Sharpe, 1997), p. 214.
36. Japan's UN Mission Internet Web site (September 1998).
37. Foreign Minister Obuchi Keizo's statement at the 52nd session of the General Assembly, 23 September 1997.
38. "What Has Become of WHO?" *Wall Street Journal,* 5 May 1993.
39. *New Scientist,* 10 April 1993; "WHO: Director-General's Travels," *The Lancet* , 5 December 1992. A journalist specializing in Japan speculated that the only feasible explanation for this desperate behavior, in the face of wide opposition, was Japan's desire to keep any "warm body"—any Japanese appointment—in office! (Discussion, Tokyo, September 1998).
40. *Japan's ODA Annual Report 1997,* p. 133.
41. For example, Edward Neilan, "Blame Japan for Much of the Asian Crisis," *Japan Times,* 18 January 1998; Kagami Mitsuhiro, "The Asian Currency Crisis: A Bigger Role for Japan," *Japan Echo* 24:5 (1997); Manning and Przystup, 1998; Donald C. Hellmann, 1998.
42. See, for example, Ming Wan, "Japan and the Asian Development Bank," *Pacific Affairs* 68:4 (Winter 1995-96).
43. Ming, 1995-96.
44. *Asian Wall Street Journal,* 3 July 1998.
45. Leitch, Kato, and Weinstein, 1995, pp. 204-205. For Edward J.Lincoln, "[f]undamental structural features of society suggest that the Japanese government will continue to have difficulty playing a strong role in international political crises. Reactions to unexpected events remain chaotic, and decisions are slow to materialize" (p. 12), and there is "failure to define a new, less commercial framework for greater participation in world affairs" (Lincoln, 1993, p. 158).

CHAPTER 4

Globalization and Regionalization

Moon Chung-in and Park Han-kyu

Japan's foreign policy is facing major challenges as it adjusts to the emerging international environment of the post–Cold War era. Japan has traditionally adopted a reactive, incremental, and risk-minimizing foreign policy, the maneuvers of which have been limited by the historical burden of imperial expansion and defeat in the Pacific War, postwar institutional constraints determined by the peace constitution, and the shadow of the American security umbrella. These historical and structural constraints have enabled Japan to avoid involvement in international politico-military affairs and, instead, concentrate on maximizing its economic interests. This policy orientation has allowed Japan to achieve, in a relatively short time, an almost unprecedented degree of economic success.

Japan's postwar national strategy has, however, produced a paradox in terms of foreign policy: the nation has often been described as an "economic giant," but a "political pygmy."[1] The disjuncture of economic and politico-military power has resulted in a foreign policy that is looked on with ambivalence by policy makers and as an enigma by the rest of the world. Given its enormous economic power and wealth, Japan could have played a more responsible role in international society. Nevertheless, the existing political and institutional structure and the postwar historical legacy of pacifism have made it extremely difficult for Japanese leaders to shift national strategy from a passive and reactive to a positive and proactive posture.

Since the early 1980s, however, Japan has been struggling to redefine its international identity and to assume a position of global and regional leadership comparable to its economic power. Such efforts have led to new debates on globalization and regionalization within Japanese society. Since the bold initiative taken by former Prime Minister Nakasone Yasuhiro aimed at achieving internationalization, a growing number of scholars and policy makers have been involved in the debate over greater assumption of global leadership and the path to globalization.[2] As evidenced by the defiant tone of Ishihara Shintaro, however, an equally large number of Japanese politicians and intellectuals are seeking Japan's new identity in Asia, arguing that Japan should strive to undertake a leadership role in the region. While the goals of global and regional leadership are not necessarily in conflict, as the two camps would have one believe, the intellectual and policy confrontation has stirred concern at home and abroad. That stems, clearly, from the sheer size of Japan's economic power, which can easily reshape the economic, political, and strategic landscape in Asia and around the world.

This chapter will elucidate the patterns of globalization and regionalization in Japan, explore foreign policy alternatives, and draw empirical and policy implications for the future. The first section presents a brief overview of recent analytical discourses on globalization and regionalization, while the second looks at historical origins, empirical dimensions, and policy options for globalization in Japan. The third part examines the dynamics of regionalization in Japan and explores policy alternatives. The concluding section discusses some empirical and policy implications for Japan's foreign policy.

Some Analytical Remarks

Before delving into a discussion of Japan's experiences, it is necessary to understand the concepts of globalization and regionalization. While scholars' interpretations of the term "globalization" differ according to their epistemological and normative orientation,[3] the concept can be meaningfully divided into two categories: spontaneous and governed globalization.[4]

Spontaneous globalization refers to the process of economic interdependence and integration through market forces that have resulted from the development of technology and world capitalism. Global diffusion of production achieved by multinational corporations, integration of movements of factors of production, transnational networks of financial transactions and equity capital, as well as the expansion of international trade serve to underscore the empirical dimensions of spontaneous globalization.

Spontaneous globalization is not always mutually beneficial and welfare maximizing. On the contrary, it can entail new constraints, challenges, and transitional traumas. The process can increase systemic vulnerability: it makes national economies more vulnerable to the transmission of external turbulence, such as the cyclical instability of international financial and capital markets, the rollercoaster effects of international commodity markets, and the transborder contagion of inflation. It can also deepen relational sensitivity, in terms of the impact and related costs of bilateral pressures. Unlike systemic vulnerability, relational sensitivity can be managed within existing policy frameworks, although domestic adjustment costs are high. A good example is the U.S. bilateral pressure that, wrapped in the principle of strategic reciprocity, is placed on Japan and other Asian trading partners. Finally, the globalization of production by multilateral corporations can undermine the economic sovereignty of host nations by cultivating structural dependency.

Further, since spontaneous globalization can be seen to variously threaten national economies, no country will be passive in the face of globalizing forces but, rather, will attempt to minimize the costs while maximizing the benefits.

Such efforts are termed governed globalization or coping strategies, and can take several forms. Countries can defy, adapt, and accommodate forces of spontaneous globalization on the one hand or, on the other, restructure them.

Defiance is rare, since the process of spontaneous globalization is grand and irreversible, but an example can be found in the self-reliance strategy adopted by North Korea and the former regimes of Albania and Tanzania. The restructuring option is also hardly feasible, since it involves a fundamental realignment of the governance structure that underlies spontaneous globalization. The creation by the United States of the General Agreement on Tariffs and Trade (GATT) and the Bretton Woods monetary system falls in this category. But other than a hegemonic power, few countries would be in a position to choose this option because restructuring the norms, principles, rules, and decision-making procedures underlying international political economy requires enormous material resources.

Most countries opt for internal or external adaptation and accommodation. Internal adaptation is predicated on the opening, liberalization, rationalization, and deregulation of the domestic economy. The core of adaptation strategy comprises the realigning of social and economic norms, ideas, and institutions to cope with the challenges and pressures of spontaneous globalization: the terms of engagement with the outside world must be changed from defensive mercantilism to open multilateralism. Cooperative multilateralism, in turn, becomes the essential ingredient of external adaptation.

It is quite difficult to make an analytical distinction between globalization and regionalization, since the latter can be conceived of as being part of the globalization process on a regional basis. As with globalization, regionalization can be spontaneous or governed. Functionalists argue that spontaneous regionalization can be defined as the process of market- or function-driven cooperation and integration among national economies in the same region.[5] According to this view, a market-driven division of labor and the subsequent formation of economic networks enhance regional economic cooperation and integration. Thus, regionalization is sui generis, evolving from the correlation of regional economic growth and interdependence.[6] Spontaneous regionalization does not require the intervention of national governments. On the contrary, such intervention can create new barriers to regional cooperation by distorting the process of market transactions.

As in the case of spontaneous globalization, market transactions and concurrent regional economic interdependence and cooperation can accompany unintended negative externalities. As a result, national governments may need to intervene in the regionalization process to cope with those threats. Governed regionalization consists of conscious government strategies to deal with the process of spontaneous regionalization, and can take one of two forms: open or soft regionalization, in which the national government fosters the process of spontaneous regionalization by removing artificial barriers and institutionalizing regional mechanisms for market-based economic cooperation; or closed or hard regionalization, in which the national government resists spontaneous globalization by forming exclusive zones of regional economic transactions and cooperation.

The concepts of globalization and regionalization do not necessarily conflict, but can be both complementary and conflictual. For example, the concept of open regionalization is a prerequisite for cooperative multilateralism; the concepts go together since they are framed on the notion of welfare maximization through market forces. But closed regionalization can hinder the process of adaptive globalization, while fostering the rise of exclusive economic blocs in the world economy. The two concepts are, thus, closely intertwined, since the choice of different paths to globalization and regionalization cannot be determined by any single variable. As with other foreign policy issues, these concepts are a function of the dynamic interplay of domestic, "inter-mestic," and international politics.

Globalization in Japan: Outside Pressures, Internal Adjustment, and Strategic Choice

Three Waves of Opening

As an island nation, Japan had traditionally been closed and inward looking, with a few exceptions such as its forays into the Korean Peninsula. It preserved its independence and maintained peace by closing its borders (*sakoku*). Since the middle of the nineteenth century, however, Japan has undergone three waves of opening and internationalization.[7] The first was triggered by the arrival of Commodore Perry's "black ships" in 1853, which eventually forced the opening of Japanese ports to foreign trade. Japan responded to its first encounter with the Western international system by undertaking the Meiji Restoration in 1868. The "revolution from above" ended the some 250 years of peace and the self-imposed seclusion of the Edo period (1600–1868), and moved Japan swiftly to adopt Western civilization to build a modern nation-state.

Ever since the Meiji era (1868–1912), there has been rivalry between the internationalists, who have wanted Japan to get out of backward Asia and join the advanced West, and the Asianists, who have sought Japan's fortune and identity in Asia. Internationalists such as Meiji educator Fukuzawa Yukichi argued that Japan should leave Asia and join the West in the interests of modernization (*datsu-Ajiaron*).[8] Fukuzawa believed that, since Asia was in decline, the only way Japan could become a modern nation-state was to adopt Western civilization and become a full-fledged member of the international community. He was an instrumental, rather than consummate, internationalist who saw internationalization as a means whereby Japan could realize the "rich nation, strong army" (*fukoku kyohei*) ideology. Nonetheless, his *weltanschauung* played an important role in sustaining the first opening of the country by preaching the virtues of Western civilization and inducing Japanese minds to accept the brave new world in an assertive manner.

The second wave of opening and internationalization came by default rather than design, as a result of Japan's defeat in the Pacific War and its subsequent military occupation by the United States. Since the early Showa era (1926–89), the Asianists had gained the upper hand over the internationalists. The historical inertia resulting from continental conquest, the prevailing logic of lebensraum at a time when there was a growing sense of isolation in the international community, and the unfolding of hegemonic rivalry in the region among the Western powers, led to the Asianists' triumph, precipitating Japanese military adventurism into China and in the Pacific. Japan's experiment with the concept of a Greater Asia in the prewar period ended with its defeat in the Pacific War. With the Allied Occupation and the conclusion of the San Francisco peace treaty in 1951, the ideology of exclusive Asianism was totally demolished as the principle upon which to build national strategy, and Japan pursued a new path to internationalization. Its tenets are well summarized in the Yoshida Doctrine, which emphasized the passive role of Japan's foreign policy under the U.S. security umbrella.[9]

Yoshida's skillful combination of political realism and economic pragmatism determined the second wave of Japan's internationalization, from the 1950s to late 1970s. While the doctrine's political realism consolidated the American security umbrella over Japan, giving it a free ride in terms of national security, economic pragmatism paved the way to an impressive economic recovery. After having resolved its status as a defeated nation by concluding the San Francisco peace treaty in 1951, Japan joined the International Monetary Fund (IMF) in 1952, the General Agreement on Tariffs and Trade (GATT) in 1955, and the United Nations (UN) in 1956. It also joined the Organization of Economic Cooperation and Development (OECD) in 1964, and began to liberalize trade and deregulate the international flow of capital. These steps were all taken under U.S. patronage, with the perceived need for the strategic containment of the Soviet Union offering the opportunity for a strong alliance between the United States and Japan. Japan fully exploited this situation by pursuing a policy of assertive economic pragmatism centering on the developmental state and neo-mercantilism.[10] The second opening, which can be characterized as outward internationalization, coincided with Japan's stunning economic success, labeled the Japanese miracle.

Japan's economic ascension eventually led to the third wave of opening and internationalization, which has placed it on an irreversible path to globalization. In the 1960s and 1970s, the economic miracle brought about phenomenal trade surpluses, precipitating enormous bilateral and multilateral pressure for Japan to open its domestic markets. Bilateral pressure from the United States, in particular, has intensified since the early 1980s. Departing from its traditional reliance on the import restrictions applied during the 1970s, the United States undertook more offensive moves under the principle of strategic reciprocity, and applied sector-specific, country-specific policies to balance out the trade deficits. Legislative pressure in the form of the Super 301 clause and the Structural Impediments Initiatives (SII) introduced by the administration of U.S. President George Bush further fostered the liberalization of Japan's economy.[11] Equally important were multilateral pressures from the OECD and GATT, with the settlement of the latter's Uruguay Round preventing Japan from continuing its neomercantilist practices in international trade.

A striking aspect of Japan's third wave of opening and internationalization is the role of outside pressure. As is discussed below, Japan has rarely voluntarily undertaken measures to liberalize its economy; its steps have been only incremental and responsive, as dictated by outside pressures. It is not only because of mercantilist characteristics deeply embedded in the Japanese politico-economic system, but also because of its political operational logic requiring consultation, consensus, and compromise.

Spontaneous Globalization: Trade, Investments, and ODA

Since the second opening, Japan has recorded the most impressive economic transformation in modern world history. Such economic dynamism has fostered the process of spontaneous globalization. Japan's share of the world's GDP was less than 10 percent in the 1970s. As Figure 4.1 illustrates, however, it rose to 16.6 percent ($2.82 trillion) in 1988 and to 18 percent ($4.14 trillion) in 1993. During this relatively short period of time, Japan has become the second largest economy in the world, next only to the United States.

The growth of Japan's economy has been closely associated with the expansion of trade. In relative terms, Japan's share of world exports has declined slightly since the mid-1980s, due to the growth of exports by the East Asian newly industrialized economies (NIEs) and China. But in absolute terms, it has substantially increased. Japan accounted for 9.7 percent of world exports in 1988, and 9.4 percent in 1994, again second only to the United States, which had a share of 11.3 percent in 1988 and 12.2 percent in 1994. Although Japan's share of world imports decreased from 6.6 percent in 1988 to 6.4 percent in 1994, it still constituted a large share.

Apart from the size of its international trade, expanding intrafirm trade illustrates another important aspect of globalization. Prior to the 1980s, Japan's intrafirm trade was relatively insignificant, but it rapidly grew over time to account for 21.6 percent of Japan's total exports in 1983 and 25.9 percent in 1992. The trend can be attributed to the proliferation of Japanese companies' overseas affiliates. Japanese companies transferred production bases abroad through foreign direct investment (FDI), and their overseas affiliates have been importing manu-

Figure 4.1: Percentage of Major Countries and Regions in World GDP

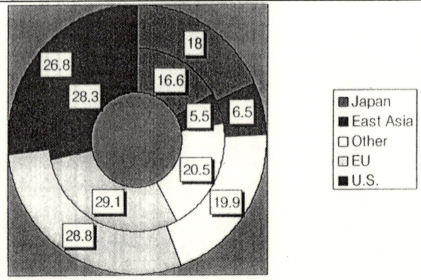

Notes: Outer Ring: $23 trillion (1993)   Inner Ring: $17 trillion (1998)
Sources: MITI, *Summary of White Paper on Trade 1996*.
   (Downloaded from www.jef.or.jp/news/wp1996/wp96_1.html, on September 25, 1998).

factured products from Japan, resulting in the increase of Japanese exports. For example, the share of overseas production of total Japanese production rose from 3 percent in 1986 to 8 percent in 1994. Compared with the United States and Germany, however, Japan's overseas production is relatively low. While offshore production has accounted for an average of 15 percent of total German production since the mid-1980s, its share in the United States has exceeded 20 percent since 1990.[12] But clearly, the changes in Japan's trade structure reflect the deepening integration of its economy into the world economic system.

The expansion of offshore production and outsourcing is naturally predicated on an increase in outbound FDI. Several factors facilitated Japan's overseas investments in the 1980s: the steep appreciation of the yen (*endaka*) following the Plaza Accord in 1985, the comparative disadvantage of Japanese domestic production due to the currency's appreciation, and inducement incentives by host nations. Before the Plaza Accord, Japanese FDI was slightly more than $10 billion; thereafter, it rose to $33 billion in 1987, and doubled to $67.5 billion in 1989 (see Figure 4.2). Increased outward FDI fostered the further integration of Japanese manufacturing into the world economy. While Japan has actively invested abroad since the mid-1980s, inward FDI has been almost negligible by comparison. As Edward Lincoln has pointed out, the disparity between Japan's overseas investment and the flow of foreign capital into Japan in the 1980s and 1990s strikes at the heart of the nation's lopsided vision of internationalization.[13] In 1993, for example, inward FDI in Japan was less than 5 percent of that in the United States.[14]

Japan's official development assistance (ODA) also reflects its deepening globalization. It currently allocates about $10 billion in ODA for the promotion of economic development in the developing countries, making it the world's top donor since the mid-1980s (see Figure 4.3). More importantly, an increasing portion of Japanese aid has been disbursed through multilateral institutions such

Figure 4.2: Japan's Foreign Direct Investment by Region

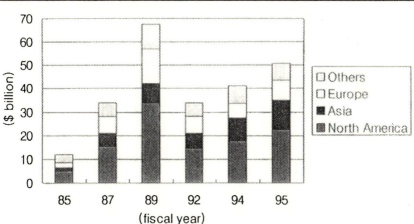

Sources: MITI, *Summary of White Paper on International Trade 1996.* (July 1996)
(Download from www.jef.or.jp/news/wp1996/wp96_1.html, on September 25, 1998).

as the World Bank and the Asia Development Bank (ADB). For example, Japan has been the largest contributor to the ADB and the United Nations Population Fund, and the second largest donor to the World Bank, the United Nations Development Programme, the United Nations High Commissioner for Refugees, and the World Health Organization.[15] Moreover, Japanese bilateral aid has increasingly become less tied to the Buy Japan policy.[16] These changes reflect a new dimension of Japan's globalization.

In the early 1990s, the Japanese government made an important change in its ODA policy. In April 1991, Prime Minister Kaifu Toshiki specified the principles that would guide the distribution of ODA. In his address to the Diet, Kaifu stipulated that ODA decisions would depend on the conduct of recipient countries in the following areas: military spending; the production of weapons of mass destruction; weapons sales and purchases; and the promotion of democratization and respect for human rights.[17] The stipulation of such conditions was intended to enhance Japan's global leadership by expanding its influence from the economic to the political domain.

Governed Globalization: Managerial Responses and Policy Choice

The process of Japan's spontaneous globalization has entailed new constraints and opportunities. On the one hand, the diffusion of spontaneous globalization and Japan's chronic trade surpluses have brought about intense bilateral and multilateral pressure for market opening. On the other hand, the added gravity of the Japanese economy—in terms of growth, trade surpluses, investments, and overseas development assistance—has focused world attention on Japan's growing role as a global leader. Facing an odd mix of constraints and opportunities, Japan's leadership has long deliberated its proper strategic positioning in the international system. Since the early 1970s, some Japanese leaders have been arguing that Japan's interests are not well served either by the pursuit of high

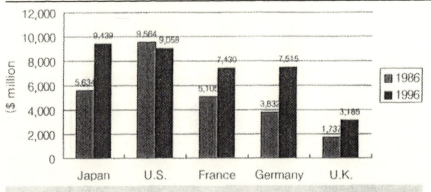

Figure 4.3: ODA among Leading Countries Belonging to OECD's Development Assistance Committee

Notes: 1996 figures are estimates.
Sources: Development Assistance Committee, OECD, 1997.

economic growth through neomercantile policies or one-nation pacifism, which have been the main tenets of Japan's postwar foreign policy. Given the higher stakes in the international politico-economic arena, they have said, it is necessary for Japan to support, and assume the lead in maintaining, the international order.

The Cabinet of Prime Minister Ohira Masayoshi (1978–80) set the tone for future lines of discourse by not only proposing the concept of "comprehensive security," but also advocating more proactive solutions to such issues as trade friction with the United States, and taking the initiative in forming an economic cooperation organization in the Asia-Pacific region.[18] However, a more aggressive initiative was undertaken by the Cabinet of Prime Minister Nakasone Yasuhiro (1982–87). He wanted to transform Japan from an economic superpower into a political superpower by consolidating a bigemonic leadership with the United States. Unlike past practices, his foreign policy initiative was proactive; he sought to transcend the psychological barriers imposed by the Yoshida Doctrine, which he regarded as passive and demeaning. Nakasone's grand design had three major tenets: 1) Japan would no longer be a follower nation; 2) Japan would be prepared for global leadership by being remade into an "international state"; and 3) Japan would assume an active role in global strategic affairs.[19] But Nakasone's initiative encountered a major setback due to both bureaucratic resistance and lack of social consensus.

The Gulf War of 1991 intensified the national debate on Japan's international role throughout the 1990s and after. This was the result of widespread international criticism of Japan for its lack of leadership in, and contribution to, maintaining peace and security in the world. Japan was criticized despite its contribution of $13 billion to the multinational forces during the Gulf War. The hesitant, reactive, and incremental character of Japanese foreign policy making precipitated such outside criticism, eventually fueling the domestic debate on its proper international positioning. In this sense, the Gulf Crisis provided Japan with a new opportunity to seriously reconsider its international contributions (*kokusai koken*) in the fields of security and economics.

The Japanese debate on international contribution is roughly divided into two camps: the neoconservatives and the neoliberals. Ozawa Ichiro, who represented the neoconservative camp, argued that Japan should be a normal state (*futsu no kuni*), fulfilling its global economic, political, and military responsibilities as a superpower. While he supported deregulation and free trade, active participation in the United Nations and regional organizations, foreign aid, and continued cooperation with the United States under the U.S.-Japan mutual security treaty, he also took a hard-line position on Japan's international military role by calling for the overseas deployment of Japanese Self Defense Forces as part of UN peacekeeping missions without first requiring a constitutional amendment.[20]

By contrast, neoliberals wanted Japan to remain a peaceful economic power by emphasizing the importance of nonmilitary international contributions. According to this camp, Japan can derive more benefit from increasing foreign aid, supporting UN humanitarian activities, playing a major role in preserving the global environment, promoting economic growth and free trade in Asia, and facilitating the stabilization of the international financial system.[21] Former Prime Minister Miyazawa Kiichi supported this line of thought by proposing the "defective state" (*kekkan kokka*), which is predicated on the preservation of the peace constitution and a small Japan through international economic, rather than military, contributions. Former Prime Minister Hosokawa Morihiro can be seen as belonging to this camp, since he placed greater emphasis on improvements in the quality of life of the Japanese people than on international issues. Since the mid-1990s, however, the debate on strategic international positioning has been overturned, not because of the resolution of the issues, but because of the economic downturn. Likewise, Japan's governed globalization has been rather slow and incremental. Domestic reforms to cope with challenges of spontaneous globalization have made little progress over the past ten years, due to resistance from the bureaucracy and vested interests in the existing politico-economic system, resulting in their failure to meet domestic and international expectations.

Equally critical is the continuing ambiguity in Japan's external management. It seems hardly feasible for Japan to revert to its former guise as a mercantile state, and it is being obliged to seek multilateral alternatives to cope with global and regional economic problems. There are two possibilities. One involves efforts to sustain and even revive the current world economic arrangement that has been wrapped in the World Trade Organization (WTO) and IMF. Japan can make an important contribution by strengthening the existing multilateral economic arrangements in several ways, which could constitute the core of this open multilateral posture: the assertive accommodation of external demands consistent with the principles, rules, and procedures of the WTO; the strengthening of its decision-making power in the IMF; facilitating the stabilization of the international financial system, including the regulation of hedge funds; and expanding overseas development assistance.

Two factors could, however, impede Japan's efforts to internationalize its economy and to support multilateral economic regimes. One is the mercantile inertia and domestic political dynamics associated with them. The other is the defection of the United States. The relatively weak and ineffective political leadership, coupled with opposition from a loose coalition of powerful bureaucrats, political cliques, and clusters of industrialists, could undercut Japan's efforts to liberalize and deregulate domestic markets. Hashimoto's failure in steering administrative and other reforms exemplified the trend. The domestic political backlash emanating from liberalization and structural reforms is likely to deter such a movement. Domestic political rigidity associated with patterned pluralism could also hinder Japan's move toward full-fledged multilateralism.

Apart from the domestic barrier, the offensive and provocative nature of American bilateral trade management could undermine Japanese efforts to achieve fuller multilateralism. Since the settlement of the Tokyo Round, the United States has become increasingly impatient with multilateral solutions, tilting toward bilateral initiatives centering on the principle of strategic reciprocity. Japan has been the main target of the U.S. bilateral offensive. As the case of its Structural Impediment Initiatives demonstrates, the principle of strategic reciprocity has yielded some concessions from Japan. However, the excessive and inertia-driven application of the bilateral offensive could easily backfire, reviving the specter of old mercantilism in Japan, as well as undermining the Japanese path to open multilateralism.[22]

Should the deepening and strengthening of the current multilateralism fail, Japan may seek the formation of a triple alliance with the United States and the European Union. This tripolar cooperation is predicated on U.S. willingness to promote shared leadership and the willingness of Japan and the European Union to assume the collective burden of leadership. Multilateral regimes can be reshaped and realigned according to the pattern of interaction among these three poles. According to this scenario, Japan is likely to play two important roles: that of regional leader, representing the entire Asian region; and that of binding agent to prevent the world's three major economic groupings from becoming rigid, exclusive blocs.

Regionalization in Japan: Closed vs. Open

Historical Context of Asian Regionalism

The idea of Asian regionalism currently prevailing in Japan originated in the prewar debates on Greater Asianism, which was designed to reassess the value of Asia and define Japan's newly acquired position in world politics in relation to Asia, as well as to overcome Asia's perceived inferiority to Europe by demonstrating its fundamental equivalence. In prewar Japan, this served as the ideological premise to rescue Japan from its growing isolation in international opinion. In the Japanese vision of Greater Asia, however, all nations and peoples were not necessarily equal. Japan, as the only modernized and industrialized nation in the region, was entitled to lead Asia. By the beginning of the 1930s, Greater Asia became closely linked to Japanese colonial expansion into the Asian continent. The concept was soon incorporated into a national policy in the late 1930s by serving as the guiding ideology for the New Order in East Asia (1938) and the Greater East Asian Co-Prosperity Sphere (1940) during the Pacific War.[23]

The prewar ideology of a Greater Asia has been occasionally resurrected in contemporary Japan, profoundly influencing the discourse on regionalization. It offers a tempting rationale for Japan's regional leadership in the economic and political arena.[24] Okabe Tatsumi, for example, calls for a regional division of labor among Japan and Asian countries by arguing that "the central task for Asia-Pacific cooperation is to carry out smoothly the adjustment of industrial structures, or the establishment of a division-of-labor structure, based on comparative superiority."[25] He envisaged a Japan-centric regional economic structure based on the principal of comparative advantage. In a similar vein, Kobayashi Yotaro, an influential business leader, has urged Japan's re-Asianization by asserting that Japan should find its identity and destiny in Asia because it cannot escape its cultural roots and geographical neighbors.[26] More provocative is Ishihara Shintaro, a leading Japanese nationalist, who argues that Japan's future lies primarily in contributing to the creation of a dynamic and ever-growing Asian economic bloc, which can counterbalance the increasingly anti-Asian West.[27] Kakizawa Koji, a member of Parliament (the Diet), goes even further by proposing Japan's contribution to peace and security in Asia through the participation in an Asian version of the UN peacekeeping force, made up of military contingents of various Asian countries.[28]

The contemporary resurgence of an Asian identity can be ascribed, in part, to the rise of anti-American sentiment, intensified by growing trade friction with the United States since the early 1990s, as well as to Japan's frustration over the disjuncture between its economic and political power in the international arena. However, the dynamic transformation of the East Asian economy and subsequently growing regional economic interdependence have played an equally important role in reviving Asian sentiment in Japan. Asia is a region the parts of which have become closely intermeshed, and its economic power has grown too large to be easily ignored; it is no longer a symbol of backwardness, immobility, and humiliation. The ascension of Asian economic power has implanted a new sense of Asian pride and confidence in Japanese minds.

Dynamics of Spontaneous Regionalization
Underlying the new Asian regionalism is the dynamics of spontaneous regionalization. Asian economic transformation over the past four decades has been remarkable. Japan and East Asian countries' share of world GDP and trade have become comparable to those of the European Union (EU) and North America. In 1960, Japan and East Asia accounted for only 4 percent of world GDP, which was insignificant, compared to 37 percent for the United States, Canada, and Mexico. In 1993, the combined economies of Japan, the NIEs, the ASEAN states, and China nearly matched the economy of either North America or Europe, accounting for about 30 percent of the world's GDP.[29]

Spontaneous regionalization has been facilitated by the complementarity of development strategies in the region. Japan was the pacesetter, while other Asian countries followed its lead, resulting in the flying geese formation of the intraregional division of labor. Emulation and replication of Japan's developmental experiences and growing intraregional trade deepened the horizontal division of labor in the region, moving steadily upward in their levels of manufacturing sophistication.[30] However, the flying geese model fails to grasp the reality of recent East Asian economies. Since the 1980s, most Asian countries, regardless of developmental level, have been moving into more value-added, capital- and technology-intensive industries. Japan, the NIEs, and ASEAN countries have all promoted cutting-edge industries such as semiconductors and computers. As a result, in contrast to the flying geese model, a horizontal, "swarming sparrow" pattern of development has become prevalent, further deepening economic competition and the friction between Japan and its regional economic rivals, based on shifts in comparative advantage.[31]

Despite the conflicting patterns of development strategy, intraregional trade has been on the rise, its share of trade in Asia having risen from 23 percent in 1980 to 40 percent in 1996.[32] During this period, intra-Asian trade grew 9.49 times—much faster than Asian exports to the United States—while trade between East Asia and the United States increased by only 5.77 times.[33] Meanwhile, during the same period, total Japanese trade with Asia grew from 31.3

percent to 42.4 percent, and in 1991, the volume of Japanese exports to Asia for the first time surpassed that of exports to the United States.[34]

A similar trend can be found in Japan's FDI in Asia, which increased dramatically due to the appreciation of the yen against the U.S. dollar since the Plaza Accord in 1985. The surging yen forced Japanese manufacturers to relocate their production lines to other Asian countries. Offshore production helped Japanese firms cope with protectionist barriers as well as ease the friction resulting from chronic bilateral trade surpluses with Asian countries. As a result, Japan's total investment in Asia rose from $2 billion in 1985 to $8.5 billion in 1995, putting Japan far ahead of the United States as the largest investor in Asia. And Japanese investment in the region has also proved very profitable. According to Ministry of International Trade and Industry (MITI) statistics, for the period 1991–92, Japanese firms in Asia gained ¥487 billion in net profits, while their North American counterparts lost ¥208 billion.[35] Japan took advantage of the increased FDI in Asia to construct a regional division of labor that sustained Japan's business expansion and facilitated its domestic economic restructuring.

But recent economic crises in East and Southeast Asia have revealed the vulnerability of the growing intraregional financial and capital interdependence. According to an OECD estimate, Japanese banks have a $270 billion-plus exposure to Asia's five crisis-hit economies, which is equivalent to 110 percent of their combined capital. To make things worse, $46 billion of the total loans to Asia is thought to represent nonperforming loans.[36] Failure to recover these loans could boomerang on Japan, and set off a chain reaction causing the collapse of the entire regional economy.

Japan has also been the number one donor of official development assistance (ODA) in Asia. Although the recipient countries increasingly have been spread throughout the world, Japanese aid is still concentrated in the Asian region. In 1994, $5.54 billion—equivalent to 57.3 percent of Japan's total ODA—went to Asia.[37] Eight of Japan's ten largest recipients in 1996 were Asian countries—Indonesia, China, Thailand, India, the Philippines, Pakistan, Bangladesh, and Sri Lanka.

Governed Regionalization and Japan's New Initiatives

As new cases of trade friction and intraregional financial vulnerability demonstrate, spontaneous regionalization has not necessarily brought about regional economic cooperation and integration. New regional dynamics of conflict and cooperation have caused Japan to rethink its regional posture, leaving it with three alternatives.

First, Japan may pursue the formation of an economic bloc through U.S.-Japan collective leadership in the Asian region. Tight bigemonic regionalism comprising the dollar-yen bloc, a free trade system, and the shared burden of regional public goods, characterizes this option. It presupposes several preconditions, namely, shared leadership between the United States and Japan, continuing Japanese adherence to political realism based on the Yoshida Doctrine, and collaboration with other regional actors. Japan has been enthusiastic about this model, but the United States has been reluctant to form this type of regional arrangement, not only because of its questionable feasibility, but also because of American unwillingness to share the leadership in this new integrative system. ASEAN has shown very little interest in, and has been suspicious of, the regional arrangement, fearing the erosion of its unity as well as a lack of immediate gain. Should Japan purse this option, however, no serious opposition is anticipated from the East Asian NIEs, since they might initially enjoy free-ride benefits.[38]

Second, Japan can also deliberate on open or soft regionalism. This type of regional initiative envisages a loose coalition of major economic powers in the region. Instead of Japan taking a leadership position, the United States, Japan, Russia, China, Australia, and the East Asian NIEs can form a less tight regional organization or regime through which they can coordinate their macroeconomic, industrial, and trade policies. It could imply the extension of the current Asian Pacific Economic Cooperation (APEC) scheme. In the post–Cold War era, this open regional arrangement could be more desirable and realistic, since it can easily incorporate China and Russia into the capitalist economic order, and can also reduce the cost of creating regional collective goods for the parties involved. According to this option, no serious domestic political opposition can be envisaged in Japan. At the same time, Japan's regional rivals are likely to favor it, since the arrangement presupposes the decentralization of economic power and collective management. Nevertheless, due to its very soft character, the consortium formula will be less effective in managing intraregional economic conflicts.

Given the increasing trend toward bloc economies, the formation of a Japan-centered trading bloc under yen hegemony cannot be ruled out. To counterbalance the euro in the EU, and the U.S. dollar bloc in North America, Japan could consider creating a yen bloc. Despite the haunting wartime memory of the Greater East Asian Coprosperity Sphere, some ASEAN countries are increasingly supportive of the idea. Malaysian Prime Minister Mahathir Mohamad proposed the idea of the East Asian Economic Caucus (EAEC), an exclusive East Asian trading bloc, to counter the emergence of protectionism and closed regionalism elsewhere in the world. The proposed idea was exclusive, in that it comprised only the eleven Asian members of APEC—excluding the United States, Canada, Australia, and New Zealand. The East Asian NIEs have been, however, less enthusiastic about the proposal, fearing Japan's economic dominance. Japan itself is divided on the issue. Ultra-nationalists such as Ishihara Shintaro advocate such an option, while mainstream political leaders and bureaucrats are much more cautious because the move could be rejected outright by the United States, further fragmenting the world trading system, and increasing the burdens of leadership.

But the recent financial crisis in Asia has increased the possibility that a loose yen bloc may emerge centering on the role of the Asian Monetary Fund. In July 1997, the Thai baht sharply depreciated because of domestic economic mismanagement and the subsequent abrupt outflow of foreign capital. But the crisis, not confined to Thailand, spread to other countries in the region and caused international lenders to panic. There followed currency crises in Indonesia, the Philippines, Malaysia, and even the Republic of Korea, where the fundamentals had been generally considered healthy. Furthermore, with the stock markets in

Hong Kong and Tokyo on the verge of crashing in the latter part of 1997, the region faced a major economic crisis.

Japan took a decisive step to cope with the Asian economic crisis, being aware that, given the size of its direct and indirect investments and external lending, failure to do so could produce an enormous backlash. As Table 4.1 shows, since the onset of the crisis, Japan has provided the largest amount of financial assistance to countries in the region. From July 1997 to November 1998, it disbursed more than $44 billion to the crisis-stricken countries through both multilateral and bilateral channels. On 30 September 1998, Japanese Finance Minister Miyazawa Kiichi announced a new initiative, totaling $30 billion, to assist countries in the region. According to the Miyazawa Initiative, $15 billion is to be made available over the medium- and long-term to help Asian countries recover economically, while the remaining $15 billion is to be preserved for short-term capital needs that might occur as a result of the implementation of economic reforms.[39] In addition, on 16 November 1998, Prime Minister Obuchi Keizo and U.S. President Bill Clinton announced the Asian Growth and Recovery Initiative, also to support crisis-hit Asian economies. The joint initiative, with the support of the World Bank and the Asian Development Bank (ADB), pledged to set up a $5 billion fund to help rejuvenate the Asian economies. Japan also agreed to donate a $3 billion national bond to the ADB, which will be used to assist Asian countries by means of credit guarantees for bond issuance and interest subsidies for bank borrowing. As part of the initiative, Japan has decided to offer an additional $4.6 billion via special low-interest yen loans for three years through its ODA.[40]

Table 4.1: International Assistance to Thailand and Indonesia

Country	Contents
Thailand (Total $17.2 billion)	Japan: $4 billion US: $0 Singapore: $1 billion Malaysia: $1 billion China: $1 billion Hong Kong: $1 billion Australia: $1 billion
Indonesia (Total: $40 billion)	Japan: $5 billion US: $3 billion Singapore: $5 billion Malaysia: $1 billion Australia: $1 billion
Indonesia (Total: $40 billion)	Japan: $10 billion US: $5 billion Singapore: $1 billion Malaysia: $1 billion Australia: $6.25 billion

Recognizing that the recovery of the Asian economy is closely tied to that of its own economy, in April 1998 Japan announced a Comprehensive Economic Measures package totaling ¥16 trillion yen (about $124 billion) to stimulate domestic demand and to promote structural reforms. Weak signs of economic recovery forced the Japanese government to come up with an additional fiscal stimulus package, totaling ¥23 trillion on 16 November 1998 (¥17 trillion for public projects and ¥6 trillion in tax cuts). The measure was undertaken in anticipation that the massive tax cuts and social infrastructure investments would put the Japanese economy back on the path to self-sustaining and domestic-demand-driven growth. It also set aside ¥700 billion (about $5.4 billion) for Asian countries, which was composed of an Export-Import Bank financing package to facilitate trade financing, ODA loans to support economic reforms, technical assistance for human resources development, and assistance in the form of food and medical supplies for Indonesia and elsewhere.

Likewise, Japan has undertaken a series of unprecedented measures to cope with the Asian financial economic crisis. It is in this context that the idea of the Asian Monetary Fund (AMF), led by Japan, began to attract public attention. The AMF scheme was originally proposed by then Finance Minister Kubo Wataru at a joint IMF–World Bank meeting in Hong Kong in September 1997. The proposal was intended to assist Southeast Asian countries experiencing financial and foreign exchange crises through the provision of stand-by loans to cover current account deficits, the extension of trade credits, and hedging against foreign exchange losses by pooling $100 billion, of which $50 billion was to be drawn from Japan, and the remainder from other Asian countries. The United States and the IMF initially opposed the idea of forming the AMF, not only because they considered the proposed body to be a duplicate of the IMF, but because they saw it as a waste of resources, and as a moral hazard associated with the relaxation of prerequisites. As the Asian financial situation worsened in tandem with the spread of the crisis to South Korea, however, both the United States and the IMF began to realize the value of the proposed fund in stabilizing financial and foreign exchange systems in the region. South Korea and crisis-laden Southeast Asian countries have also regarded the AMF as an alternative regional scheme to the IMF. Despite the region's growing interest in the AMF, however, Japan has been rather reluctant to promote it. As Obuchi stated explicitly in an interview with a South Korean newspaper, the Japanese government does not seem to have any immediate plan to establish the AMF.[41] Thus, Japan is likely to pursue the existing method of bilateral management in dealing with the Asian economic crisis, rather than opt for the AMF formula.

Conclusion

Debates on globalization and regionalization are not new in the Japanese context. Since its initial opening up by the Meiji Restoration, Japan has been struggling with strategic positioning in the international system, oscillating between internationalism and Asianism. The strategic choice has not been easy, but a desirable and even feasible path seems to be the simultaneous pursuit of multilateralism and open regionalism in a changing world. Japan should not abandon its global responsibility for maintaining a stable international economic system. Nonetheless, there is no need for Japan to avoid its constructive role in the Asian regional economy; it can ensure shared global leadership, as well as promote a regional leadership role in overcoming the Asian economic crisis and setting the future economic agenda for the region. However, retreat to the old pattern of an Asian identity, or adherence to closed regionalism could have catastrophic results for Japan, Asia, and the world. A beggar-thy-neighbor policy on the part of a Japan obsessed with its parochial national and regional interests could have adverse results: retaliation, the spread of the crisis, and panic behavior.

The path toward open regionalism and multilateralism might not be easy. However, domestic political structures, overall economic health, and the international system will continue to influence the nature and direction of Japan's foreign economic policy. Weak political leadership and fragmented domestic consensus, long-lasting economic downturns, and international political and economic instability could deter such a move, eventually plunging Japan, the Asian region, and the world into a black hole of disorder and conflict. Japanese foreign policy in the new millennium should be designed and conducted to minimize the probability of such a scenario.

Notes

1. For excellent accounts on postwar Japanese foreign policy, see Takashi and Daniel I. Okimoto, eds., *The Political Economy of Japan vol. 2: The Changing International Context* (Stanford: Stanford University Press, 1987); Gerald Curtis, ed., *Japan's Foreign Policy After the Cold War* (NY: M. E. Sharpe, 1993); and Kenneth B. Pyle, *The Japanese Question: Power and Purpose in a New Era* (Washington, D. C.: The AEI Press, 1996).
2. For a detailed discussion of the debate on internationalization in Japan, see Kamo Takehiko, ed., *Nihon no kokusaika: Sekikan no sekaiseiji* [Internationalization of Japan: World Politics Between Centuries] (Tokyo: Nihon Heironsha, 1994).
3. For the different concepts of globalization, see Kenichi Omae, *The Borderless World* (London: Collins, 1990); James H. Mittelman, ed., *Globalization: Theory and Practice* (NY: Frances Printer, 1996); Richard Falk, "Resisting 'Globalization-from Above' Through 'Globalization-from Below," *New Political Economy* 2:1 (1997): 17–24; Dani Rodrik, "Sense and Nonsense in the Globalization Debate," *Foreign Policy* 107 (1997): 19–36.
4. For more detailed explanation on difference between spontaneous and governed globalization, see Chung-in Moon, "Democratization and Globalization as Ideological and Political Foundations of Economic Policy," in *Democracy and the Korean Economy*, eds. Jongryn Mo and Chung-in Moon (Stanford: Hoover Institution Press, 1999), pp. 1–33.
5. For the functionalist theories of regional integration, see Amitai Etzioni, "The Dialectics of Supranational Unification," *American Political Science Review* 56 (1962): 927–55; Ernst B. Haas, "International Integration: The European and the Universal Process," *International Organization* 15 (1961): 366–92.
6. Peter Drysdale and Ross Garnaut, *Asia Pacific Regionalism: Readings in International Economic Relations* (Pymble: Harper Educational Publishers, 1994).
7. Globalization and internationalization are analytically differentiated. But in the Japanese context, both terms are interchangeably used. An official use of the term globalization is relatively a new phenomenon. See Economic Planning Agency, Comprehensive Planning Bureau (Keizai Kikakucho Sogo Keikakukyoku), ed., *Keizai shingikai nijuisseki sekaikeizai iinkai hokokusho* [Report of the Twenty-first Century World Economy Committee of the Economic Council] (Tokyo: The Economic Planning Agency of Japan, 1997).
8. See Yukichi Fukuzawa, "On De-Asianization," in *Meiji Japan through Contemporary Sources*, vol. 3, ed., Center for East Asian Cultural Studies (Tokyo: Center for East Asian Cultural Studies, 1973), pp. 129–33.
9. Kenneth B. Pyle, "Japan and the Twenty-first Century," in Inoguchi and Okimoto, 1987, p. 454.

10. For the developmental state argument, see Chalmers Johnson, *MITI and the Japanese Miracle: The Growth of Industrial Policy, 1925–1975* (Stanford: Stanford University Press, 1980).
11. For a comprehensive analysis on the SII, see Leonard J. Schoppa, *Bargaining with Japan* (NY: Columbia University Press, 1997).
12. Tadahiro Sekimoto, "Manufacturing: Japan's Key to the Twenty-first Century," *Japan Echo* 23:4 (1997).
13. Edward Lincoln, *Japan's New Global Role* (Washington, DC: The Brookings Institution, 1993).
14. Alan Kitchin, "Japan: A Place in the Sun," *Director* 51:2 (1997): 77–80.
15. Ministry of Foreign Affairs of Japan, *ODA Summary 1995* (1996), chapter 1.
16. T. J. Pempel, "Transpacific *Torii*: Japan and the Emerging Asian Regionalism," in *Network Power: Japan and Asia*, eds. Peter J. Katzenstein and Takashi Shiraishi (Ithaca: Cornell University Press, 1997), pp. 67–68.
17. Ministry of Foreign Affairs, *Diplomatic Bluebook 1991: Japan's Diplomatic Activities* (Tokyo, 1991), p. 1.
18. Yuichiro Nagatomi, ed., *Masayoshi Ohira's Proposal to Evolve the Global Society* (Tokyo: Foundation for Advanced Information and Research, 1988).
19. Pyle, 1996, pp. 88–89.
20. See Ozawa Ichiro, *Nihon kaizo keikaku* [Plan for restructuring Japan] (Tokyo: Kodansha, 1993) [English edition, *Blueprint for a New Japan* (Kodansha International, 1994)].
21. Yoichi Funabashi, "Introduction: Japan's International Agenda for the 1990s," in *Japan's International Agenda*, ed. Yoichi Funabashi (NY: New York University Press, 1994), pp. 1–27.
22. Chung-in Moon, "Managing Regional Challengers: Japan, the East Asian NICs and New Patterns of Economic Rivalry," *Pacific Focus* 6:2 (1991): 43–44.
23. Kimitada Miwa, "Japanese Policies and Concepts for a Regional Order in Asia, 1938-1940," in *The Ambivalence of Nationalism: Modern Japan between East and West*, eds. James W. White, Michio Umegaki, and Thomas R. H. Havens (Lanham, MD: University Press of America, 1990), p. 135.
24. J. V. Koschmann, "Asianism's Ambivalent Legacy," in Katzenstein and Shiraishi 1997, p. 83.
25. See *Posuto reisen to Ajia–Taiheiyo no shinchoryu* [Post-Cold War and the New Asia-Pacific Trend], Roundtable Discussion, *Gaiko forum* (February 1991).
26. Yotaro Kobayashi, "Japan's Need for Re-Asianization," *Foresight* (April 1991).
27. Ishihara Shintaro and Morita Akio, *No to ieru Nihon* [The Japan that Can Say No] (Kobunsha, 1991) [English edition: *The Japan That Can Say No*; Simon and Shuster, 1991].
28. Koji Kakizawa, "Japan Should Back an Asian Peace Force," *Japan Times Weekly*, 29 April–6 May 1991.
29. Peter J. Katzenstein, "Introduction: Asian regionalism in Comparative Perspective," in Katzenstein and Shiraishi, 1997, p. 12.
30. For the "flying geese" and the horizontal division of labor argument, see Watanabe Toshio, *Nishitaiheiyou no jidai: Ajia shinsangyo kokka no seiji-keizaigaku* [The Era of the Western Pacific: The Political Economy of Asian Newly Industrializing Countries] (Bungei Shunju, 1989).
31. Moon, "Managing Regional Challengers," pp. 23–47; Gordon Bernard and John Ravenhill, "Beyond Product Cycles and Flying Geese: Regionalization, Hierarchy, and Industrialization of East Asia," *World Politics* 47 (1995): 171–209.
32. Ministry of International Trade and Industry (MITI), *Tsusho hakusho 1998* [White Paper on Trade 1998] (Tokyo, 1998), chapter 1.
33. Ministry of International Trade and Industry, 1998, chapter 1.
34. Ministry of International Trade and Industry, 1998, chapter 3.
35. Yong Deng, "Japan in APEC: The Problematic Leadership Role," *Asian Survey* 37 (1997), p. 355.
36. *Economist*, 18 April 1998, p. 30.
37. Yanagitsudo Hiroyuki, "Japan's Economic Assistance after the Cold War," *Japan Times Weekly*, 4–10 December 1995, p. 5.
38. Moon, 1991, p. 43.
39. *The Japan Times*, 30 September 1998.
40. *Nihon keizai shimbun*, 15 December 1998.
41. *Joongang ilbo*, 30 December 1998.

CHAPTER 5
===

Japanese Foreign Policy and Human Rights

Ian Neary

You have to look very carefully in the writing about Japanese foreign policy before the mid-1990s to find any mention of human rights. There were some references to the ambivalent attitudes adopted by Japan in the mid-1970s, when the United States began to stress human rights concerns in its criticisms of the Soviet Union, and there have been some passing comments on Japan's voting record on human rights resolutions in the UN. Mostly, though, the issue has not been mentioned at all. However at the end of the 1990s human rights issues play a much more important role in both domestic and foreign policy agendas. Two committees exist, attached to the prime minister's office, to consider detailed domestic policy changes and to promote human rights awareness in the UN decade of human rights education.

Almost every year now the Ministry of Foreign Affairs has to prepare a report for submission to the UN about some aspect of Japan's human rights record, which provokes nongovernment organizations (NGOs) within Japan to produce "alternative" reports. Japanese government officials have thus become involved in discussions of human rights matters within Japan at the same time as being drawn into the debate about the compatibility of human rights and Asian values at international seminars and conferences. Rights issues have come to play an important part in the development of the parameters of current policy making and also raise difficult questions about Japan's identity in international affairs. In the following discussion of some aspects of human rights dimensions of Japan's foreign policy, we will seek to trace the nature of Japan's response to the development of an international treaty regime that tries to insist that states take rights seriously.

Human Rights

Human rights emerged in a form relevant to international relations within documents produced from the mid- to late-1940s at the time of the founding and early development of the United Nations. Later, we will review the process in which these ideas have been elaborated, but first we need to clarify what is meant by "human rights."

It is common in the literature on human rights to distinguish between three generations of rights. The first generation is composed of civil and political rights whose main focus is to protect the individual from the state. The struggle for civil and political rights was central to the American and French revolutions of the 1780s and 1790s, and these ideas were developed in the constitutional struggles in western Europe and North America in the eighteenth and nineteenth centuries, based on liberal notions of equality and freedom. They include the right to vote, the right to free speech and press, and the right to due process of law.

Working class and other social movements that developed in the nineteenth and twentieth centuries protested that, firstly, the ruling groups in the liberal states did not always implement these ideas consistently to protect the rights of the whole population—women and the unpropertied classes, for example. Secondly, they argued that civil and political rights had little meaning if significant sections of society were deprived of subsistence or social services such as health care or education. Thus there emerged demands for second generation rights—economic, social, and cultural rights—which it was the state's duty to provide in order to ensure the survival and development of all its citizens. First formal recognition came in the constitution of the German Weimar republic in 1919, but most constitutions produced after 1945, including that of Japan, contain reference to these second-generation rights.

More recently, and more controversially, demands have been made, mainly by Third World countries, for the protection and promotion of what are called "solidarity rights." These include a right to a healthy and balanced environment, the right to economic and social development, and the right to peace. These are demands not made on particular states but on the international system in general and more specifically on the economically advanced nations of the "North" whose actions, it is alleged, fail to protect the interests—the rights—of the "South."

Thinking of rights in terms of "generations" has the unfortunate consequence of suggesting a hierarchy of rights and has led to a discussion about which set of rights should have priority in policy implementation. Should the need for economic development, which will enable the state to ensure economic, social, and cultural rights, have priority over demands for civil and political rights that protect the individual but at the cost of the collective? This has led to the suggestion of a holistic notion of basic rights that would consist of the rights to physical security, economic subsistence, and political participation. This gives equal attention to the various aspects of rights, but also to the balance between individual and collective rights.

Human Rights and the Asian Values Debate

During the Cold War era, Western criticism of violations of civil and political rights by governments in the communist bloc provoked the response that socialist states had a much better record in the protection of the economic and social rights of citizens thanks to the socialized welfare programs and low rates of unemployment. It was suggested that there was an inevitable trade-off between the two kinds of rights, and that overall the West did not perform much better than the East. The collapse of the Soviet Union and the reform of its former allies in Europe made this debate irrelevant, but a new frontier of the human rights debate was recreated in Asia as the United States, and its allies were presented as attempting to impose their human rights ideas on such countries as China and Singapore with quite different cultural values and different levels of economic development. Such outspoken Asian leaders as Lee Kwan Yew and Mohammed Mahathir argue that human rights ideas are inappropriate in Asian societies and will undermine (and in some versions of the argument are intended to undermine) East Asian growth and its domestic law and order. The Chinese argue the case for human rights or development. That is, that the cost of civil and political liberties is too great for developing countries and their fulfillment has to take second place to economic growth. At its most extreme, the Western enthusiasm for human rights is described as a new form of cultural imperialism.

A UN-sponsored meeting of the representatives of 40 Asian states—including Japan—was held in Bangkok in March 1993 in preparation for the World Conference on Human Rights to be held in Vienna in June. There the governments of Indonesia, China, Singapore, and Malaysia argued strongly that many of the human rights values were alien to Asia and that there was a danger that they would be imposed on the region by the West. Meanwhile Japan, South Korea somewhat less vociferously, and some other governments maintained the UN line on the universal applicability of human rights standards. In the Bangkok Declaration produced after the conference, Asian governments declared that developed countries should not tie aid to human rights considerations, should respect the sovereign rights of states to manage human rights within their borders, and should not promote human rights through the imposition of incompatible values on Asia.[1] Although Japan was also a signatory to this, it later announced it had reservations to the "Bangkok" approach. Japan has had considerable difficulty in reconciling its desire to maintain solidarity with Asia while remaining loyal to its commitment to support Western, mainly U.S., policy on human rights.

The United Nations and Human Rights

The UN Charter commits its members to ensure that rights and basic freedoms are guaranteed, irrespective of race, sex, language, and religion. On the other hand it endorses the principle of absolute national sovereignty and forbids interference in another country's internal affairs. At first the UN, in particular the Commission on Human Rights (CHR), placed most emphasis on respect for sovereignty. Nevertheless, in a relatively short time the CHR produced a draft of the Universal Declaration of Human Rights (UDHR), which was adopted by the United Nations General Assembly (UNGA) in 1947. A declaration is little more than a statement of good intentions, it has no legal force so it was decided to devise a covenant that countries would be asked to sign and ratify. Such a covenant would be equivalent to a multilateral treaty that, once ratified, would incorporate the ideas and standards of the covenant into the country's legal system.

At this early stage of the development of the Cold War, there was already disagreement over priorities in human rights, so it was decided to draw up two separate, but complementary documents, one covering political and civil rights, the other economic, social, and cultural rights. The two covenants were completed and presented to the UNGA in 1954, although it was to be more than ten years before they were adopted and another decade before they came into effect. Thereafter, apart from the Declaration on the Rights of the Child (1959) and a draft on Rights of Asylum (1960), the UN initiated very little human rights standard setting until 1966. There was no obvious desire to push ahead with the rights agenda, and the CHR sought no role other than to deal with relatively uncontroversial topics, such as genocide, slavery, refugees, and stateless persons. Between 1946 and 1966, its official position was that it had, "no power to take any action in regard to any complaints concerning human rights."[2]

In the 1960s, many newly independent Asian and African nations joined the UN. This introduced a third force that undercut the control of the U.S. and Soviet blocs, neither of which, for different reasons, were interested in developing the UN's human rights machinery. The Third World countries were more interested in rights issues and were particularly alarmed by the development of apartheid policies in South Africa. In December 1965, the UNGA had adopted the Convention on the Elimination of All Forms of Racial Discrimination (CERD), which included provision for the submission of complaints against states that accepted the procedure. This new climate of opinion made possible reconsideration of the two draft treaties, on civil and politics rights (the ICCPR) and economic, social, and cultural rights (the ICESCR), ready since 1954, which were finally adopted by the UNGA in December 1966. However they did not come into force until they had been ratified by 35 countries and this did not happen until March 1976.

All states ratifying these covenants have an obligation to produce periodic reports, though only those states that have ratified the first optional protocol allow appeals to the Human Rights Committee (HRC) from individuals who allege rights violations by their state. The HRC was set up in 1977 to consider reports from and complaints against the states party to the ICCPR. After an initial report submitted within a year of ratification, subsequent reports are due every five years. Between 1977 and 1991, the number of states party to the ICCPR increased from 35 to 96. This had gone up to 140 by 1998, with 92 countries having ratified the first optional protocol.

Parallel to the HRC, which supervised the complaints and reporting system under the ICCPR, in 1979 the UN Economic and Social Council established arrangements to monitor states' compliance with the ICESCR. After "eight years of thoroughly ineffectual monitoring," a committee on economic, social, and cultural rights was created that held its first session in 1987.[3] The following year a reporting system was devised so that each state party should present a report at five-year intervals. Since then, the committee has endeavored to work out ways to develop an effective monitoring system that maintains dialogue between the committee and the states. Although still developing, this system is much less effective than one that monitors civil and political rights.

Other major UN conventions on human rights have also incorporated reporting obligations and set up committees to consider reports and otherwise supervise the implementation by states of the rights defined in the conventions. By 1991 the CERD had been ratified by 129 states, not including Japan. It requires submission of a report one year after the report comes into effect and every two years thereafter. The Convention on the Elimination of Discrimination against Women (CEDAW), which entered into force in 1981 (Japan ratified in 1985), requires reports within a year of it coming into effect and every four years thereafter. The Committee against Torture (CAT) was set up by the Convention against Torture and Other Cruel, Inhuman or Degrading Treatment or Punishment, which entered into force in 1987. It, too, expects to receive a report within a year of ratification and then every four years. Two years later the Convention on the Rights of the Child (CRC) was passed, incorporating similar reporting procedures.

Japan and Human Rights to the Late 1980s

Japan has been constitutionally committed to the protection of the human rights of its citizens since the coming into effect of the 1947 Constitution. Popular sovereignty is one of three ideas central to the postwar political structure. Secondly, there is "pacifism" to which Japan apparently commits itself in Article 9, and, thirdly, there is the commitment to human rights, which is present in three places in the Constitution. There is indirect reference in the preamble:

We recognize that all peoples of the world have *the right to live in peace, free from fear and want.*

We believe that no nation is responsible to itself alone, but that laws of political morality are universal; and that obedience to such laws is incumbent upon all nations who would sustain their own sovereignty and justify their sovereign relations with other nations.(Emphasis added.)

Secondly, there is Chapter III of the Constitution, which in articles 10-40 lists those rights in some detail. Finally, Article 97 states that "the *fundamental human rights* [granted] by this Constitution . . . are fruits of the age-old struggle of men to be free . . . and are conferred upon this and future generations in trust, to be held for all time inviolate." (Emphasis added.)

As a former "enemy power," Japan was not involved in the process that created the United Nations, that led to the drafting of the UDHR, or even the drafting of the ICCPR or the ICESCR. Japan did not join the UN until early 1957, and although Japan was committed, then as now, to a "UN centered" foreign policy, this has not meant that it has been actively seeking new initiatives to strengthen the United Nations. On the contrary, "Japan's early years in the world body were marked by a nearly total absence of initiative."[4] Rather like the

Third World nations who joined in the 1960s, they seem to have felt it was a club founded by the old colonial powers.

Japan was not one of the 35 states that had ratified the ICCPR and ICESCR when they came in to force in March 1976. Japan did not ratify them until 1979, when the UN human rights monitoring structure was starting to operate and the Jimmy Carter administration was taking an interest in human rights diplomacy. At the time Japan did ratify them, it was party to only two international rights treaties: on political rights of women (July 1955) and the suppression of the traffic in persons and the exploitation of the prostitution of others (May 1958). During the 1980s, Japan ratified the Refugee Covenant and the Protocol relating to the Status of Refugees (October 1981 and January 1982) and CEDAW in 1985. There was no haste to join the emergent international human rights regime, and one might speculate why this was so.

It may be that, as the supporter of "Asian values" might argue, there are cultural reasons that deter the Japanese government from taking human rights issues on board. However, as we will see below, most of the reservations referred to by Japan on ratifying the covenants have concerned economic, not social or cultural issues. More persuasive is that Japan has followed the line set by the United States. As far as the UN and human rights were concerned, U.S. policy was set out by John Foster Dulles in 1953 when he declared the United States intended "to encourage the promotion everywhere of human rights and individual freedoms, but to favour methods of persuasion, education and example rather than formal undertakings."[5] The United States, he went on, did not intend to become party to the draft covenants then nearing completion and would not even submit them to the Senate for consideration. The view of Japanese officials was "while the UN may identify common categories of rights, it may neither set specific international human rights standards nor impose sanctions,"[6] a view remarkably similar to that expounded by Dulles in 1953. Finally it might be that the Japanese government, the Liberal Democratic Party (LDP) in particular, did not want to draw attention to its human rights record nor to provide its domestic critics with the opportunity to use external arena to criticize its policies.

When Japan ratified the two main covenants, it entered reservations: to Article 22 of the ICCPR and Article 8 of the ICESCR, which meant that workers in the public sector would continue to be denied the right to organize and strike, and there were objections to another part of Article 8, which would have allowed unions to join international federations. There were also reservations on Article 7 of the ICESCR on the right to remuneration on public holidays— union and opposition party voices of protest were not listened to. Japan announced reservations on Article 13 of the ICESCR, which commits government to work toward free secondary and higher education. Finally Japan was opposed to Article 41 of the ICCPR, which empowers the Human Rights Committee to deal with claims between states. This latter is of only theoretical interest as it is not a function that the HRC has sought to develop, but it is consistent with the Japanese government's attitude, which was to oppose giving the

HRC more to do than simply review periodic reports. Japan did not ratify the first optional protocol of the ICCPR, which would have allowed residents of Japan to appeal to the UN of violations of the covenant by the Japanese government.[7] The LDP/government position is that this would be unconstitutional and contrary to Asian practice, even though it has now been accepted by the governments of South Korea, Mongolia, the Philippines, and Nepal.

Japan submitted its initial report on civil and political rights in October 1980. It was brief, just 12 pages, three of general remarks and nine that commented briefly on the 27 substantive articles of the covenant. Most notorious was the comment on Section 27, which referred to minorities. The Japanese government reported that minorities of the kind mentioned in the covenant did not exist in Japan, completely ignoring the existence of the Ainu, not to mention the Korean community resident in Japan. Hardly anyone was aware of the report or that it was considered by the Human Rights Committee. Meanwhile the committee, being poorly informed about Japan, did not know enough to ask the government representatives about its ethnic minorities.

The second report was due in 1986, but in the summer of that year the prime minister, Nakasone Yasuhiro, made some unguarded remarks about the homogeneity of Japanese society compared to the racial diversity of the United States, which aroused criticism both at home and from American minority group leaders. This seems to have caused a delay in the submission of the report until December 1987. Once again there was no consultation with groups outside government in the process of writing the report, and NGOs only got to see the report after it was published by the UN. On this occasion, however, there was sufficient time for 12 NGOs based in Japan plus the World Council of Churches to submit counterreports.

To summarize: until the late 1980s Japan was not an enthusiastic proponent of human rights within the UN. First, it participated in the bodies dealing with human rights issues only reluctantly and tended to respond defensively to proposals it considered at variance with Japanese law or practice. This is in part a result of Japan following the U.S. lead in human rights policy, as in most other areas of foreign policy. Second, Japan was also reluctant to expose itself to criticism from abroad and did not want to give indigenous human rights organizations the opportunity to use international standards or institutions to exert pressure from outside. Third, Japan has resisted measures that might interfere with the process of economic growth.

Japan and Human Rights Post–Gulf War, Post–Cold War

At the end of the 1980s, the Japanese government had only ratified seven of the 22 human rights treaties, and in the reports made to the UN, there was often less than full disclosure; but during the 1990s one can detect a qualitative change in the Japanese approach. At the governmental level, we can see the Ministry of Foreign Affairs taking the lead in the signing and ratifying of a number international human rights covenants and playing a more positive role in human rights promotion at UN conferences worldwide and within the region. At the nongovernmental level, too, groups and organizations have started to locate their demands for human rights within an international context and to seek to contribute to a broader awareness of rights issues regionally and internationally.

In May 1994 Japan ratified the Convention on the Rights of the Child and the following year the Convention on the Elimination of all forms of Racial Discrimination. In 1997 the Ministry of Foreign Affairs began working on preparations for the ratification of the Convention Against Torture and other Cruel, Inhuman or Degrading Treatment or Punishment. Meanwhile the government produced two periodic reports in 1993 and 1998 under the terms of the ICCPR, which were accompanied by alternative reports from a large number of organizations including the Japan Federation of Bar Associations (JFBA) and the Japan Civil Liberties Union (JCLU). There have also been new policy initiatives in human rights education and to aid victims of human rights violations. For perhaps the first time, there was a feeling that human rights were being taken seriously within central government and that the NGOs were keen to ensure that government live up to its international commitments.

Japan's change of attitude toward the international human rights regime can be explained by three interlinked factors. First, the Gulf War showed the new significance of the UN in the post–Cold War world. Moreover, there was widespread criticism of Japan for its policy immobility and inability to deal with an international crisis of this proportion. This was not only a matter of international politics. It was Japan's conspicuous failure to respond effectively to the Gulf crisis that moved Ozawa Ichiro to demand reform in the structure of Japan's party politics and administration, which contributed to the LDP's loss of power in 1993 and the uncertainty at the center of Japan's political life that still (in 1999) has not been completely resolved. What Japan should do was not clear, but no longer could Japan afford to sit on the sidelines of international politics contributing only cash, whether that be in the form of overseas development assistance (ODA) or finance for the peacekeeping efforts.

Second, during the early 1990s, international attention focused on the regional human rights conference held in Bangkok in April 1993, which was a prelude to the world conference held in Vienna in June that year. These conferences forced Japan and many other nations to clarify their positions toward human rights. At both conferences the Japanese delegation made clear that it took the universalist view in opposition to the views expressed by the representatives of China, Singapore, and other Southeast Asian countries that insisted on placing human rights in the context of "Asian Values." Nevertheless there were conservatives at home who criticized the government for following the U.S. "excessive human rights policy" so slavishly.

The third major change was that by 1990, a consensus had been achieved in the Ministry of Foreign Affairs to actively pursue Japan's candidacy for a permanent seat on the UN Security Council if and when there is any reform of UN structures. Public debate about this started in 1992-93. The more positive attitude of the Ministry of Foreign Affairs to the international human rights regime was no doubt part of the attempt to win domestic support for more positive involvement in UN activities. It would be difficult for Japan to press its case if it continued to ignore the demands in the international community that it ratify at least some of the outstanding human rights treaties.

The third and fourth periodic reports on civil and political rights submitted to the HRC in December 1991 and June 1997 were substantially longer than their predecessors, stretching to 49 and 101 pages, respectively. The NGOs are critical of the way the Ministry of Foreign Affairs continues to compile these reports without any input from the groups representing the various minorities and women, but there has been an increase of cooperation between them. Both reports were made public immediately after submission to the UN, and the "list of issues" that came from the HRC after it had read the report was passed straight on to the NGOs. Meetings took place between the NGO representatives and government officials who were going to Geneva. Twenty-three "counter-reports" were prepared and submitted prior to the Human Rights Committee hearing in 1993, and 80 lobbyists were in Geneva for the meeting. In 1993, the Japanese government was represented by not only the Ministry of Foreign Affairs but also by bureaucrats from Ministry of Justice, the National Police Agency, and the Management Agency. In 1998, the Ministry of Labour, Ministry of Education, and Ministry of Health and Welfare were also represented in the official party of 26, and there were 50 representatives of more than ten NGOs at the meeting with the HRC.

The JFBA produced very substantial counterreports in 1993 and 1998—each over 250 closely printed pages, which focus heavily, though by no means exclusively, on criminal procedure.[8] Despite their long-term commitment to promoting human rights ideas within Japan, there is said to have been a feeling among lawyers before 1990 that to point out the inadequacies of the government report to an international audience was somehow shameful, unpatriotic. This is no longer a problem. Neither the JFBA nor any other human rights NGOs have such compunctions, and they have become enthusiastic about exposing Japan's human rights record to international scrutiny.

The fifth report is due in 2003. There are suggestions that the HRC be invited to consider the Japanese report and reports from other Asian countries at a session held in Tokyo. This would focus the attention of the world on Asian issues.

Through the regular process of report and counterreport, the Japanese government has been forced into a dialogue not only with the international experts on the HRC but also domestically with the home NGOs. The growth in the length of the periodic reports over the years is not simply due to the questions that have come from the experts on the committee but also are a result of the government making an effort to maintain its position as the legitimate interpreter of the state of human rights in Japan. The scale of the response from the NGO side has generated a very large amount of data and conflicting interpretations of events. It also demonstrates the wide range of groups now involved in rights issues in Japan.

Toward a Coordinated Human Rights Policy?

Another factor that focused government attention more closely on rights issues was that on 30 June 1994, the Japan Socialist Party (JSP) agreed to join the LDP to form a coalition cabinet and Murayama Tomiichi became prime minister. Very quickly, the JSP dropped most of its more radical policies, especially related to foreign policy, but it did maintained its commitment to human rights issues. In the summer of 1995. a high profile committee was created within the Prime Minister's Office to formulate Japan's plan for the UN Decade of Human Rights Education. This was formally chaired by the prime minister and contained five senior ministers plus the deputy vice minister from all the main agencies and ministries. It was the first time such a high profile committee had been set up to promote human rights with the authority to coordinate policy across all government departments

In January 1996, the CERD became effective in Japan, but in the same month Murayama resigned as prime minister. Although his successor, Hashimoto Ryutaro, had a right of center image, the momentum behind the push toward giving human rights a higher profile continued as the JSP remained a member of the coalition cabinet. In December 1996 a Law for the Promotion of Human Rights Protection was passed by the Diet, effective from March 1997. This clarified the duty of the state to promote human rights through the promotion of human rights education and protection of the victims of human rights infringements. It established a committee, Policy Council on Rights Protection, of 20 members nominally chaired by the prime minister to produce a report within two years, recommending legislative measures on human rights education and, within five years, suggestions for policy to give redress to victims of human rights violations. The aim is to resolve human rights problems including the Burakumin minority problem.

In July 1997 the Prime Minister's Office published its detailed proposals for the UN Decade of Human Rights Education. As well as including detailed discussion of the overall aims of the program—in brief, equality before the law and respect for the individual—it discusses nine specific areas: women, children, the elderly, the disabled, Burakumin issues, Ainu, foreigners, HIV patients, and former prisoners. Even those critical of the inadequacy of government policy admit that, though there is still a need to address the roots of its discriminatory culture, Japan is now at the start of the implementation of the Constitution's human rights principles.

Human Rights and Development Aid Policy

In April 1991 Prime Minister Kaifu Toshiki announced "Four ODA Principles" that the Japanese government would take into account when deciding on development assistance. The first three were concerned with military spending, but the fourth factor concerned "efforts to promote democratization, secure human rights, and move toward a market-oriented economy." In June the following year, the Ministry of Foreign Affairs announced revisions in its ODA charter to include reference to the securing of basic rights and freedoms in the recipient country. This apparent commitment to human rights was tempered by the assurance that it would implement this policy only in accordance with the principles of the UN Charter, which promises respect for sovereignty and nonintervention in domestic matters. As protection of sovereignty is the most common grounds for rejecting criticism on human rights policy, especially by states such as China, there was an in-built difficulty with this policy right from the start.

The government was criticized from a number of quarters. First there were those who argued that, as a matter of principle, government should not politicize its aid policy and should keep politics separate from economics, an echo of a theme in the wider foreign policy debate since the 1950s. Second, there were those sympathetic to the "Asian values" argument who suggested that Japan should not collude with the U.S. and other Western leaders in trying to impose Western values on the countries of Asia using the leverage of foreign aid. From a different perspective, the advocates of human rights and democracy argued that the government was not serious about these principles and doubted whether they would really play a part in the application of development assistance policy.

Japan's initial response to the repression of protest in China in June 1989 was to resist domestic and international pressure to impose punitive sanctions. Nevertheless a freeze on aid projects was imposed, and it was announced that the new aid package would be delayed. The freeze was lifted in August 1989, however, and the new five-year package due to begin in April 1990 went ahead in June 1990 following token concessions by the Beijing government. The authorities in Japan were not sympathetic to students protesting about Tiananmen Square and its aftermath. They neither impeded nor protested the activities of embassy or consular officials who harassed and intimidated prodemocracy Chinese students studying in Japan. There were numerous cases of disregard of the rights of individual Chinese to political asylum, and students were not allowed to extend their stays in Japan despite official pledges that they would be permitted to do so.[9]

This was, of course, before Kaifu's announcement of the new guidelines for ODA policy that arguably marked the launch of a new phase in its international human rights policy. So what is the evidence from the 1990s? Following a detailed analysis of the provision of ODA 1990-94, Hoshino Eiichi has concluded that, "Japanese ODA is not accounted for by human rights practices in recipient countries" and therefore, "Japanese foreign aid is not used as a conditioning tool to reward or punish in any systematic way with respect to human rights."[10]

The 1996 ODA White Paper distinguishes between the use of foreign aid policy as a positive and negative sanction. Where favorable moves are observed, Japan will "reward" the country through extending aid. Where unfavorable moves appear they will freeze, reduce, and finally, if no change in policy is forthcoming, cease foreign aid provision. Hoshino's research only covered the period prior to the announcement of this policy but there is no reason to revise his conclusion about ODA practice. It remains constrained both by the principle of nonintervention in domestic matters and by the importance attached to considering "Japan's bilateral relations with the recipient country." Particularly when these factors can be said to coincide, they are allowed to override the use of aid provision as either a negative or positive sanction in human rights policy.

Conclusion

During the 1990s, the Japanese government has become increasingly engaged with the international human rights structures. There has been pressure on Japan to adopt a more proactive human rights policy both from domestic NGOs and within the international community. Human rights became more obviously part of the domestic policy-making process in the 1990s but, despite the much publicized changes in the ODA charter, rights considerations do not seem to have made much difference to the way Japan allocates its economic aid. The gap between its stated policy and practice on ODA provision allows it to nominally adhere to UN/U.S. rights-promoting policy while doing nothing that might damage trading relations within the region.

The Convention Against Torture (CAT) has not been widely ratified by Asian countries. It would be possible for the Japanese government to make a positive commitment to human rights by ratifying the CAT and promoting its implementation in Asia. This could amount to the start of Japan taking a lead in human rights diplomacy in Asia. Given the perception of Japan's colonial activity in Asia in the twentieth century, it is difficult to imagine the Japanese government being easily accepted as *the* leader of an Asian human rights promoting group, but there is no reason why Japan could not become one of a number of countries, perhaps including South Korea, who might by example and by their activities within UN organizations elaborate an Asian perspective on human rights that would rival that of the "Asian values" view favored by Singapore, China, and Malaysia.

Since the 1950s, Japan has been reluctant to become actively involved in human rights promotion. Within the arena of international politics, policy makers were content to follow the U.S. lead, but despite its periodic enthusiasm for "human rights diplomacy" the United States does not have an unblemished record of encouraging the spread of UN standards. Within Japan both bureaucrats and LDP politicians have sought to limit the impact of liberal and social democratic ideas, as incorporated, for example, in the postwar Constitution and educational system. However, both domestic and foreign constraints within the policy-making process are changing. The way is now open for Japan to move out of the shadow of the United States and develop a distinctive human rights dimension to domestic and foreign policy as it creates a new identity that is based on being Asian, industrialized, and rights sensitive. Within this process there is the possibility of Japan taking a lead in human rights in Asia and from there the world.

Notes

1. David Arase, "Japanese Foreign Policy and Human Rights in Asia," *Asian Survey* 33:10 (October 1993): 940.
2. Quoted in Philip Alston, "The Commission on Human Rights," in *The United Nations and Human Rights: A Critical Appraisal,* ed. Philip Alston (Oxford: Clarendon Press, 1992), p. 139.
3. Philip Alston, "The Commission on Economic, Social and Cultural Rights," in Alston, 1992, p. 473.
4. John M. Peek, "Japan, the United Nations, and Human Rights," *Asian Survey* 32:2 (February 1992): 218.
5. Quoted in Alston, 1992, p. 133.
6. Peek, 1992, p. 222.
7. Peek, 1992, p. 223–26.
8. Japan Federation of Bar Associations, ed., *A Report on the Application and Practice in Japan of the International Covenant on Civil and Political Rights* (Tokyo, April 1993); Japan Federation of Bar Associations, *Alternative Report to the Fourth Periodic Report of Japan on the ICCPR* (Tokyo, September 1998).
9. Arase, 1992, pp. 943–45.
10. Hoshino Eiichi, "Human Rights and Development Aid: Japan," in *Debating Human Rights,* ed. Peter Van Ness (London and New York: Routledge, 1999), pp. 225.

CHAPTER 6

Japanese Environmental Foreign Policy

Ohta Hiroshi

Japanese environmental foreign policy, as does other foreign policy, evolves out of intertwined domestic and international factors. The well-being and economic prosperity of Japanese are ever heavily dependent on a stable international political and economic order. Free and open access to and steady supply of food and energy are Japan's primary security concerns. As to the diplomatic means for sustaining economic prosperity, postwar political arrangements continue to set its parameters. The no-war clause of the Constitution has prohibited Japan from taking any militarily aggressive foreign policy; it has abided by the spirit and obligation stipulated in the Charter of the United Nations advocating peaceful resolution of international disputes.[1] At the same time, the U.S.-Japan security treaty has continuously provided Japan with military security as one of the regional security arrangements that comes within the purview of the UN Charter.[2] The established consensus about Japan's postwar foreign policy is that, although it has the right to defend itself, Japan cannot take part in any collective security activity. Since the end of the Cold War and the Gulf War of 1991, however, this foreign policy framework has come under scrutiny both inside and outside Japan.

The fundamental issue has been: can Japan contribute to the enhancement and maintenance of international public goods, such as a stable international political and economic order, through the existing foreign policy framework, while further pursuing the well-being and prosperity of the Japanese? There are two main alternatives. One option is to pursue a foreign policy involving military activity that would eventually require major political rearrangements including amendment of Article 9 of the Constitution.[3] The other is to further pursue foreign policies not involving military activity that can make substantial international contributions within the purview of the existing tenets of the country's foreign policy. Japan's environmental foreign policy represents one aspect of the latter option.

Thus, the basic domestic political framework and the quest for international contribution through nonmilitary means mentioned above generated the rationale for the government to take initiatives in environmental diplomacy. Yet, how could it launch such a policy?

Japan experienced severe industrial pollution, widely known as *kogai* in Japan.[4] During the years of rapid economic growth, especially throughout the 1960s and into the first half of the 1970s, nowhere in the world was as polluted as many industrial areas of Japan. Minamata and *itai-itai* (ouch-ouch) diseases, both caused by toxic chemical compounds—methyl-mercury and cadmium, respectively—became known to the world, together with Yokkaichi asthma caused by air pollution in the vicinity of a petrochemical industrial complex. During this period, Japan was, as one scholar put it, the "showcase of environmental pollution."[5]

However, about a decade later, the report "Environmental Policies in Japan," issued by the Organization for Economic Cooperation and Development (OECD), concluded: "Japan has won many pollution abatement battles, but has not yet won the war for environmental quality."[6] In fact, by that time, various industrial pollution problems had been considerably ameliorated and the air surrounding large cities and industrial areas had become much cleaner than before. Out of this effort, Japan has developed the technology and the market for pollution-prevention devices, such as desulfurizer and denitrification devices.

Japan's past experience of severe environmental degradation and its achievement of having overcome those problems have yielded various techniques, technologies, and human resources for protecting the environment. They include antipollution policies and institutions, trained experts in the public and private sectors, and technologies effective in mitigating or preventing environmental degradation. These are the hard-won assets that have given rise to Japan's environmental diplomacy. These factors, which established the conditions for Japanese initiatives in environmental diplomacy, however, cannot fully explain the emergence of such initiatives. Japan's domestic political arrangements and the quest for ways to contribute to international society are also behind Japan's environmental initiatives.

Let us now turn to the genesis, basic tenets, players and structure, as well as some current initiatives of Japanese environmental foreign policy.

Toward the World Commission on Environment and Development

It was the early 1970s when Japan's environmental diplomacy first began to form, and three international events were catalytic. The first report of the Club of Rome's project on the predicament of humankind of 1972 was alarming. However, it was the United Nations Conference held in Stockholm in 1972 (the Stockholm Conference) that first brought the crisis of international environmental destruction to the attention of Japanese policy makers. They were further influenced by the U.S. government's *The Global 2000: Report to the President,* which sparked efforts at building institutions to tackle global environmental problems.[7] In September 1980, soon after the publication of *The Global 2000,* under the direction of then Prime Minister Suzuki Zenko, an "informal advisory institution" consisting of "persons of learning and experience" was established under Kujiraoka Hyosuke, director general of the Environment Agency (EA). This advisory council was called "Discussion Group on Global-scale Environmental Problems," and its chairperson was the late former minister of foreign affairs, Okita Saburo.

The first and second reports of the Discussion Group deserve special attention. The first report deals with basic ways to tackle global environmental problems. This report was submitted to the director general of the EA in 1980. It defined the scope of global environmental problems and outlined the fundamental directions environmental policy should take. The second report of 1982 articulated some frameworks for international efforts and resulted in the creation of the World Commission on Environment and Development (WCED, also known as the Brundtland Commission). As one of its achievements, the WCED helped publicize the notion of "sustainable development," which is development that "meets the needs of the present without compromising the ability of future generations to meet their own needs."[8]

The global environmental issues outlined in the Discussion Group's first report includes population, food, the ecosystem, forests, deserts, flora and fauna, the oceans/water, the air/climate, energy, chemical substances, and human habitats. The report proposes that it will become extremely difficult for the ever-increasing world population to obtain enough resources to assure people can live decent lives. At the same time, it foresees that the human environment will likely be under mounting pressure from growing population. Acknowledging the interconnectedness and recursive dynamics of these issues, the report emphasizes that environmental degradation could threaten the life-maintenance systems of the earth itself. Once damage and destruction to the environment passes a certain threshold, the report points out, not only will restoration require tremendous cost and time, some damage will be irreversible. The report warns of the danger of nonaction. Even though it may be difficult to provide hard evidence for forecasts of future environmental decline for each issue, it warns, it is likely to be too late if no immediate countermeasures are taken due to scientific uncertainty.[9]

The importance of Japan's role as a member of the world community is also underscored in the report. With respect to indigenous climatic, geological, ethnic, as well as cultural diversity, the review of the Japanese developmental aid policy and projects is called for so as not to destroy the local ecological system. The report classifies Japan as a nation that depends heavily on energy and food of foreign origin. That imperative, it points out, makes all the more important Japan's obligation to contribute the preservation of forests and soil throughout the world for the sake of global environmental protection. The report also stresses the desirability of Japan's contribution to dealing with the causes of global environmental devastation, drawing on its past experiences of overcoming such problems.[10]

The second Discussion Group report of 1982 resulted in a recommendation for the establishment of a world commission that would primarily examine the global environmental predicament. It was Hara Bunbei, then director general of the EA, who proposed the creation of such a commission at the tenth anniversary for the Conference on Human Environment held in Nairobi in 1982. In the following year, with Japan's contribution of ¥1 billion for its creation, the WCED (or Brundtland) Commission was established by the General Assembly of the United Nations.[11] The WCED launched its activities in May 1984 in pursuit of a vision for the global environment as the twenty-first century approached. The WCED had seven meetings, in Geneva, Jakarta, Oslo, São Paulo, Ottawa, Harare, and Moscow, before it completed its mission at the close of the final meeting in Tokyo in February 1987.

The Tokyo Declaration of the Brundtland Commission's final meeting, on 27 February 1987, called upon the nations of the world to "build a future that is prosperous, just, and secure." Nations were urged to integrate the concept of sustainable development into their goals and to implement the principles of the new policy.[12]

Although the concept of sustainable development and its attendant principles provide the world with a general direction, the concept itself is elusive and ambivalent. It is elusive since no clear development goals or priorities or qualities of life that can be achieved by "sustainable development" are articulated.[13] Therefore, the interpretation of this concept varies widely among environmentalists, industrialists, financiers, and politicians, as well as between people of the developing and developed countries.

In addition, the concept is ambivalent. While the previously unqualified developmental concept and projects can now be modified, the means, methods, and administrators needed to achieve the vague goal of "sustainable development" are technologies, risk-management skills, and technocrats that have been partly responsible for today's global environmental predicament. There has been no public debate on or consensus formed on clear developmental goals, priorities, and the quality of life in sustainable development, or discussion about "how society should live, or what, how much, and in what way it should produce and consume."[14]

Nonetheless, the concept of sustainable development, at least, has offered policy makers and the general public alike a great chance to check inappropriate and destructive developmental concepts and projects that devastate both regional ecosystems and thus the "decent lives" of people.

Aside from the conceptual issues mentioned above, the prime minister's Discussion Group began to discuss the implementation of the WCED's principles and perspectives after receiving the final WCED report, entitled *Our Common Future,* in 1987. Its fourth report resulted in establishing the Headquarters of Policy Planning and Promotion for Global Environmental Protection under the Office of Administrative Vice Minister of the EA in August 1988. Meanwhile, the EA's annual White Paper, the *Quality of the Environment (Kankyo hakusho),* of May 1988 featured global environment issues as its main theme for the first time.

International Environmental Diplomacy and Japan's Response

Japan's internal momentum might have been strong enough to carry out further environmental policy changes. Yet, the speed and scope of changes would have been much slower and more limited if it had not been for the ever-growing international diplomatic concerns about global environmental degradation.

By 1989, the competition in international environmental diplomacy and politics had intensified, especially among West European countries. In March 1989, then British Prime Minister Margaret Thatcher hosted a three-day international conference on the issue of the depletion of the stratospheric ozone layer. The following week, the governments of France, the Netherlands, and Norway jointly held an international conference in the Hague. The main subjects of this conference were the depletion of the ozone layer and climatic change caused by global warming.[15] In June, the Greens gained 19 seats at the election of the European Parliament. As the result, they had a total of 39 seats out of the 518-seat assembly.[16] In addition to these developments, the Group of Seven's annual meeting, held in Paris in July 1989, symbolically highlighted environmental diplomacy. The economic declaration of this G-7 meeting devoted 19 out of 56 paragraphs to environmental issues, including climate change, ozone depletion, and deforestation.[17]

In 1989, the waves of environmental diplomacy rolled into Japan. The Tokyo Conference on the Global Environment and Human Response toward "Sustainable Development" was held from September 11 to 13. This conference was jointly hosted by Prime Minister Kaifu Toshiki, Secretary General Mostafa Tolba of the UN Environment Programme (UNEP), and Secretary General G.O.P Obasi of the World Meteorological Organization (WMO). Other participants were representatives of international organizations, widely respected scientists, and experts on global environmental problems. The main themes of the conference were the issues of the changing atmosphere and development and the environment in developing countries."[18]

At the same time, a people's forum, called "International People's Forum: Japan and the Global Environment," was held also in Tokyo from 8–10 September.[19] It should be noted that a different prioritization of various environmental problems and perceptual gaps on key issues and concepts, such as "sustainable development," did exist between the NGO representatives at the forum and the prominent policy makers attending the Tokyo Conference.

The policy makers' Tokyo Conference had been proposed initially in August 1988 by then Prime Minister Takeshita Noboru. He had begun to perceive the importance of the protection of the global environment while discussing the issue with other leaders at the G-7 summit meeting in Toronto in June 1988. After the Toronto summit, he became the prime caretaker for the global environment issues, especially when it came to financial ways and means.[20]

It was Takeshita, especially after the Toronto summit, who began to affirm that "Environmental problems have become a mainstream political issue."[21] He also maintained on several occasions, "Politicians who do not know and act for environmental issues are those who lack intelligence, education, and courage."[22] His rationale for Japan's financial contribution to the cause of the environment was his policy reference to the two postwar U.S. aid projects to Japan: namely, Government and Relief in Occupied Areas and Economic Rehabilitation in Occupied Areas (GARIOA-EROA). These two pieces of the United States legislative programs during the post–World War II era authorized funds for economic relief and reconstruction in occupied countries.[23] In 1962, the United States and Japan agreed on the figure of US$1.8 billion as Japan's total GARIOA debt to the United States for postwar assistance and on the sum of $490 million as the amount that Japan would pay over 15 years in settlement.[24]

The amount of US$1.8 billion approximated 6 percent of Japan's GNP at the time. Takeshita proposed to disperse "largesse" of about 6 percent of today's Japanese GNP, or roughly US$100 billion, to the least developed countries, in return for the kindness that Japan had received in the past. Since Japan has thus far spent about US$50 billion as official development assistance (ODA) over the years, the rest of $50 billion was considered the "spirit of GARIOA-EROA." According to Takeshita, this amount of money should be spent for the sake of the global environment.[25]

Takeshita certainly played a significant role in domestic environmental politics and diplomacy in the late 1980s and early 1990s, particularly pertaining to financial matters. At a special meeting for world leaders who assembled at the Earth Summit, after pointing out the importance of financing for the new international cooperative effort for the improvement of environmental dilemmas, he stated:

> Japan will be expected to make an appropriate contribution in this regard, and I will personally do my best to work out a way to make such a contribution possible. I strongly urge that all countries—especially developed countries—consider seriously how additional financial demands will be met.[26]

Despite his negative popular image as a typical pork barrel politician, Takeshita has been considered an expert on financial issues and taxation. In fact, it was Takeshita who as prime minister was able to enact a consumption tax law after several unsuccessful attempts by his predecessors, including Ohira Masayoshi and Nakasone Yasuhiro. By passing the consumption tax law, he boosted his political credibility among bureaucrats, especially those in the Ministry of Finance.

The Quest for "Internationalization of Japan" and "International Contribution"

Public polls revealed the strength of Japanese desire for *kokusaika* or the "internationalization of Japan" in the latter half of the 1980s. For instance, the Prime Minister's Office's monthly *Public Opinion Poll* of 1987 began to include an item on the "internationalization of Japan" as a regular feature.[27] This rise of self-awareness about Japan's role in the world coincided with the rapid evaluation of the yen after the Plaza Accord of September 1985 and its aftermath.[28] In one year after the Plaza Accord, the exchange rate of the Japanese yen to the U.S. dollar skyrocketed from ¥240 to ¥120 to US$1.00. This sharp hike in the value of the Japanese yen struck a crushing blow to the export-oriented industries in Japan. In order to salvage them, the Bank of Japan adopted an easy-money policy, lowering the official discount rate. For over one year from January 1986, the

Bank of Japan lowered the official rate five times until it stood at 2.5 percent. This easy-money policy, however, resulted in the so-called bubble economy, which began to inflate in 1986 until the bubble burst from 1990.[29]

The high-value yen and the "bubble" economy at home served to inflate the aspiration for Japan's internationalization. This aspiration can be seen in the general trends in the *Public Opinion Poll* on foreign policy from 1987 to 1992.[30] One question was asked about public views on the "internationalization of Japan." Except for the poll of 1987, the largest number of respondents chose Japan's "international obligation as a great power" as the reason why Japan needed to promote its internationalization. The next popular reason was to "maintain Japan's mid- and long-term prosperity." Actually, the support for these two answers during the period between 1987 and 1992 was very close; on average 44.8 and 42.0 percent, respectively.[31] A distant third, representing 20 percent of those polled, chose "for the spread of Japanese culture."[32]

As to the role Japan should play in the world, the statement that received the greatest support was to "contribute to solving global environmental problems." During the period between 1990 and 1992, the rate of selection of the category of "contribution to the global environment" was 47.5 percent, while "contribution to mediating local conflicts" was 34.5 percent on average. In addition, "contribution to sound growth of world economy" was 33.8 percent.

Thus, the second wave of the global environmental movement following the United Nations Conference on Environment and Development (UNCED) became the beneficiary of the general public's aspiration for Japan to play a greater international role. Many writers saw Japan as a "great surplus power," one "inflated" by a high-value yen and a "bubble" economy and overdue in its contribution to the world.[33] One business leader articulated the mood of the times succinctly when he described this heightened sense of obligation as *kokusai koken byo* (the "international contribution disease"). But what kind of contribution should the Japanese make? In his view, most of the general public and the politicians were not comfortable with the idea of sending the Self-Defense Forces (SDF) to the Middle East and Cambodia. They were happy, he felt, to contribute to solving global environmental problems.[34]

At the diplomatic front of the UNCED, especially in the process of negotiating the final terms of the UN Framework Convention on Climate Change (UNFCCC), Akao Nobutoshi, an experienced career diplomat of the Ministry of Foreign Affairs (MOFA), took charge as Ambassador for Global Environmental Affairs and Asia-Pacific Cooperation. This ambassadorship was a recent creation to match the status of negotiators of other countries. Before assuming his new position in January 1991, Akao had served as the director general of the United Nations Bureau of MOFA since February 1990 and had met stiff political opposition when the PKO bill was shelved in the fall of that year. (After the Gulf War, the government had made strenuous efforts to pass the PKO bill that aimed at legalizing the participation of the SDF in UN peacekeeping operations within the framework of the Japanese Constitution, but was forced to withdraw the bill in the face of overwhelming opposition. A modified bill was passed through the Diet in June 1992.)

Dealing with global environmental affairs was much easier than dealing with the PKO bill, Akao testified during an interview. Unlike the case of the PKO bill, there was no political opposition to Japan's contribution to the betterment of the global environment, he said.[35] This is not to say that the government was united in its policy on climate change. There existed tension between the principal beliefs of "economic growth" and "development," and "environmental protection"; that is, the tension between the Ministry of International Trade and Industry (MITI) and Environment Agency (EA) at the bureaucratic level. Nevertheless, both camps had reached an agreement, however reluctantly, on the importance of a new world view of "sustainable development" and the belief in the causal effect of greenhouse gases on the global climate. This fundamental agreement kept their differences from burgeoning into a serious domestic issue at the political level. The fact was that politicians of both the ruling and opposition parties showed strong support for and interest in global environment-related questions. In terms of the "international contribution" so much desired by all, Japan was able to make both financial and technological contributions to protect the global climate.[36] While engaged in the final round of negotiations in New York for the UNFCCC, Akao put it this way:

> We tend to see Rio and the environment as offering Japan a key leadership role. It is tied directly to what we call *kokusaika*—the internationalization of policy, which is essential. *Kokusaika* is almost an obsession with our political and business leadership and with our people in general. Our media bombard the public with articles about how we must internationalize. Rio is happening against that background. It was tailor-made for us.[37]

This view was shared widely in Japan. In addition, Akao underscored the importance of Japan's contribution to the area that other leading states, such as the United States, could not.

The Politicians Climb on the Bandwagon

Five influential Liberal Democratic Party (LDP) politicians, with heavily powdered faces and wearing colorful *kimono* and *geta* (wooden clogs), and holding *bangasa* (coarse oil-paper umbrellas), posed at a show for the formal introduction of a kabuki all-star cast. The title of their skit was the *Five Men of the LDP Environmental Policy Tribe*. In the middle, there was Takeshita Noboru. On his right is Hashimoto Ryutaro and on his left Aichi Kazuo. Takemura Masayoshi is next to Hashimoto, and Aoki Masahisa is next to Aichi. The popular weekly magazine *AERA* introduced the event in an article entitled, "Objectives of the New LDP Environmental Policy Specialists: Transformation from Advocates of Development."[38]

As noted earlier, Takeshita projected the image of an ardent advocate of the new "creed" of global environmentalism. Particularly before the Earth Summit, speculation about Takeshita's transformation was ripe at "Nagatacho" (the Japanese equivalent of "inside the Washington, D.C. beltway"). One theory argued that he wanted to reestablish his reputation impaired by the Recruit scandal. Yet another speculated that he was seeking a comeback to the center of power.[39]

We will not know for sure what the late former Prime Minister Takeshita was thinking especially before the Earth Summit at Rio de Janiero. However, it seems plausible that he wanted to protect his old political stronghold and expand his influence over the area of the environment, in addition to aiming at rehabilitating himself. The global environment was now a growing issue area with a rapidly expanding popular concern and national budget. Expanding environmental policy areas included measures to arrest global warming, preservation of biological diversity, and affrestation. Takeshita was known as one Japanese political leader who hesitated to move politically until he had constructed a broad consensus of opinion behind him and he maintained extensive contacts with opposition leaders.[40] Thus, when he moved, there was a good chance that he would achieve his goal.

In addition, financial assistance to developing countries for the preservation of the environment became one of the most contentious issues between developed and developing countries in the months preceding UNCED. The world community longed for Japan to resolve this issue, especially by making a financial contribution. Needless to say, by becoming the mediator for this matter, Takeshita (and his party) was able to fully exploit Japan's national quest for "internationalization" and "international contribution" for his own political gain. Furthermore, taking the leadership in global environmental issues was politically safe. Takeshita was quoted as saying, "Whereas Japan's participation in the UN peacekeeping operations stirs up political controversy, the protection of the global environment is an issue area to which Japan can contribute without hesitation."[41]

In sum, there were several plausible reasons why Takeshita became a new "greenish" political leader: to redeem his honor; to protect his and his faction's "vested interests" from the intrusion of "environment" policies; to broaden his (and his party's) political support from potential voters of the "new politics"; and to exploit for his (and LDP's) political gain the national quests for "internationalization of Japan" and "international contribution" through efforts to arrest global environmental degradation.

In February 1992, an informal group, the Kankyo Kihon Mondai Kondankai ("Discussion Group for Fundamental Environmental Issues"; hereafter the Hashimoto Discussion Group) chaired by Hashimoto Ryutaro, was established by the LDP to support Takeshita's political endeavor. On top of the five new LDP environmentalists (Aichi Kazuo, Aoki Masahisa, Takemura Masayoshi, Takeshita, and Hashimoto) mentioned above, other influential senior politicians belonging to the Hashimoto Discussion Group included former Prime Minister Kaifu Toshiki; chairperson of the Mitsuzuka faction Mitsuzuka Hiroshi; former LDP Secretary General Obuchi Keizo (the late prime minister); then Chief Cabinet Secretary Gotoda Masaharu; and former General Director of the Environment Agency, Hara Bunbei.[42]

However, the Hashimoto Discussion Group did not invite several veteran and ardent LDP environmentalist Diet members such as the former EA directors general, Kujiraoka Hyosuke and Kitagawa Ishimatsu. The latter was very sympathetic with the movement against the construction of a dam at the mouth of the Nagara River, which is the last major Japanese river without a dam or other man-made alteration of the water flow. Kujiraoka in 1981 urged then Prime Minister Suzuki to submit an environment impact assessment bill to the Diet, holding his letter of resignation in his hand. Moreover, during its preparation period, the Hashimoto Discussion Group did not consult with veteran LDP environmentalist Kosugi Takashi. Kosugi was active in other areas, engaging himself in global environmental issues as a member of the Global Legislators Organization for a Balanced Environment (GLOBE), which was established in 1989 by parliamentarians from the European Community (now EU) and the United States. (Soon after, Japanese legislators joined GLOBE.) During the two-year term between 1990 and 1992, then U.S. Senator Al Gore, now vice president of the United States, served as the president of GLOBE International. Kosugi succeeded Gore as president in 1992.

The near exclusion of long-time "green" politicians and the like may imply what was the real objective of new "greenish" political leaders who gathered under the banner of the Hashimoto Discussion Group. As we have examined earlier, the connotation of "environmental issues" has changed qualitatively and expanded. The vague and elusive concept of "sustainable development" is a case in point. Environmental problems in Japan had long been seen as synonymous with local pollution (*kogai*) that has been closely associated with industrial pollution since the late 1950s. The late 1980s and early 1990s brought new emphasis with the recognition of emerging urban and global environmental problems. Moreover, by manipulating the internationally accepted concept of sustainable development, now even long-time advocates of development, or the "old politics" of material prosperity can project their "greenish" image, even though they stress not the environment but development. In any case, "brownish" politicians of old politics have begun to invade and colonize the realm of environmental policy areas.

Another important factor in the rise of global environmental concerns among Japanese politicians is the collapse of the Cold War system. Aside from such unsolved problems in world politics as ethnic conflict, the relationship of the environment to development has become one of the most salient political issues between the North and South. The constitutional constraint on the option of military foreign policy formed one indirect cause for Japan to consider environmental diplomacy a viable policy option. According to several public opinion polls of 1991 and 1992, well over a majority of the respondents had come to recognize the legitimacy of the SDF, even though the second paragraph of Article 9 of the Japanese Constitution prohibits the maintenance of any military force. In reality, Japan's military expenditure in 1991 was the fifth largest in the world.[43] However, the same polls indicated that the majority of the respondents opposed the SDF's participation in settling international military conflict and opposed the revision of the Constitution, particularly Article 9.[44] This means that the Japanese still, at least in 1991 and 1992, supported Article 9: that is, the prohibition of the use of force to solve international disputes. Thus, environmental diplomacy became a viable option for Japan's contribution to the world.

To be sure, there exists a group of people who advocate a more assertive foreign policy, including the participation of the SDF in a multinational force, such as the one led by the United States during the Gulf War of January 1991. The so-called Ozawa Chosakai (Ozawa Commission),[45] a special research circle within the LDP on Japan's fundamental security policy, reported such a policy proposal to then Prime Minister Miyazawa Kiichi in February 1992, calling for a policy review concerning the SDF's possible participation in UN forces.[46]

The Hashimoto Discussion Group and the Ozawa Commission differed in their foreign and security policies. The Hashimoto Discussion Group favored the continuation of nonmilitary diplomacy and called on Japan to make its international contribution to the betterment of the global environment. The Ozawa Commission proposed a much more active Japanese foreign policy, including a military option. As of the early 1990s, this foreign and security policy contest was still in progress, but the policy debate now went beyond the LDP. The school of new and "muscular" foreign policy was led by Ozawa, de facto leader of Shinshinto (president of the Liberal Party at this writing in autumn 1999), who has been insisting that Japan become a "normal country" (*futsu no kuni*).[47] Komeito (Clean Government Party), Hosokawa Morihiro's Nihon Shinto (New Japan Party), Minshato (the Democratic Socialist Party, DSP), and some independent politicians who left the LDP joined the school that advocates the "normalization" of Japan. According to Ozawa, a normal country plays major political and economic roles in the world.[48]

Many politicians wanted to go to Rio even though the deliberations for two important bills were to reach the final stage at the Diet during the UNCED, and the election for the House of Councilor was to be held in the summer. Until June 22, the Diet was to deliberate on the political reform bill and a bill regarding UN peacekeeping operations (hereafter the PKO bill). Above all, the PKO bill was extremely contentious between a policy coalition of the LDP, Komeito, and DSP, on the one hand, and the Socialist Democratic Party of Japan (SDPJ) and Japan Communist Party, on the other hand. The crux of the debates was whether or not Japan should or could send the SDF abroad for UN peacekeeping operations. The UNCED was convened from 1–12 June when the Diet deliberations about the PKO bill were to reach its last phase. Yet, about 80 parliamentarians from both the ruling and opposition parties expressed their strong desire to take part in the Earth Summit. Some were veteran politicians who worked for the protection of the environment; others were extempore environmentalists.[49]

Eventually, a contingent of 13 politicians from different parties went to Rio. Takeshita led the main contingent of ten politicians, consisting of five from the LDP, two from the SDJP, two from the Komeito, and one from the DSP. In addition, three senior politicians, Kaifu, Hashimoto, and Mitsuzuka, also participated in the UNCED separately. However, only former Prime Minister Takeshita and then acting Prime Minister Miyazawa had a chance to deliver a speech, and Miyazawa could not attend due to the pending debates on the PKO bill. Thus, most of the politicians who went to Brazil did not have anything to do with the proceedings. Nevertheless, the delegation was quite substantial compared to the Stockholm Conference of 1972, when no politicians accompanied the official delegation led by Oishi Buichi, then EA director general.[50]

Nongovernmental Organizations Become Active
Since the Stockholm Conference of 1972, the United Nations had considered the role of the nongovernmental organizations (NGOs) crucial for the solution of international environmental problems. As to the UNCED, an international NGO conference, called the 92 Global Forum, was to be convened independently of the official conference. Responding to this forum, the 92 NGO Forum-Japan was organized by various grassroots groups in May 1991. Ever since, Japanese environmental NGOs have organized themselves and helped to raise popular concerns. This visibility and collective voice became a social pressure, albeit an insufficient one, to influence the national policy directly.[51]

Among various activities, they drew up with their own report, identifying global environmental problems, and explaining how humankind came to face these problems, and how to ameliorate them. The report entitled *People's Voice of Japan: I Have the Earth in Mind, the Earth Has Me in Hand* was completed in May 1992 and submitted to the Earth Summit. Even though some policy proposals needed much more scrutiny to become viable policy alternatives, the report was as a whole a comprehensive expression of grassroots views on the issues of the environment and development.

Businesses also joined in. On 23 April 1991, Keidanren (Japan Federation of Economic Organizations) adopted its Global Environment Charter. The new leadership of Keidanren led by Hiraiwa Gaishi, the former chairperson of Tokyo Electric Power Company, played a crucial role in articulating the charter. In early January 1991, at his first press conference as the chairperson of Keidanren, Hiraiwa alluded to doing something relating to global environmental concern during his tenure; he expressed his aspiration to link the three concepts of earth, human beings, and the market. For his basic policy guideline issued on 22 January, Hiraiwa included environmental issues as one of five agenda items for Keidanren. Soon after, the Environment Safety Committee, consisting of chief executive officers of 100 major Keidanren-affiliated companies, began to work on the issue. After a series of discussions, they decided that what was needed was a code of conduct on global environmental issues for private corporations.[52]

The charter consists of an introduction, basic philosophy, and guidelines for corporate action on 24 items within 11 fields, and an appendix. It is based on three perceptions. The first stresses the inevitability of a new approach to the problem. In the past, Japanese industry was successful in containing industrial pollution and in developing energy conservation technology. However, a new set of urban environmental problems, such as household garbage, waste water, and air pollution caused by ever-increasing numbers of automobiles, cannot be solved solely by antipollution measures and technology, nor can global environmental problems be dealt with effectively by technological solutions or by Japan alone. The second perception is that the current social and economic system must be fundamentally reexamined while seeking technological breakthroughs.

And third, cooperative efforts among the private sector, public sector, individuals as consumers, and academia are essential factors for success. Unlike past industrial pollution problems, which created a confrontational relationship between producers and consumers, today's urban and global environmental problems require cooperation between the two.[53] The charter's basic ideology indicates a change in the attitude of the CEOs of major Japanese corporations.

In September 1992, Keidanren embodied the ideals of its Global Environment Charter in a major global environmental project, the establishment of Keidanren Nature Conservation Fund.[54] This is considered a model case of cooperation between private companies and environmental NGOs. The objective of the fund is to develop human resources for international cooperation for nature conservation activities in developing countries and for nature preservation in general. Its activities include: to cooperate for nature preservation projects, such as debt-for-nature swaps (DNS),[55] to support nature conservation projects of private corporations indirectly; to foster talent and create a network; and to diffuse knowledge and understanding about nature conservation. The immediate target for the projected amount of the fund was ¥300 million; ¥250 million from companies and ¥50 million from individuals.[56]

Official representatives from 172 countries and international organizations participated in the intergovernmental UNCED. One hundred and fifty governmental officials led by EA director general Nakamura Shozaburo were sent from Tokyo to Rio. They formed one of the largest contingents but lacked the presence of the head of government.

On top of the governmental representatives, 13 politicians led by Takeshita took part in the UNCED. About 50 Japanese NGOs that had registered for the UN Global Forum 92 were at the UN Forum site. Many different grassroots environmental organizations took part. Some were groups concerned about the depletion of tropical rainforests; others were environmentally conscious lawyers' organizations; and yet others were representatives of victims of industrial and air pollution. Ten industrial organizations were also enlisted as NGOs and participants in Global Forum 92. They included Keidanren and the Petroleum Federation, to mention just a couple.[57] It is reported that 18,680 people representing 7,946 organizations from 187 countries participated in the NGO's Global Forum.[58] The Japanese contingents were highly visible in both the official UN Earth Summit and the NGO forum.

Japan's Initiatives in International Environmental Cooperation

Corresponding to the emerging environmental diplomacy during the Arche Summit of 1989, the Japanese government launched its environmental ODA policy. The main features of the policy include: (1) the expenditure of about ¥300 billion in bilateral and multilateral environmental assistance for the three years beginning in 1989; emphasis on forest conservation and related research programs, especially for tropical rain forests; (3) emphasis on capacity building in ODA recipient countries; and (4) the enhancement of environmental considerations in its assistance programs.

One year prior to the UNCED, international environmental diplomacy kept its high steam, and the Japanese government added some extra features for environmental ODA. At the London Summit of 1991, on top of Japan's mission for developing countries to share its experience about overcoming industrial pollution problems in the past, the policy objective to deal with the linkages among poverty, population growth, and environmental degradation was added to the focal policy areas in Japan's environmental ODA.

The 1992 UNCED (Earth Summit) held in Rio de Janeiro adopted the UNFCCC and the Convention on Biological Diversity. The former convention became effective in December 1993 and the latter in March 1994. Another Convention to Combat Desertification was adopted in June 1994. These agreements helped strengthen the existing international legal framework for the protection of the environment.

Responding to these international developments and, at the same time, aiming at further articulating Japanese environmental foreign policy, the ODA Charter, one of whose principles addresses the betterment of the environment, was adopted by the Cabinet on 30 June 1992. Furthermore, the Basic Environmental Law of 1993 (hereafter, the Basic Law) and the Basic Environmental Plan (the Basic Plan) that was established within the purview of the Basic Law's call for initiatives in protecting the global environment and assisting developing countries in the fields of environmental protection.

The activities of international environmental cooperation funded by ODA have various aspects. They include research about desirable projects, developmental studies, as well as the dispatch of technical experts to and acceptance of trainees from developing countries. In terms of the manner of giving, there are grants, loans, and financial contributions to international organizations, such as the UNEP and the International Tropical Timber Organization (ITTO). In 1991, the Global Environmental Facility (GEF) was founded to provide developing countries with financial resources to tackle the problems of global warming, the loss of biological diversity, the problems relating to international waters, and the depletion of the stratospheric ozone layer. Operated jointly by the World Bank, United Nations Development Programme (UNDP), and UNEP, the GEF started in 1994 after a three-year pilot period, with an increased amount of funding. Japan has been actively participating in the GEF, providing it with about ¥45.7 billion since fiscal 1994, the second largest contribution after the United States.[59]

Environmental ODA

The ODA Charter of June 1992 specifies four ODA principles. They include:

1. Environmental conservation and development should be pursued in tandem.
2. Any use of ODA for military purposes or for aggravation of international conflicts should be avoided.
3. Full attention should be paid to trends in recipient countries' military expenditures, their development and production of mass destruction

weapons and missiles, their export and import of arms, etc., so as to maintain and strengthen international peace and stability, and from the viewpoint that developing countries should place appropriate priorities in the allocation of their resources on their own economic and social development.
4. Full attention should be paid to efforts for promoting democratization and introduction of a market-oriented economy, and the situation regarding the securing of basic human rights and freedoms in the recipient country.[60]

In addition, the Charter includes international cooperation for tackling global environmental problems as one of five focal issue areas.[61]

At the UNCED, Japan pledged to significantly expand its environment-related ODA between ¥900 billion and ¥1 trillion over five years starting in fiscal 1992. By the end of the fourth year, Japan had disbursed about ¥980 billion, thus meeting its target a year ahead of the original schedule. The contents of this environmental ODA include grants, loans, and technical and multilateral assistance, among which loans are the largest. The amounts of each type of ODA from 1992 to 1995 are listed in Table 6.1.

Table 6.1 Various Types of Environmental ODA (unit: ¥100 million)

Year	Grants	Loans	Technical	Multilateral	Total (%)
1992	310.6	2,212.5	174.1	105.7	2,803 (16.9)
1993	377.1	1,526.5	214.1	162.0	2,280 (12.8)
1994	414.3	1,055.7	234.2	253.3	1,942 (14.2)
1995	428.2	1,708.2	222.9	400.3	2,760 (19.9)
Subtotal	1,530.2	6,502.9	845.3	921.3	9,785

The figures in the parentheses represent the share of the total ODA for each individual type.

Source: Economic Cooperation Bureau, Ministry of Foreign Affairs, *Japan's ODA: Annual Report 1996* (Tokyo: Association for Promotion of International Cooperation, 1997), p. 156.

Technical support and capacity building are the main ingredients of the specific policy areas subject to Japan's environmental ODA. Specific areas include air and water pollution control measures, energy conservation, improvement of the residential environment (relating to water supply, sewage systems, and disposal facilities), natural disaster prevention through flood prevention technology, forestry conservation, as well as nature conservation in general. Regarding the area of capacity building for arresting environmental degradation in developing countries, the principal measure is to foster human resources through the support for establishing and operating research and training centers for environmental protection in developing countries.

Some concrete projects of Japan's environmental ODA in 1995 are as follows: (1) India—Gujarat Afforestation and Development Project (loan aid); (2) Bulgaria—Industrial Pollution Project in Plovdiv (loan aid); (3) Indonesia—the Biodiversity Conservation Project (grant aid); (4) Egypt—Project for Improvement of Solid Waste Management in Alexandria City, Phase II (grant aid); (5) Zimbabwe—Water Pollution Control Project in the Upper Manyame River

Region (development study); (6) Chile—the Master Plan Study on Industrial Solid Waste Management in the Metropolitan Santiago Region in the Republic of Chile (development study); (7) PRC—the Japan-China Friendship Environmental Protection Center (project-type technical cooperation); and (8) Mexico—the National Center for Environmental Research and Training (project-type technical cooperation).[62]

The Implementation of Environmental ODA

The implementation of ODA projects, particularly its technical aspect, is the responsibility of the Japan International Cooperation Agency (JICA), an ODA executive agency. The annual expenditure of JICA's projects for environmental cooperation in 1995 was ¥22.3 billion, or 8 percent of Japan's total environmental ODA. Its major policy foci include the improvement of living conditions (drainage, waste management), disaster prevention, antipollution measures, forest preservation, and the conservation of biological diversity.[63]

JICA's environmental policy has five distinctive characteristics. Two of them are environmental studies relating to the planning stage of ODA projects: that is, project identification and formation studies for environmental protection. JICA stresses the importance of its early involvement in environmental cooperation, above all, in the initial stages of environmental ODA project formation. The main reason for this is that developing countries are often incapable of identifying or formulating environmental protection measures partly due to the lack of experience or expertise and partly due to the fact that the policy priority of environmental protection tends to be lower than that of economic development.[64]

Third, JICA has also set up environmental guidelines and issued manuals for project development. Since 1991, JICA has been making environmental guidelines for 20 fields of developmental projects such as the construction of ports and harbors, roads, water supply and drainage, mining and manufacturing industries, forestry, and fishery. JICA has also published manuals for preparatory and full-scale studies, and a guidebook, *Q&A for Environmental Considerations* (Tokyo: JICA, 1994), to promote environmental considerations and help facilitate JICA's staff training.

The fourth and fifth features are related to human resources and capacity building, respectively. As another new feature since 1992, even when a developmental project does not directly deal with environmental issues, JICA has been including specialists for environmental assessment in any developmental study team if a proposed project requires environmental considerations. Since then, environmental assessment by specialists has become another distinctive feature of JICA's environmental policy and the number of such involvement of specialists increased, for example, from 65 in 1993 to 92 in 1995. As to capacity building in recipient countries, JICA provides them with the programs, which help improve environmental management, research, and monitoring activities, and execute technical cooperation projects and training programs. The salient examples of these assistant programs are the establishment of environmental management or research centers. They include the Environmental Research and Training Center in Thailand, Japan-China Friendship Environmental Protection Center in

China, Environmental Management Center in Indonesia, National Center for Environmental Research and Training in Mexico, and National Center for Environment in the Republic of Chile.

The evaluation of these environmental programs is out of the scope of this chapter's objective. However, some statistics clearly show the increase in environmental consideration in the formation and implementation of ODA projects. For instance, the number of trainees accepted increased by five times from 314 in 1989 to 1,572 in 1997. The number of environmental experts sent to developing countries also substantially increased from 152 to 309 in the same period. In 1997 the largest number of trainees were trained in the field of disaster prevention (286), followed by forest preservation (184), air pollution control (143), water pollution control (125), water supply (119), and others. Forest conservation specialists (30) were most needed for JICA's project in 1997, and the second, third, and fourth from the top were water pollution control (19), disaster prevention (18), and water supply (17). Finally, the total expenditure for JICA's environmental cooperation in the same period increased from about ¥10 billion (10.1 percent of the total) to about ¥30 billion (19.2 percent).

Along with JICA, the Overseas Economic Fund-Japan (OECF) also plays an indispensable role, particularly in terms of financial flow for international environmental cooperation. The OECF was established in 1961 as a development finance institution of the Japanese government. Since 1966, the OECF has been providing long-term, low-interest-rate loans to assist developmental projects in developing countries. ODA loans account for 40 percent of Japan's ODA, rendering its role in international cooperation pivotal.[65]

OECF commitments of all types in the fiscal year (FY) 1997 amounted to ¥1,029.9 billion (decreased by 19.4 percent from the previous year), and disbursements were ¥649.6 billion (5.4 percent increase from the previous year). As a result, cumulative OECF commitments as of March 1998 reached ¥17.3 trillion, exceeding ¥17 trillion for the first time in OECF's history. At the same time, the regional breakdown for ODA loans in FY 1997 reflected its long-term trend of the total loan, 83.6 percent went to Asia, in comparison with 9.0 percent to Latin America and the Caribbean, 4.3 percent to Africa, 2.1 percent to East Europe and others, 0.7 percent to the Middle East, 0.2 percent to Oceania.[66]

While the regional bias for the ODA certainly remains obvious, the emphasis on environmental projects also becomes observable. After having reviewed the environmental aspects of ODA projects financed by the OECF's loans, in October 1989 the OECF issued the first Environmental Guidelines (the second version issued in 1995) to articulate its environmental considerations. Adopting the OECD's recommendations relating to environmental protection, the OECF's environmental guidelines aims at assisting developing countries' self-help efforts for managing their own development in an environmentally sound way. In FY 1997, the number of environmental projects was 26, 18.8 percent lower than the number for 1996. The total loan amount for environmental projects decreased by 33.4 percent from the previous year, when the figures for both were the largest in OECF's history. However, the 1997 levels were about the same as those for FY 1995. The total amount for environmental projects accounted for

20.6 percent of the total amount of ODA loans committed in FY 1997 and was the second largest since OECF's establishment (Table 6.2).

The figure reflected the great need for ODA loans for environmental projects in developing countries. Above all, the OECF committed ODA loans to China amounting to ¥202.9 billion in FY1997, earmarked for six environmental projects aimed at improving the air and water situation, and mitigating the impact of acid rain. In the case of loans to Brazil, the total loan amount (¥37.6 billion) in FY1997 was for three environmental projects designed to arrest global warming, one of which was a wind power generation project, using a new and renewable energy source. The new and most concessional interest rate for special environmental projects (introduced in FY 1997), was applied to four projects amounting to ¥31.7 billion, and the most concessional rate for consulting services was applied to 11 projects amounting to ¥10.4 billion.[67]

Table 6.2   Environmental Projects   (unit: ¥ billion/commitment basis)

Fiscal Year	Cumulative commitments	Numbers of loan projects	Share in the Entire ODA Loans (%)
1993	181.2	18	18.1
1994	108.4	19	12.3
1995	220.2	26	20.1
1996	318.9	32	21.1
1997	212.3	26	20.6

Source: "OECF Operations in FY 1997," OECF Press Release, 28 April 1998.

Some of the concrete projects of the yen loans include Thailand (Electricity Energy Efficiency Promotion Project, Flue Gas Desulfurization Plant for Mae Moh Power Plant, Bangkok Water Supply Improvement Project); Sri Lanka (Greater Colombo Flood Control and Environment Improvement Project); Argentina (Reconquista River Basin Sanitation Improvement Project); Hungary (Municipality Utilities Project of the Varpalota Region Environment Program); Philippines (Calaca I Coal-fired Thermal Plant Environmental Improvement Project); India (afforestation); and Indonesia (Bali Beach Conservation Project, Environmental Soft Loan for Pollution Abatement Equipment, Bapedal Regional Monitoring Capacity Development Project).[68]

On top of all these, the technical aid to help Eastern Europe combat its aggravating environmental problems has been enhanced since 1991, when then Prime Minister Kaifu Toshiki visited the region, and pledged Japan's assistance. In fiscal 1995, Japan started accepting trainees from the region, and two programs got under way in Hungary, one to conduct a development study for drawing up measures to cope with air pollution and the other (in yen loans) to assist in environmental improvement. Every year since fiscal 1991, Japan has been making a financial contribution to the Regional Environment Center for Central and Eastern Europe, founded in Budapest to fight environmental problems in the region, a contribution that amounted to $1.7 million in fiscal 1995.

Lastly, the role of the MITI in this new policy area deserves our attention, albeit being mentioned briefly. With regard to technological assistance for developing countries, MITI has its own project. Its version of international environmental cooperation was first proposed in August 1991. It is called the Green Aid Plan. This plan is designed to provide comprehensive support for developing countries in accordance with their particular needs and circumstances. As of fiscal year 1992, the allocated budget for the Green Aid Plan amounted to about ¥2.7 billion (about US$20.8 million). Concrete measures are policy dialogue and comprehensive energy and environmental cooperation. The latter includes human resources development programs to train personnel in the areas of energy conservation and environmental technology.[69]

In March 1990, the International Center for Environmental Technology Transfer was established in Yokkaichi, Mie Prefecture. The center undertakes training programs for overseas personnel and research activities commissioned by MITI.[70] Relating to the issue of global warming, the Research Institute of Innovative Technology for the Earth (RITE) seeks various kinds of technological solutions. Although RITE's activities are still in the phase of laboratory experiments, it has developed quite powerful CO_2 separation membranes from flue gas. For research and experiment, RITE also "mobilizes" tangles and "wakame" seaweed that breed microorganisms to absorb carbon dioxide, but there exists tremendous difficulty in finding the way of disposing of CO_2 after its fixation. Nonetheless, private corporations, such as electric power, chemical, and construction companies, have joined and engaged in RITE's research and development of each project.[71]

Current Environmental Initiatives

At the June 1997 Special Session of the United Nations General Assembly on Environment and Development, Prime Minister Hashimoto Ryutaro announced Japan's comprehensive medium- and long-term plan for environmental cooperation. This plan, called the Initiatives for Sustainable Development Toward the Twenty-first Century (ISD), indicated the ways Japan would support programs in developing countries to address a wide variety of environmental problems, including global warming, air and water pollution, waste disposal, deforestation, and loss of marine and terrestrial biological diversity. Furthermore, as the host of the Third Conference of Parties to the UNFCCC that was held in Kyoto in December 1997, Japan presented the Kyoto Initiative. It consists of strengthened environmental support that focuses on assisting developing countries in arresting global warming, in the policy framework of the ISD. The Kyoto Initiative, like ISD, will be implemented mainly through the Japanese government's ODA program.

The fundamental features about what Japan does or can do for arresting the degradation of the global environment are well articulated in the "three pillars of (environmental) assistance" in the Kyoto Initiative. The three pillars of assistance consist of cooperation in capacity building, official development assistance loans at the most concessional conditions, and utilization and transfer of Japanese technology and know-how.

In the five years beginning in FY 1998, Japan will train 3,000 people in developing countries in the fields of air pollution, waste disposal, energy saving technologies, and forest conservation and afforestation. As to the second pillar, Japan will grant ODA loans with the most concessional terms available internationally (0.75 percent interest rate, 40-year repayment period) to actively promote cooperation in the fields of energy-saving technologies, new and renewable energy sources, and forest conservation and afforestation. Lastly, using technology and know-how acquired through Japan's own experience of overcoming its severe pollution and energy problems, Japan will (1) send teams to diagnose global warming prevention measures in manufacturing plants; (2) set up information networks related to global warming prevention technology; (3) develop and transfer technology suited to developing countries' needs; and (4) hold workshops on global warming prevention.

U.S.-Japan Common Agenda for Cooperation in Global Perspective

In July 1993, in an effort to resolve serious global issues facing future generations, Japan and the United States established the Common Agenda, one of the most important bilateral cooperation initiatives participated in by the two countries. The projects handled in the Common Agenda comprise the four initiatives in promotion of health and human development, measures to meet challenges regarding the stability of human society, global environmental protection, and progress in science and technology.[72]

The policy areas of U.S.-Japan cooperation pertaining to global environmental problems include: (1) preservation policy; (2) assistance in environmental development; (3) regional global change research network and organization; (4) global observation information network (GOIN); (5) research and forecast of global change; (6) environment and energy technology; and (7) environmental education. The contents and some results of these cooperation are described in Table 6.3.

Table 6.3 U.S.-Japan Common Agenda in the Area of Global Environmental Problems

1. Preservation Policy
    a. Coral Reef Preservation: Every country has been lobbied to participate in the International Coral Reef Initiative (ICRI), which aims at promoting efforts among government and private individuals for protecting valuable coral reefs. In addition, assistance is being given to the Palau government for the establishment of a coral reef protection research center.
    b. Forest Preservation: Joint capital investments are being made for forest preservation, which is presently at a critical level.
    c. Swampland Preservation: Training programs are conducted for personnel managing swampland preservation activities in accordance with the Ramsal Treaty.
    d. Environmental Policy Dialogue: Dialogues are being held with regard to the feasibility of Japan-U.S. cooperation in international environmental issues, such as global climate change, biological diversity, toxic waste, and ozone depletion.
    e. Ocean Preservation: Oceanographic research is being conducted to identify the causes of climate change.
2. Assistance in Environmental Development
    Japan and the United States are jointly extending financial assistance to NGOs

through a nature preservation project for the preservation of the bioecological diversity of Central and South America. Specifically, assistance will be given toward the reservation of 100 million acres of nature in Central and South America and the Caribbean region through the year 2000 under this project.

3. Regional Global Change Research Network and Organization
Regional networks will be established in North and South America, Europe, Africa, and the Asia Pacific to achieve breakthroughs in earth science, and efforts will be aimed at developing an international network that connects these regional networks.

4. Global Observation Information Network (GOIN)
This project is aimed at providing a wide range of users in both Japan and the United States with global observation information that contributes to global change research as well as to the observation, forecast, and warning of environmental disasters.

5. Research and Forecast of Global Change
Cooperation in research will be extended to the International North Pole Research Center in Alaska and to the International Pacific Basin Research Center in Hawaii for the research and forecast of global change.

6. Environment and Energy Technology
Information is being exchanged on CO_2 isolation, and technical development is being undertaken for the development of alternatives for ozone-depleting CFCs.

7. Environmental Education
The GLOBE Program will be expanded to include developing countries. At the same time, environmental education programs will be developed through the establishment of an Asia-Pacific environmental education forum, and the method of nurturing personnel will be studied.

Source: Ministry of Foreign Affairs, "U.S.-Japan Common Agenda for Cooperation in Global Perspective," in "Global Environmental Problems: Japanese Approaches." http://www.mofa.go.jp/policy/global/environment/pamph/index.html (June 1997).

U.S.-Japan relations are often described as conflicting as their trade frictions are occasionally intensified whenever major organized economic interests collide with each other's. However, it is useful for us to remind ourselves that there exists some common agenda for playing a leading role in the world. Although U.S.-Japan cooperation to arrest the degradation of the global environment might not be as significant as the security relations between the two nations, such cooperation certainly adds a positive feature to the overall bilateral relation, albeit a minor one.

In Lieu of Conclusion

Further study about Japan's environmental diplomacy is needed to evaluate how effective these environmental initiatives are. This chapter also lacks substantial description about the roles of the private sectors, both for-profit and not-for-profit sectors. Yet, the main objective of this chapter is to identify the main factors that generate Japan's environmental foreign policy and to describe some major environmental initiatives. In short, while the domestic political framework has been forcing Japan to seek nonmilitary foreign policy, the arrest of global environmental degradation is a ready-made foreign policy in which Japan can make a substantial contribution by fully utilizing its financial, technological, as well as human resources. It is also doubly convenient since Japan's environmental diplomacy can satisfy Japan's quest for internationalization without raising any serious regional and international political repercussions.

Political climates within and outside Japan are rapidly changing. New Japanese political parties have still split, merged, or formed a temporary alliance. The security atmosphere in the North East Asia has become increasingly cloudy after North Korea tested its ballistic missile that could even fly over the Japanese territory into the Pacific Ocean. While strengthening the bilateral security relations by acting under the renewing U.S.-Japan defense cooperation guidelines, Japan may seek a more active role even in military-political foreign policy in the future. However, unless Article 9 of the Constitution is amended, Japan's environmental diplomacy will continue to be one of the vital means for Japan's international contribution.

Notes

1. See in particular, Article 2, Paragraph 3, and Chapter 6 (Articles 33–38) of the Charter of the United Nations.
2. Refer to Article 51 and Chapter 8 (Articles 52-54) of the UN Charter.
3. Article 9 of the Japanese Constitution reads:

    Aspiring sincerely to an international peace based on justice and order, the Japanese people forever renounce war as a sovereign right of the nation and the threat or use of force as means of settling international disputes.

    In order to accomplish the aim of the preceding paragraph, land, sea, and air forces as well as other war potential, will never be maintained. The right of belligerency of the state will not be recognized.

4. *Kogai* is defined by seven types of disruption of the environment, namely, air, water, soil, and noise pollution, abnormal vibration, and land subsidence, as well as offensive odor, each of which "inflicts damage to human health or the living environment" (Paragraph 1, Article 2, Kogai Taisaku Kihonho, or the Basic Law on Antipollution Measures, promulgated in 1967.)
5. Helmut Weidner, "Japanese Environmental Policy in an International Perspective: Lessons for a Preventive Approach," in *Environmental Policy in Japan*, eds. Shigeto Tsuru and Helmut Weidner (Berlin: Edition Sigma, 1989), pp. 481–82.
6. OECD, *Environmental Policies in Japan* (Paris: OECD, 1977), p. 83.
7. Donella H. Meadows, Dennis L. Meadows, Jorgen Randers, and William W. Behrens III, *The Limits to Growth* (NY: Universe Books, 1972); Gerald O. Barney, *The Global 2000 Report to the President of the United States* (Oxford: Pergamon, 1980).
8. The World Commission on Environment and Development (WCED), *Our Common Future* (Oxford: Oxford University Press, 1987), p. 8. This concept itself, however, had already been introduced in *The World Conservation Strategy*, compiled and published in 1980 by the International Union for the Conservation of Nature and Natural Resources (IUCN) and the United Nations Environment Programme (UNEP).
9. Tanaka Tsutomu, "Chikyuyteki kibo no kankyo mondai ni taisuru waga kuni no taio" [Japan's Response to Global Environmental Problems], *Kikan kankyo kenkyu* (Tokyo: Environmental Research Center) 33 (1981), p. 7.
10. Tanaka, 1981, p. 8.
11. Interview with Hara Bunbei, speaker of the House of Councilors (and former director general of the Environment Agency) on 2 September 1993. The Environment Agency (EA), *Kankyo-cho*

nijunen shi / The Twenty-Year History of the Environment Agency (Tokyo: Gyosei, 1991), p. 366; and the EA, *The Quality of the Environment* (1992), p. 236.

12. The Tokyo Declaration states that a bright and constructive future depends upon whether or not all states adopt "the objective of sustainable development as the overriding goal and test of national policy and international co-operation," WCED 1987, p. 363. Eight principles are listed as the guidance for each state's policy: (1) revive growth; (2) change the quality of growth; (3) conserve and enhance the resource base; (4) ensure a sustainable level of population; (5) reorient technology and manage risks; (6) integrate environment and economics in decision making; (7) reform international economic relations; and (8) strengthen international cooperation (WCED 1987, p. 364–65).
13. Lynton Caldwell, *International Environmental Policy* (Durham: Duke University Press, 1990), p. 207.
14. Wolfgang Sachs, "Environment," in *The Development Dictionary*, ed. Wolfgang Sachs (London: Zed Books, 1992), p. 36.
15. Lester Brown, "The Illusion of Progress," in *State of the World: 1990,* eds. Lester Brown et al. (NY: W.W. Norton and Company, 1990), p. 13.
16. "Is Europe Turning Green?" (editorial), *New York Times,* 22 June 1989.
17. Ministry of Foreign Affairs, Global Environmental Section of Economic Division in the United Nations Bureau (Japan), ed., *Chikyu kankyo sengenshu* [Collected Declarations on the Global Environment] (Tokyo: Ministry of Finance Printing Bureau, 1991), pp. 53–61.
18. Environment Agency (EA) Planning Division, Global Environment Department, *Chikyu kankyo jidai* [The Era of Global Environment] (Tokyo: Gyosei, 1990), pp. 247–63.
19. With about 1,500 Japanese and foreign NGO representatives, the "Tokyo Appeal" called for citizens' participation in environmental policy making. The main themes of six workshops included: (1) global warming and extreme climates; (2) destruction and preservation of tropical rain forests: what should Japan do?; (3) biodiversity and preservation of its habitat; (4) toxic waste: burdens on the future generations; (5) measures to strengthen "environmental consideration" for Japan's environmental aid; and (6) restoration of regional recycling.

    Foreign guests and participants included indigenous people from the Amazon, along with environmental activists and lawyers from Southeast Asia, Africa, Europe, Australia, and the United States. The Executive Committee of "People's Forum for the Global Environment," *Proceedings* (Tokyo, November 1989).
20. The late Prime Minister Takeshita resigned in the spring of 1989 due to the Recruit stocks-for-favors scandals.
21. Quoted during an interview with Dr. Morita Tsuneaki (Environment Agency/Prime Minister's Office), 12 December 1991. This statement was also repeated during the interview with Aichi Kazuo, then Liberal Democratic Party's (LDP's) House of Representative (and former director general of the EA) on 20 December 1991.
22. At the opening reception for the second meeting of the U.S.-Japan Task Force on the Environment and the Search for a New World Order, sponsored by the Carnegie Council on Ethics and International Affairs held at Kayu Kaikan, in Tokyo on 14–16 October 1992. The first meeting was held in New York City, 6–7 April 1992.
23. Contributions to Japan under these programs from 1947 to 1951 amounted to about US$2.1 billion. Major items were food, fertilizer, petroleum, medical supplies, and industrial raw materials; some civilian costs were also paid for by GARIOA funds. Soybeans, among the first commodities shipped to Japan, later became a major export item for the United States (Richard Finn, "GARIOA-EROA," in *Kodansha Encyclopedia of Japan,* vol. 3, pp. 11–12).
24. *Encyclopedia of Japan.*
25. Interview with Dr. Morita, 12 December 1991.
26. Speech by Takeshita, former prime minister of Japan at Leadership Dialogue, a special event sponsored by the Secretariat of the United Nations Conference on Environment and Development (UNCED), in Rio de Janeiro on 4 June 1992.
27. This questionnaire, distributed in October 1986, polled 3,000 Japanese over the age of 20.
28. Finance ministers of five developed countries, including the United Sates, then West Germany, and Japan, agreed to coordinate their respective international policies to pursue a low exchange rate to the U.S. dollar. The main objective of this policy coordination was to correct U.S. international payments deficit.
29. For instance, see Economic Planning Agency, *Kokumin keizai keisan nenpo 1993* [Annual Report of National Economic Account 1993] (Tokyo: Ministry of Finance Printing Bureau, 1993).

30. As of 1994, this inquiry still continues in the Prime Minister's Office's *Monthly Public Opinion Poll*, but in this section I just look at the trend until 1992 when the Earth Summit was convened.
31. The poll conducted in October 1991 reflected the outbreak of the Gulf War in January. People selected "Japan's obligation as a great power" as the need for internationalization more than usual. The percentage choosing this answer was 48.2 percent. Yet, in the following year the choice of this answer returned to the near average rate of 44.1 percent.
32. Prime Minister's Office, *Monthly Public Opinion Poll*, 1988–93.
33. The term *kuroji taikoku* (literally, "black-ink great power") or *boeki kuroji taikoku* (a "great trade-surplus country ") and *kokusai koken* ("international contributions") were omnipresent in newspapers, magazines, and speeches and conversations of politicians, bureaucrats, businessmen, and the general public.
34. Interview with Ichikawa Hiroya, then director of industrial policy of Keidanren, 2 June 1993.
35. Interview with Ambassador Akao Nobutoshi, 23 February 1993.
36. Akao, 1993.
37. John Newhous, "The Diplomatic Round: Earth Summit," *The New Yorker*, 1 June 1992, p. 68. During the interview with Ambassador Akao on 23 February 1993, it was confirmed that this anonymous quotation was his statement.
38. Mago'ori Akihiko and Shigeri Katsuhiko (Illustration), "Kaihatsu-ha kara no henshin: Jiminto shin-kankyo zoku no nerai" [Objective of New LDP Environmental Policy Specialists: Transformation from Advocates of Development], *AERA* 5:22 (2 June 1992): 6–9.
39. Mago'ori and Shigeri, 1992, p. 6.
40. J. A. A. Stockwin et al., *Dynamic and Immobilist Politics in Japan* (Honolulu: University of Hawaii Press, 1988), pp. 1, 15.
41. The Press Corps for the Earth Summit, "'The Earth Summit Is at Risk,'" *Asahi shimbun*, 18 February 1992.
42. Mago'ori and Shigeri, 1992; and Akira Sato, "The Eve of Dissolution of A Political Party," *AERA* 5:13 (24 March 1992): 7.
43. If the former U.S.S.R.'s figure could be converted into U.S. dollars, it would have been the second largest. In that case, Japan's military expenditure would become the sixth. (Stockholm International Peace Research Institute [SIPRI], SIPRI Yearbook 1992 [Oxford: Oxford University Press, 1992], pp. 259–63.)
44. (1) While 33 percent of the poll respondents favored the revision of the Constitution, 51 percent opposed to the revision ("Poll Results Show 45 percent Say the Constitution Becoming Outdated," *The Daily Yomiuri*, 2 May 1991).
    (2) Asahi Shimbun Sha, "Nihon no kokusai koken to koto no fukei (Kyoto, Nara, Kamakura) [The National Public Opinion Poll on "Japan's International Contribution and the Landscape of the Ancient Capitals (Kyoto, Nara, and Kamakura)] (June 1991).
    In this poll, although over 60 percent of the respondents considered that Japan should play a more active role in solving international disputes, the majority opposed the use of military force. 56 percent of the respondents answered that the "renunciation of war" clause (in Article 9) should be strictly observed, whereas 35 percent of the respondents approved a flexible interpretation.
    (3) The Jiji Press, *Jiji Public Opinion Poll* (July 1991): At this poll, 80 percent of respondents approved of the SDF.
    (4) Japan Broadcast Association [Nihon Hoso Kyokai (NHK)], *The Public Opinion Poll on "Japanese and the Constitution"* (March 1992): At this poll, about 75 percent of the respondents considered that Article 9 had contributed to maintaining peace and security of Japan. While about 48 percent agreed the legitimacy of the SDF under this clause, over 62 percent opposed the revision of Article 9. For more details about these public opinion polls, see for example, Prime Minister's Office, *Heisei 4-nen ban seron chosa nenkan—Zenkoku seron chosa no genkyo* [Public Opinion Polls Yearbook 1992: The Current Situation in National Public Opinion Polls] (Tokyo: Ministry of Finance Printing Bureau, 1993).
45. The real name of this commission was Kokusai Shakai ni Okeru Nihon no Yakuwari (Special Commission on Japan's Role in the International Society).
46. The members of the Ozawa Commission included Ozawa Ichiro, Kakizawa Koji, Funada Hajime, (all three left the LDP, but Funada later returned), Kato Koichi, Yamazaki Taku, and Moriyama Mayumi (who remained with the LDP). See "Jieitai no kokurengun sanka teigen: Ozawa chosakai" [Proposal for SDF Participation in the UN Forces: LDP Ozawa Commission], *Asahi shimbun*, 21 February 1992; also Sato, 1992.

47. The term "muscular" foreign policy is used by Gerald L. Curtis in his article "Political Change Comes to Japan," prepared for deliberation at the Modern Japan Seminar at Columbia University, 1 October 1993.
48. Ozawa Ichiro, *Nihon Kaizo keikaku* (Tokyo: Kodansha, 1993) [English translation, *Blueprint for A New Japan: The Rethinking of a Nation* (Tokyo: Kodansha International, 1994)]. Some recent major changes in Japanese political party politics are the establishments of Minshuto (Democratic Party) in September 1996, which is led by Kan Naoto and Hatoyama Yukio, and Jiyuto (Liberal Party) in January 1998, which is led by Ozawa. Jiyuto was born after the split of Shinshinto in December 1997, three years after its establishment. And at the same time, the former Komeito politicians, who once joined and then left Shinshinto, formed Shinto Heiwa (New Party Peace). Yet, in November 1998, Shinto Heiwa and Komeito were reunified. As of April 1999, the Democratic Party is the largest opposition party (93 lower house and 49 upper house representatives), followed by the Liberal Party (40 and 12) and the Clean Government Party (Komeito: 38 and 24). The LDP and Liberal Party have been forming a policy alliance and obtained the stable majority in the lower house (with 264 LDP members). However, they cannot reach the majority in the upper house (with 104 LDP members). Seeking stable and speedy Diet deliberations, the LDP is approaching Komeito. In this context, Komeito now has a casting vote in Japan's political party politics.
49. Yoshida Takafumi, "Chikyu samitto waremo waremo" [Vying with One Another to Go to the Earth Summit], *Asahi shimbun*, 3 March 1992.
50. Yoshida, 1992. Yamanaka Sadanori was the first director general of the EA but served just for five days due to a Cabinet reshuffling under the Sato Eisuke administration. Thus, Oishi Buichi was the de facto first EA director general, from 5 July 1971 to 7 July 1972. During his tenure, he stopped the construction of an interprefectural highway joining Gunma, Niigata, and Fukushima, which would have destroyed the Oze marshlands. He also established a legal concept of "no-fault liability" for polluters, which had been a public pledge of the Sato administration but was not fulfilled due to MITI opposition. Oishi's attempt was successful partly because of popular support for him and partly because of Wagatsuma Sakae's cooperation with him as a special legal adviser. Wagatsuma is one of the most authoritative legal scholars of the Civil Code. Furthermore, the EA acknowledged "Minamata disease" as pollution-related disease for the first time. Since he retired from public service as a parliamentarian, Oishi has been active in global environmental issues. He is now president of the Fund for Defending the Green Earth, which promotes such projects as tree planting. "A Symposium: 10-Year History of Environmental Policy," *Jurisuto* 749 (15 September 1981): 21–22.
51. For a more detailed account (and for the following section on the Japanese business sector's response), for instance, see Hiroshi Ohta, *Japan's Politics and Diplomacy of Climate Change* (Ph.D. dissertation, Columbia University, New York, 1995), pp. 219–38.
52. Interview with Ichikawa Hiroya, 2 June 1993. He was then director of industrial policy at Keidanren and in charge of this project.
53. *Keidanren Global Environmental Charter* (English version) (Keidanren, 23 April 1991), p. 3.
54. During the same period, Keidanren also established the Industrial Waste Foundation.
55. Since the late 1980s, mainly U.S. nature conservation groups have undertaken to purchase some of the foreign debts of developing countries in exchange for agreements to protect natural environment. For instance, the first swap was carried out in 1987 by Conservation International, a U.S. environmental nonprofit organization. This organization paid US$100,000 for an uncollectible US$650,000 that the government of Bolivia owed to Citicorp. The group then agreed to wipe out Bolivia's debt in exchange for protecting a 3.7-million-acre buffer around the Beni Biosphere Reserve and spending the equivalent of $250,000 in local currency to manage and maintain the reserve. (See Peter Passell, "Washington Offers Mountain of Debt to Save Forests," *New York Times*, 22 January 1991 (Science Times Section) .
56. Interview with Dr. Ichikawa on 2 June 1993; Ichikawa, "Companies and the Earth Charter," p. 15; and a pamphlet on Keidanren's Fund for Nature Preservation; also see "Keidanren kankyo suwappu sannka" (Keidanren Participates in Debt-for-Nature Swaps), *Asahi shimbun*, 5 February 1992.
57. Takeuchi Ken and Yoshida Takafumi, "Kankyo koken mienu 'Nippon'" [Japan's Environmental Contribution is Invisible], *Asahi shimbun*, 6 June 1992; and report crew for the Earth Summit, "NGO inarabu seifu zaikai jin" [Government Officials and Industrialists Line Up with NGOs], *Asahi shimbun*, 8 June 1992.

58. Kamei Naomi (Friends of Earth Japan), "Gurobaru foramu ni sanka shite" [Participating in Global Forum], 92 *NGO Forum Japan*, 2 July 1992, p. 8.
59. Ministry of Foreign Affairs, "Japanese Economic Cooperation in the Environmental Sector" <http://www.mofa.go.jp/policy/global/environment/pamph/199706/evn_sect.html> (27 June 1996).
60. Ministry of Foreign Affairs, *Japan's ODA: Official Development Assistance, 1992* (Tokyo: Association for International Cooperation, 1993), pp. 193–94.
61. The five priority issues include (1) global issues such as the environment and population; (2) basic human needs; (3) human resource development and research and other cooperation for improvement and dissemination of technology; (4) infrastructure improvement; and (5) structural adjustment. Ministry of Foreign Affairs (1993), p. 194.
62. Ministry of Foreign Affairs, 1996.
63. Environment, Women in Development (WID) and Other Global Issues Division, Planning Department of JICA website, "Environmental Assistance of Japan International Cooperation Agency." http://www.jica.go.jp/E-info/E-earth/E-env/E-env-cont/E_env001.html
64. JICA website. I refer to the same source for the following sections on JICA's environmental policies.
65. OECF, *What's the OECF* (Tokyo: OECF, 1990), p. 3.
66. "OECF Operations in FY 1997," OECF Press Release http://www.jbic.go.jp/english/release/oecf/press98/1998/0428-e.htm> (28 April 1998)
67. OECF, 1998. The OECF and the Export-Import Bank of Japan (JEXIM) merged to become the Japan Bank for International Cooperation (JBIC) on 1 October 1999.
68. International Cooperation Initiatives, in "Japanese Approaches to the Suppression of Greenhouse Gas Generation," <http://www.mofa.go.jp/policy/global/environment/warm/japan/chap6.html>
69. Ministry of Foreign Affairs, "Japan's Energy Conservation" in "Global Environmental Problems: Japanese Approaches" (June 1997). <http://www.mofa.go.jp/policy/global/environment/pamph/index.html>
70. Refer to MITI's pamphlet of the International Center for Environmental Technology.
71. Refer to MITI's pamphlet of the Research Institute of Innovative Technology for the Earth.
72. "U.S.-Japan Common Agenda for Cooperation in Global Perspective," in Ministry of Foreign Affairs, 1997.

CHAPTER 7

Japanese Role in PKO and Humanitarian Assistance

Caroline Rose

The Ministry of Foreign Affairs identifies the "two main pillars of Japan's international peace efforts" as contributions to international humanitarian relief operations and participation in UN peacekeeping operations (PKO), and it could be argued that these efforts have constituted some of the more positive aspects in the evolution of Japan's foreign policy in the 1990s. Prompted by international negative reaction to Japan's immobility in the run up to and during the Gulf War, the implementation of the International Peace Cooperation Law (IPCL) in 1992 has resulted in a number of successful PKO missions and a greater commitment to humanitarian relief. This aspect of Japan's foreign policy is in line with the concept of a UN-centered diplomacy, revived by Prime Minister Kaifu Toshiki in 1990, and it could provide one way forward to a more proactive foreign policy in the twenty-first century. However, Japan's participation in peacekeeping operations has not been without controversy both domestic and international, raising the sensitive issues of constitutional revision, the constitutionality of the Self-Defense Forces (SDF) and their overseas deployment, and Japan's role in the UN and in the international arena.

The following sections outline Japan's role in the UN since its entrance in 1956, and the expansion of that role after the Gulf War. The discussion will continue with an evaluation of the PKO missions in which Japan was involved in the early 1990s, before considering the opportunities for, and constraints on, greater participation in the future.

Japan in the UN

When Japan gained UN membership in 1956, Prime Minister Kishi Nobusuke made support for the United Nations one of his important political principles. This early commitment to "UN-centrism" (*Kokuren chushinshugi*) was made at a time when hopes were high about the role of the UN in the maintenance of international peace and security. Such idealism faded quickly, however, and UN-centrism did not produce any concrete measures beyond conducting Japan's foreign policy in line with UN principles, which were in any case identical to those of the Japanese Constitution.[1] Successive prime ministers often referred to Japan's international role as a "contributor to peace" to a greater or lesser degree, but "UN-centrism" did not become a focal point of Japan's foreign policy again until the 1990s, when it became politically useful.[2]

In the intervening period, however, Japan's role in the UN was not insignificant. Since becoming an economic power, Japan has been a major financial contributor to the UN. Japan's assessment for contribution to the 1998 regular budget was 17.981 percent. This was set to rise to over 20 percent in 2000, representing the second largest contribution after the United States, which contributes 25 percent. In terms of the contribution of personnel, the record is less impressive. With the exception of a handful of high-profile posts (Ogata Sadako, Akashi Yasushi) Japanese representation in UN organizations is somewhat low-key. The number of Japanese staff working at the UN Secretariat has regularly fallen short of the "desirable range" of over 200. In 1996, for example, there were only 108 Japanese staff. Japan's late entry to the UN, difficulties of secondment, and a general lack of interest and expertise in international affairs have been cited as reasons for this shortfall, but in the late 1990s the government was actively seeking to recruit international civil servants to redress the balance.[3]

In the 1980s Japan began to play a key role in a number of projects, for example, initiating a committee to discuss streamlining of the UN, proposing the creation of an international arms shipments register and a "Reserve Fund" for UN peacekeeping. But all of these, Ronald Dore argues, were "costless" initiatives, in that they were fairly uncontroversial.[4] In the late 1980s and early 1990s, Japan's "political activism" increased. Primarily, Japan started (and continues) to push for reform of the Security Council, mainly with an eye to securing a permanent seat. Although Japan has regularly been elected as nonpermanent member to the UN Security Council (UNSC), its lack of a permanent seat excludes it from key decision-making posts, and therefore greatly limits Japan's political influence. Another area of recent activity is peacekeeping, although this has been hampered by external and domestic considerations.

Japan and Peacekeeping

Peacekeeping refers to activities that ensure international peace and security. More specifically this is "impartial and non-threatening activity in the cause of peace which takes place with the consent of the host state or states and the cooperation of all the direct disputants."[5] It has "traditionally" involved the deployment of peacekeepers to implement an agreement after a cease-fire is in place. Humanitarian assistance refers to those activities under the remit of bodies, such the United Nations High Commissioner for Refugees (UNHCR) or the World Health Organisation (WHO), concerned with aiding refugees or victims of conflicts. Humanitarian assistance can take the form of assistance in the relief and repatriation of victims of conflict, provision of food, clothing, medicine and medical care, and reconstruction of infrastructure. Since 1948 there have been almost 50 UN peacekeeping missions, but the majority of those took place after 1988 (36 up to 1998). Post–Cold War operations have related more to internal conflicts than border or bilateral conflicts, often reflecting the reemergence of internal ethnic or religious conflicts, which had been held in check by the East-West balance of power. With this increase in peacekeeping activity, the UN has been forced to request greater contributions from its members for peacekeeping and humanitarian relief, and the scope of activities has expanded beyond the "traditional" concept to include political education, electoral monitoring, law and order tasks, repatriation, rehabilitation, human rights, and administration.[6]

Japan's contribution to UN peacekeeping efforts has mirrored its role in the UN as a whole. As a member of the UN, Japan has an obligation to assist in peacekeeping and indeed the first principle of Japan's 1957 Basic Policy for National Defense (*kokubo no kihon hoshin*) is to support the activities of the United Nations and promote international cooperation, thereby contributing to the realization of world peace. Yet support for peacekeeping activities has materialized in the form of financial rather than "physical," human contributions. In 1997, Japan provided $195 million, which constituted 15 percent of the UN peacekeeping budget (compared to the United States 25 percent, Germany 9 percent, France 7.8 percent). Personnel involvement began in the late 1980s, and only then in relatively small numbers. For example, one Ministry of Foreign Affairs official took part as a political officer in the UN Good Offices Mission in Afghanistan and Pakistan in 1989, and another in the UN Military Observer Group in Iraq-Iran 1988–89. Election monitors were also sent to Namibia, Nicaragua, and Haiti in 1989–90. Participation in these missions attracted little attention and caused no domestic political or legal problems, given that participants were either foreign ministry officials or local government officials seconded to the foreign ministry, and therefore "officially" involved in diplomatic activities. In addition, the missions were successful, and no loss of life was incurred. When compared with numbers of participants from other countries, Japan's involvement is decidedly lightweight, but greater participation in PKO activities would necessitate the dispatch of troops—and it is this very issue that has been particularly problematic, given the contradictions in Japan's laws and Constitution, the national consensus, and potentially adverse regional reactions.

Legal Constraints: The Peace Constitution and Its Interpretation

Article 9 of the Constitution states that "the Japanese people forever renounce war as a sovereign right of the nation and the threat or use of force as a means of settling international disputes." In addition, the 1957 SDF law prohibits overseas deployment of the SDF (for collective self-defense under the U.S.-Japan security treaty). In sum, Japan's legislation prohibits SDF personnel from participating in UN peacekeeping operations where use of force would be involved, although civilian personnel are under no such restrictions (again, provided they are involved in noncombat operations). Thus, UN requests for Japanese personnel assistance (notably in 1958 for the UN Observer Group in Lebanon and the

United Nations Operation in the Congo in 1961), were rejected on the grounds that Japanese participation would violate Japanese laws,[7] and this was to remain the official line whenever the issue of overseas deployment of Japan's SDF was raised in relation to UN peacekeeping or matters of collective self-defense. This "minimalist interpretation" has received much criticism, however, and Japanese and foreign analysts have argued that Article 9 has often been invoked as a means of shirking responsibility. Furthermore, it is argued that the authors of the Peace Constitution did not intend it to be interpreted in such a way that would prohibit Japan from fulfilling its responsibilities as a member of the UN as stipulated in Article 43 of the UN Charter.[8]

Public Opinion

The "minimalist interpretation" of the Constitution enabled the low-key foreign policy posture advocated by Prime Minister Yoshida Shigeru and his successors to become widely accepted in the minds of the public. Indeed, the idea that use of force is a successful means of settling disputes is greeted with skepticism by many who adhere to an "economic interdependence" rather than realist point of view. By the 1980s, even though the majority pacifist view in Japan began to acknowledge that Japan should bear more global responsibilities, it was only on condition that those responsibilities do not exceed constitutional bounds. Discussion about possible revision of the Constitution was considered taboo until the early 1990s when a series of events brought about a shift in opinion (to be discussed below). Nonetheless, Inoguchi argues that in the mid-1990s a majority of Japanese still favored a "self-interested, inward-looking pacifism over enhanced security efforts."[9]

Asian Fears

Another significant constraint on Japan's international behavior stems from the legacy of history and the mistrust with which many Asian countries regard Japan. Given its colonialist record, and its failure to come to terms with and take responsibility for World War II events, regional fears are never far from the surface when the issue of an "enhanced" Japanese security role is raised. Japan's Peace Constitution, along with the U.S.-Japan security treaty, have been viewed by many East and Southeast Asian nations as the cap on the bottle, so to speak, or a safeguard against a revival of Japanese militarism. When Japan began to inch toward a more active role in the early 1990s, albeit in the sphere of UN peacekeeping, it raised suspicions in Asia. China and South Korea were the most vocal opponents, but leaders in other countries, such as the Philippines and Singapore, also voiced their worries about Japan's long-term aims.[10]

Developments in the 1990s

Japan's higher-profile role in the UN in the 1980s can be seen as a result of changes in East-West relations and attempts to revitalize the UN. When he became prime minister in 1989, Takeshita Noboru attempted to continue

Nakasone Yasuhiro's policy of internationalism, pledging, for example, to develop "cooperation for world peace" through "positive participation in diplomatic efforts, the dispatch of necessary personnel and the provision of financial cooperation aiming at the resolution of regional conflicts."[11] Takeshita's promises were soon tested during the Gulf crisis when Japan was called upon to put his words into action. The crisis is generally seen as a turning point in Japan's role in PKO activities.

Many Asian countries felt either that the Gulf crisis was a regional problem that did not directly concern them, or that U.S. and European actions were excessive and reminiscent of a not-so-distant colonial past.[12] Either way, the Asian response was low-key. For Japan though, the crisis was to be highly significant. At a "personal" level, the Iraqis took over 100 Japanese hostages. At a national level, Japan was at that point reliant on the Gulf for 70 percent of its oil (though only a small percentage originated from Iraq and Kuwait) and any prolonged disruption of supplies would have undermined the national economy. Finally, at an international level, the crisis represented a threat to world peace and security and called into question Japan's role as a contributor to that peace and security. It is, therefore, worth considering Japan's response in more detail.

The events leading up to the Gulf War prompted a domestic debate about whether or not Japan should, or indeed could, get involved in the multinational efforts, given its constitutional and legal restraints. Domestic public opinion was initially opposed to involvement beyond a financial contribution, but by the end of the crisis had undergone a transformation. Government and opposition opinion on an appropriate response was divided and slowed down the decision-making processes. Even though eventually Japan made a significant financial contribution to the costs of UN operations, foreign governments criticized the Japanese government for its inability to act quickly and decisively, accusing it of using "checkbook diplomacy." External pressure is often seen as the key influence on the government's decision to increase the amount of monetary assistance and to introduce new legislation that would lead to a physical contribution in future PKO activities, but domestic politicking by the Liberal Democratic Party (LDP) must also be taken into account.

Japan's immediate response to Iraq's invasion of Kuwait in August 1990 was to impose a ban on trade with Iraq (which meant prohibiting oil imports, exports, loans, and investments) and to cancel Prime Minister Kaifu's impending visit to the Middle East. The government then pledged an initial $1 billion to contribute to the multinational effort, but at U.S. insistence increased that amount by an additional $3 billion by mid-September. After the start of Desert Storm in January 1991, a further $9 billion was pledged, bringing the total financial contribution to $13 billion, which amounted to 20 percent of the cost of the war. Various plans were put forward to provide aircraft for transportation and a medical team, but these failed to materialize for various reasons.[13] The only human contribution to the war took place from April to October 1991 when six Maritime Self-Defense Force (MSDF) vessels were sent to the Gulf to carry out minesweeping. Domestically, the mission was interpreted as necessary for maintaining the safety of commercial shipping lanes (which Japan used) and was therefore not in violation of the Constitution.

From UN Peace Cooperation Bill to International Peace Cooperation Law 1992

In response to U.S. criticism that Japan was not making a "physical" contribution, the LDP had introduced the United Nations Peace Cooperation Bill (UNPCB, Kokuren Heiwa Kyoryoku An) to the Diet in October 1990. The bill would have allowed SDF troops to assist in UN peacekeeping operations in the Gulf in a noncombatant role. One of the chief proponents of the bill was Ozawa Ichiro, a powerful figure in the LDP who argued that Japan should play a more active role. In the face of strong opposition (within the LDP as well as from opposition forces), a lack of LDP majority in the Upper House, and potentially adverse public reaction, the bill was withdrawn in November. It was not abandoned totally, however, and was to be reintroduced some months later.

In the intervening period, a number of changes took place, facilitating the smoother passage of the second bill. First and foremost, the LDP worked hard to develop a larger support base for the bill, particularly in the Upper House. Through a series of lengthy and complicated negotiations (not necessarily directly related to the Gulf crisis), Ozawa and his supporters managed to persuade key opposition parties like the Komeito and Democratic Socialist Party to vote for the proposed legislation, albeit with various changes. Another major change was a shift in public opinion. In the early stages of the Gulf crisis, public opinion had been very much against Japan's involvement beyond economic support. A poll carried out by the Asahi Shimbun in November 1990, for example, revealed that nearly 80 percent of those polled opposed any overseas dispatch of SDF personnel, judging such an action to be unconstitutional, 54 percent opposed the dispatch of a civilian peace cooperation organization, and 58 percent opposed the UNPCB. Kaifu's handling of the crisis, along with cooperation with the United States was also greeted with high levels of dissatisfaction.[14] A year later in November 1991, however, public opinion had shifted considerably, and nearly 60 percent of respondents in a Kyodo poll supported overseas deployment.[15] The combination of such factors as exposure to debates on Japan's international roles and constitutional revision, in addition to the success of the minesweeping mission, no doubt contributed to the shift of opinion.

These factors in turn paved the way for the reintroduction of the PKO bill in September 1991 and its successful implementation as the International Peace Cooperation Law (IPCL, Kokusai Heiwa Kyoryoku Ho) in June 1992, although it should be noted that there was still considerable opposition to the bill, not least from the Socialist Party, which attempted to delay voting in the Diet using the "cow-walk" tactic.[16] The aim of the law was to provide a mechanism to enable the overseas dispatch of SDF personnel as part of a UN peacekeeping mission for a period of up to two years. Duties would involve supervision of civil administrative affairs, election monitoring, installation and repair of transport and communication facilities, medical care, and assistance in environmental restoration. These fit in with regular UN peacekeeping activities of logistical support and humanitarian assistance. SDF participation in the more dangerous activities associated with peacekeeping, such as cease-fire monitoring, patrol in buffer zones, monitoring of arms traffic, collection and disposal of abandoned weapons, relocation and disarmament of warring factional forces, assistance in creating cease-fire lines, and assistance in the exchange of prisoners of war, were written into the law but "frozen," pending a review of the law in 1995.[17] The intention, therefore, was not to produce a law that would allow Japan SDF participation in frontline activities of UN peacekeeping operations. Indeed, in addition to the limited activities allowed under the IPCL, dispatch of personnel was further restricted by a number of "conditions" (five principles) that must be met before Diet approval can be given:

- a cease-fire agreement between conflicting parties must exist,
- participation of Japanese personnel can take place only with consent from conflicting parties,
- peacekeeping operations must be conducted impartially,
- the Japanese government has the right to withdraw if any of the above requirements break down,
- weapons (small arms) may be used in self-defense only.

Japan's PKO and Humanitarian Assistance: An Evaluation

With the IPCL in place, Japan participated in five PKO missions between 1992 and 1998 (Angola, Cambodia, Mozambique, El Salvador, Golan Heights) and one humanitarian relief operation to assist Rwandan refugees. These operations involved a combined total of more than 1,900 personnel, ranging from civilian electoral observers to SDF engineers. Each operation varied in scope, time span, and the number of personnel dispatched. Japan's participation in the Angola and El Salvador missions, for example, was restricted to monitoring of the electoral process and involved relatively small numbers of personnel (three and 30 respectively) over a period of a few weeks. Mozambique was a larger operation involving 169 personnel variously engaged in electoral monitoring, transportation, and administrative duties over a period of 18 months. Three teams of more than 45 personnel each were sent to the Golan Heights for transportation, road repair, and administrative duties between February 1996 and August 1998.[18]

The largest missions in terms of numbers of personnel were in the United Nations Transitional Authority in Cambodia (UNTAC), described below, and in the United Nations Assistance Mission in Rwanda, where personnel were involved not in peacekeeping operations but in humanitarian relief efforts. In the case of the latter, in addition to a pledge of $44 million, the Japanese government responded to a request from the UNHCR by sending 400 members of the SDF to countries bordering Rwanda in September 1994 with the primary aims of providing medical and sanitary care, supplying food and water, and building accommodation at camps. In line with the IPCL, Japanese personnel were not allowed to enter Rwanda proper, but were based in Zaire and Kenya.

UNTAC stands out as Japan's first major involvement in a UN peacekeeping operation after the enactment of the IPCL. Prior to 1992, and in addition to providing financial aid to Cambodia, Japan had also played an influential role in the peace process, holding one round of negotiations in Tokyo in 1990. Further involvement came in mid-1992 with the appointment of Akashi Yasushi as head of UNTAC. Between September 1992 and September 1993, the Japanese government dispatched more than 1,300 personnel (cease-fire and electoral observers, SDF engineering units, and civilian police) to oversee the implementation of a new electoral system.

It is viewed as significant that Japan's first major peacekeeping mission took place within Asia. Seen as a regional confidence-building measure, the mission could be deemed a success. Despite worries expressed by China, South Korea, and Singapore about the dispatch of Japanese troops overseas, sentiment among other Southeast Asian nations was supportive if not welcoming. Public opinion at home was mixed. A high-profile public relations exercise that emphasized Japan's new positive role was juxtaposed against the harsh reality of the dangers inherent in peacekeeping activities. The death of two Japanese peacekeepers in Cambodia (one a volunteer involved in electoral monitoring, the other a civilian policeman) raised understandable concerns about the safety of operations and levels of training, and led to domestic demands that the Japanese contingent be withdrawn. But in response to fears expressed by other participants in UNTAC that Japan's withdrawal might jeopardize UNTAC as well as ruin the credibility of Japan's newly attained peacekeeping role, the Japanese government stood firm, allowing the Japanese contingent to remain in Cambodia until September 1993 with no further casualties.[19]

As of 1999, Japan had not been involved in any missions on as large a scale as Cambodia or Rwanda but did maintain a modest presence in some peacekeeping and disaster relief operations in late 1998 and early 1999. For example, a 16-member advance relief team was sent to Honduras under the disaster relief law in November 1998 to assist in the wake of Hurricane Mitch, and in May 1999 the government announced its intention to send several electoral observers to Indonesia in June, and to send a survey mission to East Timor with a view to cooperating with the UN in a referendum proposed for August 1999.

The process of review of the "frozen" sections of the IPCL began in 1995, and a report produced in September 1996 by the International Peace Cooperation Headquarters attached to the Prime Minister's Office suggested that the review process focus on the key areas of use of weapons and relief assistance. It took a further two years before the law was revised, but in June 1998 the Diet passed the amended law stipulating that weapons for self-defense can be used only under orders of the commanding officer (rather than at the individual's discretion), and material aid can be supplied without a cease-fire agreement in place.[20] Thus the activities of Japan's SDF in UN peacekeeping operations remained highly restricted as of 1999, prompting further debate about how, or indeed whether, the scope of activities could be expanded in the future.

Japan and Wider Peacekeeping: An Expanded Role?

There was much criticism in the early 1990s that UN peacekeeping had failed to achieve long-term results, that operations were marred by bureaucratic inefficiency, or exceeded the "traditional" scope of peacekeeping to such an extent that the task became unmanageable and unsuccessful (Somalia and Bosnia, for example, were viewed as disasters). Various propositions were put forward in response to such criticisms. Former Secretary General Boutros Boutros-Ghali's "Agenda for Peace" suggested an extension of UN peacekeeping to "peace enforcement." He suggested, for example, that preventive action be taken where outbreak of conflict is feared by one or both parties to that potential conflict. In addition, he suggested that UN forces be allowed to enforce the terms of a cease-fire agreement if a party failed to comply. While the concept of "wider" or "muscular peacekeeping" was not universally welcomed initially, there was a consensus that peacekeeping still had an important role to play. Positive evaluations of UN PKO missions in Namibia and Cambodia, for example, indicated that peacekeeping could still make a valuable contribution to international peace and security in the post–Cold War era. Indeed, given what seems to be an inexorable rise of local conflicts throughout the world, not least an increase in local tensions in Southeast Asia in 1998 and 1999, there is widespread agreement that the demand for a range of UN peacekeeping and humanitarian services will not decline in the foreseeable future.[21]

As such, Japan's participation in UN peacekeeping activities could develop beyond its current limited role, and represents one way in which Japan could play a greater political role in regional and global affairs. As Ueki Yasuhiro points out, UN-centrism is a "convenient cover under which Japan can justify its assertive political role and which helps quiet the lingering domestic opposition to Japan getting involved in *real politique*. It also dispels fears of its Asian neighbors about Japan's assertive political behavior."[22] While dissatisfaction has been expressed about Japan's hesitant and limited role in UN PKO in the 1990s,[23] there is a growing body of sentiment that envisages an expanded PKO role as the ideal way for Japan to enhance its international standing. Ambassador to the UN Owada Hisashi is a keen advocate, for example, of a "new innovative approach to peacekeeping," including preventive diplomacy and rapid deployment forces, but the exact nature of Japan's role in this is still open to debate.[24]

Domestic Debate in the 1990s

It was noted above that Nakasone and Takeshita were in favor of a stronger role for Japan in the 1980s. In the 1990s, that point of view has grown in popularity, prompted by the Gulf War and in part by the success of Japan's various peacekeeping and humanitarian missions.

The most vocal group in favor of an expanded role for Japan is represented by politicians like Ozawa Ichiro who argue that Japan should acquire "normal statehood" (i.e., with a "normal army" and permanent representation on the UNSC). Ozawa's concept of "active pacifism" rather than "passive pacifism" adopts a realist view in which military power is seen as necessary to preserve international peace. This would, by necessity, involve some revision of the Constitution and the SDF law to provide a legal framework for participation in collective security operations. For this group, a full peacekeeping role for Japan would be one way in which Japan could "ride to international rehabilitation and restoration as a fully functioning global power."[25]

An alternative view suggests that Japan should continue to play a nonmilitary role in PKO since this would be more suited to Japan's experience and legal constraints. Japan's PKO participation has been praised for "the generally solid work of the Japanese troops and civilians . . . in terms of self-discipline, effectiveness, low profile and generosity."[26] Given the UN's commitment to a broader interpretation of the concept of peacekeeping, which fits in more readily with the demands of post–Cold War conflicts, Japan could be well-placed to expand its activities that may not necessarily include a combatant role. Inoguchi suggests, for example, that based on experience gained thus far, Japan's future strengths could lie in intelligence (e.g., "assessment of local situations") or in engineering projects.

By contrast, advocates of Japan as a "global civilian power" argue that Japan has successfully proved that peace and prosperity can be brought about by economic power. Underlying this argument is the majority pacifist view that continues to eschew the "use of force" as stipulated in the Constitution, and is skeptical about the role of the SDF in peacekeeping missions. Proponents of this school of thought argue that Japan can play a more valuable role by helping to resolve global problems, such as environmental issues, than by participating in peacekeeping.[27]

At present, it appears that Japan is keen to continue its involvement in UN peacekeeping and humanitarian missions. Should future Japanese governments decide to seek an expanded role, then their success will be determined largely by their ability to deal with the constraints noted above—constitutional and legal issues, public opinion, and Asian reaction. In addition, Japan's leaders face a further obstacle in the form of a lack of permanent seat on the UNSC.

Previously a taboo subject, the topic of constitutional revision was brought out into the open again for the first time since the 1950s on the occasion of the Gulf War. In the early 1990s, LDP politicians began to call for a reexamination of each article of the Constitution to ensure its suitability for the twenty-first century—referring specifically to the possibility of revising or amending Article 9. Such calls were not just restricted to the LDP or to politicians. Some Japan New Party (Nihon Shinto) politicians advocated changes to the Constitution that would allow for Japan's full participation in UN peacekeeping activities, such as a supplementary clause to be added to Article 9 allowing UN standby units to be mobilized under UN command. In addition, Komeito head Ichikawa Yuichi advocated lifting the taboo on constitutional revision and the chairperson of Rengo, Japan's largest federation of trade unions, agreed there should be a reexamination of the Constitution. Ozawa was a keen advocate of constitutional revision, not for the purpose of allowing Japan to become a militarist power, but rather to eliminate the contradictions between Article 9 and reality.

The issue of constitutional revision was taken up by a study group attached to Japan's leading newspaper, the *Yomiuri*. The paper's 1994 draft proposed, among other things, the deletion of the second paragraph of Article 9 (referring to land, sea, and air forces and the right of belligerency of the state) and the introduction of a paragraph allowing for the creation of "an organisation for self-defence to secure [Japan's] peace and independence" under the command of the prime minister. This would legitimize the existence of the SDF but would prevent fears that such a revision would unleash a militarist revival by stressing the prime minister's authority in addition to a ban on conscription. The draft proposal also allowed for Japan to play a greater international role through "positive contributions" to "natural and man-made disasters."[28] Other suggestions for revision of Article 9 have been made by Japanese and foreign observers, but the debate is still in its early stages and unlikely to result in actual revision in the near future.[29]

It is unlikely that discussion of constitutional revision in political and media circles would have gone so far had the public mood not changed to accommodate it. Surveys in the 1990s showed a shift in favor of some revision of the Constitution. A *Yomiuri* poll of 1993 revealed that for the first time a majority of respondents were in favor of revising the constitution. The main reasons for revision were that the Constitution "cannot cope with problems that have arisen in areas like international contributions" and because of the confusion caused by constantly "modifying its interpretation and application." Yet although Article 9 is seen as "problematic," the majority view is to retain it rather than revise it to allow for the existence of armed forces.[30]

The results of these various surveys indicate the continuing underlying fear among Japanese themselves that their democratic system is not yet strong enough to "withstand a resurgence of militarism,"[31] a fear still shared in some parts of Asia. In the mid-1990s, Japan was still dealing with a number of Asian countries on sensitive issues left over from the war. To name but a few, compensation claims were being filed against the Japanese government by Chinese, Indonesian, and Filipino victims of Japan's wartime aggression and labor mobilization programs, the content of Japan's history textbooks was still a bone of contention for the Chinese and Korean governments, anti-Japanese sentiment in Korea was particularly high over the "comfort women" issue, and Japan was negotiating with the Chinese government over the disposal of abandoned chemical weapons. These issues serve as a constant reminder of Japan's militarist past, and the Chinese government, in particular, is keen to warn against a resurgence of that behavior. By the late 1990s, however, it seemed that Japan had managed to make some progress in reassuring the region that its intention was not to revive a prewar-style militarism and that a serious attempt had been made to reflect on and apologize for the events of World War II. A series of fairly successful summit meetings with the Northeast Asian leaders in late 1998 and some resolution of issues relating to the legacy of history paved the way for a more "future-oriented" diplomacy based on mutual trust and cooperation.

Another major stumbling block remains Japan's lack of a permanent seat on the UN Security Council. Criticized for its poor decision-making mechanism and for being undemocratic, the Security Council is long overdue for reform.

Many people feel it is inappropriate that economically powerful countries like Japan and Germany are not permanent members of the council. There has been much debate in Japan in recent years as to whether Japan should seek a permanent seat or not. Not surprisingly, those most in favor of Japan's permanent membership are "internationalists" like Ozawa, seeking Japan's rightful place in the international community. On other hand, some in the LDP and Social Democratic Party of Japan (SDPJ) are reluctant to support the idea of permanent membership because of implications for military involvement in UN peacekeeping operations and the constitutional revision that would entail.

Since Prime Minister Miyazawa Kiichi announced in 1992 that Japan was seeking a permanent seat "in the near future," subsequent governments have attempted to progress the issue albeit always within the context of reform of the Security Council and its functions. Thus the official line in recent years has been that Japan seeks to play a greater role in a reformed Security Council and in peacekeeping activities, though firmly within the bounds of Japanese law. This view is reflected in the 1998 Diplomatic Blue Book, which states that "there is also an increasingly large role to be played by countries which are able to contribute not just with regard to military aspects but also in social and economic areas. To adapt to these new circumstances, new members able to make a global contribution must be added to the Security Council."[32] Japan's regular, if low-key, participation in UN activities since the early 1990s has been seen as a means of strengthening the case for a permanent seat on the UNSC, but progress on the issue of UN reform is extremely slow.[33]

The Way Ahead

The changes in Japan's PKO and humanitarian relief operations in the 1990s should be viewed within the context of sweeping political and economic changes at home and abroad, numerous changes in Japan's regional and global policy brought about by the end of the Cold War, attitudinal changes about the scope and nature of the peacekeeping concept, and a resultant expansion of PKO activities. All of these factors created both problems and opportunities for Japan in terms of developing a new international role.

An acknowledgment that Japan should play a greater role in burden-sharing has been accompanied by a willingness to take more proactive steps in a number of foreign policy areas. Gradual improvements in Japan's major bilateral relationships and a greater role in joint operations under the revised U.S.-Japan security guidelines are encouraging indicators. At the same time though, caution is taken not to raise concerns among Asia-Pacific neighbors that Japan is exceeding the bounds of the U.S.-Japan alliance or seeking regional hegemony. Japan's staunch support for a regional security dialogue has been welcomed as a step in the right direction, although China and North Korea remain suspicious of Japan's intentions.

Given the nature of the Japanese decision-making apparatus and the constraints working upon it, it is clear that Japan's role in peacekeeping (whether military or nonmilitary) will not expand rapidly in the near future. That Japan remains excluded from the key decision-making forum of the UN, and key sections of the IPCL remain frozen certainly represent major obstacles to a greatly expanded role at present. Yet domestic political developments (such as Ozawa's entry into the ruling coalition, the ongoing debate about Japan's international role, changing attitudes on constitutional revision) combined with external forces noted above indicate that incremental changes leading to a more proactive UN-centered diplomacy could provide one possible "path to peace" that might be acceptable both at home and abroad.

Notes

1. Bert Edstrom, *Japan's Evolving Foreign Policy Doctrine* (Basingstoke, Hampshire: Macmillan, 1999), p. 41.
2. Edstrom, 1999, pp. 166, 174; Ueki Yasuhiro, "Japan's UN Diplomacy: Sources of Passivism and Activism," in *Japan's Foreign Policy*, ed. Gerald L. Curtis (New York and London: M. E. Sharpe, 1993), p. 350.
3. See, for example, *Gaiko Forum* 123 (November 1998), special issue devoted to the UN and NGOs.
4. Ronald Dore, *Japan's Internationalism and the UN* (London: Routledge, 1998), p. 112.
5. Alan James, "Peacekeeping in the Post–Cold War Era," *International Journal* 50 (Spring 1995): 247.
6. James, 1995, p. 248.
7. Milton Leitenberg, "The Participation of Japanese Military Forces in United Nations Peacekeeping Operations," *Asian Perspective* 20:1 (1996): 8–13.
8. That is, UN members make available to the Security Council armed forces for the purposes of maintaining international peace and security. See Kenneth B. Pyle, *The Japanese Question* (Washington: AEI Press, 1995), p. 124.
9. Inoguchi Takashi, "Japan's United Nations Peacekeeping and Other Operations," *International Journal* 50 (Spring 1995): 339.
10. See Brian Bridges, *Japan and Korea in the 1990s* (Aldershot, Vermont: Edward Elgar, 1993), p. 57, for the Korean response; Iseri Hirofumi, "Clearing the Mist from the Peace-keeping Debate," *Japan Echo* XIX:3 (1992): 46, for other Asian reactions.
11. Leitenberg, 1996, p. 12.
12. Charles Smith, "Loyalties under Fire," *Far Eastern Economic Review*, 24 January 1991, pp. 10–12.
13. For details of Japan's response to the Gulf crisis and the constraints involved, see Inoguchi Takashi, "Japan's Response to the Gulf Crisis: An Analytic Overview," *Journal of Japanese Studies* 17:2 (1991): 257–73.
14. J. A. A. Stockwin, *Governing Japan* (Oxford: Blackwell, 1999), p. 74.
15. Opinion polls are not consistent, and results tend to differ over time and between pollsters. For example, an Asahi poll conducted in late 1991 found only 33 percent in favor of deployment.
16. The "cow walk" is a tactic used by opposition parties to try and block the passage of legislation in the Diet by shuffling slowly to the ballot box to cast their votes, so that voting can take hours to complete.
17. Leitenberg, 1996, pp. 41–42.
18. Hayashida Kazuhiko, "PKO ruporutaju" [PKO Reportage], *Gaiko forum* 78 (1995): 52–55.
19. For a discussion of issues raised by the Cambodia mission, see Suzuki Yoji, "Kanbojia no kyoshun" [The Lessons of Cambodia], *Sekai* 584 (July 1993): 22–30; Chuma Kiyofuku, "PKO: dainiji ronsen e" [The PKO Toward a Second Round of Debate] *Sekai* 584 (July 1993), p. 38. See also, *Sekai* (March 1993) and various articles in *Japan Echo* XX:3 (1993); 6–22.
20. Defense Agency, *Boei hakusho* [Defense White Paper] (Tokyo: Ministry of Finance Printing Bureau, 1998), pp. 182–84
21. Song Young-sun, "Japanese Peacekeeping Operations: Yesterday, Today and Tomorrow," *Asian Perspective* 20:1 (1996), p. 66.
22. Ueki, 1993, p. 354.
23. Song, 1996, p. 61.
24. Owada Hisashi, "Statement at the Special Committee on Peace-keeping Operations," <http://www.mofa.go.jp/policy/un/pko> (1997).

25. Aurelia George Mulgan, "Japan's Participation in UN Peacekeeping Operations: Radical Departure or Predictable Response?" *Asian Survey* XXXIII:6 (1993): 573.
26. Inoguchi, 1995, p. 335.
27. See Hanns W. Maull, "Germany and Japan: The New Civilian Powers," *Foreign Affairs* 69 (1990): 91–106; Aurelia George Mulgan, "International Peacekeeping and Japan's Role: Catalyst or Cautionary Tale?" *Asian Survey* XXXV:12 (1995): 1,102–117.
28. Stockwin, 1999, p. 170
29. See, for example, Dore, 1998; Ozawa Ichiro, *Blueprint for a New Japan* (Tokyo: Kodansha International, 1994). The process for constitutional revision requires a two-thirds majority in each house, followed by a national referendum.
30. See Stockwin, 1999, p. 171; *Japan Echo* XX:2 (1993), XXIV:3 (1997).
31. See, for example, Ueki, 1993; Reinhard Drifte, *Japan's Foreign Policy in the 1990s* (Basingstoke, Hampshire: Macmillan/St. Antony's Press, 1996).
32. Ministry of Foreign Affairs, *Gaiko seisho* [Diplomatic Blue Book] (Tokyo: Ministry of Finance Printing Bureau, 1998), pp. 35–36. (For the English version of *Diplomatic Blue Book*, see <http://www.mofa.go.jp>.)
33. Mulgan, 1995, p. 1,109.

CHAPTER 8

Ironies in Japanese Defense and Disarmament Policy

Tsuchiyama Jitsuo

A man who has recently lost all the money he had earned, his job, house, children, and wife is probably not interested in buying insurance. If security is defined as "the absence of threats to acquired values,"[1] most Japanese who had nothing to lose but their lives could not afford to think about Japan's military security when the Pacific War ended, like the man just described. But, of course, this is not to say that the Japanese government did not have any security policy at all at that particular moment. It may sound paradoxical, but Japan's surrender itself was a strategic choice to protect 72 million Japanese lives, the homeland, and the political regime, though one may wonder if Japan had any other choice but surrender.[2]

Defense means all measures taken to prepare to resist a (military) attack by every means, especially militarily. They include all policy planning, such as strategy making, weapons procurement and deployment, logistics, defense budgetary making, defense intelligence, economic sanction, etc.[3] Yet, in the case of postwar Japan, its defense policy making and implementation cannot be well understood without realizing two factors—the new Constitution, which renounced war, and the U.S.-Japan alliance that came into effect after the Occupation ended in 1952. These two factors also influenced Japan's disarmament policy. The first sections of this chapter focus on the decisive impacts of these two factors based on the assumption that the first several years immediately after World War II are more important than the last four decades for understanding Japan's defense and disarmament policy. I take note of the contradictory relation between Japan's defense policies based on the U.S.-Japan alliance and the Article 9 of the Constitution. I will then trace the evolutionary process of Japan's defense and disarmament policy, especially focusing on its turning point in 1975–1976. I shall also reexamine the recent redefinition of defense and alliance policies, the new Guidelines for U.S.-Japanese Defense Cooperation in particular, which aim at coping with the post–Cold War world.

The New Constitution and Renunciation of War

Two weeks after the Pacific War ended, Japan was occupied by the Allied forces under the Supreme Commander for the Allied Powers (SCAP) headed by Douglas MacArthur. More than 430,000 troops were stationed in Japan by the end of 1945. Everything was under the control of SCAP—all publications were subject to strict censorship, and telephone conversations of key figures considered dangerous to the U.S. Occupation were even tapped. SCAP built the very foundations of postwar Japan, guided by two principal policy goals—demilitarization and democratization. SCAP's major activities revolved around disarmament of the Japanese war machine, political purge, dissolution of the *zaibatsu*, agricultural reform, and most importantly, drafting and promulgation of the new Constitution, which became effective on 3 May 1947.

With reference to defense policy, one of the most significant clauses in the new Constitution was Article 9, which reads:

> Aspiring sincerely to an international peace based on justice and order, the Japanese people forever renounce war as a sovereign right of the nation and the threat or use of force as means of settling international disputes.
>
> In order to accomplish the aim of the preceding paragraph, land, sea, and air forces, as well as other war potential, will never be maintained. The right of belligerency of the state will not be recognized.

Article 9, which was an amalgam of MacArthur's realism and his peculiar "anti-military" idealism, symbolizes SCAP's demilitarization policy up to the spring of 1947. It represented realism, because it intended to incapacitate Japan's war potential. It might also have carried the implication of punishment for war crimes, in line with the Tokyo War Crimes Trial. But it also demonstrated idealism, because it was drafted after the model of the antiwar Kellogg-Briand Pact of 1928. Article 9 was hastily drafted by the officers in the Government Section, led by Charles Kades. The drafting process of the new Constitution was, according to Prime Minister Yoshida Shigeru, more like "treaty making" with a foreign country than writing a constitution.[4]

Soon, however, the Cold War emerged, and by early 1948 the U.S. government was convinced that the greater threat in East Asia was not Japan but the Soviet Union and the rise of communism in Asia. Under the new circumstances, Washington reappraised the Occupation policy with a view of containment of the Soviet Union. George F. Kennan, the chief of the Policy Planning Staff (PPS) of the Department of State and the author of the "X article," which had just appeared in the July 1947 issue of *Foreign Affairs,* called for "the restoring of a balance of power in Europe and Asia" in PPS13 (6 November 1947).[5]

After his timely visit to Tokyo in February–March 1948, Kennan recommended to a shift in Occupation policy from democratization to industrialization. Contrary to the approach to Japan held by SCAP, Kennan, who laid greater emphasis on economic components as the most significant ingredient in the balance of power, stressed the strategic importance of Japan against the Soviet threat.[6] In retrospect, Kennan's visit to Japan became a turning point in U.S. Occupation policy.

Even while the new Constitution was being drafted in 1946, some Japanese were wondering whether Article 9 renounced all kinds of war, including the war of self-defense. Actually, the original text of MacArthur's "three points" (3 February 1946) prohibited a war "even for preserving its own security." But, this phrase was excluded in the drafts prepared by Government Section (13 February 1946), and it was never restored.

Though Article 9 is certainly not a spontaneous but an imposed norm, at least at the beginning,[7] the first paragraph of Article 9 can possibly be read that it does not prohibit all sorts of war as means of settling international disputes. In expectation that Japan might face conflict in the future, it has been explained that Ashida Hitoshi, a chairman of the lower house subcommittee to review the draft constitution, inserted the phrase "in order to accomplish the aim of the preceding paragraph" at the beginning of the second paragraph to make possible and clear that armaments for self-defense could be permitted. Officially, as Prime Minister Yoshida presented the draft constitution to the Diet for deliberation in 1946, it was told that Article 9 prohibits war even for self-defense purposes, because most wars in the past have been waged in the name of self-defense. Tacitly, however, it was understood among top policy makers, including the Occupation authorities, that the threat or use of force as means of self-defense was still permissible. This interpretation of the Ashida amendment was made public by SCAP when the Korean War broke out.[8]

While Occupation forces in Japan were transferring to Korea, MacArthur issued a de facto order on 8 July 1950 to the Japanese government to create the "National Police Reserve" of 75,000 men. It was ironic that SCAP, which had placed the ban on armed forces, now had to order Japan to rearm. And yet, it did not amend Article 9, probably because Article 9 was a monumental piece of MacArthur's Occupation policy, and because it was practically impossible to amend it even at that time.[9]

At first glance, although most Japanese did not realize what the National Police Reserve implied, they soon came to understand what the U.S. policy makers were intending. The National Police Reserve started to take shape in August 1950, then it was reorganized as the National Safety Force about a year later, and finally it became the Self-Defense Forces (SDF) in 1954. Legally, the SDF does not have any war potential. In reality, however, it does. Ever since, this contradiction has paralyzed Japan's defense policy. The wide gap between principle and reality has forced the government to devote enormous energy to legal interpretations of its defense policy.

For example, the Yoshida government maintained the position that Japan does not have war potential, i.e., the capacity to fight a "modern war." Accordingly, neither the National Police Reserve nor the National Safety Force possessed such capacity. However, this interpretation has fluctuated from time to time. For example, the Hatoyama Ichiro government, which succeeded Yoshida's, took the position that the possession of a "minimum level" of military forces for self-defense is not unconstitutional, therefore, the possession of the capacity to fight a modern war is not necessarily unconstitutional. Kishi Nobusuke, who succeeded Hatoyama, went even further. He told the Diet that even nuclear weapons are not necessarily unconstitutional as long as they are for defensive purposes, although the general public was more skeptical of Japan's nuclear option. Much later, in 1978, the Defense Agency took the position that the permissible level of forces as a means of self-defense is "relatively determined" by such factors as the prevailing international environment and the level of military technology. According to this interpretation, the military forces prohibited by Article 9 would be only such weapons as those used for offense, such as ICBMs or bombers.[10]

An antimilitary culture existed in Japan immediately after the war, and it still remains strong among the public. Accordingly, Japan's defense policy is still heavily restrained by such principles or policies as the three nonnuclear principles (no production, possession, or importation of nuclear weapons), no offensive weapons, no export of weapons or equipment necessary for their manufacture, no SDF combat overseas, a 1-percent ceiling of GNP for defense expenditures, an all-volunteer SDF, and strict civilian control. Compared to any other developed democracy, Japan has pursued a defense policy that tightly limits the threat and use of military forces as an instrument of conflict resolution.

In retrospect, Article 9 has had dual functions: constraint on the remilitarization of the society as well as guideline for defense policy making. Hence Article 9 has been the most significant norm of postwar Japan's foreign policy. Due to the constraints of Article 9, Japan has been very reluctant to resort to the use of force even for self-defense, to exercise the right of collective self-defense, and to bolster defense expenditures. In this sense, it may not be an exaggeration to say that "it [Article 9] became the very essence of the Japanese regime or polity."[11]

Alliance First, Defense Second

The U.S. government initiated studies on an occupation policy for Japan soon after the Pacific War started. Toward the end of the war (1944), the State-War-Navy Coordinating Committee (SWNCC) formulated specific reform plans to be implemented after the war. Once the war ended, it was the United States that sent large forces to Japan. SCAP headquarters were staffed almost exclusively by U.S. military as well as civilian personnel.

Soon, SCAP's demilitarization and democratization policies were implemented, as we have just reviewed. Yet, by the end of 1946, the international political scene had gradually intensified. Some Japanese leaders, like Ashida, were aware of these changes. In the summer of 1947, as foreign minister of the Katayama Tetsu Socialist coalition government, Ashida suggested to U.S. government officials that Japan would be able to permit the United States to maintain its military bases in Japan even after the conclusion of the peace treaty that would end the U.S. Occupation. In return, the United States should guarantee Japan's security in case of an emergency.[12]

Further dramatic changes in international politics took place in the years 1949–1950, including the end of American monopoly on atomic weapons (September 1949) and the victory of the Chinese communists (October 1949). With these new developments, Kennan's influence declined in Washington, and Paul Nitze, who was concerned with the Soviet threat, became the new chief of the PPS. In early 1950, Nitze drafted the document, later to be known as *NSC* (National Security Council)-*68*, which viewed the world as a confrontation between the communist bloc and the West. Despite the fact that *NSC-68* was "a deeply flawed document,"[13] the world it painted was widely accepted by the outbreak of the Korean War in June 1950.

Under these circumstances, in May 1950, Prime Minister Yoshida conveyed a message similar to the Ashida memorandum to the United States through the hands of finance minister Ikeda Hayato and Yoshida's protégé Shirasu Jiro. Ikeda met Joseph M. Dodge (fiscal adviser to SCAP) and expressed the desire for an earliest possible peace treaty.[14]

By the outbreak of the Korean War, the U.S. bases in Japan proved to be a critical factor in securing U.S. strategic interests in East Asia. The United States was well aware of its strategic interest in Japan in fighting a war in Korea, and it knew for a fact that the Japanese also well recognized this.[15] The Japanese government attempted to sell to the United States the right to retain its bases at the highest price possible in order to obtain a U.S. guarantee of security of Japan on Japanese terms.

Balancing and Bandwagoning

The Japanese strategy was clear: Japan wanted a U.S. security guarantee after it regained sovereignty in exchange for its acceptance of U.S. military bases in Japan, which could be used not only to defend Japan, but also for the protection of U.S. strategic interests in East Asia. By concluding a security treaty with the United States, Yoshida expected to obtain U.S. support to enter into such international institutions as the UN and international economic regimes, including the Organization for Economic Cooperation and Development (OECD), General Agreement on Tariffs and Trade (GATT), and the International Monetary Fund (IMF). In return for the U.S. commitment, the United States retained their military bases in Japan.

In this sense, Japan's diplomatic behavior is basically what political scientists call "bandwagoning" (meaning to go with a strong power), although Japan does not necessarily exclude the balancing (go with a weaker side against a stronger power) rationale in its diplomatic moves. The same pattern was observed in Japan's calculations to form and maintain the Anglo-Japanese alliance of 1902–22. On the one hand, when Japan enters into an alliance, what the Japanese decision makers had in mind were the political as well as economic benefits to be obtained from such an alliance, in addition to national safety (the upper right of Figure 8.1). On the other hand, Japan's allies, Great Britain and the United States, in those cases, formed alliances and extended their military assistance to Japan to maintain the power balance in East Asia (Figure 8.1, upper left). In the case of the Axis Pact of 1940 among Italy, Germany, and Japan, Japan's rationale was again bandwagoning for profit, whereas Germany formed it for balancing vis-à-vis the United States. Many of the mid-European powers turned to Nazi Germany, too. But they did it out of fear—bandwagoning for survival (Figure 8.1, bottom right)—not out of calculated gain.[16]

The San Francisco peace treaty and the U.S.-Japan security treaty were concluded in September 1951, while the Korean War was still going on. Thus, the Korean War became a catalyst for making the U.S. security system in East Asia in which Japan was embedded. It was not only a derivative of the U.S. security policy in East Asia; it was also a result of Japan's calculations. Ever since, Japan's reliance on the United States became the first condition of Japan's defense policy. Nishimura Kumao, a head of the Treaty Bureau of the Ministry of Foreign Affairs at the time, characterized the U.S.-Japan security treaty of 1951 *as an interim base-lending agreement.*[17] In fact, during the security treaty negotiations, the treaty was expected to hold good for only 15 years.[18]

Yet, as time went on, Japan became increasingly dependent on the U.S. military forces in Japan. For example, the very first defense policy principle, "Basic Policy for National Defense," taken by the National Defense Council and by the Cabinet in 1957 adopted the principle "to deal with the external aggression on the basis of the Japan-U.S. security arrangements . . . in deterring and repelling such aggression."[19] The Japanese expected at that time that the U.S. commitment to defend Japan and its military bases in Japan would in themselves serve to deter external aggression. In other words, the external security can be assured mainly by the U.S. commitment and U.S. forces. As far as Japan could depend on U.S. forces, the SDF, especially the Ground SDF, was expected to deal with internal threat at least during the 1950s, and less so in the 1960s. Despite the significant changes that have followed since then, that defense policy has remained intact for more than 40 years, and the basic logic and character of the 1951 treaty has remained unchanged.[20]

Cognitive Dissonance in the Yoshida Doctrine

As a result of the catastrophic outcome of the Pacific War, there was a strong rejection of military thinking as well as resentment toward military organizations

Figure 8.1 Four Forms of Alliance Formation

		Patterns of Alliance Behavior	
		Balancing	Bandwagoning
Factors of Alliance Formation	Power	Balance of power (go with a weaker side balancing against a stronger side)	Bandwagoning for profit (go with a dominant power)
	Threat	Balance of threat (go with a weaker threat against a stronger threat)	Bandwagoning for survival (go with a threatening power)

Source: Tsuchiyama Jitsuo, "International Relations Theories of the U.S.-Japanese Alliance: Views from Realism, Liberal-Institutionalism, and Constructivism," *Kokusai seiji* 115 (May 1997): 166.

in Japan. Such rejection and resentment were well institutionalized in Article 9, so that the majority of the public welcomed the "peace constitution."

Although the U.S.-Japan security treaty was not popular at first, the public gradually came to accept it out of necessity. Thus, both Article 9 and the security treaty became the two pillars of postwar Japanese politics; what Japanese political scientists call the "Article 9/security treaty system."[21] Guided by these norms, Japanese foreign policy has come to display three distinctive characteristics: (1) minimal level of military establishment for Japan's defense, (2) military reliance on the United States, and (3) heavy emphasis on economic growth. In popular parlance, this foreign policy orientation is known as the "Yoshida Doctrine," named after Prime Minister Yoshida, though it is doubtful that Yoshida had such a clearly defined strategy during his prime ministership.

Here is the dilemma: if one reads Article 5 of the U.S.-Japan mutual security treaty of 1960, one will quickly find a contradiction between the treaty obligation and Article 9. The U.S.-Japan alliance requires Japan to take collective military action to meet a common danger, whereas the Constitution renounces war and the threat or use of force as a means of settling international disputes. A strict reading of these documents can indicate that it is unconstitutional to have the SDF and to be allied with the United States. There is an apparent contradiction between those two documents. Since then, the Japanese have not been free from this cognitive dissonance problem.

To cope with this cognitive dissonance, however, Japanese leaders have not chosen to rely either on the alliance and the SDF or Article 9. Instead, the pragmatic approach they chose was to maintain a balance between the two. While the Japanese had a "fear of entrapment" (a fear that Japan may be unwillingly involved in U.S. conflict in Asia) during the first two postwar decades, Japan avoided taking collective military action with the United States. The immediate reason for this is that the war in Korea was still going on when the security treaty was concluded and there were crises and conflicts in Asia, such as the Quemoy and Matsu (Taiwan Strait) crises that took place between the United States and China in 1958, and the Vietnam War. The fear of entrapment is the very reason why the Japanese government kept insisting that Japan would not exercise collective self-defense. Accordingly, the Japanese government has held that it is not obligated to defend U.S. territories or U.S. forces deployed outside of Japanese territory. Nor has the Japanese government committed itself to sending the SDF abroad.

Furthermore, the Japanese government inserted the prior consultation clause in the revised security treaty of 1960 in the resolve not to involve Japan in Asian regional conflicts.[22] It was understood that, without Japanese agreement, no more than one Army division, one Navy task force, or one Air Force division of U.S. forces in Japan can be deployed or withdrawn, nor can the United States bring nuclear weapons into Japanese waters or territory. Nor can the United States undertake military combat operations from their bases in Japan. At least until the Sato-Nixon meeting of 1969, the prior consultation clause was considered within the U.S. government as the Japanese "veto" against U.S. requests.[23]

Disarmament Policy and Japan's Dilemma

Since Japan was disarmed after World War II, the Japanese tend to believe that they can best contribute to world disarmament by refraining themselves from the use of force. They generally consider that the risk of a war in which Japan might take part in the future has been greatly reduced by the constitutional renunciation of war.

It was partly due to this belief that signing the Nuclear Non-Proliferation Treaty (NPT) was controversial for Japan. When the NPT was concluded among the United States, the U.S.S.R., and Great Britain in 1968, China had gone nuclear a few years earlier, and the United States was steadily pursuing its Anti-Ballistic Missile (ABM) program. Yet, the most difficult and sensitive diplomatic issue that the Japanese government confronted at the time was the reversion of Okinawa: How would Japan have the United States remove its nuclear weapons (reportedly including 96 Mace-B missiles) deployed in Okinawa? How would the prior-consultation clause be implemented once a nuclear-free Okinawa was returned to Japan without creating any damage to the U.S. security guarantee? In the Sato-Nixon meeting of 1969, the United States came to an agreement with Japan on the withdrawal of nuclear weapons. However, according to secret documents made public only recently, the U.S. government obtained, through back-channel negotiations, the Japanese government's assurance that Japan would meet the U.S. requirement of the reentry of nuclear weapons or transit rights in Okinawa in the case of a great emergency with the prior consultation provision.[24]

Thus Japan's NPT problem was tacitly linked with the Okinawa negotiations. If Japan wanted the return of a nuclear-free Okinawa, it should in theory conclude the NPT. Yet, there were some strong voices against the signing of the NPT, calling for a free hand for Japan, i.e., leaving the nuclear option open for the future. After heated debate Japan did sign the NPT in 1970, but it was six years before the treaty was ratified. At least it must be said that the Miki Takeo administration ratified it not out of strategic calculations, but rather because the administration regarded the nuclearization of Japan as neither politically feasible nor desirable in terms of domestic and international norms.

By the same token, the Japanese believe that Japan's defense policy and its force structure, which are designed for self-defense purposes only, should contribute to the reduction of the security dilemma between Japan and its neighboring states. Limiting defense expenditures to the level of 1 percent of the GNP is also expected to reassure Japan's neighbors that it has no intention of becoming a big military power.

In a similar vein, the Japanese government formulated the three nonnuclear principles in 1967, and they were adopted as a Diet resolution in 1971. The principle of the nonexport of military arms was also introduced in 1967, and updated by the Miki government in 1976. All of these defense policy principles have functioned not only as policy guidelines for Japan's defense policy, but also as a disarmament policy.

The 1975–76 Defense Policy Watershed

During the first quarter of the 1970s, the focus of Japan's defense and disarmament policies diversified as the biggest postwar issue, namely the Okinawa reversion, was resolved by the Sato-Nixon meeting of November 1969. Furthermore, alliance cohesion was reduced by the emerging détente in U.S.-Soviet as well as the Sino-U.S. relations. A series of such events as the U.S.-Japan textile trade dispute, Sino-U.S. rapprochement ("Nixon shocks"), the collapse of the Saigon regime, the Soviet military buildup in the Far East, and U.S. moves to withdraw its ground forces from South Korea together worked to arouse Japan's "fear of abandonment" (that is, that Japan might be abandoned when assistance is urgently needed).

Because of these developments in the international arena, the Miki administration undertook four security policy initiatives: (1) the National Defense Program Outline (*boei taiko*) of 1976, (2) a 1-percent barrier on defense expenditures, (3) the ratification of the Nuclear Non-Proliferation Treaty, which was signed in 1970, although not ratified by the Diet by that time, and (4) the efforts that resulted in the Guidelines on U.S.-Japan Defense Cooperation of 1978. The NDPO was based on the newly formulated "Standard Defense Force" (*kibanteki boeiryoku*) concept, which emphasized the cadre concept rather than readiness. The NDPO stated that "Japan will repel limited and small-scale aggression, in principle, without external assistance,"[25] and called for cooperation with the U.S. forces in dealing with higher levels of aggression. It was somewhat similar to what Nakasone Yasuhiro tried to do when he was director general of the Defense Agency in 1970–71. Nakasone's "autonomous defense" (*jishu boei*) plan, however, failed by the opposition of almost all political forces, notably by the United States. Against nuclear threat, the NDPO stated that Japan would rely on the nuclear deterrent capability of the United States. And yet, it has actually dual functions: self-constraint as appropriate to the age of détente and enhancement of SDF capabilities.

The second policy initiative taken by the Miki administration was to fix defense expenditure levels by limiting defense budgets to 1 percent of the GNP. On the one hand, the 1 percent barrier was a way of preventing waste of money on defense. On the other, however, it was a guarantee that SDF can secure increasing budgets as long as the GNP grows steadily. To fix the defense expenditure level at 1 percent of the GNP without calculating the external threat sounds unrealistic, even dangerous, but it did have substantial impact on Japan's actual defense posture. According to John C. Campbell, the 1-percent rule institutionalized Japan's non-decision-making patterns.[26] And yet, it is ironic that a such non-decision-making pattern has provided a better defense environment than before.

The ratification of the NPT reflected the political preference of Prime Minister Miki Takeo, who was more modest than other leaders in the Liberal Democratic Party. Miki pushed the ratification to strengthen the NPT regime and to remove American disbelief caused by Japan's long delay in ratifying the treaty.

The Guidelines for U.S.-Japan Defense Cooperation were initiated by Sakata

Michita, director general of the Defense Agency during the Miki administration. The guidelines aimed at ensuring coordinated action in military operation, intelligence, and logistics between the SDF and U.S. forces in Japan in a case of a crisis in the Japan area. This was the policy to which Japan had avoided making a explicit commitment, while the United States had expected it to be forthcoming for many years. Japan made the commitment to coordinated joint action at that time, partly because its fear of being allied to the United States shifted from the fear of entrapment to the fear of abandonment during the mid-1970s. Therefore, it was logical that the Guidelines of 1978 emphasized situations under which Japan might be attacked—the so-called Article 5 situation. The four policy initiatives taken by the Miki administration therefore constituted a watershed of the postwar Japan's defense policy.[27] In 1978, the Japanese government also committed itself to increasing financial support for the U.S. military presence in Japan—Japan's host nation support, and it had grown rapidly.[28]

The New Cold War and Japan's Military Buildup

The "new Cold War," caused by such incidents as the Soviet invasion of Afghanistan, accelerated Japan's military buildup and encouraged Japan's further defense commitments. For example, the Suzuki Zenko government committed itself to extend protection of sea-lanes of communication (SLOC) to 1,000 miles from Japan's main islands. Then, the Nakasone administration decided to adopt the Mid-Term Defense Program in 1985, which contained extensive weapons procurement programs. The Nakasone government decided to make an exception to Japan's ban on arms exports and to permit the transfer to the United States of military technology that could be used to develop the Strategic Defense Initiatives (SDI) project being pursued by the Reagan administration. Nakasone's decision to remove the Diet's resolution limiting defense budgets to 1 percent of GNP also marked a symbolic gesture that his administration moved one step closer to U.S. defense policy priority.

Changes in Japan's defense policy between 1975 and 1985 reflected Japan's perception of declining U.S. strength, growing Soviet military buildup in the Far East, and its own fear of abandonment. Despite Japan's extensive military buildup and enhanced cooperation with the U.S. government during that time, its fear of abandonment—the cognitive dissonance problem mentioned earlier—had not been removed; the secondary roles and missions of the SDF had not changed much either. Again, despite removal of the limit of 1 percent of the GNP for the defense budget, actual defense outlays remained basically unchanged in percentage terms. In absolute terms, however, Japan's military expenditures grew more rapidly than any other developed country in the 1980s.

The End of the Cold War and Japan Problem

Japan's defense and disarmament policies faced severe challenges between the late 1980s and the early 1990s. There were several reasons, but a fundamental problem was that the Western democracies lost their common military threat, the Soviet Union. Contrary to the U.S. perception of the reduced Soviet threat resulting from Mikhail Gorbachev's "preemptive concessions," there had been growing consensus in the United States that it was losing its competitiveness vis-à-vis Japan. The Japanese "bubble" economy came to be perceived as a new threat to the Western democracies, especially for the United States. Such American observers as Samuel P. Huntington argued that "the United States is obsessed with Japan with the same reasons that it was obsessed with the Soviet Union."[29] Huntington even predicted an economic Cold War between the United States and Japan.[30] James Fallows went even further to say that Japan should be "contained" just like the West had contained the Soviet Union during the past four decades. As the Cold War ended, American perception of the economic disadvantages in its relations with Japan came to far outweigh the political advantages.

At the same time, Japan's FSX (fighter support-experiment) aircraft project became the most controversial defense issue in U.S.-Japan relations. Under heavy U.S. pressure, the Japanese government changed its favored option of wholly domestic development of FSX to the license manufacturing of modified F-16s with Japan's acceptance to guarantee maximum level of U.S. participation, but without obtaining U.S. assurances to provide "source code" guidance software.

Then, the Gulf crisis in 1990–91 widened the gap further between the two. Japanese were puzzled by the critical U.S. reaction to Japanese policy toward the Gulf. Japanese government sent minesweepers to the Gulf in 1991 besides its contribution of US$13 billion to the United States supporting the activities of multilateral forces. These acts were unprecedented and significant steps toward Japan's more active defense policy. Again, however, Japan's behavior during the crisis was severely criticized. The U.S.-Japan friction indicated that the "Article 9/security treaty system" of postwar Japan faced the most critical test since its inception.

With the sudden collapse of the Soviet Union toward the end of 1991, Japan's defense policy lost one of its key rationales for the SDF and the U.S. forces in Japan. Japan's defense policy-making organizations were faced with the most fragile conditions in the early 1990s. All of the recent developments—the end of the Cold War, the collapse of the Soviet Union, the FSX controversy, the Japanese bubble economy, and the Gulf Crisis—were connected to each other, and they constituted the "Japan problem" in the United States. Japan's fear of abandonment reached a critical point. That was one of the very reasons why the Hosokawa Morihiro government, which ended the 38 years of unbroken Liberal Democratic Party rule, commissioned the Defense Problem Advisory Board (Boei Mondai Kondankai) to draw up a report on Japan's new defense policy. The board's report, which came out in August 1994, cleared the way for the government to adopt a new NDPO, which made possible for Japan to take crisis management measures *outside* Japan, and to strengthen the security relations with the United States.

On the U.S. side, there were at least three factors that urged Washington to cope with the U.S.-Japan problem between 1993 and 1995. First, the draft report of the Defense Problem Advisory Board shocked the U.S. defense policy makers, because it placed priority on a multilateral security framework over the

U.S.-Japan alliance. They were concerned about whether an "independent Japan" was emerging. Second, dealing with the crisis caused by North Korea's nuclear development in 1993–1994, they came to realize that Japan might not be able to take meaningful joint action even if a war broke out on the Korean Peninsula—the Guidelines of 1978 had to be updated. Third, a tragic incident in which three U.S. marines raped a schoolgirl in Okinawa took place in September 1995, setting off a strong antibase movement there. Prompt and appropriate action was needed in Washington. One outcome was the U.S.-Japan Joint Declaration on Security issued by Prime Minister Hashimoto Ryutaro and President Bill Clinton in April 1996, in which they reaffirmed the security commitments of the two governments.

Japan's Defense Policy Beyond the Cold War

As we have seen, Japan's defense and disarmament policy after World War II has been intrinsically based on the "Article 9/security treaty system." Yet, with the ending of the Cold War system, can we expect the very foundation of Japan's security policy to erode? As a common military threat—the Soviet Union—was lost, is the principal purpose of the Western alliances, especially in the case of the U.S.-Japan alliance, fading away? Or, are they transforming themselves from traditional military alliances aimed at preparation for collective defense to international institutions for coping with such global security issues as peacekeeping and disaster relief? If the latter is the case, should Japan send the SDF abroad to participate in those military operations conducted, for example, by the UN? Or, should Japan strengthen military cooperation with the United States, which the new Guidelines for U.S.-Japanese Defense Cooperation (1997) are trying to make possible; or should Japan move to form a multilateral security framework replacing the U.S.-Japan alliance?

It may be too early to give definitive answers to these questions. To be brief, despite the dramatic changes that took place both in Japan and the global political scene in the 1990s, the "Article 9/security treaty system" remains intact. In order to deviate from the current defense policy line, the prevailing norms and institutions must perish and be replaced by others. However, such a wholesale revision of Japan's domestic norms are not taking place at this point, though it may occur in the wake of a "big bang," such as an unexpected U.S. decision to terminate the U.S.-Japan alliance, for example. So far, Japan's defense policy based on two significant norms, the peace constitution and the U.S.-Japan security treaty, has outlived the Cold War.

Since the principal rationale of Japan's diplomatic behavior is basically bandwagoning, the demise of the Soviet Union led to neither automatic termination of the alliance relation with the United States nor Japan's autonomous defense posture. However, if the balance of interest between Japan and the United States became unfavorable to either party, there is a possibility of alliance disunity, or ultimately, termination.

Two ongoing defense policy initiatives could invite trouble, if the governments fail to manage the defense and alliance policies properly. One of those defense policy initiatives is the renewed Guidelines for U.S.-Japanese Defense Cooperation, for which the Diet passed the Law Concerning Measures to Ensure the Peace and Security of Japan in Situations in Areas Surrounding Japan in May 1999.[31] It would enable the SDF to extend rear-area support and engage in search-and-rescue operations with U.S. forces in "situations in areas surrounding Japan." U.S. forces would be able to access Japanese civilian airfields and ports in such situations. The U.S. government has regarded the new guidelines as long overdue, while Japanese public has considered them a symbols of overcommitment. Japan's new role, expected to be taken under the new guidelines, goes beyond the stipulations of Article 6 of the security treaty, just as NATO is expanding its area of responsibility beyond NATO members' territories. Similar to the situation in which Russia was alarmed by NATO's adoption of the New Strategic Concept during the 1999 Kosovo crisis, Japan's moves may trigger the anger of its neighbors, especially China. If Sino-U.S. relations were to deteriorate further in the years to come, there may be such an outcome.

Two potential problems of the new guidelines are worth mentioning here. First is the problem of definition of situations in areas surrounding Japan. When the Diet passed the guidelines bill, the Japanese government presented six possible scenarios; two of them are cases in which "internal disturbances" or "civil war" take place in certain countries. But, it will be very sensitive and difficult to define the conditions under which both Japan and the United States are expected to take action in these cases. Second, when the review of the guidelines began in 1993 and 1994, Tokyo and Washington were not particularly concerned about China but about North Korea. Since the Hashimoto-Clinton meeting was held just after the March 1996 Taiwan "missile" crisis, however, the focus of the new guidelines appears to have, perhaps unintentionally, shifted from North Korea to China. In fact, the summit meeting was originally scheduled for November 1995, but Clinton canceled the meeting for domestic reasons.

Ultimately, the alliance should redefine the missions and roles that are satisfactory not only to Japan and the United States but also to Japan's neighbors. In this regard, the new guidelines would become the litmus test for crisis management, whether the two governments can control a future crisis. In the meantime, the current defense and alliance policy will continue for at least another decade because all parties will feel insecure without a U.S. military presence in Asia. In short, the U.S.-Japan alliance would function as reassurance in East Asia, whereas Japan's defense and disarmament policy will continue to play a subordinate role in that system.[32]

The second policy initiative is the Theater Missile Defense (TMD) program to which the Japanese government decided to become a joint research participant with the United States. This was shortly after North Korea fired a missile known as Taepodong 1 over Japan in August 1998. Japan's participation in joint research is by no means an indication that Japan will deploy TMD in Japan, however. During the Nakasone administration, Japan had similar problems with regard to the SDI project. Although Nakasone's decision was more like a diplomatic measure than serious defense planning, Japan's decision to participate in the TMD program appears to be more than just a diplomatic measure. Notwithstanding the government's decision, the public was ambivalent for the following reasons. First, Japanese remain unconvinced of TMD's feasibility and desirability. Second, though both the U.S. and Japanese governments are insistent that TMD is a defensive weapon system, some of Japan's neighbors, including China, regard it as an offensive system, taking the renewed defense guidelines and even U.S. action in Kosovo into consideration. If this situation were exacerbated by the future deployment of TMD in Japan, a security dilemma spiral could emerge in East Asia.

Despite much debate over whether the SDF should participate in UN-sponsored conflict resolution outside Japan, Japan has not arrived at a consensus on what it should do. In a similar vein, it has not reached a consensus over whether a multilateral security framework, such as Asian version of Organization for Security and Cooperation in Europe, is desirable and workable. The majority of Japanese people still consider the multilateral framework as an academic argument because security interests are shared unevenly among Asian powers and because there appears to be no such common identity as "we" in East Asia. Due in part to this, multilateral security institutions have not functioned well in the region. For most Japanese, defense policy based on the U.S.-Japan alliance will continue to be considered as a better option than any other alternative.[33]

Conclusion

Since policies are formulated out of hope, fear, crude calculation (and miscalculation), misperception, psychological and organizational inertia, and accidental events, there are a number of ironies and contradictions in the ongoing policies. Yet, we are often faced with difficulties in straightening them out. Japan's defense policy is such an example, full of ironies and contradictions. Accordingly, Japanese have experienced cognitive dissonance problems. Maintaining a delicate balance between Article 9 of the Constitution and the U.S.-Japan alliance, for example, is virtually political acrobatics.

As the Cold War ended, Japanese are forced to ask themselves once again what defense and disarmament can mean for their country. The meaning of alliance will also be redefined in this context. The effort to redefine the defense policy was not completed when the Diet passed the Guidelines bill, it has just begun. To redefine them, however, Japanese are not free from where they came from and where they stand today. Any forecast of Japan's defense and disarmament policies should be based on assumptions about the past as well as the present. How far Japan can go beyond its current defense policy depends upon its capability to link the past and its future. To move the nation forward, Japanese need not only a correct understanding of their power and interests but also those of their identity, norms, and culture. Going back to the first postwar years of Japan's defense policy making is necessary for understanding where it comes from. Only from there could we go back to the future.

Notes

1. Arnold Wolfers, *Discord and Collaboration* (Baltimore: The Johns Hopkins University Press, 1962), p. 150.
2. See, for example, Robert J. C. Butow, *Japan's Decision to Surrender* (Stanford: Stanford University Press, 1954).
3. Cathal J. Nolan, ed., *The Longman Guide to World Affairs* (London: Longman, 1995), p. 87.
4. Shigeru Yoshida, *Kaiso junen* [Reminiscences of Ten Years], vol. 2 (Tokyo: Shinchosha, 1957), p. 30.
5. John L. Gaddis, "The Strategy of Containment," in *Containment*, eds. Thomas H. Etzold and John L. Gaddis (NY: Columbia University Press, 1978), p. 27.
6. Kennan wrote in NSC 49 (June 1949) that:

    If the United States influence predominates Japan can be expected, with planned initial United States assistance, at least to protect herself and, provided logistic necessities can be made available to her, to contribute importantly to military operations against the Soviet in Asia, thus forcing the USSR to fight on the Asiatic front as well as elsewhere. (Quoted in Etzold and Gaddis 1978, p. 231.)

7. The distinction between "spontaneous" and "imposed" norms are borrowed from Oran Young's differentiation of regimes. See, Oran R. Young, *International Cooperation* (Ithaca: Cornell University Press, 1989), chapter 4. See also, Thomas Berger, "Norms, Identity, and National Security in Germany and Japan," in *Culture and National Security*, ed. Peter J. Katzenstein (NY: Columbia University Press, 1997), pp. 317–56.
8. According to recent studies, Ashida made an amendment without realizing that his amendment could make such interpretation possible. For example, see Koseki Shoichi, *Shin kenpo no tanjo* [The Birth of the New Constitution] (Tokyo: Chuo Koron Sha, 1985), especially chapter 9. See also, Theodore McNelly, *Politics and Government in Japan*, 2nd ed. (NY: Houghton Mifflin, 1972), pp. 241, 32–36.
9. Amendment procedure requires the concurring votes of two-thirds or more of all members of both houses, and then necessitates the voter's ratification that requires the affirmative vote of a majority of the votes cast.
10. Kyoiku-sha, ed., *Boeicho* [The Defense Agency] (Tokyo: Kyoikusha, 1979), pp. 93–94.
11. Tetsuya Kataoka, *Waiting for a Pearl Harbor: Japan Debates Defense* (Stanford: Hoover Institution Press, 1980), p. 5.
12. Nishimura Kumao, *Sanfuranshisuko Heiwa Joyaku* [The San Francisco Peace Treaty] (Tokyo: Kajima Kenkyujo Shuppankai, 1971), pp. 19–52. See also, Martin E. Weinstein, *Japan's Postwar Defense Policy* (NY: Columbia University Press, 1969).

    Ashida, who assumed power after Katayama in March 1948, however, lost in October after being involved in the so-called Showa Electric Industry Scandal. Then, Yoshida came back to power in October 1948, and he substantially succeeded to Ashida's foreign policy initiatives toward the United States.

13. John L. Gaddis, *Strategies of Containment* (Oxford: Oxford University Press, 1982), p. 106.
14. There Ikeda said:

    As such a treaty probably would require the maintenance of U.S. forces to secure the treaty terms and for other purposes, if the U.S. Government hesitates to stipulate certain terms, the Japanese Government will try to find way to offer them. (Quoted in Miyazawa Kiichi, *Tokyo-Washinton no mitsudan* [The Secret Talks between Tokyo and Washington] (Tokyo: Jitsugyo no Nihon Sha, 1956), pp. 44–46.)

15. For example, Marshall Green of the State Department wrote in his secret memorandum (in August 1950) that "Japanese leaders must be fully aware of this fact," and it is logical for them "to intimate that the price for these bases in Japan is greater than the United States had perhaps reckoned." United States Department of State, *Foreign Relations of the United States, 1950, VI, East Asia and the Pacific* (Washington, DC: U.S. Government Printing Office, 1976), p. 1264.
16. On bandwagoning, see, for example, Randall L. Scheweller, "Bandwagoning for Profit: Bringing the Revisionist State Back In," *International Security* 19:1 (1994): 72–107.

17. Nishimura Kumao, *Kaitei shinban, Anzenhosho joyaku-ron* [Revised Edition, On the Security Treaty] (Tokyo: Jiji Press, 1967), p. 59.
18. Martin E. Weinstein, "Strategic Thought and the U.S.-Japan Alliance," in *Forecast for Japan: Security in the 1970s,* ed. James William Morley (Princeton: Princeton University Press, 1972), pp. 35–84.
19. See, for example, Japan Defense Agency, *Defense of Japan: Response to a New Era* (1996), p. 259.
20. See, for example, Nishimura, 1967.
21. Sakai Tetsuya, "Kyujo-Anpotaisei no shuen" [The End of the Article 9/Security Treaty System], *Kokusai mondai* (March 1993), 32–45.
22. The provision for prior consultation as contained in the exchange of notes reads:

    > Major changes in the deployment into Japan of United States armed forces, major changes in their equipment, and the use of facilities and areas in Japan as bases for military combat operations to be undertaken from Japan other than those conducted under Article 6 of the said Treaty, shall be the subject of prior consultation with the Government of Japan.

23. John K. Emmerson, "Japan, Eye on 1970," *Foreign Affairs* 47:2 (January 1967): 348–62.
24. Wakaizumi Kei, *Tasaku nakarishi o shinzemu to hossu* [I Want to Believe We Had No Alternatives] (Tokyo: Bungei Shunju, 1994), p. 447.
25. Japan Defense Agency, 1996, p. 272.
26. John C. Campbell, "Hikettei no Nihon no boei seisaku" [Non-Decision making in Japan's Defense Policy], in *Sekai seiji no naka no Nihon seiji* [Japanese Politics in World Politics], eds. Tomita Nobuo and Sone Yasunori (Tokyo: Yuhikaku, 1983), pp. 71–100.
27. On the Miki administration's defense policy, see Otake Hideo, *Nihon no boei to kokunai seiji* [Japan's Defense Policy and Domestic Politics] (Tokyo: San-ichi Shobo, 1983). See also, John E. Endicott, "The Defense Policy of Japan," in *The Defence Policies of Nations,* eds. Douglas J. Murray and Paul R. Viotti (Baltimore: The Johns Hopkins Press, 1982), pp. 446–67.
28. Japan's host nation support, at present, totals over $5 billion annually.
29. Samuel P. Huntington, "America's Changing Strategic Interests," *Survival* 33:1 (January–February 1991): 3–17, 8.
30. Huntington, 1991, p. 10.
31. Japan Defense Agency, *Defense of Japan* (1999), pp. 135–142.
32. See Jitsuo Tsuchiyama, "The End of the Alliance?: Dilemmas in the U.S.-Japan Relations," in *United States-Japan Relations and International Institutions after the Cold War,* eds. Peter Gourevitch et al. (San Diego: University of California, 1995), pp. 3–35.
33. According to the recent opinion poll taken by the government, 62.2 percent of the public supports the current defense system based on the U.S.-Japan security treaty, whereas 7.1 percent supports the autonomous defense system, which does not have U.S. assistance to protect Japan. *Boei handobukku* [Defense Handbook] (Tokyo: Asagumo Shimbun, 1999), p. 708.

CHAPTER 9

Official Development Assistance (ODA) as a Japanese Foreign Policy Tool

Fukushima Akiko

Over the past five decades, Japan initially received from and subsequently provided economic assistance to the developing world. The amount of Japanese aid over the years has surged commensurate with the recovery and growth of the Japanese economy, making Japan the top world donor in the 1990s. According to the latest statistics, in 1997, it disbursed bilateral aid totaling ¥793 billion ($6.55 billion), down 11.2 percent from the previous year. Conversely, disbursements of Japanese aid through multilateral institutions totaled ¥340 billion ($2.81 billion). The Japanese government has not provided aid for charity reasons but with a purpose, most notably as a foreign policy tool. While various explanations of this practice have been made by Japanese and non-Japanese scholars, the reasoning behind it has also evolved over time. Domestically, the government has to explain to its taxpayers the reason Japan provides economic assistance to other countries and these explanations have also evolved. With the protracted economic slump and intensifying fiscal crisis, this job is tougher than ever. Nonetheless, the public has shown fairly strong support for official development assistance (ODA) disbursements. Meanwhile, notwithstanding the large sums of aid offered by Japan, from time to time it has also sparked criticism from both aid recipients and other quarters.

This chapter looks at how Japan's engagement in economic assistance, particularly ODA, has evolved over the years in quality and quantity to make Japan the top world donor in the 1990s. It will also scrutinize how the rationale behind ODA has shifted as Japan reconstructed and developed its economy and as the Cold War ended. It concludes by querying the problems, need for reform, and future challenges of Japanese ODA, particularly at a time when Japan can no longer treat the quantitative expansion path it did in the past due to budget retrenchment. How, furthermore, does Japan intend to use its ODA as foreign policy tool in the coming millennium?

Evolution of Japanese ODA

How did the Japanese government explain its aid to the public? What did it hope to achieve by providing economic assistance to other countries? How have such rationales changed over time?[1]

What is ODA?

Of various forms of economic assistance provided to developing countries, ODA is that made by governments with concessionary elements in terms of lower interest rates and longer repayment periods than in the case of loans; it contains the so-called "grant element." The grant element is 100 percent in the case of grant aid, while it is zero percent in the case of a loan with a commercial interest rate. In between, the grant element is calculated by the margin of concessionality compared to commercial loan conditions. In any case, aid cannot be labeled ODA unless the grant element is over 25 percent. Government aid that is outside the scope of ODA is called "other official flows" (OOF).

In Japan, ODA is provided through the Japan International Cooperation Agency (JICA) and the Overseas Economic Cooperation Fund (OECF), while OOF goes through the Export-Import (EXIM) Bank of Japan. (In April 1999, the Japan Export-Import Bank, JEXIM, and the OECF were merged to form the Japan Bank for International Cooperation. ODA accounts, formerly OECF operations, and non-ODA accounts, formerly JEXIM operations, are kept separate.) There are two types of ODA, namely technical cooperation and financial assistance. In technical cooperation, Japan receives trainees, dispatches experts, provides equipment, conducts feasibility studies, and dispatches Youth Cooperation Units. In terms of financial assistance, Japan provides both grant aid that does not require repayment and yen loans that require repayment under concessionary conditions. Grant aid is provided from tax revenues, while ODA loans or yen loans are provided from the Fiscal Investment and Loan Program (FILP), using monies from postal savings and pension funds.

In addition to bilateral ODA, Japan also provides multilateral aid through multilateral development agencies such as the United Nations Development Program (UNDP). Japan also provides contributions and subscriptions to international organizations such as the United Nations, the World Bank, and the Asia Development Bank, which are categorized as multilateral grants. (See Table 9.1)

Japan as a Recipient

Japan's first involvement with economic assistance was as recipient. Faced with a nation reduced to ashes by the end of World War II, the first and foremost mission of the Japanese government was to reconstruct. From 1945 to 1951, Japan received assistance under the Government and Relief in Occupied Areas (GARIOA) and Economic Rehabilitation in Occupied Areas (EROA) plans through which the United States funneled funds for postwar reconstruction. The Japanese government used the GARIOA-EROA funds to purchase food, pharmaceuticals, and other necessities for its people as well as to procure raw materials for industry. From 1946 to 1951, Japan received $2 billion worth of credits from the EROA fund.

Table 9.1 Japan's ODA in 1996 (by type)

		$ million		\100 million		Share of total (%)	
Type of Aid	Aid provided	Actual	1995/96 Growth rate (%)	Actual	1995/96 Growth rate (%)	ODA total	Bilateral
Grant aid		2,395.50	-19.4	2,606.79	-6.8	24.9	28.7
	(excluding aid to Part II)	2,311.88	-19.6	2,515.79	-7.0	24.5	28.2
Technical cooperation		3,180.92	-8.1	3,461.48	6.3	33.1	38.1
	(excluding aid to Part II)	3,125.84	-8.7	3,401.54	5.7	33.1	38.1
Total grants		5,576.42	-13.3	6,068.27	0.3	58.0	66.7
	(excluding aid to Part II)	5,437.72	-13.7	5,917.33	-0.1	57.6	66.3
Government loans		2779.84	-32.6	3,025.02	-22.0	28.9	33.3
	(excluding aid to Part II)	2,769.46	-32.8	3,013.73	-22.2	29.3	33.7
Bilateral ODA total		8,356.26	-20.8	9,093.29	-8.4	87.0	100.0
	(excluding aid to Part II)	8,207.19	-21.2	8,931.06	-8.9	86.9	100.0
Contributions and subscriptions to international organizations		1,251.83	-70.0	1,362.24	-65.3	13.0	
	(excluding contributions to EBRD)	1,232.04	-69.7	1,340.71	-65.0	13.1	
ODA total (including Eastern Europe and EBRD)		9,608.10	-34.8	10,455.53	-24.5	100.0	
	(excluding aid to Part II)	9,439.23	-34.9	10,271.77	-24.6	100.0	
Nominal GNP preliminary estimates ($Λbillion)		4,647.78	-10.2	505,771.00	3.9		
Percentage of GNP (%)							
	(including Part II and EBRD)	0.21		0.21			
	(excluding Part II and EBRD)	0.20		0.20			

Note 1: As of 1996, the following countries had graduated from ODA recipient status: The Bahamas, Brunei, Kuwait Qater, Singapore, and The United Arab Emirates.
Note 2: Part II: Aid to Countries and Territories in Transition.
Note 3: DAC exchange rate for 1996: $1=\108.82 (down\14.75 yen from 1995).
Note 4: Totals do not add up exactly because of rounding.
EBRD: European Bank for Reconstruction and Development.

Furthermore, from 1953 (when the Tonegawa Dam was built) to 1966 (when the Tomei Expressway opened), Japan received funding in the amount of $880 million from the World Bank for major projects, mainly infrastructure projects such as the construction of the No. 4 Kurobe Dam for hydroelectric power generation, the Tokaido Shinkansen (superexpress bullet train line), and the Tomei/Hanshin expressways linking industrial regions in Tokyo, Nagoya, and Kobe. Japanese postwar reconstruction owed much to assistance from abroad. Japan completed its repayment of these funds to the World Bank in 1990.

ODA as War Reparations

While still a recipient of foreign aid itself, Japan began providing development assistance in the form of war reparations to other countries in Asia. Pursuant to the San Francisco peace treaty of 1951, Japan was required to pay war reparations to 12 countries in East Asia to compensate for damages inflicted on them during

ODA as a Japanese Foreign Policy Tool   155

World War II, a condition to be met before it could rejoin the international community. In November 1954, Prime Minister Yoshida Shigeru signed the first agreement on reparations and economic cooperation with Burma. Subsequently, Japan entered into reparations agreements with the Philippines in 1956, Indonesia in 1958, and quasi-reparations (grants in lieu of formal reparation commitments) with Laos and Cambodia in 1959. Until Japan completed its payment of reparations to the Philippines in July 1976, reparations to East Asian countries constituted the central aspect of its economic cooperation overseas.

This background of Japanese aid has had a strong bearing on subsequent developments. The destinations of Japanese ODA and the focus on infrastructure development are symbolic. Asia has consistently been the top destination of ODA even in the 1990s, although the share has gradually declined in the 1990s. In 1970, Asia received the remarkable share of 98 percent of all Japanese ODA. In 1996, geographical distribution was still skewed toward Asia, but the percentage of other regions such as Africa and Latin America is growing, as shown in Figure 9.1.

Figure 9.1 Trend in Japan's Bilateral ODA (by region)

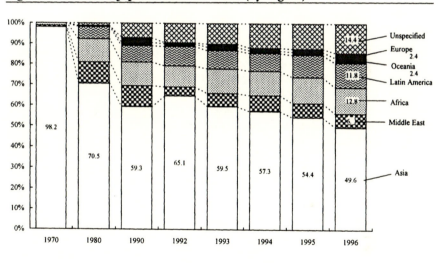

Note: Disbursements to Europe in and after 1990 include those extended to Eastern Europe.

From Reparations to Export Promotion

Japan's first foreign aid[2] to developing countries was provided in the form of multilateral aid through its participation in the Colombo Plan for Cooperative Economic and Social Development in Asia and the Pacific in October 1954.

The Colombo Plan was originally launched in 1950 in Colombo, Ceylon (now Sri Lanka) in order to facilitate economic and technical cooperation among the member countries of the British Commonwealth of Nations. Subsequently the recipient areas of this aid program were expanded. In 1955, Japan provided US$100,000 for technical cooperation under the Colombo Plan. Since then, technical cooperation has remained an important element of Japanese ODA.

In 1958, Prime Minister Kishi Nobusuke signed Japan's first agreement to give yen loans to India, again in the form of multilateral aid, through the World Bank Consortium for India. Yen loans also began playing an important role in Japanese ODA, but more as a form of bilateral aid.

Providing aid in the late 1950s was a hard political decision to make, since Japan could not yet satisfy its own financial needs. The rationale used during this time period was that war compensation could be based not only on reparations agreements but also take the form of yen loans and technical cooperation. In February 1957, Prime Minister Kishi elaborated upon the Japanese philosophy of foreign aid in his foreign policy speech as follows, "First of all, Japan's aid to Asian countries which are in the midst of their respective nation building will enhance the national welfare of those countries. Secondly, reparation and economic cooperation towards these countries will eventually secure a new export market for Japanese industries and will ultimately contribute to the Japanese economy."[3] Thus, giving aid was explained as war compensation, repaying indebtedness through postwar reconstruction and export promotion.

Japan Becomes Member of DAC

In 1960, the Organization for European Economic Cooperation (OEEC) established the Development Assistance Group (DAG) as an ad hoc meeting in order to coordinate aid giving by donor countries. In 1961, the OEEC became the Organization for Economic Cooperation and Development (OECD), and the DAG was reconstituted as a standing organ as the Development Assistance Committee (DAC). It was the DAC, in fact, that introduced the concept of official development assistance (ODA). Although not yet a member of the OECD, Japan joined the DAC as a founding member along with Belgium, Canada, France, West Germany, Italy, the Netherlands, Portugal, the United Kingdom, and the United States. Behind Japan's membership in the DAC—despite the fact that Japan was not a member of the parent body—was said to be the U.S. motive of encouraging Japan to provide more aid to Asian nations. The United States concentrated on persuading West Germany and Japan to recognize special obligations to provide aid as former recipients of aid by Allied Nations and as nations that spent little on defense, in other words, as civilian powers.[4] For Japan's part, there was a strong wish to be a member of the club of advanced nations, the OECD, and membership to the DAC was perceived as important in promoting Japan's membership in the OECD even if, as a result, its aid policies would come under the scrutiny of DAC. Alan Rix argues that "Japan joined the DAC originally to give herself a foot-hold in the group of more powerful states and gain greater influence in both world and regional affairs where it had both commercial and political interests."[5] Whether Japan's DAC membership helped or not, three years later Japan was accepted into the OECD. Members accepted Japan not only to encourage its aid but also to encourage its trade liberalization pursuant to the codes and rules of the OECD, which Japan did. Through the DAC and the OECD, Japan over the years aligned its aid policies with the other industrialized countries.

At the DAC meeting in London in March 1961, the United States asked for the group's target for aid to be set at one percent of the GNP. Japan accepted this target at the Second United Nations Conference on Trade and Development (UNCTAD) in 1968. In order to live up to its commitment, Japan began to provide general grant aid from 1969 in addition to its yen loans and technical assistance. Japanese grant aid started when Japan took part in realizing grant food aid for developing countries prepared by the signatories of the GATT Kennedy Round negotiations in 1968. The scheme was expanded to nonfood areas from the following year. However, Japanese aid then was far below one percent of the GNP and is still significantly lower than one percent of the GNP today. In fact, Japan disbursed an ODA sum equivalent to 0.22 percent of the GNP in 1997, thus ranking 19th out of 21 DAC member countries. As a matter of fact, the ratio was hovering at around 0.3 percent as shown in Figure 9.2. In fact, the only countries that have reached a level close to 1 percent are Norway, Denmark, and Sweden, whose total GNP is smaller than other donors. (See Figure 9.3.) In any event, Japan must be aware of the fact that its ODA, though the largest in the world in absolute amount, is still far below the target of 1 percent of the GNP.

Figure 9.2 Trend of Japan's ODA/GNP Ratio (Excluding Eastern Europe)

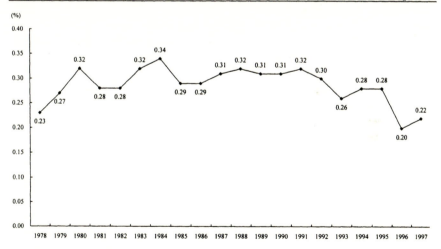

Figure 9.3 ODA/GNP Ratios of DAC Member Countries (1996) (Excluding Eastern Europe)

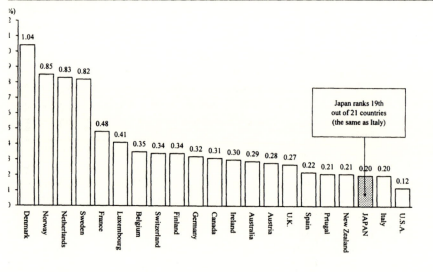

Source: 1997 DAC Press Release

The DAC has influenced Japanese ODA policy making since its inception. Japan has aspired to be a well-performing donor and has striven to align its aid policy as much as possible to the DAC agreed rules and norms.

From Export Promotion to Interdependence Rationale

Japan continued to expand its ODA and in 1964, the amount totaled US$100 million. In 1976, Japan became the second largest donor in OECD's DAC.

In the 1960s and 1970s, Japanese ODA grew not only in quantity but also in quality. These were also decades when Japan came under severe criticism as it achieved rapid economic growth under the protective umbrella of the security provided by the U.S.-Japan security treaty and the free trade policies introduced by the Bretton Woods system. Criticisms about Japanese ODA came from peer donors. It was criticized as being too commercial and highly tied, aimed directly at export promotion of Japanese goods. Tied aid means that recipients are limited to procuring equipment and services from companies of the donor nation, and is often used by donors who are not very competitive in the international market. Japan's export promotion rationale backfired overseas as Japan's aid was seen as being too commercially oriented. In response to this criticism, Japan started to untie its ODA, enabling recipients to use suppliers and contractors of any nationality instead of only Japanese. Japan revised the legislation of the OECF and the Export-Import Bank of Japan to allow these organizations to make untied loans in 1972. Pursuant to the DAC agreement of June 1974, all loan agreements concluded after 1 January 1976 by Japan were in principle LDC-untied. There are two types of untied assistance, namely general untied, which does not have restrictions on where recipients procure equipment and services, and LDC-untied, which limits procurement sources to development countries and the donor, i.e., if the source of procurement is an advanced country, it must be the donor.

The export promotion rationale for Japanese ODA started to crumble with the growth of such untied aid, at least in the direct sense, although there is no denying that economic growth of developing countries will, ultimately, provide markets for Japanese goods and services. As shown in Figure 9.4, Japan has untied all its yen loans. Grant aid, however, is still tied.

Figure 9.4 Trends in Procurement Conditions on Japan's ODA Loans

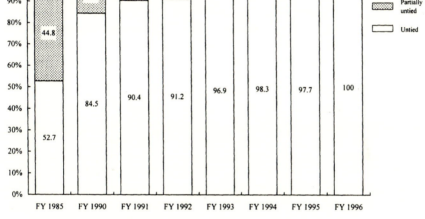

Based on Exchange of Notes

In the 1970s, interdependence, in place of export promotion per se, became Japan's main aid rationale. This notion of interdependence was clearly reflected in the 1970s MITI annual report on economic cooperation, which described Japan's relations with the less developed economies (LDCs) as having "an importance not seen in relations with advanced nations. Whether or not the LDC economies can show healthy growth has a serious bearing on our own country.... We cannot afford to neglect friendly economic relations with the LDCs. Our position is that Japan's economic cooperation is not simply an international responsibility but an unavoidable requirement for the smooth management of our own economy."[6] Ancillary to these major rationales were regional stability, bilateral leverage, promotion of political stability in recipient countries, and improved relations with other donor countries.

This interdependence rationale was further enhanced after the oil crises in 1973–74 when OPEC countries declared an oil embargo that drove home the message of interdependence. The case was truly serious for Japan, which lacks domestic oil resources. MITI's 1976 report on economic cooperation identified economic interdependence between Japan and the developing countries as its aid rationale.[7] Supply security of resources and raw materials became an important element of the aid rationale, particularly in the eyes of MITI in the post oil-crisis period. This change in aid rationale subsequently changed the geographical distribution of Japanese ODA, spreading gradually more widely to non-Asian regions, particularly to the Middle East.

Tool for Global Positioning
After completing its reparations with its final payment to the Philippines in July 1976, in 1978[8] Japan added role in and contribution to international society to its aid rationale and expanded its ODA volume through a series of medium-term ODA plans that doubled the ODA disbursement in five-year intervals. (See Figure 9.5.) In May 1978, at the time of the Bonn Summit, Prime Minister Fukuda Takeo announced the first mid-term plan to double the level of 1977 ODA within three years, accelerating the original plan of five years. This decision to expand ODA was made despite the tight budgetary situation of a zero ceiling on other items. This goal was achieved, thanks to the appreciation of the yen, and the quantitative expansion of Japanese ODA moved ahead at full throttle. The second target adopted in 1981 involved another doubling of ODA over a five-year period. Following the third target, yet another target was announced as the fourth medium-term aid plan to double the 1987 ODA volume during the 1988–92 period, including a commitment to raise the real national contribution of ODA. The doubling plan ended with the fifth medium-term plan (1993–97). Through this series of ODA doubling plans, Japan steadily rose to the position of top donor in 1989. Although it became the second largest donor after the United States in 1990, Japan was at the top again in 1991 and has remained there since, as of fiscal year 1997. The absolute amount of ODA peaked in 1995, at US$14.7 billion, and has been declining since. In fiscal 1996 Japan's ODA receded 34.9 percent from the previous year to US$9.44 billion, excluding aid to Eastern Europe, reversing the trend of annual increases in aid that Japan had maintained for so long. This reduction in assistance is due to the declining value of the yen, a downswing in Japan's fund contributions to various international financial institutions, and an increase in the repayment of funds extended earlier as yen loans.[9] According to the OECD/DAC announcement of 18 June 1998, Japan's ODA extensions during 1997 marked a slight dip in value of 0.9 percent below the preceding year. In absolute value of such aid, however, Japan maintained its leading position worldwide[10] while continuing to untie its ODA. (See Figure 9.5)

Along with these quantitative leaps in ODA disbursements came policy articulations by Japanese prime ministers on economic cooperation. During the visit to ASEAN in August 1977, Prime Minister Fukuda launched his policy of heart-

ODA as a Japanese Foreign Policy Tool 161

to-heart diplomacy, promising a total of ¥407.804 million to ASEAN projects and to the member countries themselves. The Fukuda Doctrine, as it became known, has been Japan's most significant statement on its relations with Asia, learning lessons from the experience of Tanaka Kakuei's visit to Southeast Asia in 1974, which provoked strong reactions in Thailand and Indonesia over the Japanese economic presence in their countries. During his visit to ASEAN countries Fukuda also announced the aforementioned first midterm ODA doubling plan in five years. In May 1988 Prime Minister Takeshita Noboru announced the International Cooperation Initiative, which identified aid as one of the major elements of Japan's contribution to the world. His International Cooperation Initiative included the expansion of ODA as well as promotion of world peace as a platform for Japan to play a greater global role.[11]

Figure 9.5 Net ODA Flow of Major DAC Countries

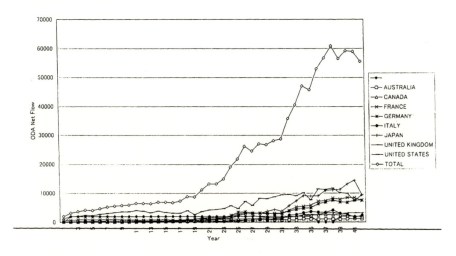

In the 1970s Japan also diversified its ODA from traditional industrial infrastructure projects to those related to basic human needs (BHN), including education, health, housing, public services, and human resource development. This humanitarian role in assisting poorer nations was another response to the accusation that Japan had not done its share as an economic power in international political affairs.

Thus, the aid rationales in this time frame were Japan's duty and global role as an economic civilian power. Having attained economic recovery and economic growth, Japan began to feel that it was its duty to contribute to world affairs, in particular world peace and prosperity, from which it had benefited directly and indirectly during the postwar reconstruction phase. Japan had received a huge amount of money from the EROA fund and then from the World Bank for its purchase of necessary items needed in infrastructure construction. Japan felt that it was obliged to repay such generosity through foreign aid. It had, after all, denounced war in its Constitution[12] and was exploring ways to contribute to international security commensurate with its economic strength.

After the oil crisis in the 1970s, this concept of a global role was further developed as comprehensive security, which was conceived by Prime Minister Ohira Masayoshi and an advisory group under him, Comprehensive National Security Study Group of the Policy Research Commission (chaired by Inoki Masamichi, former president of the National Defense Academy). Comprehensive security was proposed with the goal of adopting a comprehensive approach to diverse sources of threat. This security concept included military and nonmilitary threats ranging from military attack, disruption of resources supplies, pollution, natural disasters, crime, and terrorism. In this context, security was broadly defined as "the protection of the life and core values of the people."[13] In order to maintain security, military power in and of itself was regarded as insufficient. It was proposed that a comprehensive approach, combining military, economic, and social policies, be implemented for the overall security of citizens, hence the phrase "comprehensive security." The first official report on comprehensive security[14] was submitted to Prime Minister Ohira[15] in 1980 by the advisory group. This concept of comprehensive security was employed in the world of foreign aid to identify ODA as a tool for playing a global role in international peace and security as well as for securing supplies of resources.

However, some scholars such as Sumi Kazuo argue that the true focus of these doubling plans was not to assist countries in poverty but to respond to the demands of industrialized countries for Japan to reduce its trade surplus. ODA was a means to alleviate strong criticism of Japan's huge trade surplus in the 1980s.[16] Moreover, in the 1990s, in order to achieve its doubling plan, Japan wanted to disburse ODA money to big projects like dams, highways, airports, and port facilities, while debt-ridden developing countries wanted to refrain from such big projects.

On the other hand, despite these arguments of Japan's commercial interests in ODA, Kato Kozo argues that Japan has tried to remove the export promotion or commercial elements from ODA and has turned ODA into a genuine tool for contributing in the international arena.[17]

Post–Cold War Rationale

After the end of the Cold War, the Western industrialized countries lost their common rationale for development assistance, namely to halt the expansion of communism by aiding the Third World. During the Cold War, the developed countries provided assistance to developing countries in need, regardless of the degree of democratic governance or military behavior on the part of the recipients. The developed countries provided assistance to countries to foster their economic development so as to halt the spread of communist regimes. Relatively speaking, Japan did not place much emphasis on strategic aid, although it did occasionally provide ODA to such recipients as Egypt, Turkey, Pakistan, Morocco, and Bolivia, with which it did not have large-scale economic ties, upon the strong urging of the United States after the 1970s. Japan's first strategic aid was provided to Pakistan and other neighboring countries after the Soviet Union's invasion of Afghanistan. In May 1981, Prime Minister Suzuki Zenko and U.S. President Ronald Reagan stated in their joint communiqué that Japan was ready to contribute to world peace and regional stability through economic assistance. Subsequently Japan provided strategic aid to Latin American and Caribbean states in response to the U.S. Caribbean Basin Initiative.[18] Nonetheless, strategic aid was not the salient feature of Japanese ODA.

The end of the Cold War removed the ideological divide between East and West. In its wake, industrialized countries have used the spread of democracy and market economies as their common rationale for offering development assistance. In May 1996, the OECD/DAC adopted the report, "Shaping the Twenty-first Century: The Contribution of Development Cooperation," which sets forth strategic orientations for development cooperation into the twenty-first century. The report underscored the importance of poverty alleviation as the target of development assistance by arguing that "in the year 2000 four-fifths of the people of the world will be living in developing countries, most with improving conditions. But the number in absolute poverty and despair will still be growing. Those of us in the industrialized countries have a strong moral imperative to respond to the extreme poverty and human suffering that still afflict more than one billion people. We also have a strong self-interest in fostering increased prosperity in the developing countries. . . . All people are made less secure by the poverty and misery that exist in the world. Development matters."[19] Looking back at the aid record of the last 50 years since its beginning with the Marshall Plan, the report argues that aid works. The DAC report also states that in the twenty-first century, the international community needs to continue ODA "in order to reverse the growing marginalization of the poor and achieve progress toward realistic goals of human development."[20] Furthermore, the DAC, mindful of ODA fatigue among donors, recommends "global development partnerships."

ODA for World Peace and Stability
Japan, too, has gone through a soul-searching process to find its own post–Cold War rationale for ODA, particularly after the 1990–91 Gulf War when it faced criticisms for not doing enough as an industrialized country and economic power. Although Japan did not dispatch its Self-Defense Forces to the Gulf in light of the constraints of Article 9 of its Constitution, it did provide financial contributions in the amount of US$13 billion. Nonetheless, this was criticized as "too little, too late." Japan's critics stated that it should have done more to contribute to the resolution of the Gulf War and to the maintenance of international security and peace. Such criticism prompted then Prime Minister Kaifu Toshiki's pronouncements on Japanese foreign aid in April 1991. Kaifu made it clear that in allocating ODA money, Japan would consider the recipient country's trends in arms spending, trends in the development and manufacture of weapons of mass destruction, arms exports, promotion of democratization, movement toward a market-oriented economy, and the protection of freedoms and basic human rights.

These principles were further developed and were adopted as Japan's Official Development Assistance Charter (ODA Taiko)[21] in 2 June 1992 by the Cabinet as follows:

1. Environmental conservation and development should be pursued in tandem.
2. Any use of ODA for military purposes or for aggravation of international conflicts should be avoided.
3. Full attention should be paid to trends in recipient countries' military expenditures, their development, and production of missiles and weapons of mass destruction, their export and import of arms, etc., so as to maintained and strengthen international peace and stability, and from the viewpoint that developing countries should place appropriate priorities on the allocation of their resources for their own economic and social development.
4. Full attention should be paid to efforts in promoting democratization and introduction of a market-oriented economy, and to the situation regarding the securing of basic human rights and freedoms in the recipient country.

The charter also emphasizes good governance and self-help efforts of recipient countries. Self-help is the element Japan has upheld as the backbone of Japanese ODA. Since the pronouncements of its ODA Charter, Japan has been true to the principles declared therein, increasing amounts provided to countries displaying positive trends in line with its principles and suspending it, except for emergency or humanitarian needs, in countries—such as the Sudan, Myanmar, Haiti, Nigeria, and Gambia—where human rights have been seriously violated or the democratic process halted. Moreover, Japan halted plans to provide new aid grants, in addition to fresh yen loans, to India and Pakistan in protest over the underground nuclear tests conducted by those countries in 1998.

Tool for Conflict Prevention: Africa

Japan sees a possible link between economic development and world peace and stability. Widening economic disparities, such as those in many countries of Sub-Saharan Africa, have made some developing states fearful that the trend toward economic globalization and interdependence could marginalize them in the world economy. This fear is manifested in the increase of intrastate conflicts occurring since the end of the Cold War. Replacing communism, poverty has become the common fear. Although poverty alone does not cause conflict, when combined with other factors like ethnic or religious divides, and weak governance, the result is sometimes instability and conflict. Japan's *Official Development Assistance Annual Report 1997* notes that "it is crucial that regional tensions be defused before they develop into full-blown military conflicts. . . . Though varying factors are usually behind the outbreak of any given conflict, human deprivation and economic confrontation are often common denominators in the equation. ODA therefore has a role to play."[22]

Mindful of the civil wars that were breaking out in various corners of the world, Japan has thus identified ODA as a tool for reconstruction of postconflict regions as well as for prevention of potential conflicts through development assistance—so-called peace building. This, Japan's new focus in aid, has been demonstrated by hosting meetings of the International Conference on Reconstruction of Cambodia (ICORC), the Tokyo International Conference on African Development (TICAD), and the Mongolia Assistance Group Meeting. During the TICAD meetings in October 1993, Japan pledged grant aid for well water development as well as to implement assistance for certain priority areas (supporting democratization, supporting economic reform, cooperation in fostering human capital, and cooperation in environmental issues).

Japan hosted the second Tokyo International Conference on African Development (TICAD II) in October 1998 jointly with the United Nations and the Global Coalition for Africa. The Agenda for Action adopted at TICAD II underscored the spirit of the ownership of African countries and global partnership in developing Africa with three themes of capacity building, gender mainstreaming, and coordination. At TICAD II, Japanese Prime Minister Obuchi Keizo announced Japan's New Assistance Program for Africa, which includes an approximately ¥90 billion aid grant to the sectors of primary education, health and medical services, and water resources over the next five years, as well as support for African countries' efforts to combat antipersonnel land mines, and for debt management capacity building.

Having benefited from world peace without having made any readily visible contribution, Japan feels obliged to make an international contribution. Today Japan sees ODA as a tool to contribute to world peace, particularly in the context of postconflict peace building, a tool to offset economic overpresence, as well as a tool to enhance its relations with developing countries by improving their economic stability.[23]

Leveling Off in Quantity

Reflecting serious fiscal strains in FY1998 Japan reduced the ODA budget allocation in its general account by 10.4 percent from the previous fiscal year. Acting on instructions of then Prime Minister Hashimoto, the government made adjustments beyond official quotas and placed allocation priority on maximizing the effectiveness of ODA. As a result, first a higher priority was placed on the environment, social development, and technical cooperation, and on UN agency programs in humanitarian fields. Second, in the interest of improved efficiency, a fraction of related ministry or agency budget outlays for technical cooperation was consolidated into or transferred entirely to the JICA budget.

Notwithstanding these efforts, in light of the currency and financial crisis that developed and spread across Asia in the second half of 1997, Japan has offered to assist Asian economies hit by the crisis. It has announced its intention to supply $19 billion to the IMF packages for Thailand, Republic of Korea, and Indonesia; Japan has also provided bilateral yen loans and grant aid to Indonesia, Thailand, the Philippines, and Laos to help them pay for essential imports. Moreover, in October 1998 Japan announced a new initiative to overcome the Asian currency crisis, the so-called New Miyazawa Initiative to assist Asian countries to weather economic difficulties.

Multilateral Aid

In addition to bilateral ODA, Japan provides multilateral aid through multilateral development institutions such as the World Bank, the International Development Association, and Development Banks worldwide as well as a range of United Nations agencies, particularly the United Nations Development Program (UNDP), the United Nations High Commissioner for Refugees (UNHCR), the World Food Program (WFP), and the Fund for Population Activities (UNFPA), and more recently to the United Nations Environment Program (UNEP). Since the late 1970s, Japan stepped up its multilateral aid, not so much to enlarge its votes at international institutions or to enhance its economic interests but because of increasing multilateral aid in proportion to its economic power in the face of the relative decline of U.S. hegemony.[24] Japan's multilateral aid has increased in reverse proportion to declining U.S. multilateral aid. This aid does not bring benefits to Japanese companies in terms of exports of equipment. Nor has this multilateral aid led to the expansion of a voting share since Japanese contributions to multinational institutions often take the form of special contributions without voting rights.[25]

In addition, this increase in multilateral aid is a reflection of Japan's concern for global issues like the environment, population, and food, areas that need to be addressed by both developed and developing countries alike. For example, Japan announced at the United Nations Conference on Environment and Development in 1992 that it would extend $7 billion in ODA for environment-related projects over a five-year period from 1992 to 1996. Also, in 1994, Japan announced a program called the "Global Issues Initiative on Population and AIDS (GII)" and decided to contribute approximately US$3 billion in ODA aimed at population and HIV/AIDS problems.

Major Problems and Issues in Aid Administration

Complicated Decision-making Process

In other donor countries, economic aid is often planned, implemented, and managed by a single agency, such as the Canadian International Development Agency (CIDA), the U.S. Agency for International Development (USAID), and Office for Development Assistance (ODA) in the United Kingdom. Japan, however, does not have a single agency to handle ODA and involves 19 ministries in the decision-making process. In the case of grant aid and technical assistance, the Economic Cooperation Bureau (Keizai Kyoryoku Kyoku) of the Ministry of Foreign Affairs is in charge of planning and management while the Japan International Cooperation Agency (JICA), which falls under the jurisdiction of the foreign affairs ministry, is responsible for its implementation. As for yen loans, the four ministry decision-making system (Yon Shocho Kaigi), comprised of the Ministry of Foreign Affairs, Ministry of Finance, Ministry of International Trade and Industry, and Economic Planning Agency, determines the course of ODA programs. Although the foreign affairs ministry is the coordinator, unless all of the other ministries and agencies agree the government or the bureaucracy cannot submit an ODA project application to the Cabinet meeting for approval. Since there are no minutes taken at interagency meetings, there is no way for the Japanese public to know how ODA decisions are made. Yen loans are provided by the Overseas Economic Cooperation Fund (OECF), now part of the Japan Bank for International Cooperation. This has led to the criticism that Japan's ODA is fragmented and lacks coordination. Alan Rix, for example, observes that "competition between those bodies has confused the purposes of Japan's aid and obstructed effective overall direction of the programme."[26] The complicated decision-making process will also demand more information transparency, and more information disclosure regarding decision making for ODA projects.

Request-First Principle
Another unique feature of Japanese ODA is that it is based on the "request first principle," meaning that a recipient government must first make a formal request for aid from Japan, after which the case will be considered. This is aimed at providing aid that is needed by recipients rather than imposing on them. This process, however, also affects the efficiency of implementation of ODA, making Japanese ODA less articulate in terms of its priorities and principles.

This approach to ODA has led to the criticism that "Japanese ODA has usually been guided by Japanese private sector interests. . . . Thus, critical questions concerning the social impact of aid in a given area are inevitably skirted."[27] Thus came the criticism that it is too commercial and often not delivered to people suffering from poverty but into the pockets of government people in recipient countries.

Application of the ODA Charter
The aforementioned ODA Charter established the norms of Japan's aid giving. However, its application has been criticized as half-baked. When China conducted nuclear tests in August 1995, Japan imposed a freeze on all grant aid other than that for emergencies, of a humanitarian nature or for grassroots assistance, but resumed the aid in March 1997 after China enacted a moratorium on further nuclear testing and later signed the CTBT. When India and Pakistan conducted nuclear tests in May 1998, Japan decided, pursuant to its ODA Charter, to halt the provision of new grant aid other than that for grassroots projects or of an emergency or humanitarian nature as well as new yen loans.

The critics point out, however, that Japan is providing ODA to countries that engage in suppression of human rights, manufacture weapons, and so forth. One example is China. Censure is particularly strong against yen loans to China, which is a nuclear state and does not hesitate to conduct nuclear tests or to infringe on human rights. Its military expenditures are constantly rising, all issues that violate Japan's ODA Charter. Another example is Myanmar. Though aid is offered on a case-by-case basis, such as for the Yangoon International Airport Expansion Project, the country's regime suppresses human rights and obstructs democratization.

The Japanese government explains that the ODA Charter states that the overall situation determines a country's eligibility. There is a provision allowing for ODA disbursement in certain cases even though the recipient may not fit all the criteria (i.e., bad human rights record, military buildup, environmental preservation); if the country is deemed to be in need, the funds are provided. In the eyes of some critics, this permits Japan to provide aid to those who violate the terms of the ODA Charter.

Japanese ODA's Commercial Nature
One of the most common criticisms of Japan's ODA is that it seems calculated only to serve the country's economic interests, through collusion with corporations and consultants, and ends up actually contributing to the suppression of human rights and destruction of the environment in recipient countries. It is said that Japan lacks criteria and principles, spreading around money, equipment, and technology at random. "Half of the aid money returns to the Japanese economy through trading companies,"[28] charges one critic. Although provided on the basis of recipients' requests, such applications are sometimes prepared by trading companies and "fed" to developing country governments. Another criticism is that Japan is aiding countries that have natural resources important to its needs, but offers little or no assistance to less-developed countries that do not have commodities for export, as in the case for example of Ethiopia, which exports little more than coffee to Japan.

Japan's ODA is also looked askance for blindly following the dictates of the United States strategic aid. An example in point is the yen loans to the Jamaican anti-Cuban regime.

According to Sumi Kazuo, Japanese aid has sometimes resulted in damage to the environment of the recipient country when it does not give sufficient attention to the needs of local people, such as in the case of dam development, when many people may suffer from being deprived of land they depended on for subsistence. For program or nonproject aid, money sometimes disappears into the pockets of the rulers, contributing to graft and corruption. In the case of authoritarian regimes, ODA money is sometimes used for oppressive purposes. In a nonproject loan to Indonesia, for example, aid money was used in a government transmigration plan called *transmigrasi*, leading to the suppression of the Melanesian indigenous population of West Papua and East Timor.[29] In Brazil, Programa Grande Carajas has been implemented to develop iron ore, railways, and port facilities. In 1980, at Brazil's request, Japan's JICA conducted a feasibility study for this project, and it was ultimately carried out. Later it was found that the Carajas development had opened a slash through the forest above the iron ore deposits with devastating consequences for the natural environment of Carajas. It also invaded the traditional homeland of the native people of the area. Sumi shows that JICA's feasibility study was partly responsible because its assessment failed to foresee the impact on the environment and the indigenous people's lives.[30] Similar examples can be found in the Narmada dam development project in India, which forced 1 million people to migrate from their farms, throwing many into unemployment. There have been other such cases where the damage has been inflicted on the environment and suffering on native inhabitants. An example is the Japanese assistance provided in Malaysia to develop prawn acquaculture, which resulted in cutting down vast tracts of topical rainforest for construction of roads and a production research center and destruction of the coastal mangrove forests. The balance between development and preservation of the environment is a very difficult topic, and finding optimum solutions is not easy. There is no denying that recipients benefit from earning hard currency, the jobs created, and the increase in income, but they also suffer when the projects have a negative ecological impact. Should Japan order its people not to eat prawns? Should we refuse to use tropical woods? The OECD and JICA have established their respective guidelines for environmental preservation.

Another question asked is whether Japanese ODA has been truly useful in alleviating poverty and in helping the recipient countries to develop. It has provided ODA to Myanmar (Burma) since 1955, initially in the form of reparations and subsequently as aid, but Myanmar was categorized as a less developed country (LDC) by the United Nations even in 1987, and is still notorious for its suppression of human rights. Was this Japanese assistance extended in vain?

On the other hand, Kusano Atsushi and Watanabe Toshio argue that Japanese ODA has promoted investment by private businesses and assisted in the overall development of such countries.[31]

Others, including Watanabe Toshio, argue that it is inevitable that ODA should be related to commercial and export promotion. Since we live in a capital market society, corporate profits and the national interest are not necessarily contradictory. It was also inevitable that a country with a tight aid budget should expand its tied aid in order to support Japanese companies. Now Japan has untied most of its ODA. If there are any profit-promising projects, any company, Japanese or not, would be interested.

Domestic Public Opinion
The Japanese public, Sumi Kazuo asserts, has not been critical of funneling of their tax funds into the phenomenal growth of ODA in the 1980s and 1990s because people believe Japan should compensate for its trade surplus in the developing world and that such assistance does help people suffering from poverty.[32] He concludes, however, that they are not well informed either about how ODA is provided or how helpful it actually is to recipients.[33]

According to opinion surveys, the Japanese public still shows strong support for the nation's ODA policies and programs. According to an October 1997 opinion poll conducted by the Prime Minister's Office, 44.5 percent of respondents felt that the country should maintain its efforts at economic assistance "at current levels." Furthermore, 31.2 percent were of the view that assistance should be increased; with only 13.6 percent responding that it should be reduced as much as possible, and 2.3 percent that it should be curtailed entirely. In other words, those who expressed support for the status quo or for expanded aid accounted for 75.5 percent of all respondents.[34]

Since Japan has become the largest donor in the world, the press has started to cover stories on ODA, including cases involving corruption. This may lead to a call for more assessments of ODA projects and their results. The current audit by the Japanese General Accounting Office may not suffice.

In the Japanese Diet, some representatives have started to question the efficacy of ODA as a foreign policy tool. Some point out that recipient countries are not necessarily aware of or grateful for Japanese aid for infrastructure building. Emphasis should be more on technical cooperation or cooperation that is more visible in nature. Some representatives from economically depressed constituencies have even suggested that, if ODA is not serving its true purpose, such funds need to be shifted to domestic assistance rather than foreign assistance.[35]

Challenge and Reform

Shrinking Budgets

On 3 June 1997, the Hashimoto Ryutaro Cabinet passed a resolution concerning structural reforms to the fiscal budget. The provisions of that resolution included reducing the ODA budget by 10 percent in 1998 from the fiscal 1997 level and not to increase that level for the following two years until 2000 while budget restructuring was taking place. Subsequently, in 1998, the Budget Restructuring Law was frozen for the sake of stimulating economic recovery, and the ODA budget was not cut too severely. However, given the protracted recession following the 1991 burst of the bubble economy, and given Japan's aging society and the trend toward smaller families, it is unlikely that a growth pattern similar to what was experienced in the 1970s and 1980s will return for some time. Japan may no longer be able to maintain its top donor status. This means that it needs to work for greater quality and efficiency in the delivery of its ODA.

Shrinking budgets and tougher struggles over budget appropriations will make assessments of ODA and its effects more severe than ever. How effective has ODA been? Has it achieved its objectives? When Indonesia was thrown into chaos at the time of the resignation of former President Suharto, questions were asked: What had Japanese ODA done to make the country more democratic and more stable? Could Japanese ODA have prevented internal strife? Could the confusion in 1997-98 be evidence that Japanese ODA has had little effect?

Proposals for Reform

Decline in ODA disbursements is not unique to Japan. It is happening in many donor countries, if not all. Now at an important crossroads, Japan has created many committees on reform of ODA. In June 1997, the Economic Planning Agency's Study Group on Economic Cooperation Policy, which was created as an advisory organ to the Director General of the Coordination Bureau of the EPA and was headed by Hoshino Shinyasu, president of the National Institute for Research Advancement, submitted its final report.[36] The Ministry of Foreign Affairs created the Council on ODA Reforms for the Twenty-first Century headed by Kawai Saburo, chairman of the International Development Center of Japan, and published an Emergency Opinion Paper on Fiscal Restructuring in June 1997 followed by a final report in January 1998.[37] MITI's Industrial Structural Council's Economic Cooperation Working Group also announced its interim report in February 1996.[38] Keidanren (Japan Federation of Economic Organizations) also announced its recommendations entitled, "Reforming Official Development Assistance in Japan" on 15 April 1997.[39]

Despite the inevitable ODA budget cuts under the three-year fiscal restructuring consolidation drive, none of the reports questioned the importance of ODA. Rather, they all underscored that ODA will remain an important instrument with which Japan can contribute to the international community to alleviate poverty, secure world peace, and grapple with the problems of interdependence, thereby pursuing Japan's national interests. A 1996 Ministry of Foreign Affairs interim report stated that "Japan's ODA is of vital importance to its continued existence, and to the goals of peace and prosperity. ODA-backed efforts to eradicate poverty and promote social and economic advances in the developing world can and do contribute to the peace and prosperity of the international community at large. In addition to these far-reaching, global benefits, ODA also contributes to the life, security, and dignity of the Japanese people. As such, it is directly in Japan's own national interest as a country striving to strengthen its ties of interdependence with the rest of the world, a world which is increasingly involved in globalization."[40] The reports also emphasized that Japan cannot live without comprehensive security, not only for itself but globally as well. Global security includes protection of the environment and natural resources, eradication of poverty, prevention of famine, securing of adequate food supplies, and population control. Population, in particular, left unchecked, will lead to conflicts that could affect Japan's security and economic well-being. If ODA can contribute to eradicating poverty in developing countries, it should in turn contribute to international peace. Chaotic conditions in the world resulting from leaving global issues unattended, in other words, would prevent Japan from sustaining its own existence. This is the source of the logic that providing ODA despite imminent budget reconsolidation needs is in Japan's national interest.

All reports of Japanese ODA studies have urged the government to deliver ODA more efficiently and effectively in order to avoid the downsizing of projects. In improving efficiency, all the reports recommend partnership as suggested by the aforementioned DAC report. They encourage role-sharing and coordination among Japan's ministries and agencies as well as with the private sector (business, NGOs, and academia), and among the advanced industrial countries and international institutions. A Ministry of Foreign Affairs report recommends the establishment of an ODA Comprehensive Policy Council (ODA Sogo Seisaku Kyogikai) with representation from all the ministries and agencies involved in ODA programming and implementation as well as to establish partnerships with developing countries, the private sector, and international institutions.[41] The Keidanren report recommends establishing distinct divisions of labor among the policy-making ministries in addition to the creation of a new aid agency, the "International Cooperation Agency," to be charged with the task of implementing assistance programs.

Conclusion

Why does Japan provide aid? Although ODA that was initially identified with war reparations and export promotion invited criticisms for being excessively commercial in orientation, Japan since the mid-1970s has shifted its rationale to contribution to the international community. This shift was manifested in its ODA doubling plans, the untying of its bilateral aid, increased contributions to multilateral institutions, and increases in its aid to Sub-Saharan Africa. Since the end of the Cold War, Japan has identified ODA as a means for conflict prevention and peace building. This shift has also been manifested in projects supported by Japan's ODA, from infrastructure building to education, health, and medical services. In today's world, infrastructure can be built with private money, taking advantage of Build-Operate-Transfer (BOT) schemes and the like, instead of using government funds. Yen loans that require repayment under concessional conditions may need to be reconsidered and redesigned. The ODA Charter, flawed though it may be, indicates that Japan is trying to use its assistance abroad in a positive way to induce countries to refrain from military buildup, suppression of human rights, and destruction of the environment. The spirit of the Charter can be further extended to make ODA a conduit for contributing to world peace and stability. In other words, Japan can explore the possibility of using ODA as a positive tool to encourage countries to move onward for the abolition of weapons of mass destruction, for environmental preservation, and for protection of human rights.

Whether Japan, with its constitutionally imposed constraints on military power, will be able to use ODA as a viable foreign policy tool in the next millennium depends on how successful it will be in redesigning ODA in the future.

Notes

1. For a critical assessment of the philosophy of Japan's foreign aid in the eyes of a non-Japanese, see Alan Rix, *Japan's Foreign Aid Challenge: Policy Reform and Aid Leadership* (London and New York: Routledge, 1993), chapter 1.
2. In describing foreign aid, different terms, such as "economic cooperation" and "development assistance" are sometimes used interchangeably. Foreign aid is used more in terms of funding developing countries on concessional terms including commercial and official fund flows. Official development assistance (ODA) as defined by the DAC is used to mean government-sponsored flows of resources made available on concessional terms to foreign governments. Economic cooperation is used in a broader sense and not limited to official resource transfers.
3. Ministry of Education Science Research Subsidy Main Area Research, "Sengo Nihon seisaku keisei no kihonteki kenkyu" [Basic Research on Postwar Japan's Policy Making], created by Professors Watanabe Akio, Yamakage Susumu, and Tanaka Akihiko. http://www.ioc.u-tokyo.ac.jp/tanaka/tanaka/htm.
4. Alan Rix, *Japan's Economic Aid: Policy-making and Politics* (London: Croom Helm, 1980), pp. 28–31.
5. Rix, 1980, p. 28.
6. Ministry of International Trade and Industry, *Keizai kyoryoku no genjo to mondaiten* [Economic Cooperation: Present Situation and Problems] (Tokyo: Trade Industry Survey Committee [Tsusho Sangyo Chosakai], 1971), pp. 116–17.
7. Ministry of International Trade and Industry, *Keizai kyoryoku no genjo to mondaiten* [Economic Cooperation: Present Situation and Problems] (Tokyo: Trade Industry Survey Committee [Tsusho Sangyo Chosakai], 1976), pp. 182–86.

8. Kato Kozo, *Tsusho kokka no kaihatsu kyoryoku seisaku* [The Development Cooperation Policies of a Trading Nation] (Tokyo: Mokkosha, 1998), pp. 65–66.
9. Ministry of Foreign Affairs, ed., *Japan's ODA Annual Report 1997* (Tokyo: Association for Promotion of International Cooperation, October 1997), p. 9.
10. "Japan Keeps on World's Top Place in 97 ODA Extending Results," *The Japan Economic Review*, 15 August 1998.
11. Ministry of Foreign Affairs, *Gaiko seisho* [Diplomatic Blue Book] (Tokyo: Ministry of Finance Printing Bureau, 1989).
12. Article 9 of the Constitution of Japan stipulates:

    Aspiring sincerely to an international peace based on justice and order, the Japanese people forever renounce war as a sovereign right of the nation and the threat or use of force as means of settling international disputes.
    In order to accomplish the aim of the preceding paragraph, land, sea, and air forces, as well as other war potential, will never be maintained. The right of belligerency of the state will not be recognized.

13. National Institute for Research Advancement, *Jiten 1990 nendai: Nihon no kadai* [The Era of the 1990s: Tasks for Japan] (Tokyo: Sanseido, 1987), p. 344.
14. Prior to this official report, Nomura Research Institute in December 1977 announced its report, "A Recommendation for the 21st Century—The Change in the International Environment and Japan's Response." This report proposed the notion of comprehensive security by likening it to insurance policy. In times of peace, in order to secure the survival of the state, it is necessary to prepare for a possible conflict by investing in various sorts of "insurance." Security should be approached comprehensively, it stated, with a sense of paying insurance premiums to cope with it before the actual crisis occurs.
15. This advisory group was established by Prime Minister Ohira in April 1979, but by the time the report was submitted, Ohira had passed away and it was actually submitted to acting prime minister Ito Masayoshi in July 1980.
16. Sumi Kazuo, *ODA enjo no genjitsu* [The Realities of ODA] (Tokyo: Iwanami Shinsho, 1989), p. 11.
17. Kato, 1998, pp. 67–68.
18. Dennis T. Yasutomo, *The Manner of Giving: Strategic Aid and Japanese Foreign Policy* (Lexington, MA: Lexington Books, 1986), p. 41; and Robert M. Orr, *The Emergence of Japan's Foreign Air Power* (NY: Columbia University Press, 1990), pp. 116–17.
19. http://www.oecd.org/dac/htm/stc/intro.htm.
20. http://www.oecd.org.
21. http://www.mofa.go.jp.
22. Ministry of Foreign Affairs, 1997, p. 84.
23. Ministry of Foreign Affairs, Economic Cooperation Bureau, Research Committee on Economic Cooperation, (Tokyo 1984), 82–83.
24. Kato, 1998, p. 80.
25. Kato, 1998, pp. 81–82.
26. Rix, 1993, p. 72.
27. Orr, 1990, p. 139.
28. Kusano Atsushi, *ODA itcho-nisen-oku en no yukue* [Where Does 1 Trillion 200 Billion Yen of ODA Money Go?] (Tokyo: Toyo Keizai Shinbunsha, 1993).
29. Sumi, 1989, pp. 18–19.
30. Sumi, 1989, pp. 61–80.
31. Watanabe Toshio and Kuwano Atsushi, *Nihon no ODA o dosuruka* [What Should We Do About Japan's ODA?] (Tokyo: NHK Books, 1991), p. 36.
32. Sumi, 1989, p. 10.
33. Sumi, 1989, p. 38–60.
34. Ministry of Foreign Affairs, Economic Cooperation Bureau, *Annual Evaluation Report on Japan's Economic Cooperation* (Tokyo, June 1998), p. 3.
35. Funabashi Yoichi, "Otoko wa damatte en shakkan de wa komaru" [Japan Can't Go On Giving Yen Loans Without Making Any Demands], *Asahi shimbun*, 4 February 1999.
36. The interim report, "Keizai Kyoryoku Seisaku Kenkyukai chukan hokoku," can be found at http://www.epa.go.jp/j-j/dpc/1996bg/1996bg5-j-j.html. The final report, *Jizoku kano na keizai*

  kyoryoku ni mukatte [Toward Sustainable Economic Cooperation], can be found at http://www.epa.go.jp/j-j/doc/houkoku1997-6-j-j.html (in Japanese).
37. http://www.mofa.go.jp.policy/oda/reform/interim.html (both Japanese and English available).
38. http://www.miti.go.jp/past/b60205bl.html (Japanese).
39. http://www.keidanren.or.jp/english/policy/po1059/index.html (English).
40. http://www.mofa.go.jp/policy/oda/reform/interim/html (Japanese).
41. *21-seiki ni mukete no ODA kaikaku kondankai hokokusho* [Report of the Council on ODA Reform for the Twenty-first Century] (Tokyo, January 1998), pp. 10–11.

PART III
The Relationships

CHAPTER 10

U.S.-Japan Relations in the Post–Cold War Era: Ambiguous Adjustment to a Changing Strategic Environment

Akaha Tsuneo

The contemporary debate in Japan and the United States regarding their alliance after the Cold War reflects growing anxiety on both sides over respective strategic requirements in the dramatically altered environment of the Asian-Pacific region. The demise of the Soviet Union and the disintegration of Russia, the growing Chinese power and independent-minded Taiwan, as well as the stalemate on the Korean Peninsula and dangerously isolated North Korea pose serious challenges to the alliance. The task of finding a new strategic relationship between Washington and Tokyo is made more difficult by the recent Asian financial and economic crises, which are now threatening to engulf the U.S. economy. The two countries alone cannot fend off the destabilizing effects of the virtually uncontrollable flow of capital across the interdependent Asian-Pacific economies and beyond. Their ability to forge a viable strategic alliance in the post–Cold War world hinges increasingly on their ability to cooperate with the other major world powers, particularly the EU—with respect to the management of the globalizing world economy—and China and Russia—with regard to the varied threats to the peace and stability of the Asian-Pacific region.

In this brief analysis, I will examine the ongoing debate in Japan and the United States regarding their bilateral relations, and discuss possible future directions. The central questions in this study are how perceptions of the power balance between the two countries in the changing regional and global context have affected each side's expectations of itself and the other's within the bilateral relationship; and how their understanding of the regional and global significance of their relations is likely to inform those relations, particularly in the realm of political security. Before we examine the contemporary situation, however, let us review briefly the evolution of U.S.-Japan relations in the postwar decades, so as to discern the factors contributing to gradual changes in mutual perceptions between the allies.

Evolution of U.S.-Japan Relations

World War II to the 1950s

U.S.-Japan relations during the decades following World War II evolved through several phases.[1] In the immediate postwar years, Japan, as a vanquished nation, was at the mercy of the United States for its domestic political reform, economic reconstruction, and international political rehabilitation. The U.S.-led occupation forces undertook sweeping political reforms in Japan, introducing the "no war" clause in the new Japanese Constitution and demobilizing all military personnel at home and abroad. They also disbanded the *zaibatsu,* whose concentrated power had kept Japan's war machine going in the prewar and wartime years.

Following the onset of the Cold War in Asia, with the emergence of communist China in 1949 and the outbreak of the Korean War in 1950, the United States took advantage of its occupation of Japan to bring Tokyo into its strategic fold. Washington concluded a security treaty with Tokyo in 1951, committing itself to the defense of Japan against foreign aggression and giving itself access to Japanese bases from which to stage military operations throughout the Far East. Also in 1951, Washington secured the San Francisco peace treaty and denied Moscow uncontested control of the Northern Territories (southern Kuriles), creating what soon became the single most important wedge between Tokyo and Moscow in the postwar era. Moreover, Washington provided direct assistance to the coalition of conservative, pro-American political parties in Japan against leftist forces, leading to the formation of the Liberal Democratic Party in 1955. Washington also made sure that the pro-Beijing political forces and business interests in Japan would not lead the Japanese government to the establishment of diplomatic relations with Beijing. All these measures succeeded in framing for decades to come Japan's basic policy direction: pro-United States, pro-West, and minimally armed for its own defense. Needless to say, this generally satisfied Japan's postwar interests as defined by mainstream Japanese, although it frustrated both nationalists, who wanted Japan to write its own constitution and develop an autonomous defense policy, and leftists, who wanted closer relations with the Soviet Union and China.

On the economic front, Washington nurtured a pro-United States, pro-capitalist policy in Tokyo. In addition to direct aid to Japan, the United States opened its market to Japanese exports to assist in the creation of jobs at home and the garnering of valuable foreign exchange. Washington also persuaded its European friends and allies to allow Japan to join the postwar world trade system and help the former enemy pursue its export-driven development strategy. The United States also brokered postwar settlements between the Japanese and their wartime victims in Asia, linking reparation agreements to Japanese access to Asian markets.

Maturation of the Alliance: 1960s and 1970s

Japan's successful economic recovery and rising nationalist sentiments on both sides of the Pacific led to a revision of the U.S.-Japan security treaty in 1960.

The new treaty obligated the two countries to take action to assist each other in case of an armed attack on Japanese territory, although it was understood that Japan would not come to the aid of the United States were the latter to be attacked. Notes accompanying the treaty required prior consultation between Washington and Tokyo, were the former to undertake major changes in its troop deployment or equipment stockpiling in Japan. The treaty was also made subject to a one-year notice of revocation after 1970. These changes reflected the gradual increase in Japan's assertion of sovereignty and U.S. accommodation. Behind the growing Japanese confidence was its successful economic growth and expansion throughout the 1950s. Japan's economic miracle continued into the 1960s.

From the end of the 1960s to the end of the 1970s, Japan's robust economy shielded the country against some major external disturbances. It survived a series of external shocks: the Nixon Doctrine (announced in Guam in 1969), the 1971 U.S.-China rapprochement, the 1971 New Economic Policy of the United States, the 1973–74 oil crisis, and the U.S. defeat in the Vietnam War and withdrawal from Indochina in 1975. Following these disturbances, Japan emerged a confident junior partner in the bilateral relationship. At the same time, however, Japan began to question Washington's political leadership. Many Japanese were disturbed, some even felt betrayed, by the sudden turnaround in Washington's policy toward Beijing. A few years later, Tokyo was jolted by yet another sudden shift in U.S. policy. In 1978, President Jimmy Carter announced Washington's plan to withdraw U.S. ground troops from South Korea. Facing protests from South Korea and Japan and from within the United States, Carter quickly retracted this decision. Following the Soviet invasion of Afghanistan in 1979, Tokyo began to realize that Washington needed its allies' support to counter the growth of Soviet military power and political ambitions under Premier Leonid Brezhnev. It was against this background that Tokyo publicly acknowledged its relationship with Washington as an alliance. Tokyo also pledged to expand its defense capabilities to protect sea lines of communication (SLOCs) to a distance of 1,000 nautical miles from its coast.

A Broader Context of Alliance: 1980s to Early 1990s
In the 1980s, Japan acknowledged it had become a full-fledged member of the Western alliance. Tokyo supported Washington's effort to bring Moscow to the negotiating table in order to limit strategic arms and intermediate-range nuclear forces. However, the continuing pressure for greater defense-burden sharing cast doubt on the will and ability of the United States to bear the cost of its security commitments to Japan and other allies. President Ronald Reagan's combined policies of tax reduction and military buildup caused the federal budget deficit to reach $22.2 billion and the outstanding federal debt to climb to $2.1 trillion by 1986. The United States had become heavily dependent on Japanese capital to finance its trade and current account deficits. The Japanese, meanwhile, were willing to increase their defense burden because they had come to believe that the era of U.S. hegemonic dominance had ended and an age of shared global responsibility had dawned.[2]

Developments from the second half of the 1980s through the early 1990s made Japan's search for a new level of relationship with the United States more urgent, but also more difficult. The dissolution of the Soviet Union and the end of the Cold War caught Japan unprepared.[3] Until recently Japan had failed to see its relationship with the Soviet Union and Russia in a broader regional and global context, having focused instead on a bilateral territorial dispute.[4] Similarly, the Gulf War of 1990–91, caught the Japanese ill prepared, subjecting their checkbook diplomacy to international ridicule. A genuine search for a post–Cold War strategic vision and for a new strategic rationale for its alliance with the United States began in the aftermath of this, the first major regional conflict following the Cold War.

Let us now examine how the end of the Cold War has affected the two countries' perceptions of each other.

Japanese Views of U.S.-Japan Relations

Post–Cold War Perspectives

In the aftermath of the Cold War, ideology no longer is *the* defining mark of the Japanese debate on U.S.-Japan relations. The right-left split on almost every major issue in the bilateral relations during the Cold War has virtually disappeared. The de-ideologization of the domestic debate offers the potential for clear-headed discussion of the U.S.-Japan alliance, its relevance to the two countries' current and future strategic environment, and the requirement for each side to sustain, revise, or terminate the alliance.

Replacing the right-left split, there are three broadly discernible trends in the ongoing debate in Japan: nationalist, regionalist, and globalist.[5] These are not necessarily mutually exclusive or individually complete and systematic schools of thought. Rather, a complex mix of globalist perspectives, regionalist sentiments, and nationalist impulses informs Japanese debate.

Globalist Views

One globalist view is that Japan must play a much more visible and substantial global role, but that it should continue to pursue the pacifist foreign policy it has followed since its defeat in World War II. This view favors the maintenance of a close U.S.-Japan alliance but opposes the projection of Japanese military power beyond its borders.[6] Some globalists part company and regard as virtually inevitable the termination of the U.S.-Japan security treaty, if not immediately, at least over some period of adjustment.[7] They nonetheless support Japan's self-imposed denial of the right to collective security.

There is disagreement among the globalists as to whether it is possible to forge a global division of labor between the United States, Japan, and Europe, in which Japan will continue to limit its international security role to economic development assistance and noncombatant functions in UN peacekeeping. Some globalists (political and economic liberals) believe it is both desirable and possible. Their argument is based on two premises: that economic development in the developing world and in transitional economies would lead to domestic and international political stability, and that international economic interdependence would enhance the prospects for global peace. They share the regionalist view noted below that Asia-Pacific countries must advance multilateral economic integration as a foundation of regional peace and stability. They want to see the Asia-Pacific Economic Cooperation (APEC) forum move beyond the dialogue phase it is now in and develop clearly defined, if not legally binding, principles governing trade, investment, and other economic transactions among the member countries. They also demand that regional arrangements be consistent with the rules of the global trade system under the World Trade Organization (WTO).

Other globalists (political realists) believe that such a division of labor, especially between the United States and Japan, would be politically untenable in view of the growing isolationist sentiment in the United States. Nor do they believe that it would be desirable for Japan to disavow its responsibility for global peace and security. They assert that it is time for Japan to end its self-imposed ban on participation in collective security and become a normal state.[8] In their view, a normalized Japan would be able to play an active role in UN peacekeeping operations, including frontline operations, and also develop a more reciprocal relationship with the United States in the bilateral alliance.[9] This view is founded on the realist premise that all great powers inevitably assume political roles commensurate with their economic power and that they require and eventually acquire well developed military capabilities to exercise effective political influence in the anarchic world. Other realists, particularly those who are focused on regional political and security issues, are less inclined to invest in the UN and other global institutions and advocate instead a balance of power, or bandwagoning cooperation, with the only remaining superpower, the United States.[10] These realists assume that a new balance of power is emerging in the post–Cold War Asia-Pacific region and that Japan, alone or in concert with the United States, should deter the emergence of any unfriendly regional hegemon, e.g., China. Although they do not necessarily see rivalry with China as inevitable, they see it as a distinct possibility.

Regionalist Views

Regionalists are critical of what they see as their government's uncritical dependence on the alliance with the United States and are hopeful that the growing economic interdependence in the Asia-Pacific region will facilitate more friendly relations among the countries of the region, particularly between Japan and China. In their view, political reconciliation and economic interdependence with China and other Asian countries, rather than enhanced defense cooperation with the United States, will ensure Japan's peace and prosperity. From their perspective, both Washington's aggressive human rights policy toward China and its demand for accelerated liberalization of Asian markets are self-centered and even counterproductive. They object to what they see as Washington's sanctimonious policy on democratization and market liberalization in the region. In this they have something in common with regionalists in other Asian countries, such as Malaysian Prime Minister Mahathir bin Mohamad. However, they do not support an Asians-only regional framework, such as the East Asian Economic Caucus (EAEC) proposed by the Malaysian prime minister. Instead, they want the APEC process to succeed in advancing the cause of regional economic cooperation.

In the security realm, Japanese regionalists do not see any viable alternative to the U.S.-Japan alliance, at least in the foreseeable future, but they recognize the need to develop a multilateral security framework to supplement the alliance. They advocate, therefore, the development of regional institutions for confidence building and economic cooperation.[11]

Nationalist Views
Nationalist themes do not coalesce into any coherent system of thought or policy prescriptions. Instead, they typically appear as impulsive reactions to international criticisms of Japan. Nationalist sentiments find their expressions in the prickly debate over defense-burden sharing with the United States, in the protracted discussion on Japanese participation in UN peacekeeping operations, and in the debate on how to respond to Chinese and Korean criticisms of Japan's militarist-imperialist past.

Japanese nationalist sensitivities have been aroused by Washington's persistent demand, beginning in the 1970s, that Japan assume a larger share of the burden for its national defense. On the one hand, it is unlikely that, without the U.S. prodding, Japan would have built up its defense spending to the current level of over $50 billion and the third largest in the world after that of the United States and Russia.[12] On the other hand, Japanese nationalists have been visibly critical of the U.S.-Japan agreement on the joint development of FSX fighter aircraft that, they believe, was an unfair deal. As well, they have resented the increasing host-nation support that Washington has demanded from Tokyo for maintaining the U.S. military presence in Japan.[13]

Nationalist sentiments also echo the growing populist resentment of *gaiatsu*, or external pressure, over trade and economic issues, particularly from the United States. The resentful mood among many Japanese has been captured by the concept of *kenbei*, literally meaning the dislike of America. It should be pointed out, however, that the mood reflects not only popular Japanese resentment of the U.S. pressure, but also frustration over the government's inability to alleviate the sources of U.S.-Japan trade and economic friction. Moreover, Japanese citizens have become visibly upset over their own corrupt politicians, inept bureaucrats, and greedy business leaders who, in their view, have caused the long-protracted economic recession since the bursting of the economic bubble.

Globalist, regionalist, and nationalist perspectives share a common awareness: the United States is no longer the global hegemon it once was. They agree that the management of world affairs today requires the sharing of power and responsibilities among the great powers, including Japan, Europe, and the United States. They differ, however, over where Japan's priorities should be, whether they should concentrate on global partnerships with the United States and

Europe, invest in reconciliation and accommodation with their Asian neighbors, or focus on the search for a uniquely Japanese identity in the post–Cold War era. As I have argued elsewhere,[14] the outcome of this debate is likely to be a mixture of these competing perspectives, the balance among them depending on the issues facing the nation at any given moment.

Official Policy
The official policy of the Japanese government is an amalgam of the contending perspectives outlined above. Tokyo is determined to continue to anchor its security policy on the bilateral alliance with Washington while, at the same time, exploring possible modes of multilateral security cooperation, not to replace but to supplement the U.S.-Japan alliance.

Most Japanese are resigned to the fact that they have no choice but to support many U.S. foreign policy initiatives. Examples include Tokyo's support for the U.S.-North Korean Agreed Framework, its participation in the Korean Peninsula Energy Development Organization (KEDO) to suspend North Korea's nuclear weapons development, and Japan's support for the extension of the Nuclear Non-Proliferation Treaty (NPT).

While reaffirming the bilateral alliance with the United States and further expanding its contribution to the effective functioning of the alliance, Japan has also begun to take some initiatives to develop a security dialogue and defense cooperation with neighboring countries. Tokyo was instrumental in establishing the ASEAN Regional Forum (ARF), while it has shown increasing interest in expanding security consultations with South Korea, developing defense cooperation with Russia, and initiating a defense dialogue with China, and is also supportive of track-two diplomacy to explore various confidence-building measures. On some issues, Tokyo no longer hesitates to part company with Washington on issues about which it feels strongly. For example, Tokyo decided, against Washington's wishes, to support the international ban on antipersonnel land mines.

This measure of independent foreign policy notwithstanding, Tokyo is determined to maintain a close alliance with the United States, a resolve that is unlikely to change soon in view of the favorable public view of the current state of U.S.-Japan relations. According to a public opinion survey by the Prime Minister's Office in September–October 1997, nearly 72 percent of the respondents believed current U.S.-Japan relations to be good or basically good, despite some problems. In contrast, only 18.5 percent of the respondents believed relations were deteriorating or dangerously bad. Comparable figures for 1990 were 63.4 percent with favorable and 24.3 percent with unfavorable evaluations.[15] Similarly, nearly 75 percent of the Japanese polled in 1997 felt favorably disposed, while 23 percent felt somewhat unfriendly or unfriendly toward the United States. These numbers do not significantly differ from the results of a 1990 poll, which showed nearly 75 percent feeling strongly or somewhat friendly, and 21 percent somewhat or strongly unfriendly, toward the United States.[16]

U.S. Views of the Alliance[17]

Multiple Issues
Public support in the United States for the U.S.-Japan alliance after the Cold War also remains strong. A Gallup poll conducted for the Japanese Foreign Ministry in February–March 1998 revealed that over 83 percent of the American respondents believed the U.S.-Japan security treaty should be maintained.[18]

Views among analysts are quite mixed. The changed balance of U.S.-Japan economic power is clearly a major factor affecting U.S. analysts' views of the strategic environment in general, and the relationship with Japan in particular. This is apparent in arguments concerning (1) Japan's regional security role, (2) prospects for Japanese militarization, (3) defense burden sharing, (4) defense technology cooperation, and (5) U.S. economic stakes in Japan and elsewhere in Asia.

First, there is consensus among U.S. analysts that Japan must play a larger international role, including a bigger part in the realm of security. There is no agreement, however, on what that role should entail. While some critics of Japan's economics-first policy urge Japan to become a normal state by making greater military contributions to international peace and security, others caution against encouraging a Japanese defense buildup for fear that the economic superpower may also want to become a military power.[19] Some observers expect a multipolar balance of power to replace reliance on the alliance with the United States and believe that a collective security system will emerge in Asia in which the U.S.-Japan alliance is one part, albeit still the most important part.

Burden sharing is not a new issue. Indeed, as noted earlier, it has been an important part of Washington's policy toward Japan since the 1970s. What is noteworthy is that, while the gaps yawned between U.S. strategic plans and financial constraints and between Japan's growing economic power and its negligible contribution to international security, the Reagan administration managed to keep bilateral trade and economic issues separate from defense issues. In fact, also as noted earlier, Washington took advantage of the growing capital flow from Japan to finance its deficit spending on defense and tax cuts. More recently, however, economic and defense issues have become linked, at least in the mainstream policy thinking that provides the background for the formulation of Washington's policy toward Japan. This is apparent in the area of defense technology cooperation.

Most American analysts advocate a more reciprocal sharing of defense technology between the two countries.[20] They correctly note that U.S. interest in Japanese defense technology is motivated by both the fear of future Japanese competition in weapons development, and the potential cost savings that bilateral cooperation represents to the U.S. defense industry.[21] Some researchers warn of the long-term implications of Japan's high-technology defense research and development for neighboring countries' defense policies.[22] Others advocate more aggressive, economics-driven security relations with Japan as part of a more comprehensive national strategy.[23]

Official Policy

It has been difficult for Washington to incorporate these varied views into a coherent policy. In fact, some mainstream U.S. analysts have complained that Washington has no coherent strategy and is poorly organized for dealing with Japan.[24] Official U.S. policy has called for continued forward deployment of U.S. forces in the Asia-Pacific region. Washington views the U.S. military presence in the region as essential to regional stability, to discourage the emergence of a regional hegemon, and to enhance Washington's ability to influence a wide spectrum of important political and economic issues in the region.[25] However, Washington is increasingly unable to bear the cost of its military presence in the region and, therefore, appreciates Japan's increasing burden sharing. Washington also needs Tokyo's cooperation in pulling the Asian countries out of their economic crisis and is openly critical of slow responses in Tokyo. It is unlikely, however, that the currency, financial, and economic crises sweeping East Asia today will affect Washington's interest in maintaining the security alliance with Tokyo.

Washington is committed to maintaining the current U.S. troop presence in Japan, including in Okinawa, despite the growing local opposition to U.S. bases there following the rape by U.S. servicemen of an Okinawan girl in 1995. Washington and Tokyo managed to reach a compromise and agreed that Japan would build an offshore heliport off Nago City in Okinawa to replace the Futenma facility. However, a public referendum confirmed Nago residents' overwhelming opposition to the proposed construction, and Okinawa Governor Ota Masahide sided with the local people. In November 1998, however, Ota lost his reelection bid to Inamine, who supports the Tokyo-Washington compromise plan for the relocation of the Futenma base. How local wishes and the central government's interests will play out is not at all certain.

The strategic importance of American bases in Japan in the post–Cold War period was amply demonstrated during the Gulf War. The Seventh Fleet was dispatched to the Middle East, including the cruiser *Bunker Hill* that launched Tomahawk missiles against Baghdad. Additionally, the U.S. Marine air base in Iwakuni is being expanded with the construction of a new runway slated to begin in two years.

The *United States Security Strategy for the East Asia Region*, issued in February 1995, makes it clear that Washington has no intention of disengaging from the region or reducing its security cooperation with Tokyo.[26] According to the report, the U.S.-Japan security alliance is the linchpin of U.S. security policy in the Asia-Pacific region. The report also speaks approvingly of Japan's greater contribution to regional and global stability through ODA and its strategic partnership with the United States, including host-nation support.[27] President Bill Clinton's February 1996 report to Congress on U.S. national security strategy asserts that the development of a new Pacific community requires the linking of security needs with economic realities and concern for democracy and human rights. Defining the United States as a Pacific nation, the U.S. strategy calls for maintaining an active presence and leadership in the region and refers specifically to the 100,000-strong troop presence as contributing to regional stability.[28]

Critics

Chalmers Johnson and E. B. Keehn have offered the most articulate yet debatable criticism against the Clinton administration's policy toward Japan. They declare that the end of the Cold War and the altered balance of power—in favor of Japan—have eliminated the only meaningful strategic rationale for the U.S.-Japan alliance.[29] They assert that the continued U.S.-Japan security alliance delays Japan's coming to terms with the problems of Article 9 of the Japanese Constitution and that the "outdated security policy" of the United States short-circuits the nascent security debate in Japan. They write: "If Japan is truly to remain the linchpin of U.S. strategy in Asia, any serious rethinking of U.S. security policy must center on rewriting or peacefully dismantling the Japan-U.S. Security Treaty." To them, "a United States that continues to distrust Japan's ability to act as a true ally" is a more serious threat to a peaceful Asia-Pacific region than is China's continued expansion.[30]

The Johnson-Keehn critique underestimates the importance of firm U.S. security commitments in the region. Northeast Asia remains a potentially dangerous region. The United States, Japan, and other East Asian countries share security concerns regarding the political uncertainty in nuclear China and nuclear Russia, and the tension on the divided Korean Peninsula.[31] Beijing's saber rattling against Taiwan during the latter's presidential election in 1995 was very disconcerting to China's neighbors. Beijing's unsettled territorial disputes with its neighbors in the South China Sea are an additional concern to Tokyo, not to mention its own territorial dispute with Beijing over the Senkaku (Tiaoyu) Islands in the East China Sea. Moreover, the Johnson-Keehn argument ignores the growing acceptance, among Southeast Asian leaders, of the need to maintain the U.S.-Japan security alliance for regional stability.[32]

From Washington's perspective, the fundamental issue is not whether Japan should or should not become a normal state, but how the United States should pursue its own national interests in the dramatically changed strategic environment of the Asian-Pacific region. In this connection, the altered balance of economic power between the United States and Japan underlies Washington's urging that Japan elevate its security role.

The New Guidelines for U.S.-Japan Defense Cooperation

New Defense Cooperation Guidelines

The central issue facing the U.S.-Japan alliance today is how to make it relevant to the broader regional situation. Tokyo and Washington's joint response to this need has been the new Guidelines for U.S.-Japan Defense Cooperation.

Clinton and Prime Minister Hashimoto Ryutaro met in Tokyo in April 1997 and issued the "Japan-U.S. Declaration on Security: Alliance for the 21st Century." The document reaffirmed the essential importance of the U.S.-Japan security treaty to both countries and the region. Among other things, the declaration noted that the Asia-Pacific region was the most dynamic area of the globe but there was instability and uncertainty. It stated that the two countries needed to enhance the credibility of their security relationship by cooperating in bilateral security consultations, review of the 1978 defense cooperation guidelines, and the prevention of the proliferation of weapons of mass destruction and their means of delivery.

The aim of the new guidelines, issued in September 1997, is defined as creating a "solid basis for more effective and credible U.S.-Japan cooperation under 'normal' circumstances," "in case of an armed attack against Japan," and "in situations in areas surrounding Japan that will have an important influence on Japan's peace and security." The section on "Basic Premises and Principles" states that the new guidelines will operate within the fundamental framework of the U.S.-Japan alliance. It also states, "Japan will conduct all its actions within the limitations of its Constitution and in accordance with such basic positions as the maintenance of its exclusively defense-oriented policy and its three non-nuclear principles."[33]

Regional Contingencies
The most controversial issue relates to the ill-defined meaning of "situations in areas surrounding Japan."[34] The guidelines do not spell out what contingencies, besides an armed attack against Japan, would call for the expanded bilateral defense cooperation, but discussions among private circles are indicative of the kind of contingencies defense planners may deal with under the new guidelines. Among the scenarios discussed by private defense analysts is a North Korean surprise attack on South Korea and taking of hostages. Some speculate that North Korea, realizing the changing balance of military capabilities in favor of South Korea, might move in to the north of the Han River and take hostages, possibly including Japanese nationals. Another scenario involves low-intensity conflicts involving North Korea, including terrorist acts, assassinations, or some other destructive actions against the South, or even against Japan. Another possibility entertained by some Japanese observers is a collapse of the North Korean regime, causing an exodus of refugees, defections, and rampant acts of terrorism and assassination.[35]

There is no firm common understanding in the government about the application of the concept to Taiwan. Liberal Democratic Party Secretary-General Kato Koichi stated during his visit to Beijing in July 1997 that the new guidelines were not aimed at China. This was contradicted by a subsequent statement by Chief Cabinet Secretary Kajiyama Seiroku that a conflict between the People's Republic of China (PRC) and Taiwan would be included in this definition. Chinese Premier Li Peng protested that this was a serious interference in the internal affairs of China. In April 1998, Vice Foreign Minister Yanai Shunji stated that the concept of "situations in areas surrounding Japan" is similar to the "Far East." This prompted Director General of the Foreign Ministry's Treaties Bureau Takeuchi Yukio to issue an equally ambiguous explanation, that the senior diplomat's statement should not be interpreted to mean that the two concepts represented the same geographical definition but, rather, that both concepts were intricately related to the security of Japan. Prime Minister Hashimoto reiterated on several occasions that the new guidelines were not targeted at "any particular area or country."

The apparent absence of a uniform understanding of the operational meaning of "situations in areas surrounding Japan" is problematic. Rather than enhancing the effectiveness of U.S.-Japan defense cooperation in promoting regional stability, the problem creates uncertainty in Japan's policy and perpetuates neighboring countries' suspicions regarding an expanded Japanese regional ambition.

The U.S. position is more explicit. In June 1997, for example, Deputy Assistant Secretary of Defense Kurt Campbell briefed visiting Japanese politicians on the U.S. view of the security situation in East Asia and the Pacific, and pointed out there were five security issues of concern to the United States: (1) instability in North Korea as an existing threat, (2) Sino-Russian rapprochement as a potential threat in the next 15 years, (3) Chinese military buildup as a non-negligible development, (4) unstable PRC-Taiwan relations as a troubling issue, and (5) the growing military spending in Southeast Asia as a point of concern.[36]

Japan's New Responsibilities

Once a crisis "situation in areas surrounding Japan" occurs, the new guidelines call on Japan and the United States to cooperate in (1) relief activities and measures to deal with refugees, (2) search-and-rescue operations, (3) noncombatant evacuation operations, and (4) activities to support economic sanctions. With respect to refugees arriving in Japan, the guidelines place primary responsibility on Japan and call on the United States to provide "appropriate support." Japan's search-and-rescue operations will be limited to Japanese territory and "at sea around Japan, as distinguished from areas where combat operations are being conducted." How Japan's search-and-rescue operations will be coordinated with those of the United States in and around the areas of combat operations remains a very difficult issue. It raises the question of whether Japanese actions might constitute an exercise of collective self-defense, which is currently prohibited. As far as civilian evacuations are concerned, the 1997 guidelines state that each government is responsible for evacuating its own nationals from a third country to a safe haven. When necessary, however, Japan and the United States will coordinate in planning and cooperate in carrying out evacuation operations. For the evacuation of non-U.S. and non-Japanese civilians, the guidelines leave open the possibility that Japan may extend assistance to third-country nationals. In carrying out economic sanctions, the guidelines call on Japan and the United States to cooperate in areas of information sharing and the inspection of ships based on UN Security Council resolutions.

The new guidelines further call on Japan to permit U.S. forces' temporary use of Self-Defense Force (SDF) facilities and civilian airports and ports, to lend rear support, and to engage in bilateral operational cooperation. Japan's rear support is expected primarily in Japanese territory, but the guidelines envisage the possibility of Japanese rear support "on the high seas and international airspace around Japan which are distinguished from areas where combat operations are being conducted." This would be problematic if unfolding contingencies required a minute-by-minute redefinition of areas of military operations. Less problematic would be Japan's rear support inside its own territory, including the transportation and medical treatment of casualties, support for the security of

U.S. facilities and areas, sea surveillance around U.S. facilities, the security of transportation routes, and information and intelligence gathering.

Finally, the 1997 guidelines require Japan and the United States to develop a comprehensive mechanism for bilateral planning and to establish common standards and procedures. This will involve not only U.S. forces and the SDF, but also other Japanese government agencies. The joint defense planning now envisaged goes far beyond what had been accomplished under the previous guidelines. Previous bilateral cooperation in this area was limited to joint studies of contingencies, whereas the new guidelines call on the two countries to conduct joint contingency planning and cooperation under normal circumstances in preparation for contingencies.

Domestic Law

What specific steps is Japan taking to meet its obligations under the new framework for defense cooperation? In April 1998, the Hashimoto government submitted to Parliament three legislative bills to give substance to its new commitments: (1) a bill for the law regarding situations in areas surrounding Japan, (2) a bill to revise the Law on the Self-Defense Force, and (3) a bill to revise the Acquisition and Cross-Servicing Agreement (ACSA) between Japan and the United States. These laws set legal rights and obligations in some new areas.

Under the first law, the government would be authorized to undertake, in the face of "situations in areas surrounding Japan," rear support, search-and-rescue operations in rear areas, and the inspection of ships. Japan would extend search-and-rescue operations to U.S. soldiers. The prime minister would be required to obtain Cabinet approval for the basic plan of action. Some critics in Japan argue that parliamentary approval should be required, but the government, presumably to ensure timely response to an impending crisis, opted for more readily obtainable Cabinet approval instead. The new law would empower the defense agency director-general to specify actions to be included in rear support, search-and-rescue operations in rear areas, and ship inspections, and to order the SDF to undertake such actions. The law would also authorize the government to require local governments and the private sector to cooperate. It leaves unclear, however, whether local governments and the private sector could decline to cooperate. Nor does it speak to the rights and obligations of individual citizens. The new law would not require the prime minister to obtain parliamentary approval but simply to report to parliament all decisions regarding basic contingency plans and any changes therein. Finally, the law would authorize SDF personnel to use weapons to protect themselves in the course of search-and-rescue operations in rear areas and in ship inspections.

The proposed revision of the Law on the Self-Defense Force would authorize the use of ships and ship-borne helicopters to transport Japanese citizens overseas in emergency situations. It would also authorize the use of weapons to protect SDF personnel and Japanese evacuees. Finally, the bill to amend the ACSA would outlaw the provision of weapons and ammunition by Japan to U.S.

forces, but would authorize the provision of goods and services in the course of actions taken in response to "situations in areas surrounding Japan."

If parliament approves these bills, Tokyo will have moved several steps closer to meeting its obligations under the new defense cooperation guidelines with the United States.

Conclusion

The end of the Cold War and the collapse of the Soviet Union spelled the end of the ideologically inspired strategic rationale of the U.S.-Japan alliance, and this has raised and continues to raise serious questions about the viability of the alliance, not to mention the costs and benefits, to the respective countries, of maintaining the security treaty. However, the changes in the strategic environment have not fundamentally altered the power relationship between the United States and Japan with respect to the bilateral security treaty system.[37] Hence, the competing views introduced earlier on the desirable or possible directions for future U.S.-Japan relations. On the one hand, those in the United States and Japan who emphasize the change in the regional strategic environment tend to call for a more drastic change in the bilateral alliance. On the other hand, those who stress the continuing unequal power relationship between the two countries tend to prefer more incremental changes in the alliance. Washington and Tokyo are faced with these competing thrusts as they seek a new strategic rationale for their alliance in the twenty-first century. As we have seen, this is by no means an easy task.

Should Washington and Tokyo fail either to maintain the U.S.-Japan Security Treaty System, or to develop a multilateral security framework to supplement or replace the bilateral alliance, Tokyo would face even more uncertain and unsettling options. They are (1) accommodation with Beijing to neutralize China's possible hostility, (2) a strategic partnership with Moscow to counter China's growing power, (3) a concert of powers including the United States, Japan, China, and Russia, and (4) defense buildup and independent security policy.

Accommodation with China would likely reduce Japan's already dubious influence in China over such issues as human rights, defense buildup, arms exports, and even territorial demands on its neighbors, possibly compromising Japan's own claims to the Senkaku (Tiaoyu) Islands. As well, it would increase Japan's financial burden to support China's economic development, which would further strengthen China's national power and weaken Tokyo's leverage over Beijing. More importantly, a Japan-China accommodation of this magnitude might seriously undermine Japan's relations with the United States, politically and economically.

A strategic partnership with Moscow that could balance China's growing power would require a full settlement of the Russo-Japanese dispute over the Northern Territories, not an assured prospect despite the visibly improving relationship between Moscow and Tokyo since 1997. Even if the two countries were able to find a mutually acceptable solution to the territorial dispute, a full-fledged strategic partnership between Tokyo and Moscow would likely entail a substantial burden on Japan: massive economic aid to the struggling Russian economy and equally substantial Japanese investment in the fledgling markets, a risk that most Japanese businesses would like to avoid.

A concert of great powers, involving the United States, Japan, China, and Russia, would require an unprecedented convergence of future visions among these powers. This is not a likely prospect. Given Japan's historical aversion to a balance-of-power-based political order in Asia, moreover, it would be surprising if Tokyo chose this option over the others.

Finally, Japan's military aggrandizement would be equally problematic. It is true that Japan has developed substantial military capabilities through direct arms purchases from the United States, defense technology cooperation with the United States, and the research and development program of its own. The experience the Japanese defense industry has thus gained is varied enough and advanced enough to provide Tokyo with some powerful indigenously developed military hardware. However, an independent Japanese defense policy would almost certainly mean the end of Japanese access to U.S. weapons technology. Japan would have to finance its military buildup entirely on its own. This might tempt Japan to go nuclear, but such a prospect would surely frighten its neighbors into a coalition against Japan. Tokyo's decision to abandon its three nonnuclear principles and to develop nuclear weapons would polarize and destabilize Japan, where pacifism and antinuclear sentiment run deep.

Clearly, then, Tokyo's best alternative is to continue its alliance with the United States and, where the bilateral cooperation is inadequate to meet post–Cold War regional security challenges, to develop bilateral and multilateral security dialogues and consultations with other countries of the region. This indeed is the alternative Tokyo has decided to pursue toward the twenty-first century.

Notes

1. For a review of the evolution of Japan's perception of the U.S. power through the 1980s, see Tsuneo Akaha, "Japan's Security Policy after U.S. Hegemony," *Millennium: Journal of International Studies* 18:3 (Winter 1989): 435–54.
2. A number of excellent analyses appeared in Japan of the structural changes in world politics during this period and implications for U.S.-Japan relations. Among them: Inoguchi Kuniko, *Posutohaken shisutemu to Nihon no sentaku* [The Posthegemonic System and Japan's Options] (Tokyo: Chikuma Shobo, 1987); Inoguchi Takashi, *Gendai kokusai seiji to Nihon* [Contemporary International Politics and Japan] (Tokyo: Chikuma Shobo, 1991), particularly chapters 5, 15, and 18, pp. 115–145, pp. 297–320, and pp. 375–412, respectively; Kamo Takehiko, *Kokusai anzen hosho no koso* [A Design for International Security] (Tokyo: Iwanami Shoten, 1990), particularly chapters 3 and 4, pp. 119–79 and pp. 181–261, respectively.
3. For a detailed analysis of the slow intellectual adjustment in Japan, see Gilbert Rozman, *Japan's Response to the Gorbachev Era, 1985: A Rising Superpower Views a Declining One* (Princeton, New Jersey: Princeton University Press, 1992).
4. Tsuneo Akaha, "The End of the Cold War and Japanese-Russian Relations," in *Russia in the Far East and Pacific Region*, eds. Il Yung Chung and Eunsook Chung (Seoul: Sejong Institute, 1994), pp. 327–56.
5. This section draws on Akaha Tsuneo, "An Illiberal Hegemon or An Understanding Partner?: Japanese Views of the United States in the Post–Cold War Era," *Brown Journal of World Affairs* (1998).

6. The description of Japan as a pacifist nation is found in virtually every Japanese work on the nation's contemporary international policy. For discussions of Japan as a civilian power, see Hanns W. Maull, "Germany and Japan: The New Civilian Powers," *Foreign Affairs* 69:5 (Winter 1990–91); Funabashi Yoichi, "Japan and the New World Order," *Foreign Affairs* 70:5 (Winter 1991–92): 65; Funabashi Yoichi, *Nihon no taigaikoso: Reisengo no bijon o kaku* [A Vision for Japan's External Policy: Fashioning a Post–Cold War Vision] (Tokyo: Iwanami Shoten, 1993), pp. 159–206.
7. See for example, Tsuru Shigeto, *Nichi-Bei ampo kaisho e no michi* [Pathway to the Dissolution of the U.S.-Japan Security Alliance] (Tokyo: Iwanami Shoten, 1996).
8. For the normal state thesis, see Ichiro Ozawa, *Blueprint for a New Japan: Rethinking of a Nation* (Tokyo: Kodansha International, 1994); Okazaki Hisahiko, "Rekishi no kyokun: Kokusai kankei no shiten" [The Lessons of History: A Perspective on International Relations], in Okazaki Hisahiko, *Kokusai josei handan: Rekishi no kyokun, senryaku no tetsugaku* [Judging the International Situation: The Lessons of History, Strategic Philosophy] (Tokyo: PHP Kenkyujo, 1996), pp. 275–317.
9. For advocacy of Japanese participation in collective security, see Okazaki Hisahiko, "Japan Should Awake to Its Right to Collective Self Defense," *Daily Yomiuri*, 4 July 1994; Sase Masamori, " 'Shudanteki jieiken' kaishaku no kai" [Association for Interpretation of the "Right to Collective Defense"], *Voice* 223 (July 1996): 128–49; and Sato Seizaburo, "Clarifying the Right of Collective Self-Defense," *Asia-Pacific Review* 3 (Fall–Winter 1996): 91–105.
10. For the concept of bandwagoning, see Stephen M. Walt, *The Origins of Alliances* (Ithaca: Cornell University, 1987); Kenneth N. Waltz, "The Emerging International Structure of International Politics," *International Security* 18:2 (Fall 1993): 44–79. For a recent Japanese analysis of the U.S.-Japan alliance dynamic from the balance of power, bandwagoning, and other theoretical perspectives, see Tsuchiyama Jitsuo, "Nichi-Bei domei no kokusai seijiron: Riarizumu, riberaru seidoron, konsutorakutibizumu" [International Relations Theories of the U.S.-Japan Alliance: Realism, Liberal-Institutionalism, and Constructivism), *Kokusai seiji* 115 (May 1997): 161–79.
11. Kazuo Ogura, "Japan's Asia Policy, Past and Future," *Japan Review of International Affairs* 10:1 (Winter 1996): 3–15.
12. Robert S. Ross, *Managing a Changing Relationship: China's Japan Policy in the 1990s*, Strategic Studies Institute, U.S. Army War College, 1996, p. 5. For a balanced assessment of Japan's military capabilities, see Michael Mandelbaum, *The Strategic Quadrangle: Russia, China, Japan, and the United States in East Asia* (NY: Council on Foreign Relations Press, 1995), p. 120.
13. See for example, Soejima Takahiko, *Zokkoku Nipponron* [Japan, a Tributary State] (Tokyo: Satsuki Shobo, 1997).
14. Akaha Tsuneo, "Nihon no mittsu no kao: Nashonarisuto, rijonarisuto, gurobarisuto to shite no shorai" [Three Faces of Japan: The Nationalist, Regionalist, Globalist Visions of the Future], Nihon Kokusai Seiji Gakkai, eds., *21-seiki no Nihon, Ajia, sekai* [Japan, Asia, and the Global System: Toward the Twenty-First Century] (Tokyo: Kokusai Shobo, 1998), pp. 775–806.
15. Prime Minister's Office, Office of Public Relations, ed., *Seron chosa* [Public Opinion Survey] (Tokyo: Ministry of Finance Printing Bureau, 1998), p. 36.
16. Prime Minister's Office, Office of Public Relations, 1998, p. 34.
17. This section draws on Akaha Tsuneo, "Beyond Self-Defense: Japan's Elusive Security Role under the New Guidelines for U.S.-Japan Defense Cooperation," *Pacific Review* 11:4 (1996): 461–83.
18. *Asahi shimbun*, 30 April 1998, p. 2.
19. For an example of the first view, see Edward Olsen, "Target Japan as America's Economic Foe," *Orbis* 36 (1992): 496. The second view has been articulated by Henry Kissinger, who has warned that Japan might not be content with its status as an economic giant and a military dwarf. See *Hokkaido shimbun*, 23 January 1993, p. 2.
20. See, for example, Robert A. Manning, "Futureshock or Renewed Partnership: The U.S.-Japan Alliance Facing the Millennium," *The Washington Quarterly* 18 (1995): 87–98.
21. Andrew K. Hanami, "The Emerging Military-Industrial Relationship in Japan and the U.S. Connection," *Asian Survey* 33 (1993): 592–609.
22. Nakamura Hisashi and Malcolm Dando, "Japan's Military Research and Development: A High Technology Deterrent," *Pacific Review* 6 (1993): 177–90.
23. See, for example, Wayne Sandholtz, Michael Borrus, John Zysman, Ken Conca, Jay Stowsky, Steven Vogel, and Steve Weber, *The Highest Stakes: The Economic Foundations of the Next Security System*, A BRIE Project (NY: Oxford University Press, 1992).

24. Joseph Nye, "Coping with Japan," *Foreign Policy* 89 (Winter 1992): 96–115.
25. Department of Defense, *A Strategic Framework for the Asian Pacific Rim: Report to Congress* (Washington, DC: Department of Defense, 1992), p. 20.
26. Office of International Security Affairs, Department of Defense, *United States Security Strategy for the East Asia-Pacific Region* (Washington, DC: Department of Defense, 1995).
27. Office of International Security Affairs 1995, p. 16.
28. The President of the United States, *A National Security Strategy of Engagement and Enlargement* (Washington, DC: The White House, February 1996), pp. 39–40.
29. Chalmers Johnson and E. B. Keehn, "The Pentagon's Ossified Strategy," *Foreign Affairs* 74 (1995): 103–10.
30. Johnson and Keehn, 1995, p. 110.
31. Robert A. Manning, "Futureshock or Renewed Partnership: The U.S.-Japan Alliance Facing the Millennium," *The Washington Quarterly* 18 (1995): 90–2.
32. Ralph A. Cossa, "Johnson and Keehn's Ossified Analysis," *PacNet* 35 (6 October 1995).
33. Office of Assistant Secretary of Defense 1997, "Completion of the Review of the Guidelines for U.S.-Japan Defense Cooperation," News Release, New York, 23 September 1997, p. 1.
34. The following discussion of the new guidelines draws on Tsuneo Akaha, "Beyond Self-Defense: Japan's Elusive Security Role under the New Guidelines for U.S.-Japan Defense Cooperation," *Pacific Review* 11:4 (Fall 1998): 461–83.
35. Roundtable discussion among Sassa Atsuyumi, Taoka Shunji, and Higaki Takashi, *Ronza* (August 1996): 10–19; reported in FBIS-EAS-96-138.
36. *Sentaku* (September 1997), p. 128.
37. Hara Yoshihisa, "Josetsu: Nichi-Bei ampo taisei jizoku to hen'yo" [Introduction: The Japan–U.S. Security Treaty System—Continuity and Change], *Kokusai seiji* 115 (May 1997): 1–10.

CHAPTER 11

Japan and the European Union

Reinhard Drifte

Approaching the European Union confronts an outside actor with many complexities: the EU is the most cohesive regional block that has so far been created, endowed with genuine supranational features, an inchoate "Common Foreign and Security Policy" (CFSP), and an expanding cluster of common policies of international relevance in all kinds of fields ranging from environmental issues to development aid. According to the Treaty of Rome, external economic relations are the prerogative of the Commission of the EU, which acts on behalf of the member states. Accordingly, any outside actor has to deal with the Commission in the economic area where the Western European states are particularly important, but there are also regular political consultations at various levels. The most visible manifestation of the EU as an international actor in itself is, for example, the Delegation of the European Community in many capitals, including Tokyo. On the other hand, the member states still pursue their own economic policies, and the CFSP is still very limited. This leads to the necessity for an external actor to deal with the individual member states as well as the Commission, creating complexities but also opportunities for the outside actor. From the outside, the EU often looks more coherent and powerful than from the inside, where people are more aware of the constant struggle to achieve consensus.

Whatever the complexities, the EU is Japan's biggest and most developed market outside of the United States (accounting for around 20 percent of world trade, compared with around 10 percent for Japan), and with the advent of the euro after the year 2000, one which will be very similar to the United States in terms of integration, but offering access to over 467 million consumers (373 million as of 1998) thanks to the EU's continuing enlargement to the East. With ongoing political integration, the EU is also gaining in importance for Japan as a political and even security partner.

After giving a brief overview of the historical development of Japan-EU relations, this chapter will analyze the economic relationship and then explore the growing links on the political as well as security level. The chapter concludes that the economic relationship is still unbalanced, but that European integration has made considerable contributions to smoothening the resulting disputes. At the same time, these disputes have also increased the incentives to deepen the political and security relationship.

The Historical Background

Japan became aware of European integration when six European states created the European Economic Community in 1957 through the Treaty of Rome. Concerned that European integration may bolster Europe's competitive edge and exclude Japan from the most important developed market outside of the United States, Japan reacted by embarking on a diplomatic offensive, sending an unending stream of politicians and business leaders to Europe. This fear was also stimulated by European resentment against Japan as a result of the past war experiences and Europe's memory of aggressive Japanese trade practices during the prewar era, as well as of postwar protectionism. As a result, the European countries had been dragging their feet concerning Japan's admission to GATT in 1955 and other international economic organizations. In 1959 Japanese exports to Western Europe amounted to 10.6 percent of Japan's total exports. At the time Japan's goal was admission to international economic organizations, to gain most-favored nation (MFN) treatment, and to end the invocation of GATT Article 35 limiting trade. Japan offered only gradual steps of liberalization, but in 1963 France became the last EEC member state to put commercial relations with Japan on an MFN basis. Most Western European countries, however, had a safeguard clause in the bilateral commercial treaties with Japan that substituted for Article 35.

In the 1960s Japan's economic expansion was increasingly felt in Europe. Japan's GNP overtook that of one country after another, including Germany's in 1969, and from 1968 on Japan has had a trade surplus with the Community, creating a series of unending trade conflicts that have varied in intensity. In contrast to EC figures, Japanese figures were lower because they are based on FOB (free-on-board) exports and CIT (cost, insurance, transit) imports. In 1970 the first book on the Japanese challenge was published in Europe.[1] In the early 1960s, Japan's exports to Europe consisted mainly of ships and textiles, followed later by ball bearings, steel, electronics, and automobiles. Europe's response has been voluntary self-restraint agreements (e.g., in the trade of automobiles, color televisions, and some machine tools) and antidumping procedures. With Japan's surplus rising and Japan's growing competitivity offsetting any European countermeasures, lack of accessibility to the Japanese market became an increasingly heated subject, mirroring in many ways Japanese-American trade conflict. But already a Japanese observer had aptly described the difference of the two trade conflicts by stating that Japan's economic disputes with the EC "linger on like the prolonged drizzle that characterizes Japan's rainy season," whereas disputes with the United States are reminiscent of a "showdown between pistol-drawing cowboys."[2]

It is against this background of trade disputes and deepening European integration that the European Community (now called the European Union) became an important partner for Japan, increasingly rivaling Japan's bilateral relationships with the individual EU member states.

The Institutional Background

In order to appreciate the value and complexity of the EU for Japan, we have to look at the institutional setup of European integration. Article 113 of the Treaty of Rome provides for a common commercial policy within the Union and toward nonmembers. It is the task of the Commission in Brussels to propose initiatives on commercial policies and to negotiate trade agreements according to a mandate of the Council of Ministers, which is sometimes agreed upon by non-constitutional summit meetings of heads of governments. The full implementation of Article 113 has taken a long time, and in the case of Japan's relations with the EU, a bilateral trade agreement has not yet been concluded, although the Commission received a negotiation mandate as far back as 1969. The reason for this failure was the insistence by member states on a safeguard clause that was unacceptable to Japan.

As the executive organ of the EU and against the background of Article 113, the Commission is very keen to gain full control over EU trade with Japan, and to expand relations with Japan in other areas that are becoming the focus of common European action. The advantage for Japan is that it needs to deal on certain items with only one interlocutor and that it achieves coherence in a specific area of policy. In trade, the role of the Commission can mean an outcome more benign to Japan's interests, overriding the resistance of particular interests of one or several member states. From a Japanese point of view, the role of the Commission as the facilitator of an open and unified internal market has often prevented more radical national proposals inimical to Japan's position. This role had a decisive influence in controlling temperatures when trade disputes were at their most intense. The downside is the length it takes to reach an agreement, and the loss of the opportunity to play one EU member state against the other or against the Commission. Moreover, agreement is often made on the basis of the lowest common denominator between the EU member states. Despite the clear mandate of the Commission in the external trade of the Union, member states often consider the Commission as a welcome lever against external trade partners, but only when national means fail.

Over the years, with growing European integration on the one hand and rising saliency of the Japan-EU relationship for Europe on the other, the Commission has gained a greater role in the relationship and expanded it from initially concerning only economic and trade issues to a growing range of other issues. The Commission's role was expanded in June 1973 with the establishment of regular high-level talks between the Commission and the Japanese government, taking place every six months alternatively in Brussels and Tokyo. In October 1975 the EC opened an office in Tokyo with diplomatic status granted by Japan, followed by a Japanese mission to the European Commission in Brussels the following year. Since 1990, the head of the EU Delegation holds the rank of ambassador.

With each major step of European integration, Japan became more aware of the role of the EU. One step was the Single European Act in 1986, followed by the Single European Market in 1992, the Maastricht Treaty in 1993, and then the Treaty of Amsterdam in 1997.[3]

In the 1970s the European member states instituted "European Political Cooperation," which became under the Treaty of the European Union (Maastricht Treaty) in 1992 the "Common Foreign and Security Policy" (CFSP). Under this concept, member states together with the Commission organize political dialogue with third countries and political groupings when deemed necessary. The political dialogue today takes place through the annual summits (Presidents of the Commission and Council, Japanese Prime Minister) since 1991, Ministerials (Commission/Japanese Government) since May 1984, and, twice yearly, Troika Ministerial and Political Directors Consultations since January 1983.[4]

EU-level cooperation now takes place through a large number of structured dialogue meetings on subjects such as industrial policy and industrial cooperation, science and technology, competition policy, social affairs, development policy, environmental issues, macroeconomic and financial affairs, and transport. Since 1996 meetings of government experts in areas meriting close policy coordination take place (Asia, Former Yugoslavia, NIS and Central Asia, the Middle East Peace Process and the Gulf). As of 1998, there are 34 forums for consultation and cooperation between the EU and Japan, most of which have been established since 1991. In addition, the European Parliament, another pillar of the European integration process with growing powers, and the Japanese Diet hold consultative interparliamentary meetings annually.

The Economic Level

With rising Japanese exports and the obliteration of several European sectors like cameras or TV by Japanese competition in the 1970s, Japan was faced with demands for so-called Voluntary Restraint Agreements and Voluntary Export Agreements for particular sectors negotiated at member state level or industrial sector level. Japan had to accept these agreements, which was only made palatable by the fear of otherwise EU-wide restrictions, the advantage of guaranteed high prices for quantitatively reduced Japanese goods in high demand, and by the possibility of exploiting differences between individual member states.

After a high-level Keidanren mission ("Doko Mission") to Europe in 1976, the European Community levied for the first time antidumping duties against a Japanese product (ball bearings) at the Community level. But Japan's trade surplus with the EU continued to increase with rising exports.

This situation brought about a greater focus in Europe on its difficulties in accessing the Japanese market, and the resulting efforts closely paralleled the American strategy to improve its trade position with Japan. One target in this respect was Japan's technical and administrative trade barriers (NTB). The EU sought to address the problem by applying Article XXIII (23) under the GATT.

The result was merely that Japan agreed to voluntary restrictions on the export of ten sensitive items under a VRA administered by the Commission on a Community-wide level.

The next step of the EU to defend itself against Japanese exports consisted of antidumping cases brought against various Japanese export items, starting with one case in 1976 (ball bearings) and rising rapidly in number. The Japanese reaction to this new defense mechanism was to increase production facilities in Europe that were initially successful in circumventing voluntary export restrictions (VERs) and antidumping procedures until the Community started to establish a local contents rule in 1984. This rule stipulated a certain percentage of European content in order for an item to qualify as a European product that could benefit from free circulation within the Community. Since the measure is illegal under the GATT rules, Japan submitted a complaint and won the case in 1990. In order to set up a single market for automobiles, Japan and the EU negotiated in 1991 a transitional arrangement (until 1999) under which Japanese exports to the EU are "monitored," i.e., "voluntarily" restricted. The negotiation of VERs at the industrial sector level became incompatible with the "single European market" project, and the Commission was able to consolidate its role as the negotiating partner of Japan.

Several developments led to an improvement of trade relations at the end of the 1980s. One was the improvement of the European economic situation. Another was the growing integration of the EU under the "single European market" project that led to Japanese concerns about the building of a "Fortress Europe." More long-lasting was the changing attitude of the Conservative Party under Prime Minister Margaret Thatcher in Britain, which increasingly saw in Japanese investment a means to reduce unemployment, the most urgent political issue, and to maintain manufacturing capacities in Britain. Embracing a free market credo that overlooked the nationality of any production site in the United Kingdom, the British government offered material incentives to lure Japanese investment into Britain, significantly enhancing Britain's other advantages as a location of investment in terms of language and socioeconomic framework. When the success of this strategy influenced some other European countries to take a more positive attitude toward Japanese investment, Japan's trade surplus began to decrease. In 1988 the British Department of Trade, in cooperation with business, created the "Opportunity Japan" campaign (1988–91), which is said to have doubled British exports to Japan and led to the adoption of many Japanese management practices. The campaign was then followed by "Priority Japan" (1991–94) and since then "Action Japan." In France this change was emulated with the official campaign "Le Japon . . . c'est possible." Government in Germany is much less involved in private trade and investment, but these campaigns had a positive effect on business perceptions of Japan there as well. At the EU level, a pilot program "Export to Japan" was begun in 1990, which became in February 1994 the "Gateway to Japan" program.

As a result, Britain has become Japan's favored destination for investment (44 percent of all Japanese investment into the EU on a cumulative basis, followed by the Netherlands with 21 percent) although trade with Germany is higher. Japan is thus the third largest investor in Britain, the United States being by far the leading investor, followed by Germany. With a total of 274 cases (as of 1998) out of a total of over 1,000 Japanese companies in the country, Britain is the preferred location for Japanese direct investment in Europe in the manufacturing sector, followed by France and Germany. The investment in Britain alone has created 65,000 direct new jobs. In fiscal year 1996–97, Britain attracted ¥387.3 billion of Japanese investment, more than three times as much as the Netherlands, which comes second.[5]

Table 11.1 Trade Between Japan and the EU (unit: million yen)

Year	Exports		Imports		Balance	
	yen	% change	yen	% change	yen	% change
1992	8,452,223	-1.4	4,256,534	-7.7	4,195,689	6.0
1993	6,688,1225	-20.9	3,655,297	-14.1	3,032,828	-27.7
1994	6,271,099	-6.2	3,959,352	8.3	2,311,747	-23.8
1995	6,600,063	5.2	4,579,682	15.7	2,020,381	-12.6
1996	6,846,534	3.7	5,362,788	17.1	1,483,746	-26.6

Source: Ministry of Finance, Japan

The EU member countries now urge Japanese business to supplement their manufacturing capacity with research and development facilities, and 150 Japanese companies in the U.K. have such facilities. However, the flow of Japanese investment into Europe has dropped off in the 1990s as it has gained pace in the direction of Asia. In 1988, around 38 percent of the foreign subsidiaries and affiliates of Japanese companies were based in Asia, compared to 29 percent in North America and 18 percent in Europe. By 1997, the percentages were 60 percent, 20 percent, and 13 percent, respectively.[6]

The other side of this investment picture is, however, characterized by the considerable imbalance of EU investment in Japan of around 8 to 1, attributable to high costs in Japan (labor, real estate, general price level), European preference for wholly-owned subsidiaries, and market access restrictions in Japan deriving from structural and policy conditions. European investment is approximately 10 percent of the Japanese foreign direct investment in the EU. The EU has even been de-investing from Japan, in the period 1992–95 by an average 300 million ECU annually.[7] According to EU statistics, total EU direct investment outside the EU stood at ECU471.91 billion, of which ECU207.18 billion was in the United States and only ECU11.05 billion was in Japan, most in the manufacturing sector, services, and petroleum (including chemicals, rubber, plastic products).[8] In 1996, EU investment in Japan increased by 72.8 percent over the previous year to ¥220.2 billion, amounting to a slight increase of the number of individual investors from 330 in 1995 to 353 in 1996. By investment volume, Dutch companies lead European investment in Japan, followed by German and British companies. With the low value of the yen, Japanese deregulation, and liberalization of financial markets, European investment is likely to increase. With its current economic problems, the Japanese side is interested in more European investment to stimulate the economy, reduce price levels, and help the poorer regions of Japan.

In addition, Japanese investment within the EU is geographically unbalanced as a result of different policies and attitudes toward foreign direct investment, which are in fact the source of intra-EU friction. Due to a lack of competence in the realm of investment, the Commission has found it difficult to influence this area except through lateral means such as antidumping (e.g., local content regulation) and competition rules (e.g., creating a level playing field for national investment incentives). As of 31 December 1997, antidumping measures against six Japanese export products were in force.

The more cooperative atmosphere between Japan and the EU has allowed the problems of trade and investment imbalances to be dealt with through monitoring and dialogue. In order to come to an agreement on trade imbalances, the so-called Trade Assessment Mechanism was set up in 1993.[9] It is a statistical mechanism between the Commission and the Japanese government for comparing the EU's performance in Japan to its performance in other comparable markets with a symmetrical exercise being conducted for Japanese exports. This has led to the negotiation of Mutual Recognition Agreements in the field of testing and certification and an industrial cooperation program. Currently, negotiations are going on for mutual recognition of test results and standards with respect to telecommunications equipment, electric appliances, medical and pharmaceutical products, as well as chemical products. Telecommunications is the sector of greatest interest to the EU.

Other measures to reduce trade frictions include the executive training program, which has so far permitted over 600 young European executives to stay in Japan for language acquisition and company internships and export promotion campaigns (e.g., "Gateway Japan," to run from 1997 to 2000). The EU-Japan Centre for Industrial Cooperation, which was established in Tokyo in 1987 and in Brussels in 1996, organizes training courses and topical missions for EU managers in Japan. It also manages the Vulcanus program, which offers courses combining language and in-company training for Japanese engineering students in Europe and for European engineering students in Japan.

Another important development that has been helping to reduce economic frictions is the number of alliances concluded between European companies and Japanese companies to enhance their competitiveness as part of the globalization process. One example is the Fujitsu purchase of British International Computers Limited (ICL) in 1989, which at the time created alarm in the European computer industry. Today, joint technological development agreements between European and Japanese companies, notably in high technology where R&D has become prohibitively expensive, are as common as between European and American companies.

Trade-related negotiations now revolve around the following clusters of issues involved with improving EU access to the Japanese market:

1. Standards for testing and certification
2. Other regulatory obstacles (e.g., public procurement and distribution)

3. Tariff barriers and quantitative restrictions
4. Structural problems (e.g., *keiretsu*)

Table 11.2. Japanese direct investment in Europe (100 Million Yen)

	1993	1996 cases	1996 amount	1997 cases	1997 amount
EU total	8,303	219	8,053	225	13,452
U.K.	2,946	77	3,873	84	5,054
Holland	2,488	36	1,238	40	4,043
Germany	884	30	643	19	898

Source: Ministry of Finance, Japan

After hitting a trade surplus record with the EU of $31.2 billion in 1992, the surplus declined in both 1993 and 1994 by more than 15 percent due to progress in many of the above four areas. In terms of products (dollar-based), machinery accounted for about 70 percent of Japan's exports to the EU. In 1997, Japanese exports shot up to ECU59 billion, an increase of 13.1 percent over the previous year, while imports from the EU increased merely by 1.1 percent to ECU36 billion (see Table 11.3).

Table 11.3 Trade between Japan and the EU (unit: million ECU)

	Exports	% change	Imports	% change
1993	52,178	-7.3	24,661	11.1
1994	53,751	3.0	29,082	17.9
1995	54,284	1.0,	32,889	13.1
1996	52,507	-3.3	35,666	8.4
1997	59,367	13.1	36,049	1.1

Source: Eurostat.

In 1996, according to EU trade statistics, Japan was the third largest trading partner of the EU after the United States and Switzerland, accounting for 7.3 percent of the total value of extra-EU trade.[10] The trade is based on manufactured goods, which in 1996 represented 98 percent of all imports from Japan and almost 86 percent of all EU exports to Japan. Machinery and transport equipment accounted for the major part with 74 percent of EU imports from Japan and 40 percent of EU exports to Japan. The EU trade deficit with Japan in 1996 resulted from the negative balance of trade in machinery and transport equipment (electrical machinery, office machines and data processing machines, road vehicles). The EU achieved the greatest trade surplus with Japan in articles of apparel, medical and pharmaceutical products, and beverages. Germany and the U.K. accounted for most of EU trade with Japan, with 30 percent and 18 percent respectively. The largest trade deficit was, in order of declining magnitude, with the U.K., the Netherlands, and Germany. Italy, Denmark, and Sweden achieved a trade surplus.[11]

Japan's economic crisis and the fall in the yen/dollar exchange rate have significantly changed Japan's overall trade surplus and particularly the one with the

EU. In 1997, Japan's total exports (custom clearance base) rose 2.5 percent year on year to $422.9 billion, while imports dropped 2.9 percent to $340.4 billion.[12] In fiscal year 1997–98 (ending March 1998), Japan's overall trade surplus expanded by 80 percent to ¥11.4 trillion. Because exports rose while imports fell, Japan's trade surplus, which had contracted for two straight years, expanded by 33.5 percent to $82.5 billion. While Japan's exports to Asia dropped for the second straight year, Japanese exports to the EU increased dramatically due to the weak yen.

EU exports to Japan fell by 11 percent in the first quarter of 1998, whereas imports from Japan grew by 20 percent. Japanese automobile exports to the EU increased by 35 percent, television sets and video recorders by 28 percent, and metals and metal products by 38 percent. Japanese imports of European automobiles, on the other hand, decreased by 17 percent.[13]

The Political Level

The rise of the political level of Japan's relations with the EU is due to the need of addressing more successfully trade disputes, the institutional momentum of European integration, and the expansion of multilateral issues.

Soon both sides realized that an expansion of relations from purely trade matters to the inclusion of political issues of common political interest might create a more benign environment for finding solutions to the rising economic frictions and inequities. The Commission for reasons of its own institutional interests was most willing to support or initiate such a move. Moreover, apart from smoothing trade conflicts, Japan discovered that gaining support from the EU as a whole for certain political issues could enhance its international position, particularly on issues on which it does not see eye to eye with the United States. At the beginning, common attitudes concerned mostly the Middle East. At the height of the Iranian hostage crisis in 1980, the Japanese foreign minister participated in a Council of Foreign Ministers meeting in Luxembourg, and the Japanese and EC ambassadors to Iran submitted a joint statement to the Iranian government requesting the release of the U.S. embassy hostages. On the Palestine issue, Japan found on occasion that the European attitude was closer to its own than that of the United States because of the latter's link with Israel.

Reflecting the more positive outlook in relations at the end of the 1980s, a Council of Ministers communication in 1988 expressed the wish to strengthen EU-Japan relations. This led in 1991 to the Joint Declaration between the European Community and Japan ("The Hague Declaration of 18 July 1991"), making the political dimension of the relationship more visible and promoting equitable access to EU and Japanese markets. Japan refused to accept a proposal from some member countries that wanted "a balance of benefits in trade" written into the declaration. The compromise was a more diplomatic formula, which recognizes that Japan has complaints about access to the European market as well, a "resolve for equitable market access to their respective markets and remov[ing] obstacles on the basis of comparable opportunities." The Joint Declaration led also to the annual Summit Meeting and established the framework for political dialogue between the European Union and Japan.

Following the Commission's paper "Towards a New Asia Strategy" (13 July 1994), the Commission proposed to the Council of Ministers in March 1995 the document "Europe and Japan: The Next Steps," which suggested new efforts for an improved relationship in view of the opportunities offered by the end of the Cold War, a greater opening of Japan, the "Common Foreign and Security Policy" (CFSP), the completion of the Internal Market, and EU enlargement. It regretted that the bilateral summits had faced great difficulties and that there had been long delays in organizing ministerial meetings with the Commission. Its criticism was that, in substantive terms, the dialogue had hardly proceeded beyond the level of exchange of views and information. The Commission had originally proposed the concept of "Europe and Japan: A New Partnership," but this did not survive further drafting stages.[14] In its draft, the Commission also proposed support of Japan's bid for a permanent UN Security Council seat, but the Council of Ministers removed this recommendation due to Italy's unwillingness to accept anything that might have a positive impact on Germany's bid for a seat. On the economic side, the paper suggested the enhancement of market access through the World Trade Organization (WTO) and the EU-Japan regulatory dialogue, distancing itself from the American approach of threatening trade sanctions that do not conform to WTO rules.

As a result of these efforts, the Japan-EU relationship evolves today around three axes: political dialogue, economic and trade cooperation, and cooperation on common and global challenges. Whereas the 1995 Paris summit was still heavily focused on trade and the economic issues, the September 1996 Tokyo summit focused more evenly on trade, cooperation, and political issues. These developments toward a higher political profile are sought by both Japan and the EU because they are interested in the expansion of political dialogue and cooperation for their own political and institutional interests. Both are eager to be seen not just as economic but as political actors. At the same time, such a high political profile creates a better environment to solve trade conflicts, and allows the creation of international political and economic regimes that are more amenable to their interests.

Current Major Issues

The major issues presently discussed between the two sides are the Asian economic crisis and Japan's role in it, as well as the forthcoming Economic and Monetary Union (EMU) and EU enlargement.

Japan hopes that the euro will be easily accessible, stable, and reliable, but at the same time, the EU is concerned that the euro's launch may suffer from the Asian economic crisis and the inability of Japan to relaunch its own economy and help Asia overcome the crisis. From January 1999 the euro will be the common currency for 11 countries and it will be used for cash transactions from 2002. One particular problem for Japan is Britain, where Japan has most of its investment, which will not join the EMU in the first stage. Concerns in this connection were highlighted by the unusual remark of Toyota's Chairman Okuda Hiroshi in January 1997, to the effect that consideration of the U.K. as a site for further investment from Japan could be endangered by its nonparticipation in the EMU. The remark may have had an influence on the new Labour government since May 1997, which has taken a much more conciliatory approach to the EMU. Continuation of the economic crisis in Asia and in Japan in particular could seriously harm the start of the EMU project as Europeans see it. The crisis and resulting worldwide currency instabilities (e.g., the fall of the dollar) could lead to the euro becoming too strong for the good of EMU members and causing deflation. For this reason the EU is pressing Japan to assume a greater role in containing the economic crisis in Asia by refloating its own economy more vigorously. It is also a concern to the EU that the Japanese government and industry are using the Asian crisis to consolidate their economic position in Asia and expand the export capacities of their subsidiaries.

As a result of the current economic crisis, Japanese investment in Europe is stagnating, and Japan's trade surplus with the EU is rising. With Japan's domestic economy faltering, demand for European goods is shrinking. Thus, not only is the primary imbalance in the economic relationship returning (i.e., Japan's trade surplus), but one of the main tools to cushion this imbalance (Japanese investment in the EU) is diminishing. In July 1998 Japan's surplus with the EU increased from a year earlier by 174.5 percent to ¥377.1 billion. Exports to EU nations rose 30.2 percent to ¥822.2 billion. Japanese exports have been given a boost by the fall of the yen against the dollar. In addition, the production of Japanese transplants in the EU and in other, third countries would have to be taken into account in order to gain a full picture of the real trade flows between Japan and the EU, and Japan's global trade flows in general.

Improving European market access has gained particular saliency since the onset of the economic crisis in 1997 and the deterioration of the trade balance for the EU. While the Japanese government clearly understands the need for deregulation in order to refloat the economy, the possibly negative short-term impact on employment has prevented steps undertaken so far, including the "financial bang" in the financial sector, from appearing wholehearted. The EU submitted to Japan a list of 200 items for deregulation. It is interesting to note that in April and May 1998, Japan proposed to the EU its own wish list for deregulation in the EU, indicating a stronger emphasis on reciprocity in its external relations.

On the political level, both sides are interested in exchanging views and seeking ways to cooperate on Russia and China. Whereas the EU has the greater knowledge and involvement in Russia, the EU can benefit from Japan's experience of China. The European Energy Charter is an interesting example in which Japan has benefited from an EU initiative initially conceived to improve energy cooperation between the EU and the successor states of the former Soviet Union. In June 1990, the European Council in Dublin proposed a plan for intensive energy cooperation to the then Soviet Union and the Central and Eastern European States. The United States, Canada, Japan, Australia, and other

OECD countries accepted this proposal. A total of 51 states from East and West, including Japan, signed in 1991 the resulting European Energy Charter. The European Energy Charter evolved then into the Energy Charter Treaty, which was signed in Lisbon in December 1994 by 49 countries and opened to ratification. Japan signed the Treaty on 16 June 1995.

Cooperation is taking place in former Yugoslavia, where Japan is helping with economic and political rehabilitation. At the time of the election in Bosnia in September 1996, Japan provided US$2 million worth of support and also at the time of the election in September 1997 in Bosnia, contributed US$1.5 million. Since March 1992, it has supported refugees in former Yugoslavia with about $340 million as of June 1998. In the Middle East both sides have a vital interest in the continuation of the peace process where Japan has notably supported the new Palestinian state. Since 1993, Japan has provided US$340.84 million to the Palestinians. The EU and Japan also share similar ideas about keeping open the lines of communication with Iran, in marked contrast to U.S. policy.[15]

The United States plays a particular role in the Japan-EU relationship because of the close relationship between the EU and the United States and Japan and the United States, which is not rivaled by the Japan-EU relationship because of the lack of a similarly strong security link. For both Japan and the EU, the bilateral relationship strengthens their hands in relations with the United States, particularly in view of forceful U.S. positions on some international economic, political, and security issues. On the other hand, the greater American leverage over Japan, the higher number of its foreign trade instruments, and its more confrontational approach to trade negotiations have sometimes given rise to concern in the EU that the United States may be given greater concessions in terms of market access than the EU, as was the case, for example, with the U.S.-Japan Semiconductor Agreement in the 1980s or the bilateral agreement on car parts during the Bush administration. The EU proposed to participate in the monitoring of the implementation of the U.S.-Japan automobile agreement of 1995, and trilateral monitoring meetings started in September 1996. This was also in Japan's interest since the EU's participation reduces American unilateral pressure on Japan. There is also concern in Europe that whenever trade relations become difficult for Japan in the United States, Japan shifts the surplus to Europe.

The EU has also demonstrated greater involvement in Asian issues that are of interest to Japan, such as aid to China, Mongolia, and Cambodia, and humanitarian aid to North Korea. On 30 July 1997 the EU signed an agreement about contributing over 5 years annually ECU15 million to the Korean Peninsula Energy Development Organisation (KEDO).[16] As part of the agreement the EU became a member of the Board of KEDO, the first such member outside of the original members (United States, South Korea, and Japan). The EU's involvement in KEDO is a clear sign that it follows up with concrete steps its professed interest in a close relationship with Asia and interest in a global nuclear nonproliferation and safeguard regime. But it is also known that it is a quid pro quo for Japan's contribution to security issues of direct relevance to Europe, such as Japan's help with the economic rehabilitation of Bosnia-Herzegovina and financial support for improving the safety of nuclear power plants in the Ukraine, Russia, Bulgaria, and Lithuania.

Other forums for Japan-EU cooperation are the ASEAN-Europe Summit Meeting (ASEM), which took place in Bangkok in 1996 and in London in 1998, the ASEAN Regional Forum (ARF) and the UN. One of the prime motives for the EU's interest in starting ASEM was its exclusion from the Asia-Pacific Economic Cooperation (APEC). For Japan, it is an additional forum that may assist in integrating China into the region and global politics in general as well as reconcile Asia with Japan's leading role in Asia. The UN has also become an arena for Japan-EU cooperation, strengthening Japan's multilateral position and adding weight to the legitimacy of its quest for a permanent UN Security Council seat. The EU and Japan, for example, cosponsored the UN Arms Registry in 1991, which covers trade in missiles, tanks, combat aircraft, warships, and other major weapon systems. Cooperation also took place on the ban of land mines and the removal of them in various countries.

Conclusions

With growing integration and enlargement, the EU is becoming ever more important as an economic and political partner for Japan. While the EU is still far from being a unitary actor, Japan's economic as well as political relations with the EU member states are more and more shaped by the structure of the EU. In the banking sector, regulations are already now at EU-level whereas in the United States, the banking sector is not regulated at federal but at state level. The Commission is clearly the driving force in the relationship by taking initiatives and trying to attract with changing success the attention of both Japan and the EU member states, expanding the relationship from trade matters to political dialogue and cooperation.

Since 1968, Japan has been enjoying a trade surplus with the EU, and the bilateral investment balance is also heavily in favor of Japan. While the presence of the EU has strengthened the hand of the member states, the EU structures have significantly contributed to reduction of tensions and have engineered a change in the approach to Japan at the end of the 1980s leading also to a greater balance between economic and political-security-cultural relations. The EU has become the source of external pressure on Japan to deregulate and open its economy to the outside, and Japan has appreciated that this is being done in a less confrontational way than by the United States. However, all the European efforts and differences in style have failed to achieve a more balanced trade and investment relationship. In addition, Japan has partly recreated an economic system in East Asia that is seen as a hindrance to European economic penetration of the region. The short-term and long-term impact of the Asian economic crisis on Europe is gradually being understood by the EU. This is leading to increased European pressure on Japan to stimulate its economy by deregulation and to open the domestic economy in order to reduce rising Japanese trade surpluses and the loss of European market opportunities.

The economic crisis in Japan is not only leading to an increase of exports to the EU (and the United States), but to a decline of Japanese investments that have become the best cushion for trade frictions. According to reports from Japan, Japanese companies are expecting to cut overseas direct investment in 1998 by 57 percent.[17] As a result we are facing a situation of Japanese trade surpluses, rising exports (of Japanese affiliates) from Asia, and deterioration of European unemployment in specific sectors and vulnerable regions due to retrenchment in Japanese investment. To compound the problem, in 1998 the EU had to abruptly halt a whole series of programs (Budget line B7/851) that included the Executive Training Programme (ETP), Vulcanus, and "Gateway to Japan" because of a successful legal challenge by Britain, until a proper legal foundation can be found. Due to the impression of a declining Japanese economy, interest in Japan is waning, highlighted by a decline of applications to the ETP from the U.K. and fewer students in Japanese studies.

The political side of the Japan-EU relationship presents a more optimistic picture. The relationship offers Japan a more diversified foreign and security policy, reducing somewhat the exclusive reliance on the United States. It demonstrates that Japan is interested in global security issues and willing to contribute to international burden sharing. The expanding political and security agenda with the EU has led to a security dialogue with NATO and in December 1996, it was given special status as a "Partner for Cooperation" within the Organisation for Security and Cooperation in Europe (OSCE), enabling it to participate in various OSCE functions.[18] This also takes care of Japan's concerns about being left isolated in the wake of NATO expansion and closer EU-Russia relations. After all, the 51-member OSCE reaches within less than two miles of Japan's northern border. In 1996 Japan was admitted as observer to the Council on Europe after France abandoned its opposition.

It is only in recent years that the proliferation of forums has started to move from the exchange of information to more substantive cooperation, attributable to the competition between individual member state activities and activities at EU level, as well as the absorption of the Japanese bureaucracy in its own feuds and proclivity to satisfy the American partner first. More substantive cooperation at the EU level is bound to increase with the EMU, more competence for the Commission, and the development of the CFSP, but the competition between member states and the Commission and the impact of the economic crisis in Asia may slow down this process or narrow its focus.

Notes

1. Hakan Hedberg, *Die japanische Herausforderung* [The Japanese Challenge] (Hamburg: Hoffmann und Campe, 1970).
2. Hakoshima Shinichi, "Mutual Ignorance and Misunderstanding—Causes of Japan-EC Economic Disputes, *Japan Quarterly* 26:4 (1979): 481.
3. The Amsterdam Treaty is reprinted in *EU Official Journal* C340, 10 November 1997.
4. Troika refers to the member state representative from the immediate past, current and next presidency of the EU, which changes every six months.
5. "Towards Global Partnership: UNICE Position on EU-Japan Economic and Trade Relations." Published by the Union of Industrial and Employers' Confederations of Europe, Brussels, 7 October 1998, p. 16.

6. Edith Terry, "Crisis? What Crisis?" Japan Policy Research Institute Working Paper, 50 (1998), p. 5.
7. Eurostat, *Economy and Finances 1997*, no. 9.
8. Statistics in Focus, 15/98. Eurostat.
9. See an evaluation of this and other mechanisms in: Simon Nuttall, "Japan and the European Union: Reluctant Partners," *Survival* 38:2 (Summer 1996): 104–20.
10. Statistics in Focus, August 1997. Eurostat.
11. Statistics in Focus, August 1997.
12. Annual White Paper on International Trade, Tokyo, 12 August 1998.
13. "Towards Global Partnership," 1998, p. 16.
14. S.J. Nuttall. "Japan and Europe: Policies and Initiatives," in *Japan's Foreign and Security Policies in Transition*, ed. Bert Edstrom (Stockholm: Swedish Institute of International Affairs, 1997), p. 113.
15. About this issue see Osamu Miyata, "Coping with the 'Iranian Threat': A View from Japan," *Silk Road* 1:2 (December 1997): 30–41.
16. The organization had been formed in October 1994 as a result of the so-called Agreed Framework between the United States and North Korea in order to have the North Koreans dismantle their nuclear program, which was suspected by the United States to aim at the development of nuclear weapons. In exchange for agreeing to the end of their indigenous nuclear program, the United States promised to organize an international consortium to build two Light Water Reactors of approx. 2,000 MW(e). Until the two reactors come on stream by the year 2003, the United States committed itself to deliver annually 500,000 tons of heating oil to North Korea.
17. *Financial Times*, 19 August 1998.
18. Japan had obtained observer status at the OSCE's predecessor organization, the Conference on Security and Cooperation in Europe, in 1992.

CHAPTER 12

The Waiting Game: Japan-Russia Relations

C. W. Braddick

> *nokori mono ni fuku ga aru* —everything comes to he who waits
> (*Japanese proverb*)

Tokyo and Moscow are on the verge of signing a historic peace treaty that will finally settle the frontier between their two countries, or so the Japanese newspaper headlines announced. Such predictions have surfaced regularly during the post–Cold War decade and yet the waiting game drags on. How is it that, despite the remarkable changes the international system has witnessed in recent years, Japan and Russia are yet unable fully to normalize their relations? In attempting to explain this paradox, others have skillfully chronicled the history of this troubled relationship; in contrast, this chapter will employ an extended game metaphor. Despite the fragmentary public record, this should enable us to discern the essential contours of postwar Japan-Russia relations.

The use of games as an analytical tool has a long history in the study of international relations. However, the game referred to here differs from both the rational quantitative methodologies of the game theorists and the role-playing crisis games of international politics departments. Instead, we will take as our model the crisis-management games described by John Creighton Campbell in a recent study of U.S.-Japan relations.[1]

According to Campbell, for such games to exist players need to fulfill four requirements, namely, they must have "differing interests," "compete for real stakes," "benefit from maintaining the relationship," and be "governed (if imperfectly) by a set of rules." In other words, this is a contest poised between concord and discord, played out according to certain precepts that constrain freedom of action, but in return offering tangible rewards to both participants.

Campbell examines an intense alliance relationship—unquestionably, postwar Japan's most intimate—but such logic can also be applied to the difficult relationship with the Soviet Union. The first three conditions are certainly met: if a question mark hovers, then it relates to rules. Campbell defines rules as "norms about what behavior is appropriate and expectations about how other players will react to various actions." It would be reasonable to assume that the rules in the Japan–Soviet game were less sophisticated and more often disregarded than in the game involving Japan and the United States, where the level of interaction was many times greater, except that the rules in the latter case performed an inverse function. It is tempting to dub Japan–Soviet relations as a crisis-maintenance game, where the rules serve to sustain a certain level of hostility. If so, then one is entitled to inquire whence these rules came. The answer is that they are an organic growth that has evolved in response to the actions of the players. Furthermore as Robert Putnam and others have shown, such games are played on multiple levels. Thus, it is necessary to identify not only the main domestic players, but also external actors, although there is no superior international body to enforce the rules.[2]

Campbell identifies a set of three separate but related games as coexisting in U.S.–Japan relations: the diplomatic, military, and economic. This was equally true of Japan–Soviet ties. All three games were played simultaneously, but during the Cold War era, each enjoyed a spell in the ascendant. For a short period following the 1956 Joint Declaration that reestablished relations, the diplomatic game was preeminent. After the Sino-Soviet conflict emerged in the early 1960s, however, the economic game became more prominent. Subsequently, with the collapse of détente during the late 1970s, the strategic game came to overshadow the others. Furthermore, it is only a slight exaggeration to say that each game revolved around a single issue: signature of a peace treaty; developing the resources of Soviet East Asia; and the military balance of power in Northeast Asia, respectively.

A decade has now elapsed since the end of the Cold War ushered in a new framework of international relations. Japan–Russia interaction has increased dramatically; relations have progressed on many fronts. Hence, it is vital to assess how far the rules and players of each game have changed under the triple impact of the end of the Cold War, globalization, and democratization.

The Cold War Diplomatic Game

The Soviet Union did not sign the San Francisco peace treaty in September 1951, and its mission in Tokyo ignored Japanese requests to leave when the treaty went into effect on 28 April 1952. However, Prime Minister Yoshida Shigeru's government stubbornly refused to recognize its legitimacy, and hence this game did not commence until January 1955, when Yoshida's successor, Hatoyama Ichiro, responded positively to a Soviet approach to normalize relations. The Joint Declaration signed on 17 October 1956 resolved all outstanding issues bar one: the territorial question. This issue, thus, came to dominate subsequent diplomatic exchanges. Japan refused to acknowledge Soviet sovereignty over several islands—the Habomai group, Shikotan, Kunashiri (Kunashir), and Etorofu (Iturup)—northeast of Hokkaido and occupied by the Soviet Army in the dying days of World War II. Moscow promised to return the first two upon the conclusion of a peace treaty, but Tokyo held out for the larger two disputed islands.[3] Japan's new premier, Kishi Nobusuke, then embarked on a successful campaign to revise the Security Treaty with the United States, in response to which Moscow unilaterally withdrew its promise on 27 January 1960.

Rules

Japan did not strive to improve political relations with the Soviet Union. From Kishi onward, it preferred a wait-and-see (*seikan*) attitude and consistently dismissed all Soviet peace initiatives as examples of insincere "smile diplomacy." Japan stubbornly refused to sign a peace treaty until the frontier issue was settled. Tokyo repeatedly claimed the disputed islands on historical, legal, and moral grounds, distinguishing them from the Kuril Islands it had renounced in the San Francisco peace treaty of 1951. Japan also insisted on all of the disputed islands being returned simultaneously (*yonto ikkatsu*). Efforts by successive Japanese premiers in December 1969, March 1973, and October 1975 to soften this stance were undermined by domestic opposition.[4] Tokyo offered no inducement to the Soviets to smooth the islands' return, but it did not break off relations: lines of communication were kept open. Moreover, Japan avoided provocative actions. It did not use, or threaten the use of, force to recover the islands, and violent confrontation was generally avoided.

Moscow, by contrast, oscillated between trying to get around the territorial problem and simply denying that it existed. Evidence suggests that the Soviets secretly renewed the "two island" offer in July 1967 and January 1972, but they did not honor Soviet President Nikita Khrushchev's October 1964 promise to return the two islands when the United States handed back Okinawa in May 1972.[5] Later, in February 1975 and again in January 1978, President Leonid Brezhnev offered to sign a friendship treaty before a full peace treaty, but to no avail.

Both sides were rigid and inflexible. The characterization of Japanese diplomacy as "know what you want and push until you get it" certainly applies in this case.[6] Consequently, negotiations were ritualistic: a display of shadow boxing. It was a boring game.

A variety of reasons have been advanced to explain why the negotiating positions of 1955–56 subsequently hardened into immutable rules. If one accepts that the disputed islands are of intrinsically limited value to either side—although not without some strategic and economic merit—then their importance must be primarily symbolic. One suggestion is that, in serving as a potent reminder of the Soviet breach of their bilateral Neutrality Pact, the dispute allowed the Japanese to rewrite the history of World War II, with themselves cast in the role of victim. A related idea is that the islands acted as an ideological antidote to the popular appeal of communism, and Japan used their "illegal occupation" as a means to poison relations. A third theory asserts that Japan suffered from a pathological condition—the Northern Territories syndrome—a severe case of irredentism. Finally, some argue that it was really a test of relative national strength or status.[7] All these reasons are plausible, if difficult to verify, but it is indisputable that a weakened Japan, aware that any immediately achievable settlement would favor the Soviets, was playing a waiting game.

Players

On the Japanese team, there were few players. Diplomats from the Ministry of Foreign Affairs (Gaimusho), especially at the Soviet desk (Sorenka) are generally acknowledged to have played a central role. The foreign ministry prided itself on "its continuity in personnel; its consistent image of the Soviet Union; and its unwavering negotiating stance."[8] The unbroken period during which the Liberal Democratic Party (LDP) had been in office reinforced the diplomats' inflexibility, although ironically the left-wing opposition party platforms made even greater territorial demands on Moscow.[9]

A number of prime ministers and foreign ministers took a deep interest in the game, but the foreign ministry discouraged individual politicians from engaging in "personal diplomacy." If planning a visit to the Soviet Union, they were urged by ministry officials to raise the territorial issue as often as possible.[10] Think tanks, such as the Council on National Security Problems led by Suetsugu Ichiro, were said to be influential behind the scenes.[11] Public opinion, as measured by polls, was overwhelmingly anti-Soviet, and yet the Japanese government felt sufficiently concerned by declining popular interest to institute a Northern Territories Day on 7 February 1981.[12] There was no significant pro-Soviet lobby in Japan.

The Soviet State was even more centralized. The Foreign Ministry and the International Department of the Central Committee of the Communist Party, for most of this period under the control of Andrei Gromyko and then Ivan Kovalenko, were responsible for formulating policy, but ultimate authority rested with the Politburo.[13] In general, both sides resisted outside interference in the diplomatic game, although in August 1956 Tokyo unsuccessfully requested Washington to convene an international conference on the territorial dispute.[14] In addition, in 1964 and again in October 1970, Japan raised the issue at the UN, eliciting a very critical Soviet response. The Americans and Chinese, allies of the principals, were naturally the most interested third parties. They were not players in the same sense as the Japanese and Soviets, but they were much more than mere bystanders. Indeed, many point to Secretary of State John Foster Dulles as the real instigator of this border-fixated game.[15] Yet, if his opposition to a territorial compromise in August 1956 had not resonated with a key Japanese constituency—the Yoshida school in the LDP and the foreign ministry—he could not have done so. In July 1964, Mao Zedong suddenly reversed Beijing's stance and proclaimed his support for Japan's territorial claim. Although privately discomfited, Tokyo did not publicly reject Chinese interference until July 1976.[16]

The Cold War Economic Game

Postwar Japan-Soviet trade was minuscule until a Treaty of Commerce went into effect on 9 May 1958, spurring rapidly increasing economic exchanges. The first Soviet hints at the possibility of direct Japanese participation in Siberian development came as early as 1960, but they did not really take concrete form until the Sino-Soviet rift acquired an economic dimension. Compared to the stagnant political game, the economic game was more dynamic but no less frustrating.

Rules

This was ostensibly a more cooperative game, with both sides sharing a common interest in developing the resources of Soviet East Asia, yet political considerations were always lurking in the background. The Japanese often appeared reluctant, but there was some genuine enthusiasm to take advantage of the limited commercial opportunities offered by the Soviet economy. During most of the 1960s and 1970s, Tokyo did not attempt to link the economic and diplomatic games (*seikei bunri*). However, to strengthen its economic security, Japan sought to diversify its sources of raw materials, increase Soviet reliance on Japanese trade and investment, and profit from the Sino-Soviet conflict.

The Soviets were again inconsistent. They frequently invited greater Japanese participation in Siberia, but then would often unilaterally change conditions: a game of carrot and stick. Emphasizing the two countries' economic complementarity, Moscow hoped to exploit Japanese business for Siberian development as well as heighten Japanese dependence on Soviet resources. The Soviets used Western European (and, much later, South Korean) participation as a kind of bait to evoke in the Japanese a fear of missing the boat. Access to Soviet fishing grounds was restricted, but the Soviets also tolerated a lot of "illegal Japanese fishing" around the disputed islands.[17]

Exceptions were rare. In June 1973, Prime Minister Tanaka Kakuei let the studied nonchalance slip and announced Japan's willingness to participate in the Tumen oil project before a summit date was set, revealing Tokyo's trump card without the foreign ministry's knowledge.[18] Tanaka's resource diplomacy put economics first. This had changed by the mid-1980s, when technological advances both reduced Japanese demand for Soviet resources and increased the strategic risks associated with technology transfers, as seen in the Toshiba scandal of April 1987.[19] Henceforth, Japan explicitly linked economic exchange to the diplomatic and strategic games (*seikei fukabun*) and refused to sign an official agreement on long-term economic cooperation proposed by Moscow.[20]

Players

Like the political game, a small number of players dominated the economic game. The Japanese government officially avoided any direct role, leaving it to the private sector. Nevertheless, the foreign ministry effectively discouraged investment through administrative guidance. It faced intermittent competition, however, from the Ministry of International Trade and Industry (MITI) and finance ministry, elements within the LDP, opposition parties, and sectors of the business community. A few trading companies (*sogo shosha*), steel and heavy machinery manufacturers (members of Keidanren's Joint Japan-Soviet Economic Committee inaugurated in September 1965), and the Hokkaido fishing industry were the most intimately concerned. Big business, supported by MITI, saw the Sino-Soviet conflict as a golden opportunity and muscled in on trade previously controlled by small companies associated with left-wing opposition parties.[21] In January 1963, the LDP's right-wing pressured MITI into announcing limits on the amount of credit that could be extended to Moscow. Yet, the

Soviet link later helped the right-wing curb pro-Chinese elements within the party.[22] Some scholars have even claimed that an unholy alliance developed between pro-Taiwan politicians and pro-Soviet business interests.[23] During the 1970s, MITI's enthusiasm occasionally threatened to override the practical concerns of industry, for example, over Sakhalin gas.[24]

As a centrally planned economy, the Soviet State maintained a monopoly on foreign economic activities. Under the overall direction of Gosplan, the Ministry of Foreign Trade and Committee for Foreign Economic Relations handled all economic relations with Japan.[25]

The United States used the Coordinating Committee for Export Control (COCOM) restrictions and direct pressure on the Japanese government and businesses to limit Japan-Soviet trade. For example, in the early 1960s, Washington sought to prevent Japanese exports of large-diameter steel pipe and imports of Soviet oil, warning Tokyo that such trade would be used later for political purposes. Such opposition was somewhat undermined by U.S. grain sales to the Soviets under President John F. Kennedy, and by 1965 the American attitude was much more positive. Nevertheless, throughout the 1960s and 1970s, Japan practiced self restraint and insisted on U.S. partners for big investment projects. U.S. opposition intensified again in the early 1980s. Washington pressured Tokyo into imposing sanctions after the Soviet invasion of Afghanistan in January 1980 and strengthening them after martial law was declared in Poland in February 1982. Japan-Soviet trade declined, but companies managed to find alternative channels to sustain the economic game. Even the U.S.-inspired Toshiba scandal of April 1987, which led to MITI strictly enforcing the COCOM code, represented but a temporary setback to the revival under President Mikhail Gorbachev.

Similarly, Beijing long acted both as an impediment and alternative channel to Japan-Soviet trade. For example, the Chinese government helped to scupper Japanese participation in the massive Tumen project in October 1974.[26]

The Cold War Strategic Game

Despite being on opposing sides in the overarching East–West confrontation, for a surprisingly long time this game was not wholly subsumed within the Cold War framework. Tokyo was scornful when Moscow signed an anti-Japanese alliance with Beijing on 14 February 1950. Although it signed a Security Treaty with Washington on 8 September 1951, Japan was long a reluctant participant in the U.S. global defense structure containing communism. The strategic game did not come of age until the late 1970s.

Rules

This game rested on mutual distrust, although neither side really saw the other as a direct threat to its security. Japan attempted to minimize its role in the strategic confrontation between the Free World and Communist bloc, and to avoid involvement in the escalating Sino-Soviet conflict. Moscow oscillated between schemes ostensibly directed at reducing tension in the region, and aggressive actions that escalated them. The Japanese were not intimidated by Soviet displays of military might, but regarded with suspicion any peaceful initiatives originating in Moscow, such as the Asian Collective Security System proposal of June 1969. As this would have involved recognition of the frontiers established by World War II, and was patently aimed at containing China, Tokyo simply ignored it. Similarly, nearly two decades later, Japanese skepticism greeted Gorbachev's new Asian policy, although it focused on arms control measures favorable to Tokyo.[27]

The primary Soviet strategic objective was to prevent encirclement by a hostile alliance. Most Soviet aggressive acts were not directed specifically at Japan. The Soviets observed a revival of Japanese militarism during the latter half of the 1970s, but the antihegemony clause in the Japan-China Friendship Treaty of August 1978 and the normalization of China-U.S. relations five months later were bigger concerns. Moscow would have liked to decouple Japan from the United States but it was unwilling even to put up the ante by returning the disputed islands.

The rift with Beijing prompted Moscow to begin a military buildup in the region in the late 1960s, but Japan did not officially identify the Soviet Union as a potential threat until the 1980 Defense White Paper. This followed a series of provocative acts, in particular the stationing of troops by the Soviet Union on the disputed islands in May 1978, and its invasion of Afghanistan in December 1979. Subsequently, the Soviet Army deployed SS-20 nuclear missiles in Asia, and shot down a South Korean airliner on 1 September 1983. Political hawks in Tokyo used this opportunity to play up the Soviet military threat to justify both strengthening the alliance with Washington and increasing military expenditure.[28] Not until 1990 did Japan change course.

Players
The foreign ministry again took the lead in this game, although the Defense Agency (Boeicho) played an increasingly vocal role, with the support of the LDP's *boei zoku* (defense lobby). The Defense Agency, which based its estimates on military capacity rather than political intentions, had been criticized by the foreign ministry for inflating the Soviet threat and intruding on foreign policy, but such differences evaporated after the Soviet invasion of Afghanistan.[29] The weakening pacifist public sentiment still acted as a constraint.

In marked contrast to the situation in Japan, the uniformed ranks of the Soviet armed forces exerted a significant influence over the strategic game, although the military remained subordinate to the Politburo.

The United States and China once more played their obstructive role of preventing a Japan-Soviet rapprochement. The United States provided Japan with an effective security umbrella and employed every available means to ensure that it remained loyal to the Security Treaty. The Sino-Soviet Alliance, by contrast, succumbed to the challenge posed by rising Chinese nationalism. Thereafter, Japan became an object of rivalry in the Sino-Soviet conflict, a competition Beijing appeared to win with Tokyo's acceptance of the antihegemony clause in their August 1978 Treaty of Peace and Friendship.

The End of the Cold War and the New Strategic Game

The end of the Cold War represented a paradigm shift in international relations. The collapse of the bipolar power structure removed the fundamental strategic obstacle to Japanese-Soviet rapprochement. Yet, whereas Western Europe, the United States, and China dramatically improved their relations with Moscow during the mid-1980s, Japan did not. The legacy of distrust is slow to evaporate. Japanese opinion is divided: some argue that the Cold War endures in East Asia and that Russia remains a regional rival, while others worry about the danger of violent unrest in Russia and a regional security vacuum.[30] Certainly, it is much easier to identify the rules that no longer apply than to discern those that have taken their place. Unlike the repetitive patterns of the Cold War period, the last decade of Japan-Russia relations has exhibited a distinctly mercurial quality.

Rules

Cautious as ever, Japan may have been loath to join the new positive-sum strategic game, but there is little doubt that it is now doing so. Security has been effectively separated from the diplomatic game and mutually reinforced through a series of confidence-building measures. The credit for initiating this process rests largely with Gorbachev. While president, he ordered drastic reductions in Soviet conventional and nuclear forces in East Asia and the Pacific, and during his April 1991 visit to Tokyo, promised to demilitarize the disputed islands—a process reportedly completed by the end of 1997.[31] In response, Japan's September 1990 Defense White Paper dropped its reference to the Soviet Union as a "latent threat." Six years later, it even ceased to describe Russia as "a factor of instability in the region." More concretely, Japan slowed its own arms buildup and helped to finance Russia's nuclear disarmament. In recent years, the process has broadened to include talks on military policy planning; the exchange of military information; visits by defense ministers, uniformed chiefs and warships; and joint search and rescue exercises.[32]

President Boris Yeltsin has tried to place the strategic game on a new level. In February 1992 the Russian leader called Japan a partner and "potential ally."[33] Three years later, Moscow extended its support to Japan's campaign for a permanent seat on the UN Security Council. Then, at the G-7 summit in Denver in June 1997, Yeltsin promised that Russian nuclear missiles would de-target Japan, saying that the two countries should become strategic partners.[34] Most recently, in the Moscow Declaration of November 1998, Prime Minister Obuchi Keizo agreed with Yeltsin to form a "creative partnership" that would benefit them strategically and geopolitically, as well as contribute to security in the Asia-Pacific region.[35] A new strategic game has begun.

Players

On the Japanese side, the central players have remained the same, although their degree of influence may have altered slightly. The Defense Agency, which became increasingly outspoken during the 1980s, was forced to accept the disappearance of the Soviet threat by a weak prime minister, Kaifu Toshiki, in 1990.

Since then, the Defense Agency's traditional hostility toward Russia has waned somewhat.

The influence that the Russian military exerts over the new strategic game does not appear to have diminished to the same extent as its offensive capabilities. Conversely, while the power of the United States and China—the sole remaining superpower and its main potential rival in the post–Cold War era, respectively—has increased, their role in the Japan-Russia game has not. Initially, the divergence between the United States and Japan on Russia policy led Tokyo to question whether Washington was still defending Japanese interests. However, the gap subsequently narrowed, helped no doubt by Moscow's open support for the U.S.-Japan Security Treaty, including the new defense guidelines. Their participation—along with that of China—in the ASEAN Regional Forum (ARF) since July 1993 also seems to have reinforced security to some extent.

Globalization and the New Economic Game

Globalization refers to the process whereby national governments are apparently losing control over what were international relations. The rubric of globalization has come to include a variety of developments—economic, political (see below), and cultural. In Japan-Russia relations, the effect of globalization has, perhaps, been strongest on the economic game.

Rules

Globalization challenges the rules of the Japan-Russia economic game from both above and below, via attempts to integrate Russia into the global economy and efforts to form a subregional economic community in Northeast Asia. The attitude of the Japanese government was initially cool toward both trends.

Tokyo was long a serious restraint on Western efforts to assist Russian economic reform. It saw little national interest in doing so.[36] In part, this reflected the established linkage to the diplomatic game, but there was also genuine concern regarding Russia's ability to absorb and use financial aid effectively. Linked to this was the fear that Washington and the International Monetary Fund, in disregarding Japan's experience with a strong developing state, were imposing an inappropriate laissez faire market model on Russia.[37] Japan has gradually overcome its reluctance to support Moscow's membership of various international capitalist economic institutions. In addition, Tokyo modified its rigid *iriguchiron* approach—demanding the disputed islands' return prior to improving economic relations—with the introduction in mid-1989 of balanced expansion (*kakudai kinko*), allowing political and economic relations to develop in tandem.[38] In January 1991, Tokyo relented and initiated small-scale humanitarian assistance to the Soviet Union. Since then, it has gradually stepped up its financial assistance to Moscow. The substantial sums promised, mostly in the form of loans, have concentrated on technical and intellectual assistance, aid for the environment, energy safety, and defense conversion. The "Hashimoto-Yeltsin plan for economic cooperation," agreed at Krasnoyarsk in November 1997, added investment promotion and is reportedly making steady progress. Nevertheless, cooperation has largely been a one-way street—Japan helping Russia—and bottlenecks have been frequent. Tokyo has been very slow to dispense the promised aid. Exploitation of Russian natural resources remains Japan's primary economic goal. In a December 1996 letter to Yeltsin, Prime Minister Hashimoto Ryutaro appeared ready to abandon any linkage to the diplomatic game in favor of a truly multifaceted approach.[39] A speech in July 1997 seemed to confirm the shift to a *deguchiron* policy—accepting the return of the islands as the result of improved relations. However, while the connection has been steadily eroded, it has not been completely severed. Foreign Minister Komura Masahiko rejected a loan request in March 1999 because of Russian stalling on the territorial issue. For him, progress on economic cooperation and the resolution of the territorial dispute are joined, like "two wheels of a car."[40]

Promotion of Japan-Russia border trade began in the early 1960s, but Gorbachev's decentralizing economic reforms provided a significant boost to such trade. Hence the revival of interest in a Japan Sea Rim Economic Zone (*kan Nihon kai keizai ken*) during the late 1980s. In Japan, local governments in the Hokuriku area (including Niigata) and Hokkaido led the way, but a lack of infrastructure and knowledge has severely limited progress.[41] One could argue that the level of decentralization is insufficient in Japan, but excessive in Russia.

The Japanese government, meanwhile, has promoted its own version of regionalism. Initially targeting resources on the former Soviet republics of Central Asia, it later added the Russian Far East, but here its hands remain tied by the territorial dispute. Since autumn 1991, Russia has proposed joint economic development of the disputed islands, but Japan has been reluctant to throw away one of its trump cards.[42] Humanitarian aid was extended to the island residents following an October 1994 earthquake, and fishing has been made an exception, but Yeltsin's latest proposal to convert the islands into a special economic zone remains unacceptable to Tokyo.[43]

All of this has done little to arrest the precipitate decline of the Russian economy. In 1998, trade was at a four-year low as Russian exports to Japan plummeted, influenced no doubt by the August 1998 devaluation of the ruble and moratorium on external debt repayments.[44]

Players
Japan's business community has exhibited relatively little interest in the Russian market. In their calculation, the members believe that the risks plainly outweigh any potential gains: any incentives offered by the Japanese government cannot compensate for the lack of Russian political, legal, economic, and financial infrastructure. In addition, they fear that the Japanese government will reverse its positive stance if a territorial settlement is not achieved by 2000.[45]

The foreign ministry remains at the core of the bureaucracy-dominated policy-making system. Now, however, in addition to competing for influence with the increasingly active finance and international trade and industry ministries, the Russia desk must share responsibility with a new foreign ministry section in charge of economic aid to the former Soviet Union, the Commonwealth of Independent States (CIS).[46] For some time after the collapse of the Soviet

Union, a shared caution allowed the three ministries to coordinate their resistance to LDP calls for Russian aid. Only intense pressure from Japan's G-7 partners tipped the scales in the politicians' favor.[47] With Russia in the grip of "gangster capitalism," it is virtually impossible to identify the main Russian players in the new economic game.

Democratization and the New Diplomatic Game

Democratization is shorthand for the staggering transformation of Russia's domestic political environment, including the protection of human rights and holding of free elections, and also, perhaps, Japan's very much less ambitious experiment with political reform. Some may point to the lack of progress: the process is certainly incomplete, but already it has greatly complicated the diplomatic game.[48]

Rules

Japan was extremely cautious about supporting democratization in the Soviet Union, as was amply demonstrated by the government's tardiness in condemning the attempted coup against Gorbachev in August 1991.[49] It was slow to perceive and respond to the rapidly changing Russian political landscape and, hence, new diplomatic rules have emerged only gradually. In essence, the new game that has evolved is the reverse of the old one. Today, Japan is the one pressing for a final territorial settlement, offering inducements and compromises.[50] At the déshabillé summit in Krasnoyarsk on 1 and 2 November 1997, Hashimoto succeeded in persuading Yeltsin to accept 2000 as a target date to conclude a peace treaty. Conversely, Russia, now in the weaker position, is trying to postpone an agreement on the disputed islands, while still seeking a political rapprochement. Since December 1988, Moscow has officially acknowledged that a territorial problem exists with Japan. Instead of denial, it now rebuts Japanese claims to the disputed islands with legal and historical arguments. In the Tokyo Declaration, signed by Yeltsin on his first official visit to Japan in September 1993, Russia recognized the validity of agreements from the Soviet era and promised to conclude a peace treaty resolving the territorial dispute on the basis of law and justice.[51]

Japan has sought to take advantage of Russia's democratization to woo public opinion and its shapers, aiming to change their perceptions of the costs and benefits of an agreement. Tokyo has certainly succeeded in raising public awareness of the territorial dispute, but in so doing, it has inadvertently turned the islands into a domestic political football in Russia. Initial efforts concentrated on the Russian Foreign Ministry and Japanologists, who appeared receptive to Tokyo's ideas, but their influence proved limited.[52] Japan has sought to avoid pinning its hopes on a single leader like Yeltsin, doubting his ability to deliver on any promise. It is noticeable that as Yeltsin's health has declined, the Russian position has hardened, but Tokyo has been left with few alternatives. The more Japan has propagated its position on the mainland, the stronger has become the opposition from Russian public opinion.[53] Only brutal economic necessity has forced the majority of the diminishing band of island residents to reverse their earlier opposition.[54] Russia, meanwhile, has exploited its newly democratic status to delay an agreement. Moscow argues that to conclude an agreement without the backing of the overwhelming majority of the Russian public, including residents of the disputed islands, would be to risk national disintegration.[55]

Japan has also turned to the international community for help in pressuring Moscow to return the islands. At first, Tokyo was suspicious of positive European and American reactions to what it saw as another Soviet peace offensive. Prime Minister Takeshita Noboru sounded out European views in 1988, but backing was lukewarm at best.[56] U.S. President George Bush urged Gorbachev to concede on the issue at their summit in July 1991, to no avail.[57] Strong Japanese pressure produced vague statements of support from the G-7 at the Houston and Munich summits in July 1990 and 1992, respectively. However, this attempt at internationalizing the problem backfired when the Europeans later criticized Japan's inflexibility and self-centered attitude, and the Americans increased their support for the Russian president. Yeltsin himself was incensed by Tokyo's actions. Like Japan, Russia had spurned earlier offers from Germany and France to mediate in the territorial dispute, but Moscow has attempted its own form of (economic) internationalization. The February 1992 fishing agreement with South Korea, and the subsequent offer of leases to foreign investors for development of the disputed islands, are examples of Russian efforts to produce a fait accompli.[58]

Another favorite Russian delaying tactic has been to eschew, as far as possible, awkward summit meetings. Gorbachev canceled a planned trip to Japan in early 1987, and in 1989 announced that he would not visit until April 1991. The most blatant example of avoidance tactics, however, was the Yeltsin shock of September 1992, when the Russian president abruptly canceled a visit on the eve of departure. Tokyo's disappointment turned to anger when Yeltsin publicly blamed Japanese pressure over the territorial dispute for his action.[59] Yeltsin repeated the trick eight months later, although on this occasion a crisis was avoided.[60]

In a series of steps during 1991–92, Japan had made significant concessions regarding the timing and method of the disputed islands' return, and offered reassurances on the rights of current residents. The foreign ministry opened a consulate on Sakhalin in late 1996—over the objections of its treaty bureau—confirming de facto that it is only interested in the four islands.[61] Then in April 1998, at the second déshabillé-summit in Kawana, Japan, Prime Minister Hashimoto went half a step further with a secret offer to draw the frontier north of Etorofu and accept a long transition period under Russian administration. In November 1998, when Obuchi paid the first official visit by a Japanese premier to Moscow since 1973, Yeltsin responded by proposing joint economic development of the disputed islands without any transfer of sovereignty. In the Moscow Declaration, they officially endorsed the 2000 deadline, but just three months later, on his first visit to Tokyo, Foreign Minister Igor Ivanov declared it impossible. After criticizing the Japanese government for feeding its people an illusion, Ivanov reaffirmed the call of the Primakov government for a treaty of peace and friendship that merely creates an obligation to resolve the border issue. Tokyo, however, still refuses to contemplate a peace treaty that does not recognize Japanese sovereignty over all of the disputed islands.[62]

Players
The foreign ministry is still the dominant Japanese player in this game, and although its monopoly has been broken, the Russian desk retains primary responsibility for day-to-day decisions. Splits have occasionally surfaced within the foreign ministry, for example, over a return to the 1956 Joint Declaration in summer 1992. Some foreign ministry officials maintain close links to LDP politicians and factions, but this has not blunted the ministry's criticism of personal diplomacy. The influence of politicians may actually have declined during Japan's brief flurry of political reform. While the LDP had held an absolute majority in the Diet, prime ministers usually regurgitated their foreign ministry briefings. However, some premiers, like Nakasone Yasuhiro, foreign ministers including Abe Shintaro and Watanabe Michio, and even power brokers such as Ozawa Ichiro and Kanemaru Shin occasionally intervened in the Japan-Russia game. Their motives may have been self-serving, but with their democratic legitimacy, they offered the only realistic counterbalance to bureaucratic inertia.[63] As novices to the game, the coalition governments that followed the LDP's 1993 fall from power lacked new ideas, and were more than ever dependent on diplomats for information and advice. With the reemergence of LDP government, however, Hashimoto Ryutaro was able to inject some urgency into the process. His resort to "personal diplomacy" may have been at the foreign ministry's behest—the Ryu-Boris friendship certainly seemed somewhat spurious—but the fact that Obuchi has retained his services as a special advisor on Russian relations suggests a genuine contribution.

Japanese public opinion on the territorial issue has changed remarkably little despite everything. The foreign ministry continues its quiet efforts to manage the debate. Amongst opinion leaders, the right of center, enjoying the strongest links to the foreign ministry, remains dominant.[64] In contrast, on the Russian side, the democratization process has resulted in a series of conflicts over the right to join the game. The Russian Soviet Federated Socialist Republic challenged the authority of the Soviet Union, forcing Japan to deal with both governments for a while. The regional government based on Sakhalin asserted its own jurisdiction, especially during nationalist Valentin Fedorov's time as governor, but the district governments of the disputed islands in turn insisted on being heard.[65] The most noticeable change, however, has been the increased influence of public opinion. The divergence of views unleashed by glasnost and democratization has greatly complicated the diplomatic game. Having mobilized popular support for a hard line, the two governments have made it harder to reach a compromise.[66] Hence the secrecy surrounding recent diplomatic maneuvers. On the other hand, an agreement supported by both peoples should be more likely to endure.

Finally, at the international level, the United States has adopted a more balanced stance, but clearly, Washington now favors a territorial settlement. China, meanwhile, maintains a discrete silence. The foreign ministry showed flexibility when relations with the United States and Europe were at stake—afraid lest Japan be blamed for the collapse of Russian democracy.[67]

Concluding Thoughts

Having examined the Japan-Soviet Cold War games, we are now in a position to highlight their most distinctive characteristics. The first thing one can say is that they were not the primary or even secondary games of either side, both parties having been reluctant players. The underlying element of danger, however, lent the games a significance that escaped many friendlier international relationships. They were essentially a mirror image of the U.S.-Japan games, with conflict concentrated in the diplomatic and security games rather than in the economic game.

For Japanese diplomacy, the guiding principle of which has been to seek good relations with all other states, the Soviet Union was a partial exception. As a rising economic power, Japan was attracted by the Soviet Union's vast natural resources, but repelled by its superpower arrogance and economic inefficiency. From Moscow's point of view, fear of a potential Japan-China axis necessitated avoiding a complete breakdown of relations, while the reality of the U.S.-Japan alliance prevented relations with Tokyo from becoming close. The Soviets were impressed by Japan's economic advances, but dismayed by what they saw as its continued subservience to the United States. The result was a set of Cold War games that always seemed to be perched precariously on the verge of breakdown, yet perversely exhibited remarkable stability. The rules simultaneously promoted conflict and kept it within certain bounds that were rarely broken during more than three decades of play.

The waiting game implies that Japan adopted a purely passive stance. Certainly, the Soviets appear to have been responsible for taking most initiatives, and as a result of Japanese obstinacy, opportunities for reconciliation were doubtless lost. Yet in Tokyo there was never a consensus in favor of compromise with Moscow. Japan was pursuing its national interest—not that of America—according to its own assessment of the best methods to achieve its objectives. The foreign ministry played an unusually prominent role in this game, its job having been to enforce the rules, not to make new ones; but it zealously resisted bold policy changes, and even blocked democratically elected politicians from making them. Tanaka, and perhaps Nakasone, were rare exceptions who managed to challenge the rules of each game, albeit only briefly. Moreover, the government had some success in conscripting public opinion.

The post–Cold War games, unlike their predecessors, appear frequently to be on the brink of a significant breakthrough, but are rather erratic. They are still in a period of transition and hence any attempt to codify their rules is probably premature.

The Cold War in East Asia differed in several important respects from that experienced elsewhere, and so it should come as no surprise that the end of the Cold War has produced dissimilar results. The old rules endured for longer in part because of the immobilism of the Japanese decision-making process. The Japanese were slow to acknowledge that Russia was no longer the Soviet Union. The Russians, on the other hand, wanted new games because they realized they could not win the old ones, but not so much that they were willing to sacrifice their trump card—the islands—from the outset. Although democratization strengthened Moscow's bargaining position vis-à-vis Tokyo, the rise of globalization and the end of the Cold War substantially weakened it. The World War II positions as victor and vanquished have been reversed, and thus it is now Russia's turn to play the waiting game.

Is the Japan-Russia game simply more intense than that of its predecessor, or have we witnessed a real qualitative change? A case can be made for the proposition that in Russia at least we are really seeing the opposite trends to those described above—a revived Cold War mentality, rising economic nationalism, and an antidemocratic backlash. Yet one can equally well argue that relations with Japan are now as good as they have ever been. The gap between the two sides has narrowed dramatically, even though it remains too wide to span in the near future. History still weighs heavily on this relationship. At base, the clash of nationalisms persists. The Cold War had merely solidified preexisting negative images and reinforced age-old mutual distrust. With the exception of the remarkable emergence of an enraged public in Russia, the players, too, remain essentially unchanged. The revised rules and, hence, the character of the new games, however, differ significantly.

It is in the national interests—strategic, economic, and political—of both Japan and Russia to improve relations. They can assist each other in many ways. In other words, there is a high cost, in terms of lost opportunities, to pay for the continuing schism. However, there can be no firm bilateral relationship without domestic stability. In the short term, this is difficult to achieve in Japan, and impossible in Russia. Japan must remain patient. It will have to wait until the Russians want to give the islands back: otherwise, they will sour relations between future generations. The waiting game will continue for as long as either side remains convinced that time will work to their favor.

Notes

1. John Creighton Campbell, "Japan and the United States: Games That Work," in Japan's Foreign Policy After the Cold War: Coping with Change, ed. Gerald L. Curtis (NY: M.E. Sharpe, 1993), pp. 43–61.
2. Robert D. Putnam, "Diplomacy and Domestic Politics: The Logic of Two-level Games," International Organization 42:3 (Summer 1988): 427–60.
3. See Donald Hellman, Japanese Domestic Politics and Foreign Policy (Berkeley: University of California Press: 1969), and Tanaka Takahiko, Nis-So kokko kaifuku no shiteki kenkyu [A Historical Study of the Restoration of Japan-Soviet Relations] (Tokyo: Yuhikaku, 1993).
4. Hasegawa Tsuyoshi, The Northern Territories Dispute and Russo-Japanese Relations (Berkeley: University of California Press, 1998), p.148.
5. Hasegawa, 1998, p. 146; Hara Kimie, Japanese-Soviet/Russian Relations since 1945: A Difficult Peace (London: Nissan Institute/Routledge, 1998), p. 140.
6. Michael Blaker, Japanese International Negotiating Style (NY: Columbia University Press, 1977), p. 213.
7. Hasegawa, 1998, pp.140–41; Hasegawa Tsuyoshi, Jonathan Haslam, and Andrew C. Kuchins, eds. Russia and Japan: An Unresolved Dilemma Between Distant Neighbors (Berkeley: University of Cali-

fornia Press, 1993), p. 422; Gilbert Rozman, *Japan's Response to the Gorbachev Era, 1985–1991* (Princeton: Princeton University Press, 1992), pp. 248, 283–84.
8. Rozman 1992, pp. 26–27, 55; Hasegawa, 1998, p.172.
9. John J. Stephan, *The Kuril Islands* (Oxford: Clarendon Press, 1974), pp. 212–14.
10. Hasegawa, 1998, p. 351.
11. Rozman, 1992, pp. 34–38.
12. For relevant polls see the *Yoran chosa nenkan* [Annual Surveys] (Tokyo: Chuo Chosasha, individual years).
13. Hasegawa, 1998, pp.172–73.
14. Memorandum of Conversation, Dulles and Shigemitsu, 19 Aug. 1956, *Foreign Relations of the United States, 1955–57*, XXIII, Part 1 Japan, p. 202.
15. Hasegawa, 1998, pp. 124–26, 148–49; Hara, 1998, pp. 42–46.
16. *Sekai shuho* 45:32, 11 Aug. 1964, Cortazzi to Bently, 17 July 1964, FO371/17600–(FJ103110/23), Public Records Office, Kew.
17. Peggy L. Falkenheim, "Some Determining Factors in Soviet-Japanese Relations," *Pacific Affairs* 50:3 (Winter 1977–78): 610.
18. Hasegawa, 1998, p.154.
19. The Japanese company had been violating COCOM rules since 1979, by selling high-tech propeller milling machines for Soviet submarines. MITI compounded the "crime" by taking no action for more than a year after learning of the transfers. *Asahi shimbun*, 16 May 1987.
20. Akaha Tsuneo and Murakami Takashi, "Soviet/Russian-Japanese Economic Relations," in Hasegawa, 1993, p. 175.
21. See C.W. Braddick, *Japan and the Sino-Soviet Alliance, 1950–1964* (Doctoral dissertation, Oxford University, 1997).
22. R.K. Jain, *The USSR and Japan, 1945–1980* (New Delhi: Radiant, 1981), p. 81.
23. Wolf Mendl, "Japan and its Giant Neighbours," *The World Today* 39:6 (June 1983): 208.
24. Joachim Glaubitz, *Between Tokyo and Moscow* (Honolulu: University of Hawaii Press, 1995, p. 120.
25. Myles C. Robertson, *Soviet Policy Towards Japan* (Cambridge: Cambridge University Press, 1988), pp. 66–67.
26. Gerald L. Curtis, "The Tyumen Oil Development Project and Japanese Foreign Policy Decision Making," in *The Foreign Policy of Modern Japan*, ed. Robert A. Scalapino (Berkeley: University of California Press, 1977), pp. 167–71; Glaubitz, 1995, pp. 102–106.
27. Glaubitz, 1995, pp. 167, 176, Hasegawa 1998, p. 230.
28. See, for example, Malcolm McIntosh, *Japan Re-armed* (London: Francis Pinter, 1986).
29. Hasegawa, 1998, p. 165; Rozman 1992, p. 26.
30. Hara 1998, pp. 152–54; Takahashi Susumu, "Toward a New Era of Russian-Japanese Relations," in *"Northern Territories" and Beyond: Russian, Japanese, and American Perspectives*, eds. James E. Goodby, Vladimir I. Ivanov, and Shimotamai Nobuo (Westport, CT: Praeger, 1995), pp. 205–206, and Shimotomai Nobuo "Japan's Russia Policy and the October 1993 Summit," in Goodby, Ivanov, and Shimotamai, 1995, p. 123.
31. Hasegawa, 1998, p. 505.
32. Reinhard Drifte, *Japan's Foreign Policy for the 21st Century* (Basingstoke: St. Antony's/Macmillan, 1998), pp. 61–65, *Japan Times*, 14 November and 5 December 1998.
33. William F. Nimmo, *Japan and Russia: A Reevaluation in the Post-Soviet Era* (Westport, CT: Greenwood Press, 1994), p. 124.
34. Hasegawa, 1998, p. 508.
35. *Japan Times*, 14 November 1998.
36. Harry Gelman, *Russo-Japanese Relations and the Future of the U.S.-Japanese Alliance* (Santa Monica, CA: Rand: 1993), pp. 43–56; Mike M. Mochizuki, "Japan and the Strategic Quadrangle," in *The Strategic Quadrangle*, ed. Michael Mandelbaum (NY: Council on Foreign Relations, 1995), p. 142.
37. Ironically, the Russians were very interested in the Japanese development model at this time. Lonny E. Carlisle, "The Changing Political Economy of Japan's Economic Relations with Russia," *Pacific Affairs* 67:3 (Fall 1994): 430; Ivan Tselitschev, "Russian Economic Reforms and Japan," in Goodby, Ivanov, and Shimotamai, 1995, pp.183–84.
38. Saito Motohide, "How Japan Should Deal with Russia," in Goodby, Ivanov, and Shimotamai, 1995, p. 192; Hasegawa, 1998, pp. 285–88, 312, 325.
39. Hasegawa, 1995, pp. 405, 503, 510–11; *Japan Times*, 15 April 1998.
40. *Japan Times*, 12, 13, 16 Mar. 1999.

41. Glenn D. Hook, "Japan and Subregionalism: Constructing the Japan Sea Rim Zone," *Kokusai seiji* 114 (March 1997), 52–53; Gilbert Rozman, "Backdoor Japan: The Search for a Way Out via Regionalism and Decentralization," *Journal of Japanese Studies* 25:1 (1999): 3–31.
42. *Japan Times* 15, 16 April 1998; Hasegawa, 1998, pp. 424, 503.
43. A January 1998 agreement grants Japanese fishermen the right to fish around the disputed islands for a fee. Hasegawa, 1998, p. 509.
44. *Japan Times*, 7 February 1999.
45. Dennis T. Yasutomo, *The New Multilateralism in Japan's Foreign Policy* (Basingstoke: Macmillan, 1995), pp. 175–76; *Japan Times*, 16 April 1998.
46. Since 1992, they have also been joined by the Ministries of Transport, Agriculture, and Posts and Telecommunications. Hasegawa, 1998, p. 472.
47. Hasegawa Tsuyoshi, "The Gorbachev-Kaifu Summit," in Hasegawa, 1993, p. 53; Gilbert Rozman, "Japanese Images of the Soviet and Russian Role in the Asia-Pacific Region," in Hasegawa, 1993, p.108; Yasutomo, 1995, pp. 160, 171–2, 175.
48. Richard D. Leitch, Kato Akira, and Martin E. Weinstein, *Japan's Role in the Post–Cold War World* (Westport, CT: Greenwood Press, 1995), pp. 147–48; Takahashi 1995, p. 206.
49. The Ministry of Foreign Affairs thought that Gorbachev had no chance of surviving. Nimmo, 1994, p. 114; Hasegawa 1998, pp. 418–19.
50. In March 1991 Ozawa Ichiro, then a powerful LDP faction leader, even offered Gorbachev $26 billion in return for recognition of Japan's "residual" sovereignty over the disputed islands. The Soviets, however, were insulted by such a crude example of Japanese "checkbook diplomacy." Hasegawa, 1998, pp. 382–86.
51. Hasegawa, 1998, pp. 267, 485, 558.
52. Saito, 1995, p. 195; Shimotomai, 1995, pp. 121–22.
53. The latest poll found 78 percent against their return and only 8 percent in favor. In addition, 62 percent were against the Hashimoto plan, while 13 percent supported it. *Japan Times*, 4 November 1998.
54. The population has fallen from 40,000 in 1980 to 15,000 today. *Japan Times*, 19 January 1999.
55. Nimmo, 1994, p. 124; *Japan Times*, 11 January 1999.
56. Rozman, 1992, pp. 248, 310. See also C.W. Braddick, "Distant Friends: Britain and Japan in the Age of Globalization, 1958–1995," in *The History of Anglo-Japanese Relations, 1600–2000: Vol. 2, The Political-Diplomatic Dimension, 1931–2000*, eds. Ian Nish et. al. (Basingstoke, U.K.: Macmillan, 2000).
57. Akaha Tsuneo, "The Politics of Japanese-Soviet/Russian Economic Relations," in *Japan in the Posthegemonic World*, eds. Akaha Tsuneo and Frank Langdon (Boulder, CO: Lynne Rienner, 1993), p.172.
58. Yasutomo 1995, pp. 158–59; Hasegawa, 1998, p.435; Akaha, 1993, p. 177; *Japan Times*, 20 January 1999.
59. Some diplomats and LDP politicians demanded retaliation but were restrained by the Chief Cabinet Secretary. Hasegawa, 1998, pp.468–69; Yasutomo, 1995, p. 163.
60. Yasutomo, 1995, p.162.
61. Akaha, 1993, p.170; Hasegawa, 1998, pp. 383, 432, 439, 470, 508.
62. *Japan Times*, 13, 14 November 1998, 22 February 1999; *Nihon Keizai Shimbun*, 7 January, 23 February 1999.
63. Hasegawa, 1998, pp. 231, 239, 344, 365–8, 387, 459, 543; Yasutomo, 1995, pp. 173, 175; Rozman, 1992, pp. 21, 24, 30.
64. Rozman, 1992, pp. 31, 39, 43, 45–49, 55, 293; Hasegawa, 1998, pp. 241, 253, 315, 362.
65. In late 1991, the inhabitants of the islands requested UN trusteeship status. Miyazawa and Yeltsin soon agreed to block this, but the Ministry of Foreign Affairs was forced to begin discussing concrete plans for the residents' post-restoration welfare. Nimmo, 1994, pp. 121–2.
66. Hasegawa, 1998, p. 331, Yasutomo 1995, p. 176.
67. Mochizuki, 1995, p. 145.

CHAPTER 13

Japanese Foreign Policy toward Northeast Asia
Kamiya Matake

Observers of Japan's foreign policy in the postwar period have generally agreed that it differs from the foreign policies of other comparable Western democracies. Few would disagree that in the second half of the twentieth century it has displayed at least three distinctive characteristics:

1. The dominant influence of the U.S. relations.
2. A passive, or reactive, posture, in which Japan attempts to achieve security and prosperity mainly through adapting itself to the existing international environment, based on the recognition that the international environment is basically a given framework that Japan is not capable of changing.
3. A posture of minimalism, in which Japan, while focusing predominantly on economic rather than political or military goals, attempts to remain aloof from the aspect of power politics in international relations as much as possible, to keep its level of involvement in political and strategic issues of the world as low as possible, and to avoid confrontations with other countries as much as possible.

These characteristics have been particularly salient in Japan's diplomatic posture toward China and Korea during this period.

China Diplomacy in the Postwar Period[1]

Japan's China policy in the postwar period prior to Prime Minister Tanaka Kakuei's visit to Beijing in September 1972 was virtually prescribed by U.S. China policy. Japan became firmly incorporated into the U.S. anticommunist global strategy when it signed the San Francisco peace treaty in September 1951, though without Moscow's endorsement, and when it at the same time concluded the bilateral security treaty with the United States allowing U.S. forces to remain on bases in Japan. Based on the agreement between the United

States and Britain, neither Beijing nor Taipei were invited to the San Francisco Peace Conference, and Japan was to choose either capital when it decided to reestablish formal diplomatic relations after recovering independence. Japan, however, had practically no freedom of choice in the matter. In order to advance the country's economic recovery under the Cold War situation, Prime Minister Yoshida Shigeru did not hesitate to conclude the security treaty with the United States and to make Japan a member of the U.S. camp. Regarding China, however, he wanted to postpone the decision to choose one of the two capitals as the legitimate government of China until a more opportune time. He believed that the Chinese market was indispensable for Japan's economic recovery. He also believed that the Americans were wrong in regarding the Soviet Union and China as monolithic, and that the two communist countries would sooner or later become estranged given the differences in their civilizations, national character of their people, and political circumstances.[2] Nonetheless, Yoshida eventually had no option but to yield to the U.S. demand to conclude a peace treaty with the Kuomintang government in Taipei.

The Japanese government, however, did not want to break off all relations with the People's Republic of China (PRC). The majority of Japanese also desired that relations with the mainland be reestablished, for several reasons. First of all, there were economic motives. Yoshida's belief that the promotion of economic relations with mainland China was indispensable for Japan's economic development was widely shared by Japanese of the time. According to statistics on the 1930s, China had been one of Japan's most important trading partners, accounting for 21.6 percent of its total exports and 12.4 percent of its total imports.[3] Second, there was a widespread sense of guilt about their country's acts of aggression on the mainland. That guilt was behind the conviction among many Japanese that their country was morally responsible for making efforts to reestablish friendly relations with China. It also moderated the views of those in Japan who were otherwise antagonistic to the communist regime in Beijing. Third, Japanese have a widely shared a sense of closeness to and keen interest in China, growing out of geographical proximity and Japan's long history of cultural ties with China.

In a public opinion poll in 1952, the year Japan concluded the peace treaty with Taipei, 57 percent of respondents were already in favor of restoring diplomatic relations with mainland China. Results of similar public opinion polls conducted in the following years indicated that the majority of Japanese citizens consistently supported the normalization of relations with the PRC during that period. In a public opinion poll in 1960, 75 percent of the respondents answered in favor of normalization.[4] In the fact of such national sentiments, the Japanese government cautiously welcomed the development of trade and other nongovernmental exchanges between Japan and the PRC.

It was by no means easy for Japan to expand trade with the PRC without having official diplomatic relations. The position of the government on the Japan-PRC trade was that political relations and economic relations were to be handled separately. In other words, Japan wanted to promote commercial exchange with Beijing without any implication of political recognition or establishment of political ties. China, in contrast, consistently upheld the principle that politics and economics were inseparable. For Beijing, trade with Japan was important not only for its economic benefits but also as a useful means of exerting influence on Japanese politics and society. In reality, it was unavoidable that the Japan-PRC trade would involve some political dimensions. Consequently, Japan-PRC trade until the normalization of the diplomatic relations between the two countries in 1972 was directly influenced by the domestic politics in the two countries, the Cold War environment in Asia, and above all U.S. policy toward China.

"Private trade" between Japan and the PRC, which was based upon the successive agreements on Japan-China nongovernmental trade of 1952, 1953, and 1955, followed a general trend toward expansion until early 1958. When the Fourth Japan-China Agreement on Nongovernmental Trade was signed in March 1958, however, political factors intervened. The agreement, which provided that each side establish a private trade representative's office with some diplomatic privileges including the right to hoist its national flag in the capital of the other party, immediately invited an angry reaction from Taiwan. Under huge pressure from Washington and Taipei, the Kishi Nobusuke administration stated on 9 April that it had no intention of granting recognition to the PRC, nor of conceding any diplomatic privileges to the Chinese private trade representative office in Japan. The Japanese decision was welcomed by Taipei, but provoked fierce criticism by Beijing. Tokyo's handling of the so-called Nagasaki Flag Incident in May added fuel to Chinese ire. The incident itself was a trivial one in which a right-wing Japanese youth dragged down a Chinese flag at a Chinese products fair held in a department store in Nagasaki. When the Japanese government made public its position that the action by the arrested youth did not constitute damage to a foreign national flag—as stipulated in Japanese criminal law because Japan did not recognize the PRC as a nation—Beijing was infuriated. On 11 May, Beijing unilaterally announced that it would break off all economic and cultural exchanges with Japan. The extreme reaction by the Chinese government clearly reflected not only Beijing's frustration with the pro-Taiwan posture of Prime Minister Kishi, but also the Chinese political climate of that time. Domestically, a momentary relaxation of thought control during the Hundred Flowers campaign of 1956 and 1957 was being replaced by the political radicalism of the Great Leap Forward, launched in 1958. Internationally, the U.S.-PRC confrontation was particularly intense. The Nagasaki Flag Incident took place on the eve of the Chinese heavy artillery bombardment of Quemoy in August, which had brought China and the United States to the brink of war.

Interruption of the Japan-PRC trade lasted until 1962. Prime Minister Ikeda Hayato, who took office in July 1960, however, believed that it was unnatural for Japan not to have a diplomatic relations with this largest of its neighbors with a population of 650 million. He also anticipated that Beijing would be admitted to the United Nations in place of Taipei in the not-too-distant future.[5] Recognizing that it was still totally unrealistic for Japan to grant recognition to Beijing while the United States maintained its contention that Communist China must be contained, the Ikeda administration attempted to expand trade with the PRC on the principle that political and economic relations were to be handled separately. Washington basically accepted Japan's attempt to promote economic exchange with the PRC, and it had no intention of intervening in the Japan-PRC trade unless Japan attempted to adopt a policy that might be damaging to U.S. strategic objectives in East Asia.[6]

Private trade between Japan and the PRC was resumed by the semi-official Liao-Takasaki agreement of November 1962, and Japan became China's largest trading partner in 1965.[7] These developments again reflected the Chinese political climate at that time. Domestically, the Great Leap Forward had proved a disastrous failure and Beijing had had to adopt a moderate policy line in the early 1960s in order to cope with the many staggering problems it created. Internationally, as the Sino-Soviet conflict developed, China found it increasingly necessary to find alternative suppliers of industrial goods. In the late 1960s, however, China under the Cultural Revolution returned to an extreme political radicalism domestically and hard-line policy externally, which proved a further setback to Japan-PRC trade. The volume of bilateral trade decreased in the years 1967 and 1968.

It should be noted that the Japanese government never deliberately disturbed trade relations with the PRC during the 20 years before normalization of diplomatic relations between the two countries in 1972. Tokyo's position was that promotion of private commercial exchanges with Beijing was both beneficial to the Japanese economy and useful for keeping open the channels of communication, as long as it was handled separately from political issues between the two countries, such as Japan's recognition of the PRC. Thus, even when the Fourth Japan-China Agreement on Nongovernmental Trade resulted in further deterioration of the bilateral relationship, Tokyo wanted to maintain private trade with the PRC. Prime Minister Kishi, a pro-Washington, pro-Taipei nationalist who advocated strengthening of Japan's relations with the United States and Taiwan in order to achieve revision of the U.S.-Japan security treaty, maintained that his administration would "provide support and cooperation" to the agreement "in order that the goal of trade expansion will be achieved" "within the limits of Japan's domestic laws and regulations, based on the fact that the government [of the PRC] is not recognized [by the Japanese government], and taking the current state of international relations into account."[8] In fact, the two serious setbacks to Japan-PRC trade during the two decades were both caused by the Chinese side. In May 1958, trade between the two countries was interrupted by a unilateral announcement by Beijing that it would discontinue all private exchange with Japan. In 1967 and 1968, while the Cultural Revolution raged in China, the volume of the Japan-PRC trade decreased.

In contrast to the expansion of the Japan-PRC trade, Japan's China policy before normalization of the relationship was strongly restrained by U.S. Asia policy. Being under U.S. military protection and firmly incorporated into the U.S. Cold War strategy, Japan had practically no option but to follow the U.S. lead with regard to China. The Japanese government appeared to have concluded long before the United States started to seek for rapprochement with the PRC that a China in isolation was much more dangerous to peace and stability in East

Asia than as a member of the international community. Japan, however, continued to recognize the Kuomintang government in Taipei as the government representing China and supported U.S. policy regarding Chinese representation in the United Nations. It also carefully avoided any official relations with Beijing. The normalization of the relationship between Japan and the PRC became possible, in fact, only after President Nixon's diplomatic "revolution" with regard to the PRC took place in July 1971, notwithstanding consistently high popular support in Japan for the idea. This fact was symbolic of the decisive importance of the U.S. factor in Japan's China policy during this period.

The Japanese posture toward China was consistently less confrontational than the U.S. posture, however. The fundamental posture of Japan's security policy during this period was to avoid becoming an active player of the Cold War in Asia by limiting its military role exclusively to self-defense while maintaining military alliance with the United States. Japan was, therefore, far from enthusiastic about strengthening security ties with Taiwan. From Tokyo's point of view, even the famous "Taiwan clause" of the Nixon-Sato joint communiqué of November 1969, which stated that maintenance of peace and security was "a most important element" of Japan's own security, did not mean that Japan agreed with the United States in taking an active pro-Taiwan, anti-PRC posture. The Japanese leaders including Prime Minister Sato Eisaku believed that Japan, in order to extract a U.S. concession on the issue of the restoration of Okinawa, had no option but to make a concession to the U.S. demand to insert that clause in the communiqué.[9]

The process of the normalization of relations between Japan and the PRC was started by Prime Minister Tanaka Kakuei as soon as he came to office in July 1972. President Nixon's visit to China in February that year had fundamentally changed the international environment surrounding the Japan-PRC relations. For Japan, which had always felt uncomfortable in following the U.S. policy line of isolating Beijing, Nixon's actions in 1971 and 1972 meant the removal of the greatest obstacle to normalization of the relationship. Tanaka visited China in September 1972 and by the subsequent joint statement issued on 29 September, Japan went a step beyond the United States in granting the PRC political recognition in place of Taiwan and establishing formal diplomatic relations with Beijing. In the following years, a series of official agreements were concluded between the two countries in a variety of fields such as trade, aviation, marine transportation, and fisheries. Finally, the Treaty of Peace and Friendship between Japan and the People's Republic of China was signed in August 1978.

What was remarkable about Japan's China diplomacy during this six-year period was that the Japanese policy makers were not very aware of the strategic implications of Japan-China rapprochement. A fundamental structural change was taking place in the East Asian international relations at that time: China was becoming reconciled with the United States while remaining in confrontation with the Soviet Union. Concern about the Soviet threat provided a basis of common interest among the United States, Japan, and China. Under such circumstances, any changes in the relationship between Japan and China would inevitably exert great influence on the strategic relationship among the United

States, the Soviet Union, and China. Japanese leaders, however, tried to separate Japan-China relations from U.S.-Soviet-China relations and deal with them bilaterally.

It still had not occurred to Japanese leaders at that time that Japan might be able to promote its national interests by participating in East Asian power politics as an active player. If such an idea ever occurred to them, they could have taken full advantage of the Sino-Soviet confrontation and made the two powers compete with each other in order to realize both a peace and friendship treaty with China *and* a peace treaty with the Soviet Union.[10] They never adopted such a strategy, however. During the negotiations to conclude a peace and friendship treaty with China, which began in late 1974, Tokyo's fundamental policy principle was that Japan would not be involved in the Sino-Soviet confrontation. Prime Minister Fukuda Takeo, who concluded the Peace and Friendship Treaty with China in 1978, advocated the "equidistance diplomacy," which meant that Japan would avoid confrontation with any country, and would not seek improvement of its position vis-à-vis any country by exploiting another.[11] The Chinese, by contrast, attempted to improve their strategic position toward the Soviet Union by inserting in the peace and friendship treaty with Japan the so-called "anti-hegemony clause," which stated that neither side should seek hegemony in the Asia-Pacific region and each would be opposed to efforts by any other country or group of countries to establish such hegemony. For the Chinese, a peace and friendship treaty with Japan was inevitably part of strategy toward the Soviet Union. Beijing's demand that the antihegemony clause be inserted into the treaty annoyed Tokyo, because it feared that Moscow would perceive the clause as anti-Soviet. The treaty negotiations consequently became long and difficult. Japan and China finally agreed to include in the treaty the so-called "third party clause," together with the antihegemony clause, and signed the treaty in August 1978. The Japanese negotiators hoped that they had successfully avoided getting their country entangled in the Sino-Soviet confrontation by inserting the third party clause, which stated that the treaty would not affect either signatory's relationship with third countries. The Soviet Union, however, still perceived the Japan-China Peace and Friendship Treaty as a product of joint anti-Soviet strategy by the two signatories and harshly criticized it.

After 1978, Japan's relations with China entered into a new stage of development. During this period, the basic trend of Japan-China relations was the massive and rapid increase in various types of mutual exchange and deepening of interdependence between the two countries. Japan's basic policy toward China was to provide economic assistance, such as low-interest "yen-loans" and official development assistance (ODA), to support Deng Xiaoping's policies of economic reform and opening to the West, based on the traditional principle of noninvolvement in the Sino-Soviet confrontation. From 1972 until the end of the Cold War, Japan's China policy appeared much less restrained by the U.S. factor than before, because of the prevailing East Asian strategic structure in which the United States, Japan, and China united with each other to face the Soviet Union. In this structure, the United States basically welcomed the development of Japan-China relations. Japan and the United States also shared the "liberal internationalist" view that China's economic development was in their own best interests.[12] Japan, therefore, did not have to worry much about the will of Washington in making policy decisions vis-à-vis China.

In this context, there were some instances when Japan attempted to actively and strategically utilize its economic strength to exercise influence on the direction of China's policy. For example, when the Japanese government under Prime Minister Ohira Masayoshi decided to extend the first yen-loan to China in December 1979, the Japanese motive was not only economic, but also political and strategic. Tokyo attempted to draw Beijing closer to the West by encouraging Deng's policies of economic reform and opening of the country.[13] The Japanese leaders also hoped that Japan could promote China's active participation in Asia-Pacific international relations through economic cooperation.[14] Japan's response toward the incident known as the "Hozan (Baoshan) shock" in early 1981 represents another example. When China, whose economy was suffering from inflation, financial deficit, and energy shortage, suddenly and unilaterally canceled several major plant contracts with Japanese firms, including the contract for the second phase of construction of the Shanghai Baoshan Iron and Steel Complex, the Japanese government saved the contracts by extending China additional financial assistance. On the one hand, this decision was due at least partially to the Japanese sentiment that they should extend to China some substitute for the reparations formally waived by Beijing in the Japan-China joint statement on 29 September 1972. On the other hand, the decision was based upon the Japanese leaders' shared belief that Japan should support Deng's modernization in order to promote peace and stability in the Asia-Pacific region.[15]

Japan's China diplomacy during this period, however, was still generally passive and nonconfrontational. One can observe in the Japan-China relations from 1978 to the end of the Cold War a cycle of alternating stages of rapid expansion of economic and other exchanges, and of political friction.[16] Particularly noteworthy is that in all the cases of political friction, the Japanese attitude toward China was reactive and conciliatory.

In January 1981, the relationship between Japan and China deteriorated because of the above-mentioned "Hozan (Baoshan) shock." The crisis was resolved by Tokyo's decision to extend additional financial assistance to Beijing, and Chinese Premier Zhao Ziyang, who visited Japan from late May to early June 1982, emphasized the importance of establishing stable, long-term friendship between the two countries. That summer, however, the dispute over the so-called "textbook problem" again changed the atmosphere surrounding bilateral relations suddenly and drastically. It started with newspaper reports in Japan in late June alleging that the Japan's Ministry of Education, through the official school textbook screening system, had ordered the publishers of school history textbooks to replace the term "aggression" (*shinryaku*) with the term "advance" (*shinshutsu*) to describe Japan's military actions in Asia before 1945. However, it was later learned that these reports contained a substantial amount of false information and that the allegation was not the case.[17] The erroneous allegation was widely taken at face value throughout East Asia, nevertheless, and the Japanese government failed to take timely action to correct the misunderstanding. In late July, the problem was politicized by Beijing and an intense anti-Japanese press campaign launched. Many Japanese were deeply perplexed by the sudden change in Chinese attitudes. In the end, the crisis was diffused through assurances by the Japanese government that it would pay attention to Asian criticism of the contents of Japanese school history textbooks and would take responsibility for making necessary corrections.

After autumn 1982, the Chinese attitude toward Japan again became friendly. In August 1985, however, an official visit to Yasukuni Shrine by several members of the Japanese Cabinet including Prime Minister Nakasone Yasuhiro caused another incidence of friction between the two countries, again leading to anti-Japan student demonstrations in Beijing and various other cities in China. Before the incident, however, Nakasone had succeeded in building such a good relationship between Japan and China that the state of the bilateral relationship in 1984 was even described as "the best in its two-thousand-years history."[18] For example, Nakasone made a statement in a session of the Japanese Diet in February 1983 admitting that Japanese war against China was an act of aggression. His statement was welcomed by the Chinese.[19] In November of the same year, he hosted Hu Yaobang in Tokyo. In March of the next year, Nakasone in turn visited China and announced that Japan would provide ¥470 billion from 1984 to 1989 as the second yen-loan to China. Without doubt, Nakasone was eager to promote friendly relations between the two countries. He did not expect that his visit to Yasukuni Shrine would have such negative influence on the Japan-China relations.

From the end of 1985 to the beginning of 1987, Japan-China relations were calm. In February 1987, however, the relationship became tense again after the Osaka High Court ruled that ownership of a student dormitory named Koka-ryo, which had been purchased by the Taiwanese government in 1952, still belonged to Taiwan even after the termination of the diplomatic relations between Tokyo and Taipei. China harshly criticized the High Court ruling and insisted that the Japanese government, which had acknowledged in the September 1972 joint statement that Beijing is the sole legitimate government of China and Taiwan is a part of China, should promptly overturn the court's decision. Tokyo, however, properly claimed that it was impossible for the Japanese government to intervene in the judicial system, which is independent.

In all of these cases of political friction, the Japanese attitude was reactive. None of these frictions were the result of initiatives by the Japanese government. In the cases of the Hozan (Baoshan) shock in 1981 and the Koka-ryo problem in 1987, tensions in the bilateral relations were brought about by Beijing's actions. In the case of the textbook problem in 1982, Beijing's erratic reaction to misreports by Japanese mass media caused a chain reaction all over the East Asia. In the case of Nakasone's visit to Yasukuni Shrine in 1985, according to the dominant explanation, the visit unexpectedly triggered stormy anti-Japanese demonstrations in China due mainly to the following three factors: growing ill feeling on the Chinese side regarding the rapidly expanding trade imbalance with Japan; the Chinese political climate at that time; and the influence of a major official campaign commemorating the Japanese invasion that was carried out earlier that year to mark the 40th anniversary of the Chinese victory over Japan.[20] A basic pattern is discernible in Japan's reaction to these problems with China. In dealing with these political frictions, the Japanese government made avoiding serious confrontation with Beijing its highest priority. Refraining from asserting its own position vis-à-vis China, it went out of its way to make concessions in order to diffuse crises. In short, the Japanese approach to friction with China during this period was generally conciliatory.

Although the influence of the U.S. relations on Japan's China policy was limited for nearly two decades before the end of the Cold War, it would be mistaken to conclude that the U.S. factor was not important at all in Japan's policy decisions toward China after 1972. Tokyo's handling of the Tiananmen Square incident in 1989 confirmed that U.S. influence on Japanese decisions was still significant where there were contradictions in the U.S. and the Japanese postures toward Beijing. In fact, Japan did have to formulate its policy toward China within the limits set by U.S. policy as long as it continued relying for its security on the alliance.

When the Tiananmen Square incident occurred in June 1989, Japan was initially reluctant to apply any sanctions against China. Tokyo did not want to isolate China, because it feared that isolation could lead to political and social destabilization of its giant neighbor; Japanese business circles, moreover, wished to maintain economic exchange. Eventually, however, Japan had to follow the position of the United States and other leading Western countries. In a few weeks, Japan changed its position and applied tough sanctions against China, including suspension of extension of the third yen loan which had been scheduled for 1990. Although Japan wished to resume its economic cooperation with China as soon as possible, it was inconceivable for it to break ranks with the Western countries, particularly the United States, on this issue. In fact, it was only after signs of improvement in Sino-U.S. relations became visible with the visit of two American senior officials to Beijing in December 1989 that Japan started to take actual steps to resume economic aid. The whole episode demonstrated that the U.S. factor still weighed heavily in Japan's China policy even as the Cold War period was coming to an end.[21]

The discussion in this section so far has demonstrated that the three distinctive characteristics of Japan's foreign policy in the post–World War II period listed at the beginning of this chapter, i.e., the dominant influence of the U.S. relations, a passive, or reactive, posture, and a posture of minimalism, were salient in Japan's China policy during the Cold War years. Have these characteristics continued to be prominent in Japan's China policy since the end of the Cold War? Have there been any changes? If so, to what extent? What have been the implications to Japan-China relations in the post–Cold War period? These are the questions to be answered in the rest of this section.

In the aftermath of the Tiananmen Square incident, Japan enjoyed a brief period of extremely good relations with China. Among the G-7 countries, it took the lead in lifting economic sanctions against China at the Houston summit in July 1990, and in August 1991 Prime Minister Kaifu Toshiki became the first leader of the G-7 states to visit Beijing since June 1989. Meanwhile, China placed special emphasis on nurturing a constructive relationship with Japan, expecting that not only that it would provide further economic assistance but also help restore Chinese relations in the international community. China refrained from bring up the history issue as a bargaining card and even endorsed Japan's desire to play a larger, more active, political role in the region and globally.[22]

In that context of improved relations, Emperor Akihito made a formal visit to China in October 1992 to commemorate the 20th anniversary of the normalization of the relationship between the two countries. It represented the first visit ever to China by an Emperor of Japan. China enthusiastically welcomed the emperor, and Chinese President Yang Shangkun remarked of the visit that it "marks the beginning of a new stage of development in Sino-Japanese relations."[23] The emperor, in turn, said in his speech that "there was a period in the past when my country inflicted untold hardships on the people of China. This remains the source of my profound personal sorrow."[24] China's *Peoples' Daily* said that the imperial visit represented proof that China and Japan were developing friendly relations, while Japan's chief Cabinet minister viewed it as "having achieved a significant result in promoting friendship and amity" between the two countries.[25]

The honeymoon between Japan and China in the early 1990s did not last long. Difficulties in managing the relationship between the two countries have gradually become salient since late 1994, and Japan has been growing nervous about China.

In June 1994, Taiwan's President Lee Teng-hui announced that he had received an invitation from the Olympic Council of Asia (OCA) to attend the Asian Games to be held in Hiroshima in October. The Japanese government worried that China would boycott the games and indicated that it would not issue a visa to Lee. When the OCA withdrew the invitation to Lee, Taiwan tried to send Deputy Premier Hsu Li-teh. Despite Chinese protests, Japan permitted Hsu to enter the country. This incident clearly demonstrated that Taiwan remains one of the most sensitive issues constraining Japan-China relations even in the post–Cold War era.

On 15 May 1995, China conducted a nuclear test, only four days after it agreed to an indefinite extension of the NPT treaty in New York and ignoring Prime Minister Murayama Tomiichi's request made earlier that month in Beijing that it abandon the test. The test aroused strong popular protest among the Japanese, among whom the strong aversion to nuclear arms transcends differences of political ideology or belief. One week after the test, the Japanese government announced that it would reduce the amount of its grant aid to China as a protest, and then moved to freeze the 1995 grants when China conducted another nuclear test in August. China, in turn, harshly criticized the Japanese moves. Claiming that Japan, as a country under the U.S. nuclear umbrella, had no right to criticize the Chinese nuclear test, China denounced Tokyo's attempt to link economic cooperation with the nuclear testing. It even brought out the history issue again in an attempt to exploit Japanese feelings of guilt and put pressure on Tokyo. For example, an article carried in the *People's Daily* on 9 September stated:

> This year happens to be the fiftieth anniversary of the winning of the world war against fascism and China's war against Japan, and, while Japan ought to be making a deep self-examination of the criminal act of aggression it committed and learn some serious lessons from history, we hear noisy clamor in Japan against China under the guise of protest against nuclear testing. Such a situation obliges us to ponder seriously as to what may really be the hidden political intentions of the Japanese.[26]

The response of most Japanese was that China's way of bringing up the history issue in this way is unwarranted and unfair.

Meanwhile, from July 1995 to March 1996, China conducted a series of major military exercises off the coast of Taiwan in order to send a clear signal to Taiwan, the United States, and any other country that might support Taiwan's independence that Beijing was in no way softening its hard-line attitude on the principle of "one China." The exercises were held in areas not far from Okinawa, Japan's southernmost prefecture, and they made the Japanese people increasingly nervous about the Chinese military buildup. In this context, after the bilateral summit meeting held in Tokyo on 17 April 1996, Prime Minister Hashimoto Ryutaro and U.S. President Bill Clinton issued "The U.S.-Japan Joint Declaration on Security: Alliance for the 21st Century," and officially declared that their alliance would thereafter serve not only the defense of Japan but also the stability of the entire Asia-Pacific region. Although the two leaders emphasized that the renewed alliance between Japan and the United States would not regard China as a threat, nor would it seek to contain China, Beijing obviously felt uneasy about the Hashimoto-Clinton joint declaration and continued to criticize the U.S.-Japan alliance from that time.

Tensions between the two countries grew further in the latter half of 1996 due to the territorial dispute over the Senkaku Islands. From 1895, when Japan officially declared its dominion over the Senkaku chain, sovereignty over the uninhabited islands had not been disputed by the Chinese until the end of the 1960s. After the Economic Commission for Asia and the Far East reported the possibility of a vast amount of oil and natural gas deposits in the seabed around the Senkakus in 1969, Beijing and Taipei both started to claim sovereignty over the islands.[27] In February 1992, China adopted the Law on Territorial Waters, which claims China's sovereignty over not only the Spratly and the Paracel but also the Senkaku islands. In August 1996, when Japanese rightists tried to construct a lighthouse on one island in the Senkaku cluster, demonstrators on many ships from Hong Kong and Taiwan gathered around the Senkaku to show their support for China's territorial claim. Tokyo's approach to this incident was remarkably conciliatory. The Japanese government decided in September not to authorize the lighthouse in order to contain the friction caused by the rightists' actions. Beijing also tried to contain the friction by not allowing the anti-Japanese demonstrations in Hong Kong to spread into China. Although the two governments managed to avoid a serious deterioration of diplomatic relations, this incident obviously hurt Japanese feelings toward China. Many Japanese were also dissatisfied with their government's handling of the incident. As one Diet member argued, many Japanese believed that their government's attitude should have been to "reasonably refute China's claim to the territory which clearly belongs to Japan."[28] Regarding the Senkaku issue, an increasing number of the Japanese feel that their government's diplomatic stance was embarrassingly weak and overly conciliatory to Beijing.

In November 1998, Japanese feelings toward China deteriorated even further with the behavior of Chinese President Jiang Zemin during his official visit to Japan to commemorate the twentieth anniversary of the signing of the Peace and Friendship Treaty. It represented the first visit ever to Japan by a Chinese head of state, and at first Japan extended a warm welcome. During his six-day visit, however, Jiang brought up the history issue on virtually every occasion, even at the state banquet held in his honor at the Imperial Palace, and repeated severe criticism of Japan's militarist past in harsh language. The majority of Japanese felt that Jiang's attitude was lacking in common courtesy. While most Japanese, including those of the postwar generation, still share a sincere sense of guilt toward China, they also believe that the Chinese should accept the apologies repeatedly made by Japanese leaders, such as Emperor Akihito's above-mentioned statement in Beijing in 1992, Prime Minister Hosokawa Morihiro's apology during his trip to China in March 1994, Prime Minister Murayama's apology during his trip to China in May 1995, and Prime Minister Obuchi Keizo's apology during Jiang's visit to Tokyo. Jiang's persistent reference to the history issue left a particularly negative impression on the Japanese people, not only because of its content but also its timing. Just a few weeks before Jiang's visit, South Korean President Kim Dae-jung had also visited Japan in early October. Kim accepted Prime Minister Obuchi's forthright words of apology for the "history" of Japan's colonial rule and expressed his willingness to put the past to rest and move ahead in promoting constructive bilateral relations. The Japanese people, who were deeply moved by Kim's attitude, saw Jiang's attitude as particularly hurtful and even arrogant.

The development of Japan-China relations since the end of the Cold War clearly demonstrates both continuity and change in the three characteristics of Japan's China policy listed at the beginning of this chapter. First, the United States still holds a central place in Japan's China policy. Why?

In East Asia, the end of the Cold War meant the disappearance of the nearly two-decades-old strategic structure in which the United States, Japan, and China united with each other to face the Soviet Union. As a consequence of the sudden disappearance of the common threat, the relationship between the United States and China has become more fluid, with the United States desiring to maintain the U.S.-led regional order in the post–Cold War East Asia and with China becoming more and more assertive. Under such circumstances, the trilateral relationship among the United States, Japan, and China is asymmetrical. Japan, with its peace constitution and resultant lack of military autonomy, is not a full player in the strategic game in East Asia played by the United States and

China. National consensus in postwar Japan has been that the country should not participate in international power politics unless it was forced. Japan has consequently chosen to depend heavily for its security upon security relations with the United States.

Despite the realist prediction that any country will seek to acquire a strong military capability in order to achieve military autonomy once it achieves economic affluence,[29] Japan has maintained the remarkably self-restrained military posture of "exclusively defensive defense," even after becoming an economic superpower. For more than a quarter century after it achieved a great-power economy, Japan has refused to adopt the usual techniques of traditional major power diplomacy and has attempted to remain aloof from the power-politics aspect of international relations as much as possible.[30] In order to maintain that posture in its external affairs, it has been indispensable for Japan to continue relying upon the United States for its security.

For the first time since the end of the World War II, since the end of the Cold War, the majority of Japanese have come to share the understanding that their country must transform its reactive foreign policy posture into a more active one. They also see that it must fulfill an obligation to participate more actively and visibly in the maintenance of regional and global peace in order to make their country a respected member of international society. The majority of Japanese, however, are against the idea that Japan should become a "normal major power," militarily speaking. They want their country to basically maintain the traditional, exclusively defense-oriented military posture. Given that orientation in Japan's public opinion, the Japanese government has decided to basically maintain in the post–Cold War era the traditional posture that Japan does not seek military autonomy and will continue relying for its security upon the alliance with the United States. The Japanese decision was made public with the new 1995 National Defense Program Outline and the U.S.-Japan Joint Security Declaration in April 1996.

The implication of the Japanese decision not to seek military autonomy even after the end of the Cold War is clear: it has decided to continue accepting its asymmetrical relations with the United States and China. In other words, it will continue to tolerate a junior status in the trilateral relationship. In this sense, this decision was a painful one for Japan. Japan, nonetheless, has accepted an unequal status vis-à-vis the United States and China, because Japanese leaders see this inequality, or asymmetry, as the basis for maintenance of stable relations among the three major players in the region in the near future.[31] They are afraid that the post–Cold War environment in East Asia might become even more fluid if Japan should attempt to seek equal status.

Special attention must be paid to two crucial points. First, the Japanese decision to accept and tolerate asymmetry in the trilateral major power relations in East Asia cannot be maintained without solid security relations with the United States. Without the U.S.-Japan alliance, Japan would have no alternative but to become a "normal major power" in order to achieve an equal status vis-à-vis the United States and China. Second, many experts agree that the security environment has become more uncertain in East Asia since the end of the Cold War. In such an environment, Japan's decision not to become a militarily autonomous power means that its capacity to control regional security challenges such as the North Korea problem and the Taiwan issue will be limited. Japan will require U.S. help to deal with these challenges. Japan's ability to influence the trilateral relations among the United States, China, and itself will also be limited. Consequently, its China policy, particularly in the strategic and security fields, is likely to be heavily influenced by the United States, and is also likely to remain reactive rather than active.

Nevertheless, it is certainly an important change that Japan has begun to show some willingness to play the strategic game in East Asia more actively. For example, Japan, as well as the United States, obviously had China on its mind during the process of redefinition of the U.S.-Japan alliance, although the redefinition was by no means anti-China. Tokyo, together with Washington, attempted to influence the direction of China's external behavior by sending the following message: unless you pursue a collision course with the rest of the countries in East Asia and disrupt regional stability, we will not regard you as a threat. We want you to cooperate with us and other regional members for the stability and prosperity of the region. The "Eurasia diplomacy" advocated by Prime Minister Hashimoto in the latter half of 1997 represents another sign of Japan's desire to be a more active player in the strategic game in East Asia. It was probably the first attempt by the Japanese government to integrate three bilateral relations—between Japan and the United States, Japan and China, and Japan and Russia—into a wider context of four-way major power relations. These changes in Japan's diplomatic posture in recent years can be understood as the expression of Japan's desire to become a political major power without becoming military major power.

The way the Japanese people view China has also changed to a considerable extent in the last several years. First of all, the Tiananmen Square incident severely damaged the image of China shared by most Japanese. Second, Japanese have started to show serious concern about the future direction China might choose. Such concern was originally sparked by China's adoption of the Law on Territorial Waters in 1992 accompanying the rapid expansion of Chinese military expenditures. Since then, the Japanese concern has grown incrementally with China's repeated nuclear testing and large-scale military exercises in the Taiwan Straits from 1995 to 1996. Third, many Japanese have begun to feel that China abuses the history issue and often politicizes it in an inappropriate manner. In recent years, China brought up the issue so often to pressure Japan, but their strategy obviously backfired. Today, the Japanese people still widely share a deep sense of guilt over their nation's act of aggression against China. But many Japanese are deeply disappointed at the way the Chinese government has handled the issue.

Thus, while Japan's approach toward China remains much more conciliatory than Washington today, voices have been growing among Japanese in recent years that Japan should assert its national interests more frankly vis-à-vis China. Fourth and finally, the popularity of China among the Japanese people has considerably declined in the late 1990s. According to the public opinion polls annually conducted by Japan's Prime Minister's Office since 1978, throughout the 1980s, around 70 percent of respondents consistently answered that they had friendly sentiments toward China. In 1989, because of the Tiananmen Square incident, the percentage dropped from 68.5 percent in the previous year to 51.6 percent ,while the percentage of those who answered that they did *not* have such sentiments sharply increased from 26.4 percent in the previous year to 43.2 percent. In 1995, the percentage of those who had friendly sentiments toward China dropped below 50 percent (48.4 percent) for the first time. In 1996, the percentage of those who did not have friendly sentiments (51.3 percent) exceeded the percentage of those who did (45.0 percent) for the first time.[32]

These changes suggest that Japan's future posture toward China is likely to become somewhat more active and assertive than before. Its unilateral application of economic sanctions against China against its nuclear testing in 1995 may be a sign of a change that has been taking place in Japan's posture. It seems that such a change, or more precisely, potential change, together with the redefinition of the U.S.-Japan Alliance, have already aroused Chinese wariness toward Japan.

Both Japan and China have obviously started to be worried about each other's future external postures. This is potentially a dangerous situation that could lead to a "security dilemma" between the two countries. However, there are ample reasons for both sides to avoid confrontation. The economies of the two countries are now deeply interdependent, and both Tokyo and Beijing obviously recognize the cost of a breakdown of the bilateral relations for them. Toward the end of the twentieth century, the Japan-China relations are at a major turning point.

Japan's Postwar Diplomacy toward the Korean Peninsula[33]

Japan's diplomacy toward the Korean Peninsula was heavily influenced by U.S. policies throughout the postwar twentieth century. When Japan signed the San Francisco peace treaty in September 1951, the Korean War was still being fought. Under the flag of the United Nations, the United States intervened extensively in the war in order to support the South Korean regime. Under such circumstances, Japan had no choice but to enter into diplomatic relations with the Republic of Korea alone. Seoul, however, was not among the signatories to the San Francisco peace treaty because Korea had been under Japanese rule until August 1945 and was not a belligerent in World War II. Japan, therefore, was first required to conclude a peace treaty with the Republic of Korea and establish diplomatic relations with that state.

The first preliminary negotiations for restoration of Japan-ROK relations started in November 1951, merely six weeks after the conclusion of the San Francisco peace treaty. Nevertheless, it took 13 years and eight months with over 1,500 meetings in total to conclude the treaty.[34] Why did it take such a long time for the two neighbors to sign a normalization treaty? From the Japanese point of view, one important reason was South Korean President Syngman Rhee's extremely anti-Japanese attitude. For example, in January 1952, Rhee unilaterally declared ROK sovereignty over a wide area of sea surrounding the

Korean Peninsula (the so-called "Rhee Line") and started to capture Japanese fishing boats that entered that area. According to Rhee's declaration, the Takeshima Islands, whose ownership had been disputed between Tokyo and Seoul since Korea regained independence, was included in the area under ROK sovereignty.[35] Such anti-Japanese policies by Rhee naturally repelled Japanese. The more fundamental reason for the delay of normalization was, however, the crucial difference in two parties' postures toward the negotiations. Korea emphasized Japanese apology and reparations for its 36-year colonial rule, while Japan emphasized the building of the future relations between the two nations. Moreover, Japanese and Koreans saw the Japanese rule of Korea quite differently. In the Korean view Japanese rule had brought them only pain. Japanese admitted that their country had inflicted tremendous pain upon Koreans, but they also believed that their rule brought at least a certain amount of material benefits to the peninsula, such as agricultural development, construction of railroads and harbors, and establishment of a modern educational system. In June 1965, after considerable U.S. pressure, when the negotiations finally came to a settlement on the basis of massive financial payments by Japan, these gaps of recognition and posture between the two sides still remained. The ill feelings between the two peoples—especially on the side of the Koreans—that existed then have not dissipated.

Some observers still believe that Japan has hardly apologized to the Koreans regarding the history of its 36-year rule of the peninsula, but they are wrong. In February 1965, four months before the conclusion of the normalization treaty, Japanese Foreign Minister Shiina Etsusaburo visited the ROK and expressed profound remorse for Japanese colonial rule. Since then, Japanese leaders have repeatedly made apologies. Japan also provided economic compensation: US$500 million in economic assistance to the ROK as quasi-reparation when relations were normalized in 1965, which helped the ROK to generate sustained economic growth. These facts, however, have not satisfied Koreans. Many continue to criticize Japan for its past behavior at every occasion. Such criticism reawakens in the Japanese a sense of guilt and shame, and represents a heavy psychological pressure. This pressure has made Tokyo's diplomatic posture toward the two Koreas much more passive, lower profile, and less assertive than otherwise. That diplomatic posture has been particularly salient in the Japanese government's handling of the Takeshima issue, and the issue of history vis-à-vis South Korea, as well as in the government attitude toward North Korea, and has been often criticized by Japanese nationalists in recent years.

After the normalization of diplomatic relations, the economic exchange between Japan and the ROK drastically expanded and the economies of the two countries became deeply interdependent. Except for the economic field, however, Japan did not regard the ROK as an important partner during the 1960s and the 1970s. During that period, it recognized the importance of the ROK mainly within the context of the U.S.-Japan relations.[36] Japan had neither the capability nor the willingness to change the strategic conditions on the Korean Peninsula, and basically followed U.S. Korea policy. Japan lacked any such capability because of its remarkably self-restrained military posture of "exclusively defensive defense" and out of its heavy reliance upon the alliance with the United States for security. It lacked the willingness because of the strong pacifist orientation of postwar Japanese and their consequent desire to avoid involvement in confrontation outside of their country as well as their sense of guilt over the nation's behavior toward the Koreans before 1945 and their consequent tendency to think that they have little right to interfere in matters on the Korean Peninsula.

Out of the fear of being dragged into overseas conflicts, Japan has attempted to remain aloof from the confrontation between the two Koreas as much as possible, but only within the limits of U.S. approval. Until 1982, when Prime Minister Nakasone entered office, Japan was far from enthusiastic about entering into official security cooperation with the ROK. In the Nixon-Sato joint communiqué of November 1969, Japan certainly recognized that "the security of the Republic of Korea is essential to Japan's own security" (the Korea clause). In fact, however, Japan attempted to limit its commitment toward South Korean security because it feared that such a commitment would bring about confrontation with communist countries in the neighborhood. As in the case of the "Taiwan Clause" in the same communiqué, Prime Minister Sato Eisaku accepted Washington's demand to insert the clause in order to extract a U.S. concession on the issue of the restoration of Okinawa.[37] The Japanese government tried repeatedly to modify or remove the clause from joint statements with both the Korean and U.S. governments in the following years.[38] The Tanaka administration shifted the emphasis of Japan's Korea policy from security of South Korea to peace and stability of the Korean Peninsula as a whole.[39] In 1981, when Korean President Chun Doo-hwan requested Japanese Prime Minister Suzuki Zenko to provide the ROK $6 billion in economic aid on the pretext of its enormous military expenditures that form a shield for Japan's security, Suzuki persisted in his refusal to link economic aid with the security issue.[40]

In the meantime, as in the case of China, Japan attempted to maintain, and if possible promote, nongovernmental exchange with the communist regime of the divided nation. In Japanese society, particularly among intellectuals and journalists, leftist forces were quite strong for a long time after the end of the war. Even in the 1980s, Japanese media reports tended to praise North Korean achievements and criticize little, while harshly censuring the political and human rights conditions under the regime in the South. Influenced by such reports, the image of South Korea under the military administrations was quite negative among Japanese. Consequently, although North Korea continuously attacked Japan as "militarist" and "aggressor," the majority of the Japanese supported the government's remarkably nonconfrontational posture toward Pyongyang. In the early 1970s, when an atmosphere of detente appeared temporarily between the North and the South, Japan even attempted to move toward the "equidistant diplomacy" to Seoul and Pyongyang.[41] After 1975, however, reacting to the collapse of South Vietnam and President Jimmy Carter's plan to withdraw the U.S. troops from South Korea, Japan again grew closer to the ROK.

The massive Soviet military buildup in the Far East beginning in the late 1970s, and the Reagan administration's strong request that Japan help bear the responsibility of supporting the defense efforts of the ROK, represented two important events that promoted political and security ties between Japan and South Korea in the early 1980s. Prime Minister Nakasone, who came to office in November 1982, attempted actively to promote friendly relations between Japan and South Korea. He made an official visit to the ROK in January 1983, the first official visit to South Korea by a Japanese prime minister in the postwar era. In September 1984 Nakasone hosted President Chun in Tokyo. This was the first official visit to Japan by the South Korean head of state. These visits represented two significant steps in improving the sensitive relations between the two countries. Since then, Japanese administrations have consistently emphasized the importance to Japan of friendly relations with the ROK.

It should be noted, however, that even Nakasone attempted to limit Japan's commitment to South Korean security. For example, when Nakasone promised to provide $4 billion in economic aid to the ROK during his visit to Seoul in 1983, he refused to link it officially to the security issue although he unofficially made it clear to ROK officials that the aid package was motivated in part by his recognition of how much Seoul's defense efforts contributed to Japanese security.[42] In the joint statement issued at that time, the Korean side wanted to include the expression "the security of the Republic of Korea is essential to Japan's own security," which had appeared in the Korea Clause of the Nixon-Sato joint communiqué of November 1969. However, after Japanese insistence, the expression that was actually inserted in the joint statement was "maintenance of peace and stability on the Korean Peninsula is essential to peace and stability in East Asia including Japan."[43] Furthermore, at a meeting of cabinet members from Japan and South Korea held in August 1983, Nakasone said that Japan ought to promote private exchanges with the Democratic People's Republic of Korea (DPRK) although the fact is unchanged that South Korea is of great importance to Japan.[44]

To summarize, the keynotes of Japan's diplomacy toward the Korean Peninsula in the Cold War period were:

1. to strengthen friendly relations with the Republic of Korea with the priority on economic relations,
2. to cooperate with the United States and the ROK to maintain peace and stability on the Korean Peninsula,
3. within the framework of U.S. Korea policy, to limit the level of its commitment to South Korean security as low as possible,
4. within the framework of U.S. Korea policy, to take a non-confrontational and conciliatory approach toward the DPRK, and to promote private exchange and establish better relations, but only as far as the international environment permits.

Since the Cold War ended, two significant changes have been appearing in Japan's Korea policy. First, Japan's posture toward the North has changed drastically. In the years right after the end of the Cold War, Japan still maintained its traditional nonconfrontational and conciliatory posture. It was not so surprising that Japan decided to start negotiations to establish diplomatic relations with

Pyongyang in the early 1990s, when the tension between the two Koreas relaxed and dialogues proceeded between them. Japan's posture toward the DPRK, however, suddenly became remarkably tougher from 1993 to 1994 when the North's nuclear and missile development programs were disclosed. Japan, for the first time, came to see North Korea as a direct threat to its security. After the DPRK shot a Tepodong missile over mainland Japan in August 1998, most Japanese came to share the perception that Pyongyang represents a serious threat to their security. The economic crisis in North Korea and the danger of collapse of its regime has deepened the anxiety of the Japanese people about its possible use of military force. In the 1990s, reports about North Korea in the Japanese mass media have become much more objective than before. Japanese are now very familiar with the strange belief system shared by the Pyongyang leaders and the reality of their anti-Japan activities, including kidnapping of Japanese nationals. These reports have seriously damaged the image of North Korea among the Japanese.

Second, as the recognition that North Korea represents a serious threat to Japan spreads through Japanese society, people's willingness to accept the idea of security cooperation with South Korea has suddenly increased. In diplomatic and security circles in Japan, it became well accepted that, in order to deal with the threat from North Korea, it is essential for Japan, South Korea, and their common ally, the United States, to promote closer security relations among them. Diplomatic and security circles in South Korea welcome such change on the part of Japan. One remarkable consequence of this new development was the first joint military exercise between the Japanese Maritime Self Defense Force and the Korean navy in the summer of 1999.

In spite of these changes, Japan's diplomacy toward the Korean Peninsula is still heavily influenced by the U.S. Korea policy. Because of its decision not to become an autonomous military power even after the end of the Cold War, Japan is not capable of controlling or changing the strategic environment on the Korean Peninsula—actions by North Korea in particular. Japan's security role on the Korean Peninsula will have to be quite limited because of the legacy of its past colonial rule and the regulations of its peace constitution. For these reasons, in order to confront the threat from the DPRK, Japan has no option but to depend upon the U.S. military protection. Consequently, Japan's Korea policy still generally follows the basic movements of U.S. policy. In 1994, although Japan was not satisfied with the Agreed Framework between Washington and Pyongyang, it had no choice but to endorse it. After the Tepodong missile fly-by in August 1998, Japan unilaterally froze its financial contribution to the Korean Peninsula Energy Development Organization (KEDO) as a sanction against Pyongyang. However, it was forced to lift the sanction only several weeks later by the pressure of the United States and South Korea.

Thus, Japan's posture toward the Korean Peninsula in the post–Cold War period has changed, though only to a limited extent, and the three characteristics of Japanese foreign policy in the postwar period listed at the beginning of this chapter, namely, the dominant influence of the U.S., a passive posture, and a minimalist posture are likely to be observed in Japan's Korea policy in the foreseeable future. Still, these changes have paved the way for a wider and deeper partnership between Japan and South Korea, not only in the economic but also in the political and security fields.

As for the problem of history, the constraints of past history on Japan's Korea diplomacy may be weakening, but by no means disappearing. For a long time after normalization of the bilateral relations, Japan's efforts to overcome the legacy of the past were not sufficient to remove Korean resentment. Japanese leaders repeatedly expressed remorse and apologies for their country's past actions, but Koreans were far from satisfied, because they viewed the Japanese apologies as lacking in sincerity. The Koreans were also irritated by the fact that regardless of the repeated expressions of apology by the Japanese government, time after time certain individual politicians would make remarks totally lacking in contrition or regret over issues that were historically sensitive. They felt that the Japanese did not understand their grievances.

During the 1990s, however, Japanese leaders' willingness to show remorse with more forthright words of apology has become increasingly clear. In May 1990, when President Roh Tae Woo visited Japan, Prime Minister Kaifu Toshiki expressed "sincere remorse and honest apologies" for the suffering inflicted by Japan on Korea during the period 1910 to 1945. Emperor Akihito also admitted that Japan was responsible for the suffering of the Koreans during Japan's colonial rule and expressed his "deepest regret." The emperor's words of apology were far more outright than the former Emperor Hirohito's remarks had been about an "unfortunate period" in Japan–Korea relations at the welcoming banquet for President Chun at the Imperial Palace in August 1984.[45] Responding to these apologies, President Roh declared that the apology question was now a closed issue.[46] In November 1993, when Prime Minister Hosokawa Morihiro visited Korea, he made an unequivocal apology for Japan's colonial rule over Korea that was widely praised by the Koreans.[47]

During the same period, however, South Korea criticized Japan regarding the history issue time and again. As in the case of China, although a sense of guilt over the history of their country's colonial rule over Korea is widely shared among Japanese, many in Japan also feel that the Koreans should accept the genuine apologies repeatedly made in recent years by Japanese leaders. An increasing number have started to ask to themselves: How many times do we have apologize before we are going to be forgiven by the Koreans? How long do we have to keep apologizing? More Japanese have come to feel that the Koreans take up the historical issues too often and politicize them in an inappropriate manner. Obviously, whether the Japanese and the Koreans can control their respective nationalistic sentiments regarding the history issue will be the key to establishing constructive future relations between the two nations.

From this point of view, the visit made by South Korean President Kim Dae Jung to Japan in October 1999 turned a new page in the troubled relations between the two countries. In the summit meeting with President Kim, Japanese Prime Minister Obuchi Keizo not only sincerely expressed "remorse and apology" for Japan's colonial rule over Korea, but also agreed to include these words in the joint statement for the first time. President Kim accepted Obuchi's apology, and in his speech at the state banquet held in his honor at the imperial palace, he did not mention the history issue and emphasized his willingness to look toward the future. Japan's relations with South Korea took a sharp turn for the better as a result of Kim's attitude and words, which deeply impressed the Japanese.

Postwar Foreign Policy toward China and Korea

Since recovering its independence in April 1952, Japan has rarely taken any diplomatic posture toward China or the Korean Peninsula not compatible with U.S. policies and intentions. This has been the natural consequence of the fact that postwar Japan has depended heavily for its security on the military alliance with the United States, rather than seeking military autonomy.

As soon as it signed the San Francisco peace treaty in September 1951, Japan found itself in a harsh security environment, located right next to the Soviet Union, and with two other neighbors, China and Korea, divided into communist and anticommunist regimes supported by the Soviet Union and the United States respectively. The Cold War had already spread to Asia, and Japan became a member of the U.S. camp by destiny rather than choice. On the Korean Peninsula, the Korean War was continuing in which the United States was fighting against the communist regime in the North and China in order to help South Korea. Japan, nevertheless, was far from enthusiastic about strengthening its military power, in spite of U.S. requests to promptly rearm, out of still-fresh memories of its defeat, not to mention a sense of guilt over their nation's role in the war. A deep pacifist orientation had spread among the people after the war was over. The postwar Japanese view anything even remotely connected with the military, not to mention militarism, with a degree of wariness that borders on total rejection. There was a strong public abhorrence of using anything military-related as a tool of external policy, even including policies on the defense of Japan. The national consensus in postwar Japan was that the country should not participate in international power politics unless it was forced to do so. In the severe Cold War security environment that surrounded the Japanese archipelago, however, postwar Japanese pacifism could only survive with U.S. protection. Under such circumstances, it was only natural that Japan's policies toward the two divided nations in Asia required U.S. consent.

Since the end of the Cold War, the Japanese government has decided to continue relying for its security upon the alliance with the United States and not seek military autonomy. The decision has already been made public with the 1995 National Defense Program Outline and the Joint Security Declaration by Prime Minister Hashimoto and President Clinton in April 1996. Consequently, Japanese policies toward China and the Korean Peninsula are likely to remain in line with U.S. policies toward the new century.

Nonetheless, the tone of Japanese foreign policy style toward China and Korea has always been quite different from the U.S. style. First, Japanese diplomacy in this region has been reactive rather than active. Without autonomous military power, Japan has not been capable of controlling the political and strategic atmosphere in the region, or, put in other words, the degree of amicability and hostility between the two Korean states, between China and Taiwan, and among the United States, the Soviet Union (Russia), and China. Japan has been forced to adjust itself to changes in the regional political environment because it has lacked the capacity to engineer changes in the environment itself.

Another factor that has contributed to the reactive nature of Japanese diplomacy toward China and the Korean Peninsula is Japan's history in the first half of this century. Among postwar Japanese, a genuine sense of guilt and repentance over their nation's behavior toward China and Korea before and during the war is widely shared, although some have certainly desired to find something positive in it. The Chinese and Koreans have assumed the moral high ground in their relationships to Japan, giving them political leverage they would otherwise lack. They have been able to utilize historical issues as bargaining chips in putting psychological pressure on Japan. This has made the Japanese attitude toward China and two Koreas far more passive than otherwise. A sense of guilt over their nation's actions against the Chinese and the Koreans before 1945 has also produced among the postwar Japanese a tendency to think that they have little right to interfere in matters in China and Korea. This tendency at least partially explains why Japan has rarely taken any active initiatives to change the status quo regarding China-Taiwan relations or the relationship between the North and South on the Korean Peninsula.

Second, Japan's posture toward China and the two Koreas has been remarkably less confrontational than that of the United States. Tokyo was willing to cooperate with Washington's Cold War strategies toward China and the Korean Peninsula only to a limited extent. The fundamental goals of Japan's China and Korea diplomacies has been the maintenance of the stability, and, if possible, the reduction of tensions, in the region. It is well known that Japan signed the peace treaty with the Kuomintang government in 1952 only after putting up considerable resistance to U.S. pressure, because Japan wanted to make peace with Beijing rather than Taipei. Despite Prime Minister Yoshida's efforts to leave the issue open until a more opportune time, Japan ultimately had to follow the U.S. lead. Even after reluctantly choosing Taipei, Tokyo's position was to welcome the development of private exchanges—trade relations in particular—with the PRC. As for the Korean Peninsula, the Japanese government consistently avoided entering into military cooperation with the ROK until the end of the Cold War; while it sought to keep the door open to promote unofficial exchanges with Pyongyang.

Japan's response to the so-called history issues represents another example of its nonconfrontational posture toward China and Korea. When the Chinese or the Koreans bring up the history issue, sometimes as a bargaining chip against Japan, the Japanese government tends to refrain from making any issue about their arguments and simply make necessary concessions. In the territorial disputes over the Takeshima Islands with Seoul and Senkaku Islands with Beijing, too, Japan's approach has been consistently marked by a remarkable degree of self-restraint. In recent years, nationalist forces in Japan often attack this conciliatory approach toward Japan's neighbors, considering such low-profile diplomacy humiliating. The nationalists complain that the Japanese government is so afraid of friction with the neighboring countries that it will not courageously assert Japan's national interests vis-à-vis China and the Korean Peninsula. Such voices of the Japanese nationalists are further proof of the nonconfrontational nature of Japan's diplomacy toward its Northeast Asian neighbors.

The nonconfrontational nature of Japan's China and Korea diplomacies in the postwar period can be understood as a consequence of several factors. First, the simplest reason is that many Japanese believed it natural for Japan to have friendly relations with neighbors with whom it has a more than two-thousand-year history of cultural and other ties. It was also believed that friendly relations with these countries were essential for Japan's economic interests. Moreover, the strong pacifist orientation among postwar Japanese led to their desire to avoid involvement in political and military confrontations with their neighbors. A sense of guilt over prewar history makes the Japanese attitude toward their neighbors even more restrained. That sense also produced a belief among a considerable number of Japanese that their country was morally responsible for making efforts to build friendly relations with China and the two Koreas. Besides, the existence of strong leftist movements in the postwar Japanese society contributed considerably to Japan's nonconfrontational approach toward the PRC and Pyongyang.

Third and finally, Japan's China and Korea diplomacies in the postwar period have been remarkably economy-oriented. In its postwar relations with China and Korea, except for negotiations to normalize diplomatic relations, territorial disputes over small islets, and friction over history issues that are occasionally brought up by Japan's neighbors, only the economic relations have been salient until recent years. This feature of Japan's postwar diplomacy toward China and Korea has made the relationships between Japan and these countries during that period rather "boring" ones with few dramatic events.

The three distinctive characteristics of Japan's foreign policy in the post–World War II period listed at the beginning of this chapter, i.e., the dominant influence of the U.S. relations, a passive, or reactive, posture, and the minimalist posture have been salient in its diplomatic posture toward its Northeast Asian neighbors throughout the second half of the twentieth century. Since the end of the Cold War, there have been some signs of change in these characteristics, but only to a limited extent. The Japanese decision to continue relying for its security on the alliance with the United States and not to seek military autonomy, the persistent pacifist orientation among postwar Japanese, and the strong sense of guilt over their country's past actions toward their neighbors all contribute to continuity of these characteristics in Japan's Northeast Asia diplomacy.

Notes

1. For a detailed study of Japan-China relations in the postwar period, see Tanaka Akihiko, *Nit–Chu kankei 1945–1990* [Japan-China Relations 1945–1990] (Tokyo: University of Tokyo Press, 1991); Ogata Sadako, *Sengo Nit-Chu, Bei-Chu kankei* [Japan-China and U.S.-China Relations in the Postwar Era], trans. Soeya Yoshihide (Tokyo: University of Tokyo Press, 1992); Soeya Yoshihide, *Nihon gaiko to Chugoku 1945–1972* [Japanese Diplomacy and China 1945–1972] (Tokyo:

Keio Tsushin, 1995); and Takagi Seiichiro, "Nit-Chu kankei no shin-dankai" [A New Phase in Japan-China Relations], in *Ajia seiji no mirai to Nippon* [The Future of Asian Politics and Japan], ed. Okabe Tatsumi (Tokyo: Keiso Shobo, 1995).
2. Yoshida Shigeru, *Kaiso junen* [Ten Years in Retrospect], vol.3 (Tokyo: Shinchosha, 1957; reprint, Tokyo: Chuo Koron Sha, 1998), p. 83 (page references are to reprint edition).
3. Maruyama Nobuo, "Nit-Chu keizai kankei" [Japan-China Economic Relations] in *Chugoku o meguru kokusai kankyo* [The International Environment Surrounding China] ed. Okabe Tatsumi (Tokyo: Iwanami Shoten, 1990), p. 78.
4. NHK Hoso Yoron Kenkyujo [NHK Broadcasting Poll Research Institute], ed., *Zusetsu sengo yoron-shi* [Postwar Opinion Polls Illustrated], 2nd edition (Tokyo: Nippon Hoso Shuppan Kyokai, 1982), p. 181.
5. Tadokoro Masayuki, "Keizai taikoku no gaiko no genkei: 1960-nendai no Nihon gaiko" [The Prototype of Economic Power Diplomacy: Japan's 1960s Diplomacy] in *Sengo Nihon gaiko-shi* [The History of Postwar Japanese Diplomacy], ed. Iokibe Makoto (Tokyo: Yuhikaku, 1999), p. 128.
6. Soeya, 1995, pp.110–111.
7. Tanaka, 1991, p. 59.
8. Quoted in Soeya, 1995, p. 84.
9. Kamiya Fuji, *Sengo-shi no naka no Nichi-Bei kankei* [Japan-U.S. Relations in Postwar History] (Tokyo: Shinchosha, 1989), pp. 136–37.
10. Ogata, 1992, chapter 6 repeatedly makes this point.
11. For the meaning of Fukuda's "equidistance diplomacy," see Ogata's interview with Owada Hisashi, in Ogata, 1992, p. 163.
12. Nakai Yoshifumi, "Chugoku no 'kyoi' to Nit-Chu, Bei-Chu kankei" [The Chinese "Threat" and Japan-China and U.S.–China Relations] in *Chugoku wa kyoi ka* [Is China a Threat?], ed. Amako Satoshi (Tokyo: Keiso Shobo, 1997), p. 109.
13. Tanaka, 1991, pp. 111–12; and Nakanishi Hiroshi, "Jiritsu-teki kyocho no mosaku: 1970-nendai no Nihon gaiko" [Groping for Autonomous Cooperation: Japan's Diplomacy in the 1970s], in Iokibe, 1999, pp. 176 and 183.
14. Nakanishi, 1999, p. 176.
15. Tanaka, 1991, pp. 114–15.
16. Tanaka, 1991, p. 108; Kojima Tomoyuki, "Gendai Nit-Chu kankei-ron, [Contemporary Japan-China Relations] in *Koza gendai Ajia 4: Chiiki shisutemu to kokusai kankei* [Lectures on Contemporary Asia 4: Regional Systems and International Relations], ed. Hirano Ken'ichiro (Tokyo: University of Tokyo Press, 1994), p. 204.
17. Research Institute for Peace and Security (RIPS), ed., *Asian Security 1983* (Tokyo: RIPS, 1983), pp. 108 and 214; Tanaka 1991, p. 120; Murata Koji, "'Kokusai kokka' no shimei to kuno: 1980-nendai no Nihon gaiko" [The Mission and Hardships of an "International State": Japanese Diplomacy in the 1980s] in Iokibe, 1999, p. 195.
18. *Konshu no Nippon*, 16 April 1984.
19. Tanaka, 1991, p. 127.
20. Tanaka, 1991, pp. 145–48.
21. Wolf Mendl, *Japan's Asia Policy: Regional Security and Global Interests* (London and New York: Routledge, 1995), pp. 87–88.
22. Kojima Tomoyuki, "Sino-Japanese Relations: A Japanese Perspective," *Asia-Pacific Review*, 3:1 (Spring 1996), p. 73.
23. "Yang Zhuxi Fapiao Jianghua," *The Renmin ribao*, 24 October 1992. Quoted in Kojima, 1996, p. 86.
24. "Tenno Heika no Yo Shokon kokka shuseki shusai bansan-kai ni okeru toji" [The Emperor's Address in Reply at the Banquet Sponsored by President Yang Shangkun] in *Nit-Chu kankei kihon shiryo-shu 1970-1992* [A Collection of Basic Documents on Japan-China Relations 1970–1992] (Tokyo: Kazankai, 1994), p.158. Quoted in Kojima, 1996, p. 86.
25. "Yang Zhuxi Huijian Mingren Tianhuang He Huanghou," *The Renmin ribao*, 23 October 1992; and "Tenno Kogo Ryo-Heika no gokikoku ni tsuite no Kato Kanbo-chokan danwa" [Chief Cabinet Secretary Kato's Remarks on the Return to Japan of the Emperor and Empress]," in *Nit-Chu kankei kihon shiryo-shu 1970-1992*, p. 467. Quoted in Kojima, 1996, p. 75.
26. Gu Ping, "Buzhi Zhi Ju," *The Renmin ribao*, 9 September 1995. Quoted in Kojima, 1996, pp. 95–96.
27. Midorima Sakae, *Senkaku retto* [The Senkaku Islands] (Naha, Okinawa: Hirugi Sha, 1984).

28. Nishimura Shingo, "Japan Must Stake Its Claim to the Senkaku Island," *By the Way* 7:5 (August–September 1997): 12.
29. For a typical example of this line of argument, see Kenneth N. Waltz, "The Emerging Structure of International Politics," *International Security* 18:2 (Fall 1993).
30. For a detailed discussion on Japan's refusal to accept the style of traditional major power diplomacy, see Soeya Yoshihide, "Ajia no chitsujo hendo to Nihon gaiko" [The Changing Order in Asia and Japanese Diplomacy], *Kokusai mondai* 444 (March 1997).
31. Soeya Yoshihide, "A Presidential Overflight Rattles Japan," *Wall Street Journal*, 7 July 1998.
32. Osaki Yuji, "Aratana Nit-Chu kankei no kochiku: Ajia-Taiheiyo ni okeru Nit-Chu kankei" [Toward the Building of New Japan-China Relations: Japan-China Relations in the Asia-Pacific] in *Nihon, Amerika, Chugoku: Kyocho e no shinario* [Japan, the United States, and China: A Scenario for Their Cooperation], ed. Kokubun Ryosei (Tokyo: TBS-Britannica, 1997), pp. 180–181.
33. For a detailed study of Japan's relations with the Korean Peninsula in the postwar period, see Chong-Sik Lee, *Sengo Nik-Kan kankei-shi* [The History of Postwar Japan-Korea Relations], trans. Okonogi Masao and Furuta Hiroshi (Tokyo: Chuo Koron Sha, 1989); originally published as *Japan and Korea: The Political Dimension* (Stanford: Hoover Institution Press, 1985); Izumi Hajime, "Chikakute tooi rinjin: Nik-Kan kokko juritsu made no michi" [Close but Distant Neighbors: The Path to Restoration of Diplomatic Relations Between Japan and Korea] in *Sengo Nihon no taigai seisaku* [Japan's Postwar Foreign Policy], ed. Watanabe Akio (Tokyo: Yuhikaku, 1985); Okonogi Masao, "Masatsu to kyocho no Nik-Kan kankei: Kanjo-teki giron o haise" [Friction and Harmony in Japan-Korea Relations: Let's Get Rid of Emotional Arguments], *Gaiko forum* 86 (November 1995).
34. Izumi, 1985, p. 163.
35. In September 1954, Japan proposed to bring the dispute over the Takeshima Islands to the International Court of Justice, but the ROK did not accept the Japanese proposal.
36. Byung-joon Ahn, "Japanese Policy Toward Korea," in *Japan's Foreign Policy after the Cold War*, ed. Gerald L. Curtis (Armonk, NY: M. E. Sharpe, 1993), p. 267.
37. Kamiya, 1989, pp. 136–37.
38. Mendl, 1995, p. 64; Nakanishi, 1999, p. 152; Lee, 1989, pp. 106, 112–13.
39. Nakanishi, 1999, p.162; Lee 1989, pp.112–13. Hajime Izumi argued in his 1985 article that since the normalization of the relations with South Korea in 1965, Japan consistently put the highest priority on peace and stability of the Korean Peninsula. Izumi, 1985, pp.179–81.
40. Ahn, 1993, p. 267.
41. Lee, 1989, pp. 103–13.
42. Lee, 1989, p.185; Ahn, 1993, p. 267.
43. Lee, 1989, pp. 184–85.
44. Fujimoto Toshikazu, "Zen Tokan daitoryo ho-Nichi no igi to Nik-Kan kankei no tenbo" [The Significance of President Chun Doo Hwan's Visit to Japan and the Prospects for Japan-ROK Relations], *Kokusai mondai* 287 (December 1984): 20.
45. Research Institute for Peace and Security (RIPS), ed., *Asian Security 1990–91* (London: Brassey's, 1990), pp. 137–38
46. RIPS, 1990, p.138; Ahn, 1993, p. 266.
47. Research Institute for Peace and Security (RIPS) ed., *Asian Security 1994–95* (London: Brassey's, 1994), p. 141.

CHAPTER 14

Japanese Relations with Southeast Asia in an Era of Turbulence

Lam Peng Er

The 30th anniversary of the Association of South-East Asian Nations (ASEAN) in 1997 was supposed to be a crowning moment for the regional grouping.[1] There was indeed much to celebrate at the beginning of that year. First, the organization had achieved a degree of coherence and cooperation that included a united front toward the great powers in the region. Its members had adopted a peaceful and conciliatory approach in order to address, or even sidestep, certain intraregional problems including seemingly intractable territorial disputes between members.

Second, ASEAN members—especially Singapore, Malaysia, Thailand, Brunei, and Indonesia—had made impressive economic gains within a single generation. Indeed, many analysts believe that these countries, along with the Northeast Asian states of Japan, South Korea, China, and Taiwan, will usher in the Pacific century.

Third, ASEAN was to become a larger bloc of ten countries. By admitting Myanmar, Cambodia, and Laos to the organization, many ASEAN leaders believed that this would lead to a more united, stable, and prosperous Southeast Asia. Moreover, an expanded ASEAN might exercise greater collective political and economic clout internationally. Admirers of ASEAN could well claim that it was, indeed, the most successful regional organization in the world after the European Community.

Contrary to ASEAN expectations, however, a perfect ten was not to be: Cambodia's admission to ASEAN was put on hold after severe political violence exploded again in July 1997. Ironically, in less than a year, the image of a stable and prosperous Southeast Asia was rudely shattered; for some ASEAN countries, their East Asian economic miracle appeared to be only a mirage. Amid multiple and mutually reinforcing economic, political, and environmental crises, ASEAN as a regional organization has thus far been almost irrelevant in addressing, let alone resolving, these problems. Moreover, Cambodia, Indonesia, Myanmar, and perhaps even Malaysia face questions regarding governance and legitimacy.

This chapter examines Japan's relations with ASEAN countries and Cambodia amid economic and political turbulence.[2] It begins with an observation: while Japan appears to have successfully exercised certain initiatives on political and even strategic issues in Southeast Asia in the 1990s, it has been relatively less successful in addressing the region's economic problems. This is indeed a puzzle. Japan has often been stereotyped as an economic giant but a political pygmy. As an economic superpower, and given the historical domestic and regional sensitivities to its playing a larger political role in Southeast Asia, one would expect Japan to more ably exercise initiatives and attain greater success in the economic rather than the politico-strategic sphere. In the 1990s however, the opposite appears to be true. Although Tokyo has adopted a more active political posture in Southeast Asia, it has been relatively reactive when it comes to the economic crisis that developed there in mid-1997.

During this decade, Japan has sought to restore domestic peace in Cambodia and Myanmar by brokering a peace settlement in Cambodia and trying to persuade the military junta in Myanmar to adopt a less hard-line approach toward its domestic opposition. It floated a proposal to establish a multilateral security forum in East Asia, the antecedent of the Asian Regional Forum (ARF), and has also tried to play a positive role in the dispute over the Spratly Islands in the South China Sea. In addition, then Prime Minister Hashimoto Ryutaro proposed, in January 1997, that a regular summit be held comprising the top leaders from Japan and Southeast Asia, and that unprecedented bilateral talks be conducted on security issues involving Tokyo and individual ASEAN countries.

In contrast, Japan appeared hesitant when it came to dealing with the severe economic crisis that struck Southeast Asia. This is despite the fact that the region is important to Japan in terms of investment, trade, markets, freedom of navigation, and foreign aid,[3] and that Japanese banks had lent billions of dollars and yen to states and companies in Southeast Asia.[4] The crisis that led to the toppling of President Suharto and the subsequent state of semi-anarchy in Indonesia potentially threaten the geopolitical interests of Tokyo. Since much of its shipping, especially oil tankers, uses sea lanes adjacent to the Indonesian islands, Japan has a stake in the political stability of Indonesia and the safety of the sea lanes.

Other than a half-hearted attempt to propose the formation of an Asian Monetary Fund (AMF) and the offering of financial aid to the region, Japan did not take a lead in addressing the crisis and has yet to move significantly beyond traditional checkbook diplomacy.

Japan can adopt a more active political and strategic stance on Southeast Asia insofar as it does not meet strong opposition from its ally the United States, the ASEAN countries, and public opinion at home. Tokyo's approach toward the region is not underpinned by military power; it relies on official developmental assistance (ODA), provides its "good offices" to help address domestic and external conflicts in Southeast Asia, and generates ideas about bilateral and multilateral arrangements to enhance mutual transparency, trust, and regional order. However Tokyo has played a relatively passive role in addressing the regional economic crisis because the United States vehemently opposed the Japan-proposed AMF scheme and because Tokyo has its own domestic economic and political crises to resolve. Despite persistent U.S. demands that Japan should act as the locomotive to pull Northeast and Southeast Asia out of the economic crisis, the problem is simply too big for Japan to chew. Tokyo seems unable to pull itself out of its economic doldrums, let alone rescue the Southeast Asian economies.[5] Ironically, despite being an economic superpower, Japan is struggling to jump-start its economy and is unable and unwilling to do more for the crisis-stricken Asian countries.

This chapter will first examine various Japanese diplomatic and strategic initiatives in Southeast Asia in the 1990s, and seek to explain why Tokyo has been relatively successful in playing a more active political and strategic role in Southeast Asia. Next, it will briefly examine the economic crisis in Southeast Asia, its domino effect, and Japan's involvement. It goes on to look at Tokyo's proposals for an AMF and, subsequently, a rescue package for the region. There follows a review of suggestions that the yen should become the key currency for regional trade, ending the almost exclusive reliance on the U.S. dollar. Next will be explained the limits to Tokyo's assistance and its inability to play the part of a locomotive to pull the region out of its crisis. Lastly, we look beyond the current economic turbulence and explore other areas in which Japanese society and local governments (rather than merely the central state) can play a positive and respected role in Southeast Asia. These areas include leadership in the nontraditional but important area of environmental protection, as well as in the fields of intellectual, educational, and cultural exchange—rather than the traditional areas of guns and butter.

Seeking a Larger Political Role

After the communist takeover of mainland China and the consolidation of its regime, Japan lost an important hinterland. Tied to the United States and its containment policy to counter the specter of global communism, Japan had to seek other geographical outlets for its natural resources, trade, and investments. Southeast Asia, with its rich natural resources, a huge potential market for Japanese goods and services, and geographical proximity to Japan, appeared attractive. To the United States, it was like killing two birds with one stone: the economic intertwining between Japan and Southeast Asia could result in mutual economic benefits that would enhance market capitalism, strengthen Japan, and obviate the attractions of communism in Southeast Asia.[6] In fact, the economic bonding between Japan and Southeast Asia reinforced U.S. hegemony in Asia during the Cold War.

Washington's expectations were not misplaced. By the early 1970s, Japan had a significant economic presence in most Southeast Asian countries, and its capital was a key factor undergirding their economic progress and political stability. However considerable, the economic ties did not necessarily lead to friendship between Tokyo and the region, and triggered feelings of anxiety and resentment among many Southeast Asians. Japan's dominance, they feared, might lead to the revival of the Greater East Asian Co-Prosperity Sphere, a euphemism for the brutal Japanese military occupation of Southeast Asia during World War II.

When then–Prime Minister Tanaka Kakuei visited Thailand and Indonesia in 1974, his trip was marred by violent anti-Japanese riots in Bangkok and Jakarta. Profoundly shocked by the eruption of latent anti-Japanese feeling in the region, Tokyo's foreign policy establishment sought to address the negative image of the nation as merely an exploitative economic animal. In 1977, Prime Minister Fukuda Takeo articulated a set of principles to inform Tokyo's relations with Southeast Asian countries. This was probably the first occasion on which post–World War II Japan had explicitly codified principles to guide its relations with any particular region.

The so-called Fukuda Doctrine made three claims. First, Japan eschews the role of a great military power in the region. Second, the nation seeks a heart-to-heart relationship with Southeast Asian countries. Third, it aspires to act as a bridge between noncommunist ASEAN countries and communist states in Indochina to address regional polarization and restore regional stability. The Fukuda Doctrine is significant because Japan explicitly expressed its desire to play more than just a singular economic role even during the Cold War era; the country was prepared to play a positive political role to enhance regional order and stability.[7]

A number of reinforcing factors explain why Tokyo has sought to play a more active political role in Southeast Asia, including its desire to deflect domestic and international criticisms that Japan is merely an economic animal, seek a political role commensurate with its status as an economic superpower, and build on Southeast Asia's more receptive attitude—by comparison with that of Northeast Asia—to Tokyo's political initiatives. Unlike China and the two Koreas, Southeast Asian states and societies are relatively less bitter about Tokyo's wartime brutality and lack of genuine contrition for its atrocities. The Japanese occupation of Southeast Asia during World War II was relatively brief compared to the decades-long colonization of Korea and Taiwan, and to its aggression against the Chinese mainland. Friendly ties with Southeast Asian states may also yield diplomatic dividends for Tokyo: diplomatic support from a bloc of ten countries is valuable, especially given its desire for a permanent seat in the United Nations Security Council. In addition, being smaller and more reliant on Japanese ODA than China and the two Koreas, a number of Southeast Asian countries appeared more open to Japanese political overtures, which include providing good offices[8] and generating ideas.

Provider of Good Offices

Indochina

Vietnam's occupation of Cambodia in 1979 made it difficult for Tokyo to play a "bridging role" between Vietnam and the ASEAN states. It eventually aligned itself with the United States, China, and the ASEAN states against Vietnam and its ally, the Soviet Union. However, the structure at the end of the Cold War created favorable conditions for Japan to pursue a more active political role in the region.[9] The loss of Soviet aid, international isolation, and a lack of economic development forced Vietnam to withdraw from Cambodia. Thus China no longer had the incentive to support the Khmer Rouge faction against the Vietnamese-backed Hun Sen faction. Exhausted by the Cambodian civil war and abandoned by its erstwhile patrons, the warring Cambodian factions were receptive to Japan's overtures, suggesting that a conference be convened in Tokyo to discuss the restoration of peace in their country. Besides offering its good offices to the factions, Japan also promised to disburse substantial ODA to assist in the reconstruction of Cambodia.

The 1990 Tokyo conference paved the way for the Paris Peace Accord the following year. This led to an agreement among the Cambodian factions to accept the United Nations Transitional Authority in Cambodia (UNTAC) and UN-supervised elections to restore normality to Cambodia.[10] This development gave Japan an opportunity to play a larger role in world affairs. It paid most of the US$3 billion cost of the operation; Akashi Yasushi, a UN civil servant and Japanese national, headed UNTAC; and, after intense domestic debate, Japan, for the first time since the end of World War II, sent a contingent of troops to Cambodia under the framework of the United Nations peacekeeping operations. Thus, unlike the 1991 Gulf War fiasco—when Japan paid out US$13 billion dollars but was still roundly criticized for engaging only in checkbook diplomacy—it played a much more positive role in Cambodia.

Civil war erupted once again in Cambodia in July 1997, when Co-Prime Minister Hun Sen launched a violent coup against his erstwhile coalition partner Co-Prime Minister Prince Ranariddh.[11] Ironically, just a month before the coup, the Group of Eight (G8) had, at the Denver Summit, endorsed a Franco-Japanese special diplomatic mission to persuade the key Cambodian leaders to resolve their differences in a peaceful way. The move was to no avail and so, after violence broke out in July, Japan again sought to play an active role to help restore peace in that war-torn country. After consultations with the ASEAN countries and the Friends of Cambodia (a loose grouping of Western countries concerned about that country), Tokyo successfully brokered an agreement between the combatants. The Japanese plan called for "the exiled Prince to cut all military ties with the Khmer Rouge, an immediate ceasefire, the trial of the Prince and the pardon by his father, King Narodom Sihanouk, if he is convicted on charges of weapons smuggling and colluding with the Khmer Rouge." It also called on "the Government to guarantee the safety and security of Prince Ranariddh on his return to Cambodia and for the Prince to take part in the polls." This paved the way for Cambodia's national elections in July 1998.[12]

Although there was intermittent violence during the elections, the international community generally accepted the results as relatively fair and clean. Even though political tension has persisted in Cambodia since the polls, the 1998 elections were an important milestone on the road to political normality. A key reason for Hun Sen having relented under international pressure, especially from Japan, is the impoverished Cambodian government's dependence on foreign aid. Tokyo provides the lion's share of international aid to Cambodia, and is thus able to use ODA as a carrot to entice cooperation from the Hun Sen government.[13]

Japan's diplomacy in Cambodia is important because anarchy in that country would raise questions about the effectiveness of the UN and its peacekeeping operations (PKOs) in the post–Cold War era. Since Cambodia has been the largest and most expensive PKO thus far in the 1990s, it had to succeed to justify and legitimize future PKOs in other trouble spots around the world. After all, the UN and its PKOs could well be an important pillar in constructing a new world order. Moreover, if Japan can assist in restoring normality to Cambodia, the nine ASEAN states could embrace Cambodia and the elusive dream of an ASEAN Ten and a more stable Southeast Asia might be realized.

Myanmar

Besides Cambodia, Tokyo also sought an active role in addressing the political instability in Myanmar. Japanese diplomats have used ODA as an incentive for Mynamar's military junta to exercise restraint toward both Aung San Suu Kyi, the Nobel peace prize laureate, and the democratic movement she leads. Tokyo seeks a calibrated ODA policy toward Myanmar; were the military regime to adopt a less repressive approach toward the democratic movement, it would be prepared to offer increased ODA to Myanmar as a reward for good behavior. This approach has not been lost on the junta; it notified the Japanese Embassy in Yangon just before it released Aung San Suu Kyi from strict house arrest. Although Tokyo was supposed to resume ODA to Yangon in 1998, heightening political repression of the democratic movement in the same year undermined the disbursement of the aid. The Japanese Embassy in Yangon has acted as a bridge for communication between Aung San Suu Kyi and the junta, but it remains to be seen whether Tokyo's good offices will be as effective in Myanmar as was in the case in Cambodia.[14]

Spratlys Dispute

Japan has also offered its good offices to the states claiming the Spratly Islands in the South China Sea[15] that, despite its name, is located in the Southeast Asian region. The Spratlys straddle important shipping routes in the South China Sea and about 70 percent of Japan's oil tankers pass through the area on their way from the Gulf region to Japan. Besides the Philippines and China, Vietnam, Malaysia, Brunei, and Taiwan also claim full or partial ownership of the Spratlys. Moreover, Vietnam and China have engaged in naval skirmishes over ownership, making the Spratlys dispute a potential flash point in the Asia-Pacific region.

In 1995, the Philippines and China had a war of words over Chinese territorial markings and structures on Mischief Reef. The reef, part of the Spratlys chain, is located close to Palawan, an island of the Philippines. When the Philippines approached Japan to act as a bridge between Manila and Beijing in the dispute, Tokyo accepted the request. On a number of occasions, top Japanese leaders, including then Prime Minister Murayama Tomiichi, raised the issue with Chinese leaders and urged Beijing to exercise restraint. However, China has rebuffed these attempts at mediation because it believes that Japan should keep out of the dispute, especially since it is not a claimant state.

In addition, Japanese diplomats have informally approached their Indonesian counterparts, who have been hosting annual workshops on the South China

Sea. These workshops are venues for second-track diplomacy where officials, scholars, and experts can informally meet to discuss problems pertaining to the South China Sea. Japan was not only prepared to foot the bill for the annual workshops but also offered its national capital as an alternative location. However, Indonesia rejected the offer on the grounds that China will not accept the Japanese offer. Even though Japan has achieved little in its diplomatic forays into the Spratlys dispute, these activities are significant because they clearly demonstrate the nation's intention to be actively involved in regional strategic issues.

Japan as a Generator of Ideas

The Asian Regional Forum

During the Cold War years, Washington was concerned that multilateral security forums in Northeast and Southeast Asia might undermine its system of bilateral alliances against the Soviet Union and its allies. However, the collapse of the Cold War structure made the United States less weary toward multilateral forums in East Asia. In 1991, Nakayama Taro, then foreign minister, proposed that the ASEAN-PMC (Post-Ministerial Conference) be expanded to become a forum to promote transparency and confidence building between states in East Asia. This bold proposal took many Southeast Asian leaders and analysts by surprise, because Japan is not particularly noted for such initiatives in world affairs. Labeled the Nakayama Initiative, this idea was the antecedent of the ARF that was established in 1994.[16] Besides advocating a multilateral security forum, Tokyo also lobbied the United States, its ally, to support the scheme.

Critics of the ARF see it as merely a venue for talking shop that has yet to engage in preventive diplomacy or address the regional flash points of the Korean Peninsula, Taiwan Straits, and the Spratlys.[17] Some Japanese analysts, too, have expressed certain reservations about aspects of the ARF, including its emphasis on Southeast Asian rather than Northeast Asian issues, and the perception that it is too much of an ASEAN-driven organization.[18] However, the ARF is still a nascent organization. Regardless of its present limitations, its presence as the only multilateral security forum in Pacific Asia is undoubtedly better than its absence: half a loaf is better than none. Although the ARF is only a supplement, and not a substitute, for the U.S.-Japan alliance, Tokyo has been both a very supportive and an active member of the organization.[19] This is for two main reasons. First, Japan has no desire to put all its diplomatic eggs in one basket (the U.S.-Japan alliance). Second, the ARF is, in part, Japan's intellectual baby. Were it to further develop and mature, the ARF would probably enhance transparency, order, and stability in the region.

The Hashimoto Doctrine: Political and Security Role for Japan in Southeast Asia

In January 1997, during his trip to Southeast Asia, Hashimoto proposed a number of bilateral and multilateral arrangements that are intended to strengthen Japan's political, security, and cultural ties with the region. Besides a wide range of potential areas for cooperation, including anti-terrorism and health issues like

AIDS, the hallmarks of Hashimoto's proposals are a regular summit between the top leaders of Japan and the Southeast Asian region, and bilateral discussions between Japan and individual ASEAN states. Despite initial reservations among some ASEAN states, the proposals were accepted and the first summit was held in Kuala Lumpur, Malaysia, in December 1997.[20] Officials from the Japan Defense Agency have also become more active in visiting their counterparts in the region.

There are at least three plausible reasons for Hashimoto's initiatives. First, Japan's aspiration is to play a more active political and security role in the region. Second is Tokyo's attempt to maintain a balance in its foreign relations, especially with the United States and the People's Republic of China. Japan hopes that the ASEAN states will understand the reasons behind its new Guidelines for Japan-U.S. Defense Cooperation. Third, closer relations with Southeast Asia would give the impression that Tokyo is not strengthening its relations with the United States at the expense of others. Better ties with Southeast Asia can also be viewed as a balance against China, which may emerge as a great economic and military power in the twenty-first century.

But Japan has not remained merely a generator of ideas. When opportunities arose in Southeast Asia, the Hashimoto government tested some of the nation's post–World War II taboos. Due to the nation's entrenched mass pacifism, its government has traditionally been very cautious about sending military planes abroad, even for humanitarian reasons. However, when law and order broke down in Phnom Penh in 1997 and in Jakarta the following year, Tokyo sent military transport planes to Bangkok in 1997 and Singapore the next year. While the aircraft were, ostensibly, on standby to ferry Japanese nationals to safety, two facts are worth noting. First, chartered civilian planes could have served the same purpose had there, indeed, been a need to ferry Japanese citizens to safety. Second, despite the residual and historical suspicions Southeast Asian countries may have of Japan, both Thailand and Singapore were obliging when Tokyo requested permission to deploy its military transport planes in those countries. The two episodes suggest that Japan's so-called burden of history and the suspicions of its neighbors are slowly eroding, at least in Southeast Asia.

Ideas: Japan and the Southeast Asian Environment

Besides ideas about political and security structures and processes in Southeast Asia, Tokyo has offered ideas on the environment and global developmental models. When then Foreign Minister Obuchi Keizo gave a keynote address titled "Japan and East Asia: Outlook for the New Millennium" in May 1998 in Singapore, he offered Japanese leadership to resolve the severe environmental problems in the region. For several months in 1997, parts of Sumatra (Indonesia), Malaysia, Brunei, and Singapore had been shrouded in smog caused by the indiscriminate burning of plantations and forests for crop cultivation in Indonesia. Many of the plantations belong to capitalist cronies of former President Suharto. Obuchi's proposal went as follows:

> The forest fires and the haze problem that are raging in this region aggravated by El Niño are another cause of concern, as they have an adverse

impact on the health and lives of a vast number of people and the ecological system in the region. In order to establish new systems of fire-risk management and anti-smoke measures, I am proposing a seminar of experts from the countries concerned as well as the relevant international organizations so that we can better draw on abundant experience and knowledge. Also in this vein, I would like to encourage the International Tropical Timber Organization (in Yokohama) to dispatch missions on fire-management.[21]

During the months-long haze, Japan sent teams from its Fire Fighting Agency to help put out the fires. While Japanese environmental assistance during the haze is commendable, one should not forget that Japan is the largest importer of tropical hardwood from virgin forests in Southeast Asia.

Ideas: State-Led Development as an Alternative to American Laissez-faire Capitalism
Since the end of the Cold War and the collapse of Marxist regimes in Eastern Europe and the Soviet Union, some intellectuals have smugly claimed that the "end of history" will usher in liberal democracy and market capitalism. Many Americans assume that the U.S. model of democracy, laissez-faire capitalism, and privatization represents the appropriate developmental model for the world. This orthodoxy has been embraced by the World Bank and the IMF, international organizations that are strongly influenced by the United States.

However, Japan has a different developmental experience and was not willing to accept as universal the U.S. model.[22] As an important contributor to the World Bank, Japan pressured the international organization into conducting a study of the state-led development of the newly industrialized economies (NIEs) of South Korea, Taiwan, and Singapore. The final World Bank report on the "East Asian Economic Miracle" acknowledged that the state in East Asia does play a pivotal role in economic development. Thus the report implies that developing countries in Southeast Asia and other regions can consider other models of capitalism besides the Anglo-Saxon one. Japan's ideological challenge to developmental orthodoxy can be interpreted as a sign of the country's increasing confidence and a new willingness to exercise intellectual leadership in international organizations that have an impact on developing East Asian countries.

The Economic Crisis in Southeast Asia

Ironically, the East Asian economic miracle proved to be ephemeral. A detailed analysis of the East Asian economic crisis and the Japanese factor is beyond the scope of this study. However, Asiaweek has a succinct interpretation:

> Flashback to 1985. Under the Plaza Accord, the G7 nations intervened to stop the dollar's surge against the yen and the mark. Tokyo also cuts interest rates to help boost Japanese demand for imports and thus cut the trade deficit with the United States. The yen strengthened, making East Asian

exports more competitive (most currencies were virtually pegged to the dollar). Japanese business built production bases in Asia. The region boomed.... China devalued the renminbi in 1994, which meant it could undercut exports from East Asia. The dollar strengthened the next year. Current-account balances deteriorated as spending on imports outpaced receipts from exports. Japan's bubble economy burst, but its interest rates were kept super low. So Japanese banks lent to Asian companies for high returns. Western lenders joined the party. Easy money funded showcase infrastructure projects and property speculation. Thai finance companies borrowed low-interest U.S. dollars to relend in high-interest baht.... No one bothered to hedge. By the end of 1996, currency speculators smelled blood. The skirmishes ended with the Thais giving up on July 2, 1997. Other Asian currencies succumbed soon after. Hot money fled. Some politicians were paralyzed into inaction. Others reneged on promises to push reforms. Today, one year later, currencies remain under pressure and foreign investors are still staying away.[23]

The collapse of the baht was the catalyst for the Asian economic crisis. This, in turn, led to political change in South Korea, Thailand, Indonesia, and Malaysia. Indonesia, the most populous state in Southeast Asia, descended into semi-anarchy, with the rupiah nose-diving against the U.S. dollar, hyperinflation, food shortages, antigovernment demonstrations, looting and burning of property, the rape of Indonesian Chinese women, the resignation of Suharto, religious and ethnic violence, and the sudden proliferation of political parties and movements.

The impoverishment of Asian countries would obviously affect their ability to repay their loans to Japanese banks and purchase Japanese products.[24] Further economic and political instability in Southeast Asia may threaten the smooth production and distribution of goods from Japanese factories in the region. The paralysis of Indonesia and the economic problems of other Southeast Asian states could damage the prestige, capability, and effectiveness of ASEAN as an organization. Tokyo believes that any diminution in ASEAN's stature or capacity is highly undesirable, because it could lead to regional instability.

In 1997, Japan boldly proposed an AMF to rescue the faltering East Asian economies. The United States strongly rejected the idea, ostensibly fearing that an alternative organization would undermine the role of the IMF. But perhaps the real reason for the negative U.S. response was apprehensive that Japan would dominate the new organization. If a hefty rescue package were denominated in yen, it could, in the long run, lead to the emergence of a yen bloc in Southeast Asia. This would undermine the U.S. dollar as the de facto international currency that, in part, continues to underpin American hegemony in the post–Cold War era.

Frustrated by the rapid appreciation of the U.S. dollar against local currencies, Malaysia proposed the use of regional currencies, especially the yen, as the medium of exchange instead of relying on a gyrating U.S. dollar. Even though many Japanese bureaucrats and businessmen might believe that this is not a bad idea, Tokyo cannot openly endorse the proposal because it would undermine a core interest of its U.S. ally that would be likely to lead to a backlash from Washington. Due to Japan's dependence on the United States for its security, and on market access to the huge American market, it is not prepared to clash with the United States over either the yen as the regional currency, or an AMF.

Initially, Japan sought to play a "bridging role" between the hard-line demands of the IMF for market reforms and the recalcitrant Suharto regime. In the wake of the IMF's failure to pressure Indonesia to embark on market reform before funds were disbursed, the Japanese Ministry of Foreign Affairs in January 1998 sent a delegation to persuade Suharto to implement the IMF reforms. In mid-March 1998, then Prime Minister Hashimoto flew to Jakarta to personally persuade Suharto to accept the reforms. The carrot was Tokyo's willingness to help Indonesia if it accepted the IMF package. There was a familiar ring to the Japanese approach: the offering of good offices, and the enticement of ODA.

Tokyo offered medical aid, and 600,000 metric tons of rice (including its old stockpile of foreign rice) to Indonesia. In May 1998, then Foreign Minister Obuchi Keizo announced a US$43 billion aid package for East Asia. In comparison, the United States offered US$12 billion, while Europe pledged US$7 billion.[25] In October of the same year, Finance Minister Miyazawa Kiichi unveiled a US$30 billion package for Southeast Asia, stating that: "At the meeting [G7], I would like to propose how Japan plans to help revive Asian countries. Japan will take the leadership role."[26]

However, Japanese claims to leadership are dubious because the country still relies predominantly on its checkbook, and is unwilling to stand up to the United States. If allies cannot agree to disagree sometimes over foreign policy measures, then perhaps that alliance is less strong and equal than the rhetorical claims by Washington and Tokyo. Moreover, despite the seeming attractiveness of Tokyo's rescue packages, the severity of the East Asian contagion is so great that the funds are grossly inadequate to pull the nations out of the recession. In addition, Prime Minister Mahathir of Malaysia openly criticized Tokyo in January 1999 for its lack of urgency in disbursing much-needed funds to his country. He also remarked that Tokyo was moving so slowly that the crisis might well be over by the time it had disbursed its aid to Kuala Lumpur.

More important than ODA, however, is the need for Japan to significantly stimulate its consumer demand and pull its economy out of a grave recession. The key to addressing the East Asian contagion is neither ODA from Tokyo nor more bitter medicine (that may kill the patient) from the IMF. Japan must pull itself out of the most severe recession it has experienced in recent decades. It must boost domestic consumer demand, clean up its financial sectors, and open its markets to enable it to absorb more products from the sputtering Southeast Asian economies. A weak yen may help Japan to export itself out of a recession, but it will make certain Southeast Asian products even less competitive in the United States and Europe.

If Japanese politicians and bureaucrats cannot demonstrate leadership at home, how can they do so abroad? Although Japanese banks have an estimated US$1 trillion in bad loans, the country also has tremendous latent resources, especially in the form of domestic savings that total an estimated US$13 trillion. However, political paralysis and a lack of political will mean that resources like Japan's huge domestic savings are not fully utilized to bail the nation out of the recession. If Japan remains mired in recession into the twenty-first century, the prospects for a speedy economic recovery in Southeast Asia are bleak indeed.

In February 1999, the Japanese Diet (Parliament) approved the largest post–World War II budget of US$682 billion to jolt the economy into growth. It remains to be seen whether this measure is adequate. Radical reforms, especially involving the conversion of farming land in metropolitan areas to allow the building of better, bigger, and multi-storied homes for ordinary citizens, seem to be beyond the capacity of Japan's parochial party politics. Radical land and housing reforms would boost construction, employment, and tax revenues. Larger houses would provide more rooms and space for more foreign products from the United States, Europe, China, and Southeast Asia. This would help reduce Japan's persistent trade surplus with other countries, including those in Southeast Asia, and give their economies a further boost.

However, such proposals are probably deemed to be impractical or unrealistic because of the powerful farm lobby and its traditional links, especially with the ruling Liberal Democratic Party (LDP). Despite the introduction of a new electoral system, Japanese domestic politics remain fluid and unstable and, since the LDP does not control the upper house, it has to compromise with the other parties over the much-needed reform of its banking system. A weak banking system in Japan will have an indirect negative impact on the Southeast Asian economies.

Toward a More Balanced Japanese Approach to Southeast Asia?

An impediment in Japan's relations with Southeast Asia is Tokyo's almost exclusively state-centered approach to the region. At present, Japanese local governments have an office with a staff of about 30 people in Singapore to provide training and assistance to Southeast Asian officials. CLAIR (Council of Local Authorities for International Relations) is thus a welcome organization that enhances relations between Japan and the region at the local level.

Even regional and second-tier Japanese newspapers, such as the *Sankei shimbun* and *Hokkaido shimbun,* maintain bureaus in Southeast Asia. Their presence ensures that news about Southeast Asia is not seen only from Tokyo's point of view. The Keidanren and other business groupings in Japan have also been very active, sending delegations to Southeast Asia to study the economic crisis.

However, local governments, regional newspapers, and business groupings are still very much a part of the establishment in Japan. What is really needed is stronger ties between the civil societies of Japan and Southeast Asia. This should include institutionalized exchanges, such as sabbaticals for academics and intellectuals from Japan and countries in the region. At present, most Southeast Asian and Japanese academics and journalists would probably prefer to conduct research in the United States and Europe. Thus, unless there are more intellectual exchanges between Japan and Southeast Asian countries, the latter are likely to remain at the periphery of the United States' intellectual hegemony.

Japanese civil society also has a strong postwar tradition of trade unions, citizen and social movements, and consumer cooperatives. Since ecological issues transcend the traditional boundaries of the nation state, and because Japan experienced severe pollution during its rapid industrialization in the 1950s and 1960s, these groups should be prepared to share their experiences with nascent civil society groups in Southeast Asia. At the state level, Japan and Southeast Asia may forge better ties, but unless and until civil societies in Japan and this region establish links, interaction will remain at the formal state level without substantial grassroots support, and the heart-to-heart relations propounded by the Fukuda Doctrine will remain elusive into the next millennium.

Conclusion

Rather than a peaceful and stable New World Order after the end of the Cold War, the world is still bedeviled by political and economic turbulence from which Southeast Asia has not been spared. The turbulence has provided Japan with opportunities to play a more active role in that region, and Tokyo has indeed achieved some successes in the nontraditional areas of politics and security in the 1990s, although it has yet to play a stronger economic leadership role in the wake of the Asian economic crisis.

That it has been able to play such an active political role in the region is due to the consultative and nonconfrontational approach it has adopted toward Southeast Asian countries. Tokyo's offer of its good offices, ODA, and ideas like the ARF have been acceptable to the region because the measures have coincided with the interests of the ASEAN countries and Cambodia. Even its unprecedented dispatch of troops for peacekeeping operations in Cambodia was tolerated because it took place within the framework of the UN. Moreover, its deployment of military planes to Bangkok and Singapore did not alarm the region because these were perceived to be nonoffensive transport planes meant for humanitarian purposes. The region also accepted Hashimoto's proposals for regular summits between Japan and the ASEAN states, as well as bilateral security talks because such measures can only improve communications between Tokyo and the states in the region. The United States does not oppose Japan's political and security initiatives in Southeast Asia because it perceives such actions as not challenging U.S. core interests.

Such was not the case, however, when Japan attempted to float the idea of an AMF. Strong U.S. opposition forced Japan to drop the idea, and it again fell back in line with Washington when it urged Indonesia to abide by the IMF's prescriptions for market reform. Other than its well-worn instruments of financial and humanitarian assistance to Southeast Asia, Japan has failed to exercise economic leadership in the region, having found it difficult to pull itself out of the recession, let alone function as an economic engine to pull the region out of the doldrums.

A major obstacle to Tokyo's leadership role in the Southeast Asian economies is its lack of political leadership within the country and its stagnant economy. If ODA is slashed because of budgetary constraints, then Japan will have fewer carrots with which to woo Southeast Asian countries. Factionalism, "new" political parties that come and go, a divided Diet and a scandal-ridden bureaucracy are simply not the domestic ingredients that underpin a leadership role in Southeast Asia.

What are the future prospects for Japan's relations with Southeast Asia in the first half of the twenty-first century? Japan is likely to play a more active political role whenever opportunity presents itself. Moreover, Tokyo's burden of history will gradually lighten, since the next generation of Southeast Asians is likely to be less emotional about the Japanese occupation of their homeland, and less suspicious of a higher Japanese profile in their neighborhood. If China emerges as a potential hegemon in the next millennium, some Southeast Asian countries may welcome a Japanese political and, perhaps, even a strategic presence to balance the growing Chinese influence.

The Asian economic crisis will eventually end and Japan will maintain a major economic presence in the region during the post-economic crisis era. Whether Japan is able to forge a genuine friendship with the region in the next century will depend, in part, on its attitude toward Southeast Asia. If Tokyo does not act unilaterally and avoids the arrogance of power, the region is more likely to accept a larger Japanese role.

Notes

1. In August 1967, Indonesia, Malaysia, the Philippines, Singapore, and Thailand became the founding members of ASEAN. Brunei joined in 1984 and Vietnam in 1995.
2. Cambodia became a member of ASEAN only in 1999.
3. Erik Paul writes: "In 1995 Japan was the world's largest investor in Southeast Asia. In ASEAN countries Japan's cumulative direct investments from 1951 to 1993 totaled over US$38 billion.... In 1993, Japan's trade with Southeast Asia represented 14.3 per cent of its total trade. Japan was the most important trading country for ASEAN.... Since the late 1970s, Japan has been Southeast Asia's largest aid donor. ODA's 1990 budget was US$6.9 million, of which more than 65 per cent was allocated for Asia and more than 25 per cent to Southeast Asia." Erik Paul, "Japan in Southeast Asia: A geopolitical perspective," *Journal of the Asia Pacific Economy* 1:3 (1996): 392–94.
4. Bruce Gale, Regional Manager of the Political and Economic Risk Consultancy in Singapore, comments: "From a financial perspective, you've got the Japanese, who have lent billions of dollars to the Indonesians, facing the possibility of having to write off those loans. Now, if they have to do that, that will have serious implications for the stability, in turn, of the Japanese financial system. Many of the Japanese banks will find themselves in a position where they can't meet capital adequacy requirements." East Asia Today, "What are the Repercussions of Indonesia's Economic Turmoil for the Rest of the Region?" BBC London, 0700 hours, 7 May 1998.
5. "In order for Asian countries to get out of economic slump, it is critical that Japan becomes the market to absorb their exports.... But given the stagnated domestic demand, it is clear that they cannot count on Japan for their economic recovery and in that sense Japan is not supporting economic recovery in Asia," says Yamato Shunta, analyst at Daiwa Institute of Research. "Japan still cannot absorb goods from Asia and Asia cannot absorb goods from Japan either," according to Suzuki Taiyo, economist at the Japan Research Institute. *Business Times* (Singapore), 23 February 1999.

6. For a historical account of Japan and Southeast Asia, see Shiraishi Takashi, "Japan and Southeast Asia," in *Network Power: Japan and Asia,* eds. Peter J. Katzenstein and Shiraishi Takashi (Ithaca: Cornell University Press, 1997).
7. Sudo Sueo, *The Fukuda Doctrine and ASEAN: New Dimensions in Japanese Foreign Policy* (Singapore: Institute of Southeast Asian Studies, 1992).
8. Ambassador Akashi Yasushi suggests the term "good offices" rather than "mediation" to describe Japan's attempts to reconcile domestic or regional protagonists. Possibly, the term "good offices" gives the impression of being less pushy and intrusive. Akashi Yasushi, "Regional Security and Preventive Diplomacy," Seminar, Institute of Defence and Strategic Studies, Singapore, 14 August 1998.
9. For more details on the end of the Cold War and permissive conditions for Japan to play a larger political role, see Lam Peng Er, "Japan's Search for a Political Role in Southeast Asia," *Southeast Asian Affairs 1996* (Singapore: Institute of Southeast Asian Studies, 1996).
10. Marvin Ott writes: "UNTAC, a civil and military organization . . . would ultimately comprise over 20,000 personnel and cost close to $3 billion. The creation and deployment of UNTAC was and remains the largest peacekeeping effort ever mounted by the UN." Marvin C. Ott, "Cambodia: Between Hope and Despair," *Current History* (December 1997): 433.
11. For a good Japanese insider interpretation of Cambodia's violent politics, see Imagawa Yukio, "The Recent Situation in East Asia and Cambodia," *Asia Pacific Review* (Spring–Summer) 1998.
12. East Asia Today, "Hun Sen Agrees to Japanese Plan to Enable Prince Ranariddh to Take Part in Elections," BBC, 2300 hours, 17 February 1998.
13. Ott writes: "Nearly two-thirds of Cambodia's annual revenue comes from foreign aid. Japan is the largest single donor, providing US$152 million in grants and technical assistance in 1996. After initially suspending aid in the wake of the coup, Tokyo announced on 26 July that it would reinstate its assistance program." Ott, 1997, p. 436.
14. "Japan trying to mediate a political pact in Myanmar," *Business Times* (Singapore), 27 August 1996.
15. Lam Peng Er, "Japan and the Spratlys Dispute: Aspirations and Limitations," *Asian Survey* 36:10 (October 1996).
16. For details of the Nakayama Initiative, see Kikuchi Tsutomu, *APEC: Ajia Taiheiyo shinjitsujo no mosaku* [Searching for a New Regional Order in the Asia-Pacific Region] (Tokyo: Nihon Kokusai Mondai Kenkyujo, 1995), pp. 264–69.
17. For a critical view of the ARF, see Desmond Ball, "Multilateral Security Co-operation in the Asia-Pacific Region: Prospects and Possibilities," Seminar paper, Institute of Defence and Strategic Studies, Singapore, 31 August 1998.
18. Kondo Shigekatsu, "The ARF and Its Future: A Japanese Perspective," Institute of Defence and Strategic Studies, Conference on the Future of the ARF, 27–28 April 1998, Singapore.
19. For a good analysis on various Japanese views of the ARF, see Tsuyoshi Kawasaki, "Between Realism and Idealism in Japanese Security Policy: The Case of the ASEAN Regional Forum," *Pacific Review* 10:4 (1997).
20. Lam Peng Er, "The Hashimoto Doctrine: New Direction in Japan's Foreign Policy?" Institute of Southeast Asian Studies, "Trends No. 78," *Business Times,* Singapore, 22–23 February 1997.
21. Obuchi Keizo, "Japan and East Asia: Outlook for the New Millennium," Keynote address in Singapore 4 May 1998.
22. The subsequent discussion is from Robert Wade, "Japan, the World Bank, and the Art of Paradigm Maintenance: The East Asian Miracle in Political Perspective," *New Left Review* 217 (May–June 1996).
23. *Asiaweek,* 17 July 1998, p. 38.
24. In the case of Indonesia alone, Japanese banks had an estimated US$23 billion in outstanding loans in 1997. *JEI Report* no. 4B, 30 January 1998, p. 10.
25. *Business Times* (Singapore), 24 September 1998.
26. *Straits Times* (Singapore), 2 October 1998. "Broadly, the scheme entails the Export–Import Bank of Japan guaranteeing loans or paying the interest on loans made to Southeast Asian countries, and purchasing their government bonds to help restore the confidence of investors in those nations."

CHAPTER 15

Japan and South Asia: Between Cooperation and Confrontation

Purnendra Jain

Japan's postwar relations with the nations of South Asia—India, Pakistan, Bangladesh, Sri Lanka, Nepal, Bhutan, and the Maldives—have been amicable. All are in Asia, but with Japan in the northeast and this region in the southwest, they are separated by significant geographic and cultural distances. The distance is magnified by differences in social, political, and economic life. Postwar, the basic tenets that have driven Japan's foreign policy have shaped Japan's bilateral and regional relations here. Thus, with neither strong strategic imperatives nor recognized potential for commercial benefits to feed Japan's industrial development, the region has not aroused Japan's deep engagement.

Official aid has been the dominant feature of relations with Japan as top aid donor to most of these countries. Economic, political, and cultural relations have remained low level, whatever the messages and intentions of high-level political rhetoric. Since the early 1990s, economic reform in South Asia, especially in India, has led to visible growth in bilateral trade with the region and has spawned Japan's rising interest in business opportunities with an increasingly active private sector. By the mid-1990s, shared optimism prevailed. It appeared that Japan and India, the subcontinent's biggest player, were on the verge of stronger, multidimensional relations with the approach of a new millennium.[1]

Yet the prospect of closer, fuller relations took a tremendous blow in May 1998, when India and then Pakistan defied the international antinuclear regime to conduct their nuclear tests. Japan's condemnation was more active than either nation had anticipated. Japan has remained quietly antinuclear in stance since suffering the world's first nuclear bombing on Hiroshima in 1945, but consistent with its low-profile involvement in international politics, Japan has never been egregious in its antinuclear actions. This time, however, the imperatives of domestic and international politics emboldened it to take more strident punitive measures (particularly through international forums) than it had yet taken against offenders of the antinuclear regime. Consequently, Japan's diplomatic

Japan and South Asia: Between Cooperation and Confrontation 267

relations with India and Pakistan reached their postwar nadir in May 1998, with consequences for Japan's relationship with the South Asian region at large.

This chapter takes a broad look at the spectrum of Japan's relationships with South Asia as they shape, and are shaped by, its overall foreign policy. I focus on the nuclear issue and its consequences for diplomatic relations, since this has become crucial to Japan's foreign policy stance toward the region as the new century approaches. Importantly, Japan's response here also gives us insights into significant developments in its foreign policy posturing, as it struggles to define its international position post–Cold War. We see Japan breaking from the past, unhesitantly taking initiatives on an international issue beyond the demands of commercial self-interest. We also observe its uninhibited use of aid as an instrument of punishment and reward. The event also shows more vigorous attempts by Japan to steer international diplomacy through international forums.

In a post–Cold War international environment where new defining structures are yet to be set firmly in place, it is clear that Japan recognizes the need for a new policy stance toward South Asia as an internally divided but internationally important geostrategic region. Japan's foreign policy makers are currently responding as if by trial to this tumult in which the region's two leading players are nuclear-capable and mutually antagonistic neighbors. Their proximity to potential flashpoints in the Middle East raises the stakes for Japan even further. It is eager to send an undiluted message to the North Korean regime about its position on the nuclear issue. And, of course, Japan would like to convince its Asian neighbors, such as South Korea and Southeast Asian nations, that it is active in diplomacy and is working in the interests of maintaining peace in the region. While Japan's position on the issue presents complex diplomatic tensions bilaterally, commercial and other nonaid relations continue little changed from business as usual. When the diplomatic confrontations of May 1998 have eased, Japan's relations with the regions' two key players are likely to broaden. This is particularly true for India, itself a regional power with new wealth, opportunity, and technological strength as well as proven nuclear capability. Elsewhere in the region, aid will dominate Japan's relations and thus continue in its place as a driving force on both bilateral and regional agendas.

Japan's Stance on Nuclear Issues and South Asia

As the only nation to have suffered nuclear bombing, Japan's government and citizens alike have taken a strong antinuclear stance. Japan ratified the Non-Proliferation Treaty (NPT) in 1976 after lengthy debate that particularly concerned the NPT restrictions, which, by discriminating between the nuclear have and have-not nations, could drive nonnuclear nations to produce nuclear weapons secretly.[2] Yet for all its cogitation on the nuclear issue, Japan does not appear to pay such careful attention to understanding the disposition of South Asia's nuclear "offenders."

Japan reacted sharply when India tested its first "peaceful" nuclear device in 1974. In a then-remarkable multipartisan move, the lower house of the Diet passed a unanimous resolution condemning the Indian test,[3] followed by mildly punitive sanctions on specific aid programs.[4] Because of its low-intensity contacts with South Asia, Japan did not make a big issue of nuclear development on the subcontinent until the May 1998 tests, though it persisted with some diplomatic efforts to convince both countries to stop their nuclear programs.[5] In February 1993, Japan sent a delegation led by Donowaki Mitsuru, ambassador for arms control and disarmament, to continue dialogue with these two nations. Yet, it was reported soon after that the Indian government did not see Japan having any useful role in mediations between India and Pakistan, and rejected the notion asserted by Japanese policy makers that South Asia presented a self-contained "security paradigm."[6]

Although Japan maintained a low profile in South Asia and kept its involvement in the region to a minimum under the Cold War situation, it supported the U.S. strategic design to play a key role in the politics of the subcontinent by injecting a massive amount of aid into Pakistan after the Soviet army marched into Afghanistan in the late 1970s. Post–Cold War, Pakistan is no longer a "front-line state," and the United States expressed its umbrage toward Pakistan's nuclear program with suspension of U.S. aid in 1990.[7] Japan has also used its aid punitively against Pakistan's nuclear program, such as when Japan postponed signing a yen-loan agreement during Prime Minister Nawaz Sharif's visit to Tokyo in 1992. At the time, an NBC television interview presented former Prime Minister Benazir Bhutto and others claiming that Islamabad was capable of putting together seven nuclear devices within hours.[8]

Japan's response to Indian and Pakistani 1998 nuclear tests was an immediate freeze on all grant aid and subsequently on new yen loans. Indeed, Japan was one of the first Organization for Economic Cooperation and Development (OECD) nations to impose a range of economic sanctions on both India and Pakistan. It also took on a role as the chief global advocate of "punishing" India for its defiance of the NPT regime, in the United Nations, at the G-8 summit, at the ASEAN Regional Forum (ARF) meeting, and at other international forums held soon after. Japan also took leadership in drafting and proposing a UN resolution that was unanimously adopted by the UN General Assembly on 6 June 1998.

The official explanations offered by Japan for its swift, severe actions included Japan's adherence to its Official Development Assistance (ODA) Charter (to be discussed below), strong antinuclear sentiment in Japan, the government's support for the NPT regime, and Japan's sincere wish to eliminate all kinds of nuclear weapons. India and Pakistan had contravened both the rules and the sentiments of Japan's aid program.[9]

Yet there were some other equally important reasons. At this time, Prime Minister Hashimoto Ryutaro confronted domestic calamities, especially in financial policy and the banking crisis, and was struggling to restore the confidence of both the international market and the domestic electorate just before an Upper House election in July. Hashimoto was also posturing to fulfill his ambition to be recognized as a proactive, internationally respected leader who could

Japan and South Asia: Between Cooperation and Confrontation   269

make swift decisions without waiting for a consensus to emerge within Japanese policy-making circles. This desired image outcome would also boost his party's chances at the July election by signaling his political aptitude. But the imperatives became more than Hashimoto's personal and partisan goals when in the middle of this scenario President Bill Clinton visited China but not Japan. The diplomatic implications of this visit made Japanese policy circles very uneasy about Japan's position in the U.S. diplomatic framework, and made them think that a signal of Japan's international clout was particularly necessary. Yet whatever the mix of motivations for such a severe official backlash, some senior Japanese diplomatic staff saw the move against India as "out of proportion" and "unnecessary."[10]

Indian officials could not agree more. They had expected Japan to impose some kind of economic and/or diplomatic sanctions and that was to be no major problem; nor were Japan's aid incentives to Pakistan not to go nuclear. Yet India was deeply aggrieved by two Japanese proposals in particular. One was Japan's proposition to invite Pakistan to attend as a full forum member to balance the presence of India at the ARF meeting in Manila. The other was the Japanese proposal that the Kashmir issue be canvassed at the level of the UN Security Council (UNSC). For the Indian side, this was outrageous and in complete violation of the spirit of the Simla Agreement requiring that the Kashmir issue be resolved bilaterally. As one Indian diplomat put it, the Indian side could not "stomach" this, from the Indian point of view "an act of unbearable diplomacy that showed how little Japanese policy makers knew about the Kashmir issue."[11]

Japan has regarded tensions between India and Pakistan on the Kashmir issue as one of the major reasons for the nuclear race on the subcontinent. There is a feeling in the Japanese diplomatic circle that resolving the Kashmir issue may bring an end to the nuclear race. Yet as Alagappa argues, "[T]he Indo-Pakistani rivalry framework tells only part of the story. It precludes discussion of the Sino-Indian dimension that largely drives the Indian nuclear program. Understanding the China-India-Pakistan nexus is critical to formulating an effective South Asia policy."[12] China has long been a major security concern for India, and it is public knowledge that China has provided technical and financial assistance to develop Pakistan's nuclear capacity.[13]

Japan, however, claims not to accept India's concern over a potential Chinese threat. In July 1998, Japan's ambassador on disarmament and scientific issues put forward the tendentious view that China does not use its nuclear capacity as a tool in international affairs, making unacceptable the Indian argument that India's nuclear tests were a response to a perceived threat from China.[14] Japan has compelling diplomatic reasons not to raise China's ire, and in this publicly stated rationale has not revealed Japan's own geostrategic imperatives.

Japanese commentators feel that the most important task for Japan in the Kashmir dispute is to help create an international framework to ease tensions between India and Pakistan. This strategy was behind the move by Japan and some other countries like Sweden to submit a draft resolution to the UNSC calling for a stop to the supply of nuclear-related technology to India and Pakistan. But the Security Council was divided—Britain and Russia are diplomatically close to India, and China to Pakistan. Thus Prime Minister Hashimoto lamented to the international media the day after Pakistan's nuclear tests that the situation could have been different if the Kashmir issue had been put on the UNSC agenda straight after India conducted its nuclear tests.[15]

Japan considers itself as facilitator rather than mediator in this dispute. It has offered to provide a venue for mediation on Kashmir but will not offer a solution. As with Japan's other steps into "Kashmir" diplomacy, however, India sees these attempts as counter to the Simla Agreement mentioned earlier.[16]

But Japan is limited in its policy options if it truly seeks to register its aversion to the nuclear stance of the two South Asian offending nations, and in the process win diplomatic renown for itself. If it chooses to adhere rigidly to an antinuclear stance and to its own ODA Charter, Japan has little choice but to continue sanctions on aid to both nations. This move involves inherent costs for Japan's relations with the region. India's economy might be able to withstand sanctions, but in Pakistan the economic situation is already serious and further deterioration is likely to induce political turmoil and renewed tension on the subcontinent. Furthermore, Japanese diplomatic grandstanding may also breed regional resentment against Japan, whose relatively severe punitive actions are seen by India and Pakistan as hypocritical, duplicitous, and self-serving, particularly while Japan shelters diplomatically under the U.S. nuclear umbrella.

Indeed, both India and Pakistan have reasons to see Japan's actions as disingenuous and not at all about what they believe to be the only real solution—elimination of all nuclear weapons. When India proposed total elimination of weapons under a time-frame at talks on the Comprehensive Test-Ban Treaty (CTBT), Japan clearly favored the Western formula that sought to eliminate new entrants to the nuclear arms race, isolating India in the process. In fact, as India's diplomatic doves see it, precisely this defeat for India at Geneva gave ammunition to hawks back home to push for the nuclear test that came in May 1998.[17] Further, Japan has used the discrimination between the nuclear haves and have-nots that is inherent in the CTBT to justify its mild response to China's nuclear tests in 1996. China, Japan claimed, was already a legitimate nuclear power, but Pakistan and India did not have that status when they conducted their nuclear tests.

Sanctions cannot "denuclearize" a nation; India and Pakistan cannot squeeze their nuclear genies back into the bombs from which they were detonated. And whether or not Japan disavows the reasoning provided by its adversaries, to India and Pakistan their proven nuclear capability is both perfectly justifiable and a necessity for their defense toolboxes. As Pakistani Prime Minister Nawaz Sharif stated on Pakistan's 51st independence-day anniversary, "We have that power which only six other countries in the world have.... This strength has given us protection and confidence."[18] For India and Pakistan, however costly, their nuclear capability is a palpable, powerful, welcome reality.

We find, then, that the Indian and Pakistani nuclear tests have exposed important limitations of Japan's post–Cold War foreign policy. Japan's aid diplomacy, its bids to initiate joint action in international forums, and attempts at mediation have been largely ineffectual here. Aid carrots to befriend and aid sanctions to punish have not achieved their intended results—neither on the score of preventing nuclear buildup nor on building Japan's reputation for effective, responsible international policy leadership.

These uses of aid in response to nuclear testing offer important signs of the contemporary direction of Japan's aid diplomacy to South Asia's key players. Yet there is much more than punishment to the story of Japan's aid policy toward the region.

Japan's Aid to the Region

Japan has been a major provider of economic aid to a large number of developing nations in the postwar period, most significantly to its Asian neighbors.[19] In 1997, Japan stood as the world's largest donor of ODA for the seventh straight year. For most of the postwar period, South Asian nations have received large amounts of aid from Japan. Some were the first to receive Japan's yen loans in the late 1950s. South Asia is even now the most economically underdeveloped subregion in Asia, with a number of least developed countries (LDCs) that depend highly on foreign economic aid. Of the ten top recipient nations of Japan's ODA in 1994, 1995, and 1996, four were South Asian nations (India, Pakistan, Bangladesh, and Sri Lanka).[20] Japan has remained the top donor to most South Asian nations and was to all of them between 1993 and 1996. Nevertheless, the level of Japan's ODA to other parts of Asia remains much higher than its ODA to South Asia. Japan's total ODA to South Asia ($8.5 billion) between 1989 and 1995 was about half the value of its aid to ASEAN countries ($16 billion) and about only 10 percent higher than the total aid to China ($7.5 billion).

In light of Japan's low diplomatic priority to South Asia and the ever-greater demands on Japan's ODA funds, officials and politicians in South Asia have been unsure of Japan's aid commitment to the region. The end of the Cold War produced additional recipients eligible for Japanese aid, and Japan claims it is committed to providing aid to some states in Central Asia. South Asian nations feared that Japan might cut back its aid to South Asia. They were relieved to hear from then visiting Prime Minister Kaifu Toshiki in 1990 that South Asia would remain as a priority area for Japan's aid. But with multiple competing demands on Japan's aid supply, there is nevertheless always a sense of trepidation in South Asia about the level of aid to come from Japan.

Like Japan's aid to other parts of the world, aid to South Asian nations is not without problems. With so many variables in an uncertain international environment, and a mix of domestic interests figuring in Japan's aid policy decisions, it is surely difficult to decide what level, and what kind, of aid Japan can most usefully provide to South Asian countries. And as discussed, the stance of India and Pakistan on nuclear programs will also be an important determining factor.

Aid as a Diplomatic Tool

It was with the end of the Cold War and increasing pressure on Japan as a global economic power to accept a greater share of diplomatic responsibilities that Japan's foreign policy makers established the ODA Charter in 1992. The charter stipulates essential considerations for determining the eligibility of recipient nations, including their military expenditures, production of weapons and missiles of mass destruction, and their international trade in arms. The charter aims to use Japan's economic might to wrest a new international political role for Japan. Japan has applied the charter to a number of states including China as mentioned previously. But South Asia may well serve as a test case for Japan's ODA Charter, for while India and Pakistan are not as important as China in Japan's foreign policy framework, both are strategically significant internationally as Asian powers, especially now that they have joined the nuclear club.

Japan has used its aid as a diplomatic tool long before it established its ODA Charter in 1992. Yasutomo's study details many instances where Japan used aid for strategic purposes to support U.S. strategic interests during the Cold War, and the case of Pakistan mentioned earlier is a strong example.[21] By setting out the criteria for assessing the worthiness of a recipient country, Japan's ODA Charter was seen in some South Asian countries as often simply a form of lip service. There was certainly speculation that Japan could use its ODA as a diplomatic lever if India and Pakistan continued their refusals to sign international antinuclear treaties. However, there had never been major diplomatic rows between Japan and South Asian nations over implementation of the ODA Charter until the May–June 1998 nuclear tests.[22]

In August 1998 the Japanese ambassador to India issued a strongly worded statement that while aid was still flowing, if India's indefinite standoff on subscription to the nuclear nonproliferation regime continued for a long time, Japan's soft loans could be reduced and eventually cut totally.[23] The diplomatic consequences of this threat may be weak. Many Indian officials and commentators have in fact almost welcomed the international aid sanctions, arguing that the time has come for India to graduate from aid dependency to stand on its own two feet. Furthermore, Japan is not the only aid donor to the region, and not the only donor nation to place sanctions on its aid to India and Pakistan.

The United States is the most important of these nations and is already considering relaxing its sanctions. On Pakistan, Japan is too. A report suggested that Japanese officials were recommending an easing of sanctions following assurances from the Pakistani foreign minister to his Japanese counterpart that Pakistan will not transfer nuclear material and technology to a third country, and that it will participate in a treaty negotiated at the Conference on Disarmament in Geneva.[24] Pakistan's economy is already paralyzed and will suffer further if Japan continues its present aid sanctions.

Here we see Japan's attempt to couple aid sanctions with treaty noncompliance. We also see Japanese initiatives to render an international antinuclear regime through the vehicle of international forums. These measures using ODA have become increasingly common in Japan's post–Cold War international diplomacy.

In an overall assessment, Japan's aid to South Asia has not lubricated economic opportunities for donor or recipients to the extent that it has in Southeast Asia. Neither has it been a great success in South Asia as a tool for Japan to induce compliance through punishment and reward. Its greatest utility may have been the diplomatic benefits that result from helping to stimulate economic development in some of the world's poorest nations in this region. Given Japan's relatively tough stance on the May 1998 tests, even that is likely to have deteriorated. As one Indian diplomat expressed his disappointment, "It's time that India also forgot all types of economic assistance provided by Japan in the past. We are back to square one."[25]

Commercial Relations

Commercial relations between Japan with South Asia remain weak, despite a very healthy start in the immediate postwar years. This weakness is apparent in both the volume of trade between Japan and South Asia and the amount of direct Japanese investment in South Asia.

Trade

In recent years, both Japan and South Asian nations have seen changes in their international trading profile. For most of the postwar period, until very recently, Japan's international trading profile was dominated by its exports of value-added products and its imports were largely restricted to commodities essential to fueling Japan's industrial powerhouses. Partly through its own efforts and also under external pressures, since the late 1980s Japan's level of imports has increased substantially.

In contrast to the Japanese trading profile, South Asian economies have hitherto been principally inward-looking, with little emphasis on trade promotion and export strategies. They generally exported raw materials and primary products, such as cotton, iron ore, and seafood, and a very low quantity of finished goods. The region's imports consisted chiefly of heavy machinery and engineering equipment that could not be produced at home. Under the Cold War regime, its trading partners in the region were severely limited. Now with moves toward liberal trade regimes in these nations, more imports are allowed, and structures are in place to promote production of value-added exports that can compete successfully in the international marketplace.

These changes in the trading profiles of both Japan (increasing imports) and South Asian nations (emphasizing exports of value-added products) enhance economic complementarity. This might suggest that South Asian countries would export more actively to Japan, yet this has not been the case. Japan's trade with South Asia still largely follows the old pattern—raw material and food exports from South Asia and heavy machinery and chemical industry imports to South Asia.[26] Until 1993, trade between Japan and South Asia showed very little upward movement. Since 1994, however, a slight jump is visible. Most of the increase was recorded in Japan's trade with India, from $3.7 billion in 1990 to about $5.3 billion in 1996. Sri Lanka also recorded a slight upward movement in its trade with Japan. While almost all countries in South Asia maintain trade deficits against Japan, India is the only exception, maintaining a surplus throughout the 1990s.

Although the trend is incipient, a broader range of products and services is forming part of the trade between Japan and India. One particularly significant area is computer software.[27] Of 785 Indian software companies in 1995, 360 focus exclusively on export. The United States has been the major overseas market for Indian software (61 percent in 1993), but the Japanese market, which took only 4 percent of all India's software exports in 1993, has registered some growth in the last two years with potential to grow further. A number of Japanese computer companies, such as Fujitsu, have invested in India's computer software, while some Indian companies have begun to put greater emphasis on developing computer programs specifically designed for Japanese needs. Between 1993 and 1996, more than 100 Japanese software companies visited India to establish business links with Indian software companies. In 1997, Japan's software company Zygox established its office in Bangalore, India's Silicon Valley, expecting to cut its software development costs by 30 percent.[28] Many hurdles, such as the language barrier, remain in the way of rapid expansion of India's software exports to Japan. Although highly optimistic, some Indian estimates suggest that by the end of the decade India will export 30 percent of its software to Japan.[29] Whether or not this level is reached, it is clear that Japan's trade relations with India have moved well beyond primary products and are likely to extend further to the service sector, including banking, telecommunications, insurance, and securities.

Market reform and liberalization measures continue to make business conditions in South Asian economies more attractive to corporate Japan. So there is at least the potential for Japan to further develop its trade relations in the region. Financial crises and economic slowdown in East and Southeast Asia will surely bite into this. South Asia is not a region on which Japan's economy is highly dependent, so does not present a pressing reason for Japan to use bailout measures to underscore the solidity of its own floundering economy.

Investment

Despite Japan's deep economic recession and the financial crisis throughout the 1990s, Japanese companies continue to invest overseas. With the much publicized stories of economic reform in South Asian countries, and the assessment that India alone has a 200 to 300 million middle-class population with huge buying capacity, one could again expect that Japanese companies might seize this opportunity and direct their investment funds accordingly. But Japanese investors remain very cautious. Simply put, the conditions in the region are not what Japanese investors find most attractive.

Comparison of Japan's investment in South Asia with its investment in the "tiger" economies of Asia and China is unrealistic, as the latter have been far more attractive than the former to Japanese investors. In some of these countries, Japan invested in just one week what it invested in one full year in all of South Asia combined. Japan's investment in Vietnam provides a more realistic benchmark for comparison. In recent years, Vietnam has attracted three times more investment from Japan than has India. Japan's combined investment in India, Sri Lanka, Pakistan, and Bangladesh barely exceeded the total Japanese investment in Vietnam in fiscal 1993, 1994, and 1995.[30] Looking at the total of

Japanese foreign investment between 1993 and 1995, Japanese investment in India, Pakistan, and Bangladesh has increased, but in proportion to Japan's investment in other Asian countries, the South Asian share remains minuscule.

India has the most promising results since 1991. On the approval basis of cumulative investment, in 1996 Japan ranked fourth on India's foreign-investment table after the United States, United Kingdom, and Mauritius. Several high-profile Japanese investment missions have visited India, including a group by Keidanren officials and the first visit ever by a Japanese minister for international trade and industry in 1995. Reports provided by these mission leaders on the investment climate in South Asia have been mixed. Only a few of India's industrial sectors, such as automobiles and more recently electronics and telecommunications, have attracted Japanese investors. The entry of Sony into the Indian market in 1995 was seen by many as a major breakthrough and a sign of the confidence of Japanese investors, but it did not induce a major flow-on of Japanese companies even though Matsushita and Toyota have also entered the market.

What inhibits Japanese investors? Clearly, South Asia is not as attractive to Japanese investors as are some East and Southeast Asian markets where commercial and living conditions are both known and generally palatable to Japanese. This is not so for South Asia where corporate Japan sees many problems. Political instability, ethnic and political violence, and inconsistency in economic policy have often been cited as some of the negative factors. Many Japanese corporate leaders still regard South Asia as not simply "distant," but out of Japan's reach and scope—a Western territory.[31] Increasing conflicts of interest between Japanese and Indian joint-venture partners have made Japanese investors even more cautious. The bitter experience of Toshiba Corporation in trying to withdraw from Toshiba Anand Batteries, and the Indian government's reluctance to allow Suzuki to expand and modernize Maruti have blotted the image of India and the region at large as an ideal market to invest.[32]

The Nuclear Factor and Commercial Relations

Various reports confirm the messages heard in this author's interviews in Tokyo. This is that nuclear-inspired tensions will not directly effect commercial ties, though there may be some slowdown largely through reduced commercial opportunities that spin off from aid projects. The Japanese government has not put direct commercial sanctions on India and Pakistan, but it does have the power to exercise caution when it considers proposals by Japanese interests for new investment overseas. Companies can be "advised" to reconsider their application, a euphemism for the Japanese government's message to "hold off" in light of diplomatic tensions. In the event, Japan's willingness to pursue trade and investment opportunities depends more on the commercial environment and domestic political stability of these nations than on the state of official bilateral relations played out at the government level.

As mentioned before, some Japanese officials think that if India and Pakistan do not change their stance on the development of their nuclear capacity, the

Japanese government may impose further sanctions. Although the chances of further sanctions are negligible, if that happens the commercial relationship will suffer dramatically.

Political, Diplomatic, and Strategic Relations

Here too we find consistency with other dimensions of Japan's relationship with the region. Under Cold War conditions, political, diplomatic, and strategic ties between Japan and South Asia remained largely undeveloped. For most of the Cold War period, the subcontinent was a minefield of interstate rivalries, conflict, and even war. Further intraregional divisions came with divisive alignments to the two Cold War titans—the United States and the Soviet Union. Japan preferred to distance itself from this where possible, seeing no immediate political or economic advantage from active engagement. Post–Cold War, both Japan and South Asian nations have tried to broaden and deepen their official engagement, but with little real result.

On the diplomatic front, there is a very limited traffic of diplomats, other government officials, and high-ranking politicians to lubricate relations. A Japanese prime minister has visited the subcontinent just once in the 1990s (Kaifu Toshiki in 1990). The July 1997 visit by a Japanese foreign minister came after a lapse of ten years. The paucity of regional institutional arrangements for regular consultations and exchange of ideas between the two also works against formation of closer ties. The South Asia Association for Regional Cooperation (SAARC) was established in the mid-1980s to promote better relationships between South Asian countries, but it has been ineffective as a regionally unifying institution and its success as a regional voice has been limited, especially if compared with a very active and influential ASEAN. Japan has a close relationship with ASEAN as a regional organization and finds it an effective vehicle for diplomacy to exchange ideas, information, and opinions with member nations. SAARC has not offered Japan a similar platform for engagement.

To promote dialogue and encourage consultations on a regular basis, in 1991 the Japanese government created the South Asian Forum, a think tank of distinguished Japanese interested in South Asian affairs, drawn from academia, business, and the mass media. By the end of 1998, Japan and South Asian countries planned to hold three joint symposiums, the latest in Tokyo in February 1994. These symposiums have provided a valuable venue to bring together South Asian and Japanese government and business leaders who have long sought to promote mutually beneficial relationships but have had no effective platform to voice their views, share ideas and information with counterparts, and thus work cooperatively toward common goals.[33]

The nuclear issue has long been a sore point in Japan's relations with India and Pakistan, though not one that inspired severe tensions. Despite some unresolved issues, until the 1998 nuclear tests Japan's political relationship with South Asian nations was free from animosity. This contrasts with Japan's relations with many East and Southeast Asian nations that remain plagued by what the latter consider Japan's failure to accept responsibility for its wartime actions. Since

Japan and South Asia: Between Cooperation and Confrontation 277

Japan has not come to terms with its own offenses against crucial Asian neighbors, it has felt unable to take a tough stance against other offenders in its neighborhood on issues like nuclear testing, human rights abuses, and militarization, as is clear in Japan's stance on China. Japan is thus in a vulnerable political position when it raises concerns on these issues with its near Asian neighbors, who usually are quick to point the finger at Japan's own past.

No such baggage from the war is carried by South Asian nations toward Japan. On the contrary, most of these nations showed a great deal of sympathy with Japan after its Pacific War defeat. This was symbolized by the dissenting voice of the Indian judge who served on the International Tribunal at the Tokyo War Crimes Trial, and the compassionate statement by the Sri Lankan representative to the San Francisco peace treaty in 1951. Freedom from wartime guilt that Japan feels in its relations with South Asia, but which by its absence restrains Japan in relations with East and Southeast Asia, helps to explain Japan's unselfconscious stridency in condemning India and Pakistan's nuclear forays while responding timidly toward China's nuclear tests. It also may be partly why Japan can use the South Asian nuclear tests as a test case for its own diplomacy—to help determine the limits of its capacity to take initiative and leadership in international forums and with ODA sanctions. Certainly, South Asia's relatively low importance to Japan underscores these actions.

Japan's security treaty with the United States and its close ties with nations aligned to the United States allowed little scope for security and defense talks with South Asia. But even then, South Asia had some strategic importance in the broader context of Japan's "comprehensive security." Japan's dependence upon energy supplies from the Middle East ensures Japan's dependence on security of shipping in the sea-lanes that carry oil out of the Gulf, through the Indian Ocean to Japan, and undoubtedly Japan has a deeply vested interest in keeping this route free of conflict.

There is no systematic security dialogue between Japan and South Asian nations, though recently some informal meetings were held between Indian military officials and officers of the Japanese Self-Defense Forces. Tension over the nuclear testing has already slowed this process.

As earlier addressed, Japan does not accept the Indian and Pakistani nuclear position; as India and Pakistan see it, Japan does not understand. From several personal interviews with high-ranking opinion leaders in India, this author's impression is that most regard Japan's diplomacy as poorly informed on some of the region's internal politics and basically ritualistic—nothing more than a support act for the U.S. stance on this issue. This suggests new diplomatic image problems for Japan in the region, and the likelihood that the image-building motivations behind the Japanese response may have backfired to some extent.

Cultural Influence

Cultural relations have been the weakest link in the web of relationships between Japan and South Asia. There is not a strong cultural or human flow from Japan to the region. The Japan Foundation is the principal government-funded vehicle for officially promoting Japan's culture overseas, but when in June 1996 this author asked the office in New Delhi about Japan's cultural relations with South Asia, the director reported that the Japan Foundation office does not maintain information on this area. Japan's low level of cultural engagement with South Asia reflected in the director's response is manifest when one compares the Japan Foundation's annual expenditures by country and region. South Asia's allocations are again relatively low. In 1996, for example, the Japan Foundation spent only 3.2 percent of its program budget on South Asian nations, as compared to 18 percent in Southeast Asia and 8.7 percent in East Asia (mainly China).[34] Similarly, the Japan Foundation has established three language centers in Southeast Asia (Indonesia, Malaysia, and Thailand), but none in South Asia.

Not only at the national level but also at the local level, cultural ties are extremely weak. Japanese prefectural and other local governments spend millions of dollars on sister relationships with overseas states and local councils, but only a trickle is directed toward this region. As compared to about 340 sister-city relations in East Asia and 35 in Southeast Asia, there are only seven in South Asia, of which three are in Sri Lanka and only one in India (which was established in the mid-1950s).[35] Some local governments in Japan have established relations with local governments in South Asia based on shared interests in specific activities. The Council of Local Authorities for International Relations (CLAIR), a Ministry of Home Affairs agency that facilitates sister relationships and promotes Japanese local governments' interests overseas, has offices in East Asia (Seoul and Beijing) and in Southeast Asia (Singapore), but none in South Asia.

Japanese NGOs work in Nepal, Bhutan, and Bangladesh, but their activities are restricted by budgets and lack of resources. European and North American NGO activities in the region overshadow Japanese NGOs. Yet it could be argued here that some flow of culture is also delivered through Japanese aid programs, particularly those that involve personal contact and training in Japan, such as many of the Japan International Cooperation Agency (JICA) programs that have taken in significant numbers of South Asian trainees over the years.

At the level of popular culture, too, there is little inflow from Japan. Language differences are not the only, nor the principal barrier. The Japan Foundation has sponsored the NHK television dramas "School Gate: Family Dilemma" in Sri Lanka, "Manga Michi" in the Maldives, and "Oshin" in India and Nepal, but the diffusion rate of Japanese popular culture in South Asia is low. By comparison, Japanese dramas in East and Southeast Asian countries are popular to the point where Taipei department stores sell videos on Sunday of Japanese programs aired the previous Friday, already dubbed or with Mandarin subtitles.[36]

It is not just the weakness of Japan's cultural diplomacy in the region. There is work to be done on both sides at government, corporate, and grassroots levels to strengthen cultural ties. The vast majority of South Asians have yet to develop a clear understanding of work ethics and cultures of other Asian societies. Japanese studies even in India—the largest country in the subcontinent—remains very weak, both in quantity and quality.[37] Expansion in scholarship and teaching about Japan, such as the Japan studies institute for New Delhi proposed by the Japan–India Goodwill Association,[38] will give the people of the region a stronger working knowledge of Japan, and help them to understand how they can move most effectively to maximize mutual benefit. South Asian professionals, such as engineers, scientists, and managers who seek to work with Japanese counterparts, lack knowledge of economic, corporate, and cultural life in Japan. At a 1997 symposium in New Delhi, former Finance Minister Manmohan Singh emphasized the need for 10,000 Indians fluent in Japanese. Without concrete steps, particularly by the private sector, which stands to gain from closer commercial ties, neither the goal nor its national benefits can be achieved.

Similarly, Japan's image of South Asia is stereotyped and traditionalist: societies divided by religion and caste, scarred by deep poverty, ethnic violence, and war. The abundant ranks of engineers, scientists, economists, and other professionals who are some of the best in the world in their fields are barely known at the popular level. The migrant workers in Japan through the 1990s, from Bangladesh, Pakistan, and India, who do menial and other "dirty, difficult, and dangerous" jobs, have not helped to correct the image of South Asia among the ordinary people of Japan. A wall of stereotypes thus distorts perspectives on both sides, a distortion that future cultural programs of all kinds can help to address.

Tourism is one means through which greater cultural awareness may be achieved. South Asia has not been a popular overseas destination for Japanese tourists. Limited perception of what the region offers and weakness of tourist infrastructure in South Asian nations present barriers. India is promoting itself as a tourist destination in Japan and experienced a 27 percent jump in 1995 over the previous year to 75,000 tourists from Japan. Air services between India and Japan have become more frequent in recent years. The region has great potential to offer tourists from Japan, but further growth will depend on development of essential infrastructure that is itself dependent on attracting Japanese investment.

The Future Relationship

Actions by South Asian nations after Japan's defeat in the Pacific War revealed the national compassion and forgiveness extended by them to Japan. Japan has reciprocated postwar with its generous aid allocations to the region. Neither are blind to the other benefits that flow back to Japan through this arrangement, and both sides have found it to be mutually agreeable. There have been no compelling reasons for Japan to change its lukewarm stance. Economic, political, and social conditions in the region have continued to work against greater Japanese interest of any kind in the region. Even under Cold War conditions, when Japan's security treaty with the United States drew it into strategic-aid diplomacy toward Pakistan in the early 1980s, Japan averred a high diplomatic profile in the region.

This situation appeared to be on the brink of change following economic liberalization in the region (particularly in India) and the breakdown of the old Cold War strategic alliances. The stage was set in some parts of the subcontinent for closer economic and diplomatic ties. These prospects suffered a serious setback as a result of the nuclear tests by India and Pakistan in May 1998. Japan's prompt and strong reaction to these tests was to "punish" India and Pakistan for their defiance of the nuclear nonproliferation regime of which Japan is a strong proponent. But for Japan this was not simply a matter of punishment; it was also an opportunity to take diplomatic initiative, to build a stronger international profile, especially in an area of diplomacy where Japan feels special expertise through firsthand experience of nuclear bombing.

Japan's sanctions and its international campaign to "punish" India have produced unprecedented ill feeling within the Indian diplomatic circle. Pakistan is also aggrieved diplomatically. Japan has used its ODA as a lever to indicate that improvements at the diplomatic level are unlikely until these nations respond in a manner that is closer to Japan's position on the two major international antinuclear treaties.

While diplomatic relations have been bruised, and Japan's sanctions will inflict a significant drop in aid to South Asia, it is not clear how seriously the sanctions and the diplomatic posturing will damage commercial and other ties. Things are close to, but not entirely, business as usual. Smaller nations in South Asia will continue to receive Japan's ODA as before. Strengthening of commercial ties will depend upon the business environment in South Asian countries and Japan's own financial status that in 1998 is less solid than in earlier times. Japan's economic recession and prudential bailing out of Southeast Asian commercial partners that help sustain its own economic strength mean that it is unlikely there will be significant increase in joint ventures and other types of Japanese investment in South Asia.

Japan's policy makers now need to come to terms with the reality that India and Pakistan are nuclear states. Until this calamity, Japan has put India and Pakistan on the periphery of its foreign policy framework. But these nations are now nuclear powers with the strategic clout and confidence that this brings. Japan will need to bring this into its diplomatic calculations. Hashimoto's diplomacy attempting to isolate these nations does not appear to have yielded the intended results—for the region's welfare or for Japan's foreign policy. What is needed in the future is engagement at bilateral and multilateral levels, not isolation and the resentment that it can breed.

Notes

1. See, for example, Purnendra Jain and Maureen Todhunter, "India and Japan: Newly Tempering Relations," in *Distant Asian Neighbours: Japan and South Asia,* ed. Purnendra C. Jain (New Delhi: Sterling Publishers, 1996), pp. 85–107; Purnendra Jain, "Will the Sun Ever Shine in South Asia?" in *Japanese Influences and Presences in Asia,* eds. Marie Soderberg and Ian Reader (Richmond: Curzon Press, 2000), pp. 187–212; also, see "Minami Ajia shinjidai e no yokan" [Anticipation of a New Era in South Asia], *Gaiko forum* 5 (May 1997): 19–74 and various essays in "Wooing Japan: A Symposium on Developing a Fruitful Relationship," *Seminar* (New Delhi) 397 (September 1992).
2. Reinhard Drifte, *Japan's Rise to International Responsibilities* (London: Athlone Press, 1990), p. 31. Also see *Mainichi Daily News,* 11 April 1993.
3. For details, see Frank Langdon, "Japanese Reactions to India's Nuclear Explosion," *Pacific Affairs* 48:2 (Summer 1975): 173–80.
4. See John D. Endicott, *Japan's Nuclear Option* (NY: Praeger Publishers, 1975), p. 75.
5. For example, see the text of the policy speech by Foreign Minister Ikeda Yukihiko delivered at the FICCI Auditorium, New Delhi, 25 July 1997, "21-seiki no Nihon to Minami Ajia no aratana

kankei o motomete" [In Search of a New Relationship between Japan and South Asia in the Twenty-first century] (Tokyo: Ministry of Foreign Affairs, mimeographed), p. 6.
6. *Far Eastern Economic Review,* 15 April 1993.
7. *Asian Security 1992–93* (London: Brasley, 1993), p. 197.
8. *Dawn,* 23 December 1992.
9. Personal interviews in relevant divisions of the Japanese Ministry of Foreign Affairs, 26 August and 2 September 1998.
10. Personal interview, 26 August 1998.
11. Interview with a senior diplomat in Tokyo, 19 August 1998.
12. Muthiah Alagappa, "International Response to Nuclear Tests in South Asia: The Need for a New Policy Framework," *Asia Pacific Issues: Analysis from the East–West Center* 38 (Honolulu: East-West Center, 15 June 1998), p. 2.
13. "A Friend Indeed: China Made Pakistan's Nuclear Tests Possible," *Far Eastern Economic Review,* 11 June 1998, p. 22.
14. *Gaiko forum* (July 1998), pp. 12–13.
15. Masayuki Iida, "Peace Diplomacy Put to the Nuclear Test," *Daily Yomiuri,* 3 June 1998.
16. *The Hindu,* 18 August 1998.
17. Jagmohan, "Need for Reorienting Indian Foreign Policy," *Hindustan Times,* 20 August 1998.
18. *Daily Yomiuri,* 15 August 1998.
19. For detailed discussion on this issue, see Fukushima Akiko's chapter on Japan's ODA in this volume.
20. See Ministry of Foreign Affairs, *ODA Annual Report 1997,* (Tokyo, 1998) p. 136.
21. Dennis Yasutomo, *The Manner of Giving: Strategic Aid and Japanese Foreign Policy* (Lexington, MA: Lexington Books, 1986).
22. The ODA annual report published by the Foreign Ministry in September 1998 outlines how the charter was applied to 21 nations including India, Pakistan, and China, see Ministry of Foreign Affairs, *Japan's ODA Annual Report 1997* (Tokyo, 1998), pp. 64–72; *Asahi Evening News,* 8 September 1998.
23. *The Hindu,* 18 August 1998.
24. *Japan Times,* 8 August 1998.
25. Personal interview in Tokyo, 19 August 1998.
26. In recent years India and Pakistan in particular have begun to export a range of manufactured goods to Japan. The volume of export from India to Japan has gone up because of its exports of finished products to Japan. See JETRO, *White Paper on International Trade Japan 1996* (Tokyo, 1997), pp. 213–24.
27. Unless otherwise mentioned, information on this section is derived from Helena Fransen, "Japanese-Indian Interaction Within the Software Field," (Stockholm School of Economics, 1997, mimeographed), and Suzuki Kenji, "Sofutoweya sangyo ko fuka kachika e no senryaku" [Strategies for Value-added Production in the Software Industry], *Shukan Toyo Keizai* 29:1 (1997): 61–66.
28. *Nikkei Weekly,* 12 May 1997.
29. See Masato Ishizawa, "India's Software Touch, Prices Entice Japan's Cost-conscious Hardware Markets," *Nikkei Weekly,* 18 September 1995. In 1997, a joint venture, JASDIC Park Co., between three Indian companies (Infosys, Satyam, and DCM) and three Japanese companies (NTT Leasing, Duskin, and Fukuoka Clinical Pharmacy) was established with its headquarters in Tokyo. *The Hindu,* 10 February 1999.
30. Information on Japanese foreign direct investment is derived from Australia-Japan Economic Institute, *Economic Bulletin* (Sydney) (June 1996), pp. 7–13.
31. Interview with a senior Mitsui official in Tokyo, 7 September 1998.
32. A similar imbroglio arose with another of Suzuki's Indian partners, TVS, the Madras-based two-wheeler manufacturer. Not only has Suzuki sought to increase its equity in the company from 26 percent, it also wishes to play a key management role as it does with Maruti. *Business India,* 6–19 November 1995.
33. Symposiums and forums to discuss bilateral, regional, and global issues have also been organized by Japanese and Indian research institutes and centers. The Japan Institute of International Affairs, the Indian Institute of Defence Studies and Analysis, and the Indian Council of International Economic Relations Centre have organized such symposiums in 1996 and 1997.

34. *The Japan Foundation, Overview of Programs 1997 Annual Report 1996* (Tokyo: The Japan Foundation, 1998), p. 155.
35. See Council of Local Authorities for International Relations, *1998 Japanese Local Government International Affiliation Directory* (Tokyo, 1998).
36. Steve McClure, "Tuning into Asia: Japanese TV Finds a Wider Audience," *Japan Scope* (Spring 1995), p. 37.
37. For details on numbers of scholars and their specialization, see *Japanese Studies in South and Southeast Asia* (Tokyo: The Japan Foundation, 1997).
38. In 1996 the Japan–India Goodwill Association (JIGA) disclosed plans to establish a Japan studies institute in New Delhi, funded by JIGA's Japanese members from small- and medium-scale industries, to commemorate India's fiftieth independence anniversary. *The Hindu,* 16 April 1997.

CHAPTER 16

Japan and Australia

Rikki Kersten

On the surface, Japan's relationship with Australia is one of the more benign, untroubled bilateral relationships in Japan's foreign policy orbit. Indeed, it could even be portrayed as a relationship that illustrates the triumph of economic complementarity over political distress. Despite the trauma of World War II—when Japan attacked Australia and visited great cruelty on Australians in POW camps across Southeast Asia—it is images of koala bear diplomacy, honeymoon tourism, and regional partnership that are associated with this bilateral relationship in the postwar era.

Trade is the great success story of the Japan-Australia connection, representing, at one stage, one of the seven largest flows of bilateral trade in the world. Consequently, much of the analysis of the relationship dwells on economics as the defining element, offering a quantitative measure rather than a qualitative perspective of the underpinning dynamics. However, both nations have exhibited disquiet over allowing the health of the relationship to be defined exclusively according to the bottom line, and have put considerable effort into broadening and deepening bilateral ties to include sociocultural, political, and defense issues. It is only when we venture into the social, political, and historical realms that a more complex picture emerges, and we begin to realize that the development of this powerful trading relationship occurred despite significant obstacles, such as a weighty historical baggage of prejudice and misguided political judgment, and a volatile global political economy.

To understand the situation, we must first identify the obstacles in their historical context. How Australia moved from being a peripheral entity and then an enemy to a core trading partner and, in the 1990s, a regional ally in diplomacy and defense is a tale that needs explaining. This is especially so when we recognize that in Japan's view, it was a target of Australian prejudice from the time of Australia's federation in 1901 until the 1970s. Legislation was even passed at one point to keep Japanese immigrants out of Australia. Meanwhile, from Australia's perspective, Japan was at the center of perceived global threats from the mid-nineteenth century until well after 1945. By the 1990s, however, Australia had come to perceive a role for itself as an "honest broker" for Japan in the Asian region and in multilateral forums such as the United Nations.

Thus, although the rhetoric accompanying the postwar trading relationship is one of "partnership," "complementarity," and "mutual dependence," there is obvious discord between the rhetoric and perception that betrays a persistent underlying insecurity on both sides, concurrent with this robust economic relationship. In this chapter, I suggest that the Japan-Australia relationship became robust precisely because these insecurities were acknowledged and addressed by the governments and peoples of both countries. Primary examples of this are the two principal instruments affirming the relationship: the 1957 Agreement on Commerce and the 1976 Treaty of Friendship and Cooperation.

The interplay between perception and future promise is the intriguing story behind Japan's bilateral relationship with Australia. The economic complementarity underpinning the Japan-Australia relationship is undeniable. What we need to understand is not so much the composition of this complementarity as what has enabled it to develop, be sustained, and adjust to changing circumstances and periodic uncertainty. Above all, we need to comprehend how a positive bilateral relationship could develop even though both nations had, over time, developed quite negative images of each other and, to an extent, continue to misunderstand each other's actions and motives. The Multifunction Polis plan for Australian-Japanese collaboration to build a technopolis in the state of South Australia (to be discussed further below) is one area of recent bilateralism that suffered this fate.

Japan's preoccupation with Australian racism is a recurring theme in the relationship. There is clear evidence that racist attitudes informed Australian policies and diplomacy toward Japan, particularly in the pre–World War II era. Since 1945, some commentators have described the controversies in the 1980s—over levels of Japanese foreign investment in Australia, and popular reactions to the ambitious Multifunction Polis project—as outbursts of racist feeling in Australia toward Japan.[1] Disentangling the separate threads of cultural difference, national interest, and racist feeling is essential to a full appreciation of the enduring strengths of this relationship. It also helps identify the existing threats, their historical foundations, and the reasons that they continue to affect the relationship.

In diplomacy, there has been a marked shift from mediated bilateralism to a concerted effort to enhance the credence of the rhetoric of partnership. In the 1990s, the future of the relationship was placed very firmly in a multilateral setting. The fine-tuning of bilateralism, in the context of developing regionalism, is the new face of the Japan-Australia relationship. It is important to gauge whether Japan and Australia share similar expectations of this new maturing relationship, or whether a mismatch of ideals might hamper the fulfillment of expectations on both sides.

The relationship is perhaps best depicted as a mutual recognition that future promise will triumph over mutual misunderstanding. But better management of ties between the two countries in the future depends on first understanding the patterns of the past and, possibly, breaking the mold. There is little doubt that success will be judged according to how well the bilateral axis performs within the multilateral setting of the Asia-Pacific region and the degree of confidence building that can be incorporated into fledgling defense cooperation.

Pre–World War II Historical Background

In recounting the history of Japan's engagement with Australia, we see from the very first official Japanese reports on the subject that Japan was quick to appreciate the potential for trade. Henry Frei writes that records of official Japanese interest in Australia date from the 1850s, when intellectual, teacher, and samurai Yoshida Shoin noted that "it would be most profitable for Japan to colonize Australia."[2] Educator Fukuzawa Yukichi included Australia in his best-selling 1869 work *Sekai kunizukushi*. The 1879 World Expo in Sydney attracted Japanese participation. The Japanese foreign ministry dispatched an official to survey Australia in the early 1890s, and by 1897 Japan had established a consulate in Sydney.[3] The pioneering trading firm, Kanematsu, commenced operations in Australia in 1890. Most historians agree, however, that despite Yoshida's ominous words, Australia was but a peripheral interest for a Japan, that was poised to become a colonial power in Asia by the turn of the century.

Here we encounter the first of several pendulum dynamics that permeate the history of Japan-Australia relations. As outlined above, Japan perceived Australia as a peripheral entity until the 1940s and, arguably, even through to the end of the Allied occupation of Japan in 1952. Yet for Australia, Japan was at the very center of perceptions of a hostile world from the early twentieth century until the 1950s. Australia was quite mistaken about its place in Japan's worldview before the outbreak of war in 1941. However, as some astute commentators have noted, the presence of Japan was instrumental in helping the young nation of Australia define its own separate national interest.[4] Tension between notions of the center and the periphery would thereafter surface periodically in the bilateral relationship, often having an intangible, illogical influence on the foreign policy management of both nations.

A second dynamic that appears early in the relationship is that of mediated bilateralism. One reason that Japan considered Australia a peripheral entity prior to 1952 is that it regarded Australia a mere subset of the larger entity of the British Commonwealth. Australia did nothing to dissuade observers of this impression. Its loyalty to the mother country was constantly on show, as it supported Britain in its foreign conflicts and made trading arrangements that advantaged Britain over other countries. Australia showed a marked reluctance to leave the orbit of the Commonwealth not only before the 1940s, but even after signing the peace treaty with Japan in 1951. This was despite the development of a very profitable trade with Japan from the 1930s (albeit in a limited number of primary products), and the demonstrable divergence of national interests between Australia and Britain during World War II.

If Australia stood out in Japan's view at this time, it was as a recalcitrant member of what was otherwise shaping up to be quite a nice alliance. The Anglo-Japanese Treaty of Commerce and Navigation of 1894 (renewed in 1911) paved the way for the 1902 Anglo-Japanese Alliance; thereafter, Japan was a (nonbelligerent) member of the victorious alliance against Germany. Technically, Japan and Australia were allies during World War I, though apart from some escorting of ships, this meant little in terms of joint activity. To the increasing annoyance of Japan, Australia refused to sign on to the terms of trade agreements with Britain,[5] and maintained its discriminatory trade practices. Japan subsequently made several concerted attempts to conclude a Treaty of Friendship and Navigation with Australia, notably in 1911, 1919, and 1926, but it would be another 50 years before Japan achieved the status it first sought in 1911.

Japan's advance to the ranks of global imperial nations was crucial in making it the focal point of fear in Australia from the late 1800s. It is important to remember that for Australia, the Japanese threat shifted from one that was derived from racial prejudices to one shaped by the concerns of power politics. Australia's infamous Immigration Restriction Act of 1902, which politicians admitted was aimed at immigration from Japan, declared the intention of the newly federated nation that it would remain essentially "white." Combined with Australia's reluctance to enter into fairer terms of trade, this convinced Japan that Australian policy, including foreign policy, was essentially racist in its orientation. This impression was confirmed by the vehemence of Australian Prime Minister William Hughes in opposing the racial equality clause put forward by Japan at the Versailles peace conference in 1919.

As Japan won wars against China in 1895 and Russia in 1905, then occupied Germany's Pacific colonies in 1914, Australia began to fear Tokyo's designs on its own territory. Intelligence chief E. L. Piesse did recognize, as late as 1926, that Australia remained essentially peripheral to Japan, and he was so disturbed by the Australian statements at Versailles that he declared "I withdraw all my optimism about our future relations with Japan."[6] By 1926, Piesse wrote that while "the habit became fixed of regarding Japan as our future enemy" after the Russo-Japanese War, this was a result of rumor and a degree of paranoia, rather than a considered policy judgment.[7]

Despite a thriving trade in wheat and wool, and a balance of trade in Australia's favor, in 1936 Australia imposed on Japanese imports a tariff from which bilateral trade did not recover until the mid-1950s. By 1937, Australia was seriously affected by Japan's trade diversion policy, and recorded its first trade deficit with Japan.[8] The belated imposition by Australia of an embargo on iron ore exports to Japan in 1939 contributed marginally to the sense of encirclement that caused Japan to slide into war throughout the Asia-Pacific region.

The failure to discriminate between issues involving race and national feelings of insecurity comprises a third dynamic in bilateral relations between Japan and Australia. From the early days of the relationship, Japan was disposed to regard trade and diplomatic difficulties with Australia as a result of racial bias against its people. Australia was certainly not alone in discouraging Japanese immigration, and Japan was by no means fixed on Australia as the only country with which it had problems of this kind.[9] For its part, Australia resisted improved trade and diplomatic engagement with Japan prior to World War II, initially to discourage Japanese immigration, but increasingly because it continued to assume that Japanese ambitions extended to its own territories.

Japan's attacks on Australia in World War II, and Japanese treatment of Australian POWs during the war merely aggravated entangled suspicions of race and envy in the minds of many Australians. The story of Japan-Australia relations in the post–World War II era is truly astonishing given this inauspicious start, but the issues of race and fears for national security would, nonetheless, cast a long shadow over the future relationship.

Post–World War II Transition

Despite the trauma inflicted on relations by the war, essentially there was continuity in the pattern of the bilateral relationship after 1945. However, during the decades of the Cold War era until 1989, these patterns took on different forms. In place of the center and the periphery, there emerged new concerns about balance and imbalance in the bilateral relationship. Part of that concern involved evaluating the relative degrees of dependence of each country on the other, particularly in economic terms. And although the relationship remained in a sense a mediated one, this time the emphasis was on security rather than diplomacy, and the intermediary was the United States instead of Britain. The vexing concerns of race and national insecurity were mitigated during this period, with Australia focusing more on the consequences of cultural, rather than racial, differences. A genuine step forward in the relationship did not come until the late 1950s, and a qualitative change was not evident until the mid-1970s, when latent insecurities were squarely addressed in the lead-up to signing of the two core documents that formally underpin the relationship.

Australia did not loom large in the imagination of the shattered denizens of postwar Japan, although Australians did serve in prominent positions, including that of president of the Tokyo War Crimes tribunal (Justice William Webb), Commonwealth representative on the Allied Council (William MacMahon Ball), and head of the British Commonwealth Occupation Force in Japan (Lieutenant-General J. H. Northcott). Not surprisingly, Australia was again considered as just one part of the Commonwealth. The only respect in which Australia did stand out was in the vehemence of its punitive attitude toward Japan. Australia raised its voice in warning and foreboding throughout the Allied Occupation of Japan (1945–52), resisting attempts by the United States to rehabilitate the Japanese economy, and protesting the decision to omit Emperor Hirohito from indictment as a war criminal. Until the advent of the Liberal-Country Party government in Australia in 1949, on the eve of the Korean War, "no country was as rigid as Australia in its efforts to ensure that Japan should never again have the capacity to commit another act of aggression."[10]

Although Australia was largely marginalized in the U.S.-dominated Occupation policy-making process, it implemented its own harsh regime for Japan. By the time Australia reestablished trade with Japan in 1948, it had a triple tariff regime in place that put Japan at the greatest disadvantage. Australia was quick to protest Japanese whaling expeditions that had been sanctioned by the United States, believing that "the presence of Japanese in Australian or Antarctic waters constitutes a threat to the security and welfare of Australia,"[11] and likewise protested Japanese pearling expeditions near Australia. Most analysts agree that it was only the emergence of a bigger threat in the form of communism that persuaded Australia to fall into line and assist the economic rehabilitation of postwar Japan. This, plus the guarantee of U.S. protection from a resurgent Japan in the form of the 1952 ANZUS treaty between Australia, New Zealand, and the United States, led Australia to join the signatories of the lenient peace treaty with Japan that finally ended the Occupation in 1952.

Japan's ultimate foreign policy priorities in the 1950s were to regain full sovereignty and full acceptance back into the global trading regime. Australia's obvious reluctance to wholeheartedly support Japan in this quest again cast it into the role of marginal irritant. A sensational trading relationship was just around the corner, but first the basic insecurities of both countries had to be addressed. Japan was confronted by a nation that would only consider a bilateral relationship mediated by the military protection of the United States. A relationship so obviously based on distrust disturbed Japanese foreign policy administrators, but Japan's more pressing need for economic recovery forced it to be pragmatic.

The 6 July 1957 Agreement on Commerce between Japan and Australia defied considerable bureaucratic and political ambivalence in Australia, and partially appeased Japanese aims of rehabilitation.[12] The Australian prime minister only took the decision to respond to Japan's calls for fairer trade with "reluctance" in 1954;[13] even so, interdepartmental foot-dragging put off the negotiation of a commercial agreement for two more years. Bilateral trade had recovered its prewar level by 1956, but even though Japan had acceded to the General Agreement on Tariffs and Trade in 1955, Australia continued to give Commonwealth imports preferential treatment. The 1957 agreement finally gave Japan most-favored-nation treatment for its imports and eased import licensing, but Australia still contrived to favor the Commonwealth in trade. Only when the protocol of amendment to the agreement was signed in 1963, was Japan recognized "as a full trading partner under the GATT."[14]

The trade boom between these two unlikely partners took off in spectacular fashion in the 1960s, as Australian raw materials fed Japan's rapid industrial growth. As the Myer Committee pointed out in 1978 in a comprehensive assessment of the Australia-Japan relationship, this trade was more than just a relationship between buyer and supplier; through feeding Japan's industrial growth, Australia's prosperity was likewise assured. In other words, this trade was not just complementary, but led to a structural enmeshment that tied the prosperity of each nation to that of the other.[15]

In the 1956–57 period, Japan was consuming 14 percent of Australian exports; by 1975–76, this had risen to 33 percent.[16] In the mid-1970s, the main composition of this export trade to Japan comprised foodstuffs (21.5 percent), iron ore (24.1 percent), and coal (22 percent).[17] Japan's exports to Australia, on the other hand, represented mainly transformed manufactures and automobiles.[18] It is easy to appreciate why this trading relationship was described as "complementary" and "inter-dependent."

It is at this stage that we see the reemergence of the familiar center-periphery paradigm in a new form. Perversely, the very success of the trading relationship between Japan and Australia prompted new concerns about the degree to which each nation was dependent on the other. This, in turn, encouraged officials in both countries to try to shore up the relationship by broadening it beyond the realm of trade. The fundamental, qualitative change in the relationship that was realized with the conclusion of the 1976 Treaty of Friendship and Cooperation was the eventual outcome of this process.

Both Japan and Australia were driven by a resurgence of insecurity to push toward this treaty. Although the 1960s were a raging success in terms of bilateral trade, the oil shocks in the 1970s changed the power relations between Australia and Japan. After 1973, Australia found it held the upper hand as a resources supplier, while Japan felt itself to be at the mercy of "resource nationalism."[19] As it had done in the 1930s, Japan responded by adopting a policy of trade diversification. Toward the late 1970s, Japan embarked on a comprehensive restructuring of its economy; as manufacturing started to move offshore, the hollowing out of Japan's economy began. It was then Australia's turn to feel vulnerable, as the old patterns of supply and demand were no longer assured. Senior commentators, perceiving the relationship to be under threat, began putting forward new formulas to cushion the reality of increasing imbalance in trade, describing the Japan-Australia relationship as one based on "qualitative dependence" in place of "quantitative dependence."[20]

It was in this environment of uncertainty and mutual reappraisal that the door was finally opened for Japan and Australia to move the relationship forward. In Australia, several other factors played a vital part in forcing officialdom out of ambivalence. Foremost among them was the advent of a Labour Party government in 1972 under the leadership of the reformist Prime Minister Gough Whitlam. Whitlam's vision for Japan not only addressed the insecurities on both sides, but recognized that its own bureaucracy was partly responsible for holding back the relationship. The Labour government reassessed how Australia managed its bilateral relationship with Japan, and articulated new versions of the old paradigms that had locked the relationship into tired, predictable patterns.

The Labour government succeeded in making the leap of imagination required to break through the tangle of mutually reinforcing insecurities that had settled into the bedrock of the Japan-Australia relationship. These insecurities were first acknowledged, then articulated, and reconceptualized. Concerns over being at the center or the periphery were reconceived as a need to broaden the relationship; the issue of Australian distrust of Japan was squarely acknowledged and dispensed with; and the problem of racism was likewise positively reformulated as a program of cultural education and exchange.

The Whitlam administration began by addressing the bogey of war. Whitlam stated, "I believe Japan is determined . . . to be the first great industrial power to break the nexus between economic strength and military strength . . . ,"[21] confirming Australia's acknowledgment of Japan's "new course" as a pacifist, economic power. In 1973, the Whitlam government removed the last vestiges of the White Australia policy. On 1 November 1974, Whitlam signed a cultural agreement with Prime Minister Tanaka Kakuei, and laid the groundwork for the establishment, in 1976, of the Australia-Japan Foundation, which had a mandate to promote knowledge of Australia in Japan. This exemplified the new tone in Australian thinking concerning Japan in the 1970s, where prejudice was replaced by a desire to transcend cultural differences. As Sir John Crawford and Dr. Okita Saburo remarked in 1976, "Japan and Australia share none of the cultural, political or sentimental links that once supported the trading relationship between Australia and the United Kingdom."[22] This concern with broadening and deepening the relationship was taken up by two other assessments of the Japan-Australia relationship in the 1970s,[23] revealing a new focus on the human dimension as a way of bolstering the economic relationship.

The 1976 Basic Treaty of Friendship and Cooperation between Australia and Japan reflected these new attitudes, and also identified future directions for the relationship. The document was designed to acknowledge and appease insecurities on both sides. The text of the treaty is replete with references to diversification of the relationship, with the objective "to extend and strengthen relations between the Contracting Parties, in particular by promoting understanding between the two countries and their peoples . . ." (Article I). A second notable feature of the treaty is that it places the bilateral relationship in a regional context, stating that it is "not only [for] their own mutual benefit but also their common interest in the prosperity and welfare of other countries, including those in the Asia and Pacific region . . ." (Preamble), thus anticipating the regional activism by Australia and Japan through APEC in the 1990s.

A third significant reference in the treaty is the one that is most frequently cited as the backbone of the document. Article V responds to the uncertainties created by the oil shocks in the 1970s by clearly designating the role of Australia and Japan as that of "a stable and reliable supplier" and a "market" for Australian exports (elaborated in Article VI as mineral and energy resources), respectively. In Article IX, the thorny matter of discrimination is referred to in the context of "business and professional activities," where guarantees are given to provide "fair and equitable treatment" to each other's nationals.

In several respects, this treaty is an accounting of the misunderstandings of the past, and is a document that retained its relevance through to the end of the century. It was ironic that after his catalytic contribution to the shift in the official Japan-Australia relationship, Whitlam did not get to sign the treaty document. But by 1975, when the Whitlam government was dismissed, the new clarity of vision toward Japan had become supra-partisan. There was a new foundation on which to deal with the evolving challenges of the relationship, and to reconceptualize the interdependent economic fortunes of Australia and Japan.

By the 1980s, the composition of bilateral trade had begun to diversify beyond the core areas of iron ore and coal.[24] New resources such as brown coal liquefaction technology were explored on a bilateral basis, and there commenced what was to become a thriving trade in LNG from rich Australian deposits in the Northwest Shelf. But what warmed the hearts of Australian officials was evidence of diversification into nonprimary resource exports and services, particularly tourism and investment. Some sections of the Australian public, however, reacted badly to the more visible evidence of Japan's enhanced economic presence, namely investment in real estate, and vertical investment in sectors such as the beef industry and tourism. This touched the nerves of observers in Japan alert to Australian revivals of anti-Japanese feeling.[25]

For its part, Japan balked at Australian restrictions on investment in the mining industry (this had been a greater problem in the 1970s), and tariffs on automobiles. But in a decade of fluctuating fortunes, Japan and Australia more or less stayed on the new positive bilateral track laid down by the treaty in the mid-1970s. They decided to embark jointly on an adventure involving the creation of a high-technology city in Australia and, surrounded by burgeoning regional economic growth, it seemed, as the 1990s approached, that prosperity would continue to underpin this maturing, bilateral relationship.

Post–Cold War Partnership

The year 1989 marks the end of the Cold War in Europe, and the start of an era of global uncertainty. For the Japan-Australia connection, some radically different directions were taken in the areas of defense and diplomacy in the 1990s, plus a bureaucratic initiative that by the mid-1990s had faltered badly. At the time of this writing, the Japan-Australia relationship of the 1990s exhibited familiar stresses as the two countries explored the potential of a greatly expanded relationship.

The security arrangements of both Japan and Australia had been premised on a Cold War alliance with the United States; in the case of Australia, this alliance also preserved the threat perceptions of World War II. For the Japan-Australia relationship, the shift in the global strategic environment would mark the advent of their first nonmediated defense relationship. Historically, the prospects for defense becoming another pillar of the Japan-Australia relationship would have seemed unlikely.[26] This is underscored by the mutual misperception concerning both nations' militaristic inclinations. At the fiftieth anniversary, in 1995, of the end of World War II, it was clear that Australia was very far from forgetting experiences at the hands of Japan. But in Japan, respected analysts of foreign relations have pointed out that, in the postwar era, it is Australia that has repeatedly exhibited belligerent tendencies, by participating in several postwar conflicts alongside the United States.[27]

In the early 1990s, both nations found that changed global and regional circumstances warranted a modest boost in this dimension of the relationship. The first political-military and military-military talks between Japan and Australia were held in February 1996, though ministerial-level visits had taken place since 1990. To date, there have been high-level bilateral consultations between political and military officials, plus an increase in goodwill visits and exchange of military personnel. These modest developments belie the significance of the enterprise, namely, that defense has been identified as an area in which the bilateral relationship can grow. Not only does this promise to directly challenge that element of distrust that has lingered in the substratum of the relationship; it also provides an alternative strand upon which to build the relationship in the future. It both bolsters and counterbalances the regional economic exercise of the Asia-Pacific Economic Cooperation (APEC) forum, in that it uses a bilateral axis to address and activate the regional institutional environment. In this sense, it is very much a creature of the post–Cold War world, and promises to help integrate both nations into the Asia-Pacific region. Reinforcing this structure of bilaterally based regionalism is Japan and Australia's membership of the regional security body, the ASEAN Regional Forum (ARF).

The concurrent development of the bilateral relationship alongside new regional multilateralism was also a feature of the diplomatic dimension of the Japan-Australia relationship in the 1990s. Japan played a key role in the APEC forum, articulated by Australian Prime Minister Bob Hawke in 1989. With the appearance of rival subregional forums such as Malaysia's East Asia Economic Caucus (EAEC) and a transregional forum in the form of the Asia-Europe Summits (ASEM), however, Australia was faced once more with the possibility of marginalization. To an extent, the success of the APEC forum would be considered by Japan and Australia as a barometer of the relevance and efficacy of the bilateral relationship. The same expectations would also be revealed in the workings of the bilateral relationship in other multilateral forums, notably United Nations peacekeeping operations.

The flurry of rhetoric extolling the "partnership" between Japan and Australia in the 1990s betrays an insecurity reminiscent of the 1930s and early 1950s. This is particularly noticeable on the Australian side, but Japan was equally keen to leap onto the "partnership" bandwagon. The 1995 Joint Declaration on the Australia-Japan Partnership stated the shared aim of building "an enduring and steadfast partnership which is a strong positive force for cooperation in the Asia Pacific region," thus locating the raison d'être of bilateral activity in the sphere of Asian regionalism. The text of the declaration went on to welcome Australia's new commitment to the Asian region in general. "The Government of Japan welcomes Australia's decision to create its future in the region and reaffirms that Australia is an indispensable partner in regional affairs,"[28] thus acknowledging the foreign policy reorientation that had proactively been pursued in Australia by the government of Labour Prime Minister Paul Keating in the 1990s. This mutual affirmation of partnership as the determining element in Japan-Australia relations is repeated in most official language throughout the decade, with the August 1997 edition of *Gaiko foramu* presenting both sides at their rhetorical peaks.[29]

Why did both Japanese and Australians feel it necessary to shore up the bilateral relationship with this kind of rhetoric? How was APEC supposed to embody this partnership? When we examine attempts by analysts and officials to elaborate on the substance of this partnership, we find various interesting explanations put forward. Some speak of the fact that both Australia and Japan are "outsiders" in the region ("both countries are in Asia yet are un-Asian"), and so they both needed a vehicle to be more effectively integrated into the economically vital Asian region. Economics can thus salvage Japan and Australia, making them "the natural axis" of the Asian regional economic zone.[30] Others opt for "overcoming the clash of civilizations" logic, presenting the Japan-Australia relationship as a model for East-West collaboration.[31] These explanations are permeated with a mutual insecurity that implicitly externalizes the source of insecurity, and presents the bilateral relationship as a defense against both nations being on the periphery of the Asia-Pacific region.

It is difficult to credit this simple explanation when we consider that Australia is also faced with exclusion from the ASEM forum (although Japan has spoken for the inclusion of Australia on the Asian side of ASEM) and the EAEC. Even given Japan's prolonged Heisei recession in the 1990s, few people could conceive of an Asian economic grouping that excludes Japan; it is probable that equally few would say the same of Australia. So what is the glue that binds Japan-Australia bilateralism to the APEC initiative?

Some analysis, from both Japanese and Australian sources, identifies Australia's role as that of an "honest broker" on Japan's behalf.[32] In other words, Australia mediates Japan's diplomatic contribution in the Asian region. According to this rationale, Australia facilitated Japan's participation in United Nations peacekeeping activity in Cambodia, and continues to perform a "good offices" role in Japan's Asian diplomacy. This perspective places great importance on Japanese Prime Minister Murayama Tomiichi's 1995 statement that Australia is Japan's "indispensable partner in regional affairs."[33] Japanese voices have responded with skepticism to this notion. Watanabe Akio has argued that there is no political dimension to the enhanced bilateral relationship of the 1990s, and that on any pragmatic level, Japan and Australia must be regarded as "queer collaborators."[34] According to Watanabe, neither APEC, nor the co-chairing of the committee at the Paris Conference on the Reconstruction of Cambodia in 1989, nor the MFP project, justified the perception that Australia was "indispensable" to Japan in the 1990s.

We thus are confronted by a paradox: both nations have built great expectations into the APEC enterprise, as a demonstration of the relevance and validity of their bilateral relationship. And yet, there seem to be quite different versions of this joint exercise in regionalism. Australia has projected itself into the center of successful Japanese regionalism, but Japan is also mediating Australia's presence in regional institutions (notably ASEM). Such variance of perceptions in the core marker of meaningful bilateralism indicates a troubling lack of consistency in the shared vision of these two regional partners, placing their partnership on shaky ground.

The tale of the ill-fated Multifunction Polis (MFP) is often cited as an example of diversification that tried to go too far, or as a case study of bureaucratic inefficiency. For this writer, the MFP was also a signal of optimism, mingled with discordant echoes of old anxieties. Australia, mindful of its reliance on Japan, wanted to move even further into new areas of mutual dependence, into such exciting fields as industrial high technology and environmental sciences. In other words, Australia was trying to move closer to the center of Japan's postwar prosperity, revealing a fear that perhaps it was slipping toward the periphery. For Japan, the MFP was probably little more than a piece of diplomatic finessing emerging from a bilateral ministerial meeting with Australia in 1987. Perhaps it was also a gesture to the new spirit of the relationship, or an attempt, on the part of Japan, to add substance to the new vision despite the dramatically changed economic environment of the late 1980s.

The MFP was a Japanese initiative that flowed from the concept of the technopolis developed by the Ministry of International Trade and Industry (MITI) in the 1980s. Often confused in Australia with the Silver Columbia Plan,[35] the MFP found its way onto the negotiating table in January 1987, at one of the regular Australia-Japan Ministerial Consultations. It was seized upon by both sides as a good-news proposal that could deliver positive press for the meeting. The first serious depiction of the project was put forward after that meeting, in a 30 September 1987 document produced by MITI's MFP Planning Committee. After a feasibility study and a bungled attempt at siting, Adelaide, in the state of South Australia, was proclaimed as the site for the MFP. There followed a sorry episode in bilateral relations, as the MFP project became embroiled in Australia's 1990 election campaign. Australian politicians rode the bandwagon denouncing the MFP as a "Japanese enclave," with one politician infamously declaring "this project reeks of oriental deception and treachery."[36] It has been downhill since then for the idea, with the project now having essentially fizzled out, leaving a Science Park in Adelaide's suburbs its only legacy.

Despite its sad end, the MFP project can be seen as a brave vote of confidence in the bilateral relationship, described by one critical commentator as "the most complex and interesting single event in the history of Australia-Japan relations."[37] It was never substantively defined, and relied heavily on vague, futuristic terminology. One definition reads, "The MFP would be a fusion of high-tech industries destined to comprise core industries in the twenty-first century and high-tech oriented industries which support creative human people accompanied by their families."[38] Ultimately, it was the bilateral focus of the project that caused it to fail in the Australian context. Its Japanese conceptualization, however, largely preserved the version of the Japan-Australia relationship encapsulated in the 1976 Treaty of Friendship and Cooperation. As the MITI document said, "Australia and Japan need to cooperate in initiating new projects likely to make a broad-based contribution to the Pacific Rim nations and pave the way for the 'Pacific Era.'"[39] In a sense, then, the rejection of the MFP was a rejection of Japan's version of how its bilateral relationship with Australia might manifest itself in the Asia-Pacific region. Again, we are struck by the disparity in the vision of bilateralism that emerges from Japan and Australia.

Despite the notes of skepticism and insecurity that permeate official expressions of optimism about Japan's relationship with Australia, one should not dismiss the considerable distance that has been covered historically between the two countries. If there is a nexus between bilateralism and multilateralism in the 1990s between Japan and Australia, this could also be seen as evidence of commendable maturity between two countries that recognized long ago that mere economic complementarity was not enough. What this new version of the bilateral relationship needs is a winning project that affirms a vision that is understood and shared by both sides. In the late 1990s, it was not clear whether APEC can deliver this much-needed success.

Conclusion

In the late 1990s, therefore, we found the gauge of the Japan-Australia bilateral relationship externalized into the realm of Asian regionalism. As Australia maneuvered to retain a place in the center of Japan's regional activism, Japan continues to demonstrate goodwill toward Australia as its regional ally. For both nations, it is clear that Asia and its regional institutions have become the new mediating entities. At the turn of the century, developments in Asian regionalism and in Australian foreign policy introduced elements of uncertainty. The EAEC (known by its new name ASEAN Plus Three, meaning the ASEAN members plus China, Japan and Korea) put down roots and assumed a permanent status as an established regional grouping. At the same time, Australia's Liberal-National coalition government stated its intention to rebalance Australia's foreign relations by reducing the emphasis on Asia. As regional security increases in importance, the extent to which the fledgling defense relationship between Japan and Australia can contribute to regional stability will bear watching, to see whether it can breathe new life into the Japan-Australia axis.

Notes

1. See for example Takabatake Michitoshi, "Keizai no teitai, Nihon no kosei ni kikikan" [Economic Stagnation, Feeling Threatened by Japan's Aggression], *Ushio* 352 (August 1988): 382–90; and "Nihon e no keikaishin to hankan no haikei" [The Background to Feelings of Foreboding and Prejudice against Japan], *Ushio* 359 (March 1989): 370–78.
2. Henry P. Frei, *Japan's Southward Advance and Australia: From the 16th Century to World War II* (Honolulu: University of Hawaii Press, 1991), p. 26.
3. The first Japanese consul, Nakagawa Tsunejiro, took up his post in Townsville in 1896.
4. Neville Meaney quoted by Watanabe Akio, "Nichi-Go kankeishi no shomondai" [Some Problems in the History of the Japan-Australia Relationship] *Kokusai seiji* 68:2 (1981), p. 2.
   See also Takeda Isami, "Hakugo seisaku no seiritsu to Nihon no taio" [The Establishment of the White Australia Policy and Japan's Response], *Kokusai seiji* 62:2 (1981); 36.
5. The state of Queensland chose a different path, negotiating a "gentleman's agreement" with Japan to limit passports to certain categories of Japanese visitors. Australia as a nation followed suit in 1905.
6. Quoted in Neville Meaney, *Fears and Phobias: E. L. Piesse and the Problem of Japan 1909–1939* (National Library of Australia Occasional Papers Series No. 1, 1996), p. 20.
7. E. L. Piesse, "Japan and Australia," *Foreign Affairs* IV:3 (April 1926): 476.
8. Sandra Tweedie, *Trading Partners: Australia and Asia 1790–1993* (Sydney: University of New South Wales Press, 1994), pp. 145–48.
9. Japan also experienced difficulty over immigration issues with the United States and Canada.
10. Alan Watt, *The Evolution of Australian Foreign Policy 1938–1965* (Cambridge: Cambridge University Press, 1967), p. 211.
11. R. N. Rosecrance. *Australian Diplomacy and Japan 1945–1951* (London: Melbourne University Press, 1962), p. 78.
12. For a comprehensive study of this Agreement, see Alan Rix, *Coming to Terms* (Sydney: Allen and Unwin, 1986).

13. No. 66, Minute 2 (PM) of the Prime Minister's Committee of Cabinet, Canberra, 17 August 1954, in Department of Foreign Affairs and Trade, *The Australia-Japan Agreement on Commerce 1957* (Canberra: Australian Government Printing Service, 1997), pp. 118–21.
14. Tweedie, 1994, p. 170.
15. The Ad Hoc Working Committee on Australia-Japan Relations, *Australia-Japan Relations* (Canberra: Australian Government Printing Service, 1978), pp. 20–26. This report is sometimes referred to as the Myer Committee Report.
16. By the early 1980s, however, this had fallen to 26 percent. See N. Meaney, T. Mathews, and S. Encel, *The Japanese Connection* (Melbourne: Longman Cheshire, 1988), pp. 21–28.
17. *The Australia-Japan Relationship: Towards the Year 2000* (Canberra and Tokyo: Australia-Japan Research Centre and Japan Center for Economic Research, 1989), p. 17.
18. *The Australia-Japan Relationship, 1989*, p. 19.
19. Watanabe Akio, *Ajia Taiheiyo no kokusai kankei to Nihon* [The International Relations of the Asia-Pacific Region and Japan] (Tokyo: University of Tokyo Press, 1997), pp. 128–31.
20. Sir John Crawford and Dr. Okita Saburo, *Australia, Japan and Western Pacific Economic Relations. A Report to the Governments of Australia and Japan* (Canberra: AGPS, 1976), p. 2.
21. E. G. Whitlam, quoted in D. C. S. Sissons, "Japan," in *Australia in World Affairs 1971–1975*, ed. W. J. Hudson (Sydney: George Allen and Unwin, 1980), p. 262.
22. Crawford and Okita, 1976, p. 1.
23. Senate Standing Committee on Foreign Affairs and Defence, *Report on Japan*. Parliamentary Paper No. 2 (Canberra: Government Printer of Australia, 1973); and Ad Hoc Working Committee on Australia-Japan Relations, *Australia-Japan Relations* (Canberra: Australian Government Printing Service, 1978).
24. The collapse in commodity prices in the early 1980s lent a particular urgency to the need for the diversification of trade.
25. For example Fujiwara Hiroshi, "Taiheiyo no yoki patona kankei" [The Relationship between Two Good Asia-Pacific Partners], *Sekai choho*, 8 January 1985, p. 25; Takabatake, 1989, pp. 371–72.
26. Alan Rix argues strongly that defense and security have always been core concerns of the Japan-Australia relationship. See Alan Rix, *The Australia-Japan Political Alignment* (London: Routledge, 1999).
27. Takeda Isami, "Aratana chiiki kyoryoku to kaihatsu sekinin o motomete" [Demanding Responsibility for New Regional Cooperation and Development], *Sekai rinji zokan* 553 (April 1991): 88.
28. *The Prime Minister of Australia, The Hon. P. J. Keating MP, Official Visit to Japan 24–28 May 1995*, p. 15.
29. *Gaiko foramu* 108 (August 1997) has a feature on cooperation between Japan, Australia, and New Zealand in APEC.
30. Manabe Shunji, "Gendai Nichi–Go kankei no ikkosatsu: posuto reisen sekai ni okeru Nichi-Go no yakuwari o tenbo shitsutsu" [One View of the Contemporary Japan-Australia Relationship: Defining the Role of Japan and Australia in the Post–Cold War World], *Kansai Daigaku hogaku ronshu* 43:6 (February 1994): 1,769–781.
31. Kotaku Isido [Ishido], "The Special New Relationship of Japan and Australia," paper delivered at the Japanese Studies Association of Australia Conference in Newcastle, Australia, 6–10 July 1993.
32. *The Australia-Japan Relationship*, 1989, p. 5.
33. Quoted in P. King and Y. Kibata, eds., *Peace Building in the Asia-Pacific Region* (St. Leonards: Allen and Unwin, 1996), p. 5.
34. Watanabe, 1997, p. 151.
35. The Silver Columbia Plan was proposed by Japanese bureaucrats in 1986–87 as an offshore retirement plan for Japan's rapidly aging population. It was regarded with considerable skepticism in Australia.
36. Rex Connor quoted in Ian Inkster, *The Clever City: Japan, Australia and the Multifunctionpolis* (South Melbourne: Sydney University Press in association with Oxford University Press, 1991), p. 120.
37. Gavan McCormack, ed., *Bonsai Australia Banzai: Multifunctionpolis and the Making of a Special Relationship with Japan* (Leichardt: Pluto Press, 1991), p. 34.
38. McCormack, 1991, p. 39.
39. MITI Planning Committee, 30 September 1987, *A Multifunctionpolis Scheme for the 21st Century*, reproduced in McCormack, 1991.

BIBLIOGRAPHY

Abe Hitoshi and Shindo Muneyuki. *Gaisetsu Nihon no chihojichi* [An Outline of Japan's Local Government]. Tokyo: University of Tokyo Press, 1997.

Ad Hoc Working Committee on Australia-Japan Relations. *Australia-Japan Relations.* Canberra: Australian Government Printing Service, 1978.

Ahn, Byung-joon. Japanese Policy Toward Korea. In *Japan's Foreign Policy after the Cold War,* ed. Gerald L. Curtis. Armonk, NY: M. E. Sharpe, 1993.

Akaha, Tsuneo and Frank Langdon, eds. *Japan in the Posthegemonic World.* Boulder, CO: Lynne Rienner, 1993.

Akaha, Tsuneo. Japan's Security Policy after U.S. Hegemony. *Millennium: Journal of International Studies* 18:3 (Winter 1989): 435–54.

———. Beyond Self-Defense: Japan's Elusive Security Role under the New Guidelines for U.S.-Japan Defense Cooperation. *Pacific Review* 11:4 (1996): 461–83.

———. An Illiberal Hegemon or an Understanding Partner?: Japanese Views of the United States in the Post–Cold War Era. *Brown Journal of World Affairs* (1998).

Akashi, Yasushi. Regional Security and Preventive Diplomacy. Seminar, Institute of Defence and Strategic Studies, 14 August 1998.

Alger, Chadwick F., Gene M. Lyons, John E. Trent. *The United Nations System: The Policies of Member States.* Tokyo: United Nations University Press, 1995.

Alston, Philip. The Commission on Human Rights. *The United Nations and Human Rights: A Critical Appraisal,* ed. Philip Alston. Oxford: Clarendon Press, 1992.

Altman, Roger C. Why Pressure Tokyo? *Foreign Affairs* 73:3 (1994).

Amako, Satoshi, ed. *Chugoku wa kyoi ka* [Is China a Threat?]. Tokyo: Keiso Shobo, 1997.

Arase, David. Japanese Foreign Policy and Human Rights in Asia. *Asian Survey* 33:10 (October 1993).

———. Shifting Patterns in Japan's Economic Cooperation in East Asia: A Growing Role for Local Actors? *Asian Perspective* (Seoul) 21:1 (Spring–Summer 1997): 37–53;

Armstrong, David Lorna Lloyd, and John Redmond. *From Versailles to Maastricht: International Organizations in the Twentieth Century.* London: Macmillan, 1996.

Aruga Tadashi, et al., eds. *Koza kokusai seiji, 4, Nihon no gaiko* [Studies of International Politics. Vol. 4., Japan's Diplomacy]. University of Tokyo Press, 1989.

Australian Department of Foreign Affairs and Trade, Prime Minister's Committee of Cabinet, Canberra, 17 August 1954, in *The Australia-Japan Agreement on Commerce 1957.* Canberra: Australian Government Printing Service, 1997.

Bailey, S. *The Secretariat of the United Nations.* London: Pall Mall Press, 1964.
Barney, Gerald O. *The Global 2000 Report to the President of the United States.* Oxford: Pergamon, 1980.
Bhagwati, Jagdish. Samurais No More. *Foreign Affairs* 73:3 (1994).
Blaker, Michael. *Japanese International Negotiating Style.* NY: Columbia University Press, 1977.
Bomberg, Elizabeth, and John Peterson. European Union Decision Making: The Role of Sub-national Authorities. *Political Studies* 2 (June 1998): 219–35.
Boutros-Ghali, B. Empowering the United Nations. *Foreign Affairs* 72:5 (Winter 1992–93): 89.
Boutros-Ghali, B. Report on the Work of the Organization. NY: United Nations, September 1992.
Boutros-Ghali, B. UN Peace-keeping in a New Era: A New Chance for Peace. *The World Today* (April 1993): 66–69.
Boutros-Ghali, B. *Building Peace and Development,* the Report on the Work of the Organization. NY: United Nations, 1995.
Braddick, C.W. *Japan and the Sino-Soviet Alliance, 1950–1964,* doctoral dissertation, Oxford University, 1997.
Bridges, Brian. *Japan and Korea in the 1990s.* Aldershot, Vermont: Edward Elgar, 1993.
Brown, Lester, et al. *State of the World: 1990.* NY: W.W. Norton and Company, 1990.
Brown, M. E, S. M. Lynn-Jones, S. E. Miller, eds. *East Asian Security.* Cambridge, Mass: MIT Press, 1996.
Bryant, William E. *Japanese Private Economic Diplomacy: An Analysis of Business-Government Linkages.* NY: Praeger, 1975.
Butow, Robert J.C. *Japan's Decision to Surrender.* Stanford: Stanford University Press, 1954.
Calder, Kent E. Japanese Foreign Economic Policy Formation: Explaining the Reactive State. *World Politics* 40:4 (1988): 517–41.
Caldwell, Lynton. *International Environmental Policy.* Durham: Duke University Press, 1990.
Carlisle, Lonny E. The Changing Political Economy of Japan's Economic Relations with Russia. *Pacific Affairs* 67:3 (Fall 1994).
Chuma Kiyofuku. PKO: Dainiji ronsen e. [The PKO: Toward a Second Round of Debate.] *Sekai* 584 (July 1993).
Chung, Il Yung, and Eunsook Chung, eds. *Russia in the Far East and Pacific Region.* Seoul: Sejong Institute, 1994.
Clark, Ann Marie. Non-governmental Organizations and Their Influence on International Society. *Journal of International Affairs* 48:2 (Winter 1995): 507–27.
Clarke, Gerard. Non-Governmental Organizations (NGOs) and Politics in the Developing World. *Political Studies* 46:1 (1998): 36–52.
Claude, I. L. Jr. *Swords Into Plowshares: The Problems and Progress of International Organization.* 4th ed. NY: Random House, 1984.
Clough, Mike. Grass-roots Policymaking. *Foreign Affairs* 73:1 (January–February 1994): 2–7.
Consulates Belong to Yesterday's Diplomacy. *Los Angeles Times,* reprinted in *Daily Yomiuri,* 17 August 1998.
Cossa, Ralph A. Johnson and Keehn's Ossified Analysis. *PacNet* 35 (October 6, 1995).
Council of Local Authorities for International Relations. *1998 Japanese Local Government International Affiliation Directory.* Tokyo, 1998.
Crawford, Sir John and Dr. Okita Saburo, *Australia, Japan and Western Pacific Economic Relations. A Report to the Governments of Australia and Japan.* Canberra: AGPS, 1976.
Crichton, Michael. *Rising Sun.* NY: Knopf, 1992.
Curtis, Gerald. *The Japanese Way of Politics.* NY: Columbia University Press, 1988.
Curtis, Gerald, ed. *Japan's Foreign Policy After the Cold War.* NY: M. E. Sharpe, 1993.
De Cuéllar, J. Pérez. Reflecting on the Past and Contemplating the Future. *Global Governance* 1:2 (1995): 153.
Defense Agency. *Boei hakusho* [Defense White Paper]. Tokyo: Ministry of Finance Printing Bureau, 1998.
———. *Boei handobukku* [Defense Handbook]. Tokyo: Asagumo Shimbun, 1999.
Dore, Ronald. *Japan's Internationalism and the UN.* London: Routledge, 1998.
Drifte, Reinhard. *Japan's Rise to International Responsibilities.* London: Athlone Press, 1990.

Drifte, Reinhard. *Japan's Foreign Policy in the 1990s: From Economic Superpower to What Power?*. London: Macmillan, 1996.

Drifte, Reinhard. *Japan's Foreign Policy for the 21st Century*. Basingstoke: St. Antony's/Macmillan, 1998.

Drucker, Peter. Trade Lessons from the World Economy. *Foreign Affairs* 73:1 (1994).

———. The Global Economy and the Nation-State. *Foreign Affairs* 76:5 (1997).

Drysdale, Peter, and Ross Garnaut. *Asia Pacific Regionalism: Readings in International Economic Relations*. Pymble: Harper Educational Publishers, 1994.

Economic Planning Agency, Comprehensive Planning Bureau [Keizai Kikakucho Sogo Keikakukyoku], ed. *Keizai shingikai nijuisseki sekaikeizai iinkai hokokusho* [Report of the Twenty-first Century World Economy Committee of the Economic Council]. Tokyo: The Economic Planning Agency of Japan, 1997.

Economic Planning Agency. *Kokuminkeizai keisan nenpo 1993* [Annual Report of National Economic Account 1993]. Tokyo: Ministry of Finance Printing Bureau, 1993.

Edstrom, Bert, ed. *Japan's Foreign and Security Policies in Transition*. Stockholm: Swedish Institute of International Affairs, 1997.

Edstrom, Bert. *Japan's Evolving Foreign Policy Doctrine*. Basingstoke, Hampshire: Macmillan, 1999.

Emmerson, John K. Japan, Eye on 1970. *Foreign Affairs* 47:2 (January 1967): 348–62.

Endicott, John D. *Japan's Nuclear Option*. NY: Praeger Publishers, 1975.

Environment Agency (EA) Planning Division, Global Environment Department, *Chikyu kankyo jidai* [The Era of Global Environment]. Tokyo: Gyosei, 1990.

Environment Agency (EA), *Kankyo Cho nijunen shi* [The Twenty-Year History of the Environment Agency]. Tokyo: Gyosei, 1991.

Etzioni, Amitai. The Dialectics of Supranational Unification. *American Political Science Review* 56 (1962).

Etzold, Thomas H. and John L. Gaddis, eds., *Containment*. NY: Columbia University Press, 1978.

Falk, Richard. Resisting "Globalization-from Above" Through "Globalization-from Below." *New Political Economy* 2:1 (1997).

Falkenheim, Peggy L. Some Determining Factors in Soviet-Japanese Relations. *Pacific Affairs* 50:3 (Winter 1977–78): 610.

Fingleton, Eamonn. *Blindside: Why Japan Is Still on Track to Overtake the U.S. by the Year 2000*. Boston: Houghton Mifflin, 1995.

———. Japan's Invisible Leviathan. *Foreign Affairs* 74:2 (1995).

Fox, Jonathan A. and L. David Brown, eds. *The Struggle for Accountability: The World Bank, NGOs, and Grassroots Movements*. Cambridge: The MIT Press, 1998.

Frei, Henry P. *Japan's Southward Advance and Australia: From the 16th Century to World War II*. Honolulu: University of Hawaii Press, 1991.

Friedman, George and Meredith Lebard. *The Coming War with Japan*. NY: St. Martin's Press, 1991.

Fry, Earl H. *The Expanding Role of State and Local Governments in U.S. Foreign Affairs*. NY: Council on Foreign Relations Press, 1998.

Fujimoto Toshikazu. Zen Tokan daitoryo ho-Nichi no igi to Nik-Kan kankei no tenbo [The Significance of President Chun Doo Hwan's Visit to Japan and the Prospects for Japan-ROK Relations]. *Kokusai mondai* 287 (December 1984).

Fujita, Hiroshi. UN Reform and Japan's Permanent Security Council Seat. *Japan Quarterly* 42:4 (October-December 1995).

Fujiwara Hiroshi. Taiheiyo no yoki patona kankei [The Relationship between Two Good Asia-Pacific Partners] *Sekai choho* (8 January 1985).

Fukushima, Akiko. *Japanese Foreign Policy: The Emerging Logic of Multilateralism*. London: Macmillan, 1999.

Fukuzawa, Yukichi, On De-Asianization. In *Meiji Japan through Contemporary Sources*. Vol. 3, ed. Center for East Asian Cultural Studies. Tokyo: Center for East Asian Cultural Studies, 1973.

———. The Global Economy and the Nation-State. *Foreign Affairs* 76:5 (1997).

Funabashi, Yoichi, Japan and the New World Order. *Foreign Affairs* 70:5 (Winter 1991–92): 58 –74.

———. *Nihon no taigaikoso: Reisengo no bijon o kaku* [A Vision for Japan's External Policy: Fashioning a Post-Cold War Vision]. Tokyo: Iwanami Shoten, 1993.

———, ed. *Japan's International Agenda*. NY: New York University Press, 1994.

———. Japan's Depression Diplomacy. *Foreign Affairs* 77:6 (1998): 35–36.

———. Otoko wa damatte en shakkan de wa komaru [Japan Can't Go On Giving Yen Loans Without Making Any Demands]. *Asahi shimbun*, 4 February 1999.

Gaddis, John L. *Strategies of Containment*. Oxford: Oxford University Press, 1982.

Gaiko Seisaku Kettei Yoin Kenkyukai, ed., *Nihon no gaiko seisaku kettei yoin* [Domestic Determinants of Japanese Foreign Policy]. Tokyo: PHP Kenkyujo, 1999.

Garby, Craig C., and Mary Brown Bullock, eds. *Japan: A New Kind of Superpower?*. Baltimore and London: The John Hopkins University Press, 1994.

Gelman, Harry. *Russo-Japanese Relations and the Future of the U.S.-Japanese Alliance*. Santa Monica, Calif.: Rand, 1993.

George, Aurelia. Japan's Participation in UN Peacekeeping Operations: Radical Departure or Predictable Response? *Asian Survey* XXXIII:6 (1993): 573.

Glaubitz, Joachim. *Between Tokyo and Moscow*. Honolulu: University of Hawaii Press, 1995.

Goodby, James E. Vladimir I. Ivanov, and Shimotamai Nobuo, eds. *Northern Territories" and Beyond: Russian, Japanese, and American Perspectives*. Westport, CT: Praeger, 1995.

Gordon, Bernard, and John Ravenhill. Beyond Product Cycles and Flying Geese: Regionalization, Hierarchy, and Industrialization of East Asia. *World Politics* 47 (1995): 171–209.

Gotoda Masaharu. *Seiji to wa nanika* [The Nature of Politics]. Tokyo: Kodansha, 1988.

———. *Naikaku kanbo chokan* [Chief Cabinet Secretary]. Tokyo: Kodansha, 1989.

———. *Jo to ri : Gotoda Masaharu kaikoroku* [Sentiment and Reason: Memoirs of Gotoda Masaharu] (2 vols.). Tokyo: Kodansha, 1998.

Gourevitch, Peter, Takashi Inoguchi, and Courtney Purrington, eds. *United States-Japan Relations and International Institutions after the Cold War*. San Diego: University of California, 1995.

Government of Australia, Senate Standing Committee on Foreign Affairs and Defence. *Report on Japan*. Parliamentary Paper No. 2. Canberra: Government Printer of Australia, 1973.

Grant, Richard L., ed. *The Process of Japanese Foreign Policy*. London: The Royal Institute of International Affairs, 1997.

Haas, Ernst B. International Integration: The European and the Universal Process. *International Organization* 15 (1961): 366–92.

Hakoshima, Shinichi, Mutual Ignorance and Misunderstanding—Causes of Japan-EC Economic Disputes. *Japan Quarterly* 26:4 (1979): 481.

Halloran, Richard. *Chrysanthemum and the Sword Revisited: Is Japanese Militarism Resurgent?* Honolulu: The East-West Center, 1991.

Hanami, Andrew K. The Emerging Military-Industrial Relationship in Japan and the U.S. Connection. *Asian Survey* 33 (1993): 592–609.

Hara, Kimie. *Japanese-Soviet/Russian Relations since 1945:A Difficult Peace*. London: Nissan Institute/Routledge, 1998.

Hara, Yoshihisa. Josetsu: Nichi-Bei ampo taisei jizoku to hen'yo [Introduction: The Japan-U.S. Security Treaty System—Continuity and Change)].*Kokusai seiji* 115 (May 1997).

Harrison, Selig S., ed. *Japan's Nuclear Future: The Debate and East Asian Security*. Washington, DC: Carnegie Endowment for International Peace, 1996.

Hasegawa, Tsuyoshi, Jonathan Haslam, and Andrew C. Kuchins, eds. *Russia and Japan: An Unresolved Dilemma Between Distant Neighbors*. Berkeley: University of California Press, 1993.

Hasegawa, Tsuyoshi. *The Northern Territories Dispute and Russo-Japanese Relations*. Berkeley: University of California Press, 1998.

Hayashida, Kazuhiko. PKO ruporutaju [PKO Reportage]. *Gaiko forum* 78 (1995): 52–55.

Hedberg, Hakan. *Die japanische Herausforderung* [The Japanese Challenge]. Hamburg: Hoffmann und Campe, 1970.

Hellman, Donald. *Japanese Domestic Politics and Foreign Policy.* Berkeley: University of California Press: 1969.

Hirano, Ken'ichiro, ed. *Koza gendai Ajia 4: Chiiki shisutemu to kokusai kankei* [Lectures on Contemporary Asia 4: Regional Systems and International Relations]. Tokyo: University of Tokyo Press, 1994.

Hobbs, Heidi H. *City Hall Goes Abroad: The Foreign Policy of Local Politics.* Thousand Oaks: Sage Publications, 1994.

Hook, Glenn D. Japan and Subregionalism: Constructing the Japan Sea Rim Zone. *Kokusai seiji* 114 (March 1997).

Hoshino, Eiichi. Human Rights and Development Aid: Japan. In *Debating Human Rights*, ed. Peter Van Ness. London & New York: Routledge, 1999.

Hosoya Chihiro and Watanuki Joji, eds. *Taigaiseisaku kettei katei no Nichi-Bei hikaku* [Japan-U.S. Comparison of Foreign Policy-making Process]. Tokyo: University of Tokyo Press, 1977.

Hudson, W. J., ed. *Australia in World Affairs 1971–1975.* Sydney: George Allen and Unwin, 1980.

Hunsberger, Warren S., ed. *Japan's Quest: The Search for International Role, Recognition and Respect.* NY: M.E. Sharpe, 1997.

Huntington, Samuel P. America's Changing Strategic Interests. *Survival* 33:1 (January–February 1991).

Ikeda Yukihiko, foreign minister. Speech delivered at the FICCI Auditorium, New Delhi, 25 July 1997. 21–seiki no Nihon to Minami Ajia no aratana kankei o motomete [In Search of a New Relationship between Japan and South Asia in the Twenty-first century]. Tokyo: Ministry of Foreign Affairs, mimeographed.

Imagawa, Yukio. The Recent Situation in East Asia and Cambodia. *Asia Pacific Review* (Spring–Summer) 1998.

Immerman, Robert M. Japan and the United Nations. In *Japan: A New Kind of Superpower?* ed. Craig C. Garby and Mary Brown Bullock. Washington, DC: The Woodrow Wilson Center Press, 1994.

Inkster, Ian. *The Clever City: Japan, Australia and the Multifunctionpolis.* South Melbourne: Sydney University Press in association with Oxford University Press, 1991.

Inoguchi, Kuniko. *Posutohaken shisutemu to Nihon no sentaku* [The Posthegemonic System and Japan's Options]. Tokyo: Chikuma Shobo, 1987.

Inoguchi, Takashi and Iwai Tomoaki. *"Zoku" giin no kenkyu* [A Study of Zoku Diet Members]. Tokyo: Nihon Keizai Shimbunsha, 1987.

Inoguchi, Takashi and Daniel I. Okimoto, eds. *The Political Economy of Japan* .Vol. 2 of *The Changing International Context.* Stanford: Stanford University Press, 1989.

Inoguchi, Takashi. *Japan's International Relations.* London: Pinter Publishers; Boulder, CO: Westview Press, 1991.

———. Japan's Response to the Gulf Crisis: An Analytic Overview. *Journal of Japanese Studies* 17:2 (1991): 257–73.

———. *Gendai kokusai seiji to Nihon* [Contemporary International Politics and Japan]. Tokyo: Chikuma Shobo, 1991.

———. *Japan's Foreign Policy in an Era of Global Change.* London: Pinter Publishers, 1993.

———. Japan's United Nations Peacekeeping and Other Operations. *International Journal* 50 (Spring 1995).

International Cooperation Initiatives, in "Japanese Approaches to the Suppression of Greenhouse Gas Generation," <http://www.mofa.go.jp/policy/global/environment/warm/japan/chap6.html>.

Iokibe, Makoto, ed. *Sengo Nihon gaiko-shi* [The Postwar History of Japanese Diplomacy]. Tokyo: Yuhikaku, 1999.

Iseri, Hirofumi, Clearing the Mist from the Peace-keeping Debate. *Japan Echo* XIX:3 (1992).

Isido [Ishido], Kotaku. The Special New Relationship of Japan and Australia. Paper delivered at the Japanese Studies Association of Australia Conference in Newcastle, Australia, 6–10 July 1993.

Ishihara, Nobuo. *Kantei 2668 nichi: Seisaku kettei no butaura* [2668 Days in the Prime Minister's Residence: The Backstage of Decision-making]. Tokyo: NHK Shuppan, 1995.

Ishihara, Nobuo. *Naikaku no shikumi to shusho no kengen* [The Mechanisms of the Cabinet and the Powers of Prime Ministers]. In *Naikaku gyosei kiko: Kaikaku e no teigen* [The Yomiuri Proposal for Restructuring the Cabinet and the Government Administration], ed. Yomiuri Shimbunsha. Tokyo: Yomiuri Shimbunsha, 1996.

Ishihara, Shintaro and Morita Akio. *No to ieru Nihon* [The Japan that Can Say No]. Tokyo: Kobunsha, 1991.

Ishihara, Shintaro. *The Japan That Can Say No.* NY: Simon and Schuster, 1991.

Ishizawa, Masato. India's Software Touch, Prices Entice Japan's Cost-conscious Hardware Markets. *Nikkei Weekly,* 18 September 1995.

Izumi, Hajime. Chikakute tooi rinjin: Nik-Kan kokko juritsu made no michi [Close but Distant Neighbors: The Path to Restoration of Diplomatic Relations Between Japan and Korea]. In *Sengo Nihon no taigai seisaku* [Japan's Postwar Foreign Policy], ed. Watanabe Akio. Tokyo: Yuhikaku, 1985.

JANIC, *NGO Dairekutori-98: Directory of Japanese NGOs Concerned with International Cooperation.* Tokyo: 1998.

JETRO [Japan Export Trade Organization]. *White Paper on International Trade Japan 1996.* Tokyo, 1996.

Jain, Purnendra. Japan's 1999 Unified Local Elections: Electing Tokyo's Governor. *Japanese Studies* 19:2 (1999): 117–32.

———, ed. *Distant Asian Neighbours: Japan and South Asia.* New Delhi: Sterling Publishers, 1996.

Jain, Purnendra and Mizukami Tetsuo. *Gurasurutsu no kokusai koryu* [Japan's Internationalization at the Grassroots Level]. Tokyo: Habesutosha, 1996.

Jain, R.K. *The USSR and Japan, 1945–1980.* New Delhi: Radiant, 1981.

James, Alan. Peacekeeping in the Post–Cold War Era. *International Journal* 50:5 (Spring 1995): 247.

Japan Broadcast Association [Nihon Hoso Kyokai (NHK)]. *The Public Opinion Poll on "Japanese and the Constitution"* (March 1992).

Japan Federation of Bar Associations, ed., *A Report on the Application and Practice in Japan of the International Covenant on Civil and Political Rights.* Tokyo: April 1993.

Japan Federation of Bar Associations. *Alternative Report to the Fourth Periodic Report of Japan on the ICCPR.* Tokyo: September 1998.

Japan Foundation, Overview of Programs 1997 Annual Report 1996. Tokyo: The Japan Foundation, 1998.

Japan International Cooperation Agency, Environment, Women in Development (WID) and Other Global Issues Division, Planning Department, website, "Environmental Assistance of Japan International Cooperation Agency: http://www.jica.go.jp/E-info/E-earth/E-env/E-env-cont/E_env001.htmlJapan Keeps on World's Top Place in 97 ODA Extending Results. *The Japan Economic Review,* 15 August 1998.

Japanese Studies in South and Southeast Asia. Tokyo: The Japan Foundation, 1997.

Jichiro Jichiken Chuo Suishin Iinkai [National Prefectural and Municipal Workers Union, Central Committee for the Promotion of Local Authority] *Jichitai no kokusai kyoryoku to jichitai ODA* [International Exchange and Local ODA]. Tokyo, 1995.

Jizoku kano na keizai kyoryoku ni mukatte [Toward Sustainable Economic Cooperation], can be found at http://www.epa.go.jp/j-j/doc/houkoku1997–6–j-j.html.

Johnson, Chalmers. *MITI and the Japanese Miracle: The Growth of Industrial Policy, 1925–1975* (Stanford: Stanford University Press, 1980).

———. *Japan: Who Governs? The Rise of the Developmental State.* NY: W.W. Norton and Company, 1995.

Johnson, Chalmers, and E. B. Keehn. The Pentagon's Ossified Strategy. *Foreign Affairs* 74 (1995): 103–10.

Kagami, Mitsuhiro. The Asian Currency Crisis: A Bigger Role for Japan. *Japan Echo* 24:5 (1997).

Kakizawa, Koji. Japan Should Back an Asian Peace Force. *Japan Times Weekly* (29 April–6 May 1991).

Kamei, Naomi (Friends of Earth Japan). Gurobaru foramu ni kanka shite [Participating in Global Forum]. 92 NGO Forum Japan, 2 July 1992.Kamiya, Fuji. *Sengo-shi no naka no Nichi-Bei kankei* [Japan-U.S. Relations in Postwar History]. Tokyo: Shinchosha, 1989.

Bibliography 303

Kamo, Takehiko. *Kokusai anzen hosho no koso* [A Design for International Security]. Tokyo: Iwanami Shoten, 1990.

———, ed. *Nihon no kokusaika: Seikikan no sekaiseiji* [Internationalization of Japan: World Politics Between Centuries]. Tokyo: Nihon Heironsha, 1994.

Kan, Naoto. *Daijin* [Ministers]. Tokyo: Iwanami Shoten, 1998.

Kataoka, Tetsuya. *Waiting for a Pearl Harbor: Japan Debates Defense.* Stanford: Hoover Institution Press, 1980.

Kato, Kozo. *Tsusho kokka no kaihatsu kyoryoku seisaku* [The Development Cooperation Policies of a Trading Nation]. Tokyo: Bokutakusha, 1998.

Katzenstein, Peter J. and Shiraishi Takashi, eds. *Network Power: Japan and Asia.* Ithaca: Cornell University Press, 1997.

Katzenstein, Peter J., ed. *Culture and National Security.* NY: Columbia University Press, 1997.

Kawasaki, Tsuyoshi. Between Realism and Idealism in Japanese Security Policy: The Case of the ASEAN Regional Forum. *Pacific Review* 10:4 (1997).

Keidanren Global Environmental Charter (English version). Keidanren, 23 April 1991.

Keizai Kyoryoku Seisaku Kenkyukai chukan hokoku, at http://www.epa.go.jp/j-j/dpc/1996bg/1996bg5-j-j.html.

Keohane, Robert O. and Joseph S. Nye, Jr. *Power and Interdependence.* Boston: Little Brown, 1977.

Kikuchi, Tsutomu. *APEC: Ajia Taiheiyo shinjitsujo no mosaku* [Searching for a New Regional Order in the Asia-Pacific Region]. Tokyo: Nihon Kokusai Mondai Kenkyujo, 1995.

King, P., and Y. Kibata, eds. *Peace Building in the Asia-Pacific Region.* St. Leonards: Allen and Unwin, 1996.

Kitchin, Alan. Japan: A Place in the Sun. *Director* 51:2 (1997): 77–80.

Kobayashi, Yotaro. Japan's Need for Re-Asianization. *Foresight* (April 1991).

Kojima, Tomoyuki. Sino-Japanese Relations: A Japanese Perspective. *Asia-Pacific Review* 3: 1 (Spring 1996): 73.

Kokubun, Ryosei, ed. *Nihon, Amerika, Chugoku: Kyocho e no shinario* [Japan, the United States, and China: A Scenario for Their Cooperation]. Tokyo: TBS-Britannica, 1997.

Koseki, Shoichi. *Shin kenpo no tanjo* [The Birth of the New Constitution]. Tokyo: Chuo Koron Sha, 1985.

Kosugi, Takashi. Interview. Ima Nihon no hatasubeki yakuwari towa: Yugosurabia de mitekita koto [What Role Should Japan Play Now? My Experience in Yugoslavia]. *Sekai* (August 1998).

Kuroda, Yasumasa. *Japan in a New World Order: Contributing to the Arab-Israeli Peace Process.* NY: Nova Science Publishers, 1994.

Kurosawa, Miwako. Accepting the Role of NGOs: Examples from the Environmental and Developmental Community. *Social Science Japan Journal* (August 1999).

Kusano, Atsushi. *ODA itcho-nisen-oku en no yukue* [Where Does 1 Trillion 200 Billion Yen of ODA Money Go?]. Tokyo: Toyo Keizai Shinbunsha, 1993.

Kyoiku-sha, ed. *Boeicho* [The Defense Agency]. Tokyo: Kyoikusha, 1979.

Lam, Peng Er. Japan and the Spratlys Dispute: Aspirations and Limitations. *Asian Survey* 36:10 (October 1996).

———. Japan's Search for a Political Role in Southeast Asia. *Southeast Asian Affairs 1996.* Singapore: Institute of Southeast Asian Studies, 1996.

Langdon, Frank. Japanese Reactions to India's Nuclear Explosion. *Pacific Affairs* 48:2 (Summer 1975): 173–80.

Lee, Chong-Sik. *Japan and Korea: The Political Dimension.* Stanford: Hoover Institution Press, 1985.

———. *Sengo Nik-Kan kankei-shi* [The History of Postwar Japan–Korea Relations], trans. Okonogi Masao and Furuta Hiroshi. Tokyo: Chuo Koron Sha, 1989.

Leitch, Richard D. Jr., Akira Kato, and Martin E. Weinstein. *Japan's Role in the Post Cold War World.* Westport, Connecticut: Greenwood Press, 1995.

Leitenberg, Milton. The Participation of Japanese Military Forces in United Nations Peacekeeping Operations. *Asian Perspective* 20:1 (1996): 8–13.

Lincoln, Edward J. *Japan's New Global Role*. Washington, DC: Brookings Institute, 1993.

Mago'ori Akihiko and Shigeri Katsuhiko (Illustration). Kaihatsu-ha kara no henshin: Jiminto shin-kankyo zoku no nerai [Objective of New LDP Environmental Policy Specialists: Transformation from Advocates of Development]. *AERA* 5:22 (2 June 1992): 6–9.

Manabe, Shunji. Gendai Nichi-Go kankei no ikkosatsu: posuto reisen sekai ni okeru Nichi-Go no yakuwari o tenbo shitsutsu [One View of the Contemporary Japan-Australia Relationship: Defining the Role of Japan and Australia in the Post–Cold War World]. *Kansai Daigaku hogaku ronshu* 43:6 (February 1994): 1,769–781.

Mandelbaum, Michael, ed. *The Strategic Quadrangle*. NY: Council on Foreign Relations, 1995.

Mandelbaum, Michael. *The Strategic Quadrangle: Russia, China, Japan, and the United States in East Asia*. NY: Council on Foreign Relations Press, 1995.

Manning, Robert A. Futureshock or Renewed Partnership: The US-Japan Alliance Facing the Millennium. *The Washington Quarterly* 18 (1995): 87–98.

Manning, Robert A., and James Przystup. From Model to Millstone. *Japan Times*, 7 February 1998.

Maruyama, Nobuo. Nit-Chu keizai kankei [Japan-China Economic Relations]. In *Chugoku o meguru kokusai kankyo* [The International Environment Surrounding China] ed. Okabe Tatsumi. Tokyo: Iwanami Shoten, 1990.

Matthews, Jessica T. Power Shift. *Foreign Affairs* 76:1 (1997): 50–66.

Maull, Hanns W. Germany and Japan: The New Civilian Powers. *Foreign Affairs* 69:5 (1990–91): 91–106.

McClure, Steve. Tuning into Asia: Japanese TV Finds a Wider Audience. *Japan Scope* (Spring 1995): 37.

McCormack, Gavan, ed. *Bonsai Australia Banzai: Multifunctionpolis and the Making of a Special Relationship with Japan*. Leichardt: Pluto Press, 1991.

McIntosh, Malcolm. *Japan Re-armed*. London: Francis Pinter, 1986.

McNelly, Theodore. *Politics and Government in Japan*. 2nd ed. NY: Houghton Mifflin, 1972.

Meadows, Donella H., Dennis L. Meadows, Jorgen Randers, and William W. Behrens III. *The Limits to Growth*. NY: Universe Books, 1972.

Meaney, N., T. Mathews, and S. Encel. *The Japanese Connection*. Melbourne: Longman Cheshire, 1988.

Meaney, Neville. *Fears and Phobias: E. L. Piesse and the Problem of Japan 1909–1939*. National Library of Australia Occasional Papers Series No. 1, 1996.

Mendl, Wolf. *Japan's Asia Policy: Regional Security and Global Interests*. London and NY: Routledge, 1995.

Mendl, Wolf. Japan and Its Giant Neighbours. *The World Today* 39:6 (June 1983): 208.

Menju, Toshihiro. Jichitai gaiko no susume [Local Diplomacy]. *Chuo Koron* (October 1998): 204–14.

Michelmann, Hans J., and Panayotis Soldatos, eds. *Federalism and International Relations: The Role of Subnational Units*. Oxford: Clarendon Press, 1990.

Midorima, Sakae. *Senkaku retto* [The Senkaku Islands]. Naha, Okinawa: Hirugi Sha, 1984.

Mikuriya, Takashi, and Watanabe Akio, eds. *Shusho kantei no ketsudan: Naikaku fukukanbochokan Ishihara Nobuo no 2600 nichi* [Decisions at the Prime Minister's Residence: 2,600 Days of Deputy Chief Cabinet Secretary Ishihara Nobuo]. Tokyo: Chuo Koron Sha, 1997.

Minami Ajia shinjidai e no yokan [Anticipation of a New Era in South Asia]. *Gaiko forum* 5 (May 1997): 19–74.

Ministry of Foreign Affairs of Japan. *ODA Summary 1995* (1996).

Ministry of Foreign Affairs, "Japan's Energy Conservation" in "Global Environmental Problems: Japanese Approaches" (June 1997). <http://www.mofa.go.jp/policy/global/environment/pamph/index.html>

Ministry of Foreign Affairs, "Japanese Economic Cooperation in the Environmental Sector" <http://www.mofa.go.jp/policy/global/environment/pamph/199706/evn_sect.html> (27 June 1996).

Ministry of Foreign Affairs. *Diplomatic Bluebook 1991: Japan's Diplomatic Activities* (Tokyo: 1991), p. 1.

Ministry of Foreign Affairs, Economic Cooperation Bureau. *Annual Evaluation Report on Japan's Economic Cooperation*. Tokyo: June 1998, p. 3.

Bibliography

Ministry of Foreign Affairs. *Gaiko seisho* [Diplomatic Blue Book]. Tokyo: Ministry of Finance Printing Bureau, 1998. (For the English version of Diplomatic Blue Book, see <http://www.mofa.go.jn>.)

Ministry of Foreign Affairs. *Gaiko seisho* [Diplomatic Blue Book]. Tokyo: Ministry of Finance Printing Bureau, 1989.

Ministry of Foreign Affairs, Global Environmental Section of Economic Division in the United Nations Bureau (Japan), ed. *Chikyu kankyo sengenshu* [Collected Declarations on the Global Environment]. Tokyo: Ministry of Finance Printing Bureau, 1991.

Ministry of Foreign Affairs. *Japan's ODA Annual Report 1997*. Tokyo: 1998. [Jain]

Ministry of Foreign Affairs. *Japan's ODA: Official Development Assistance 1992*. Tokyo: Association for International Cooperation, 1993.

Ministry of Foreign Affairs, ed. *Japan's ODA Annual Report 1997*. Tokyo: Association for Promotion of International Cooperation, October 1997.

Ministry of Foreign Affairs. *Peacekeeping: Japan's Policy and Statements*. Ministry of Foreign Affairs, 1997.

Ministry of International Trade and Industry (MITI). *Tsusho hakusho 1998* [White Paper on Trade 1998]. Tokyo: 1998.

Ministry of International Trade and Industry. *Keizai kyoryoku no genjo to mondaiten* [Economic Cooperation: Present Situation and Problems]. Tokyo: Trade Industry Survey Committee [Tsusho Sangyo Chosakai], 1971.

Ministry of International Trade and Industry. *Keizai kyoryoku no genjo to mondaiten* [Economic Cooperation: Present Situation and Problems]. Tokyo: Trade Industry Survey Committee [Tsusho Sangyo Chosakai], 1976.

Mittelman, James H., ed. *Globalization: Theory and Practice*. NY: Frances Printer, 1996.

Miyamoto, Masao. *Straitjacket Society: An Insider's Irreverent View of Bureaucratic Japan*. Tokyo: Kodansha International, 1994.

Miyata, Osamu. Coping with the "Iranian Threat": A View from Japan. *Silk Road* 1:2 (December 1997): 30–41.

Miyazawa, Kiichi. *Tokyo-Washinton no mitsudan* [The Secret Talks Between Tokyo and Washington]. Tokyo: Jitsugyo no Nihon Sha, 1956.

Mo, Jongryn, and Chung-in Moon, eds. *Democracy and the Korean Economy*. Stanford: Hoover Institution Press, 1999.

Moon, Chung-in. Managing Regional Challengers: Japan, the East Asian NICs and New Patterns of Economic Rivalry. *Pacific Focus* 6:2 (1991): 43–44.

Morse, Ronald. Japan's Drive to Pre-Eminence. *Foreign Policy* 69 (1987–88).

Mulgan, Aurelia George. International Peacekeeping and Japan's Role: Catalyst or Cautionary Tale? *Asian Survey* 35:12 (1995): 1,102–117.

Muramatsu, Michio, Ito Mitsutoshi, and Tsujinaka Yutaka. *Nihon no seiji* [Japanese Politics]. Tokyo: Yuhikaku, 1992.

Murata, Koji. Boei seisaku no tenkai [Development of Defense Policy]. In *Nihon seiji gakkai nenpo* (1997): 79–95.

Murayama, Tomiichi. *So ja no* [Well, Let's See]. Tokyo: Dai-san Shokan, 1998.

Murray, Douglas J., and Paul R. Viotti, eds. *The Defense Policies of Nations*. Baltimore: The Johns Hopkins Press, 1982.

Muthiah, Alagappa. International Response to Nuclear Tests in South Asia: The Need for a New Policy Framework. *Asia Pacific Issues: Analysis from the East-West Center* 38. Honolulu: East West Center, 15 June 1998.

NHK Hoso Yoron Kenkyujo [NHK Broadcasting Poll Research Institute], ed. *Zusetsu sengo yoron-shi* [Postwar Opinion Polls Illustrated]. 2nd ed. Tokyo: Nippon Hoso Shuppan Kyokai, 1982.

Nagatomi, Yuichiro, ed. *Masayoshi Ohira's Proposal to Evolve the Global Society*. Tokyo: Foundation for Advanced Information and Research, 1988.

Nakai, Yoshifumi. Chugoku no "kyoi" to Nit-Chu, Bei-Chu kankei [The Chinese "Threat" in Japan-China and U.S.-China Relations]. In *Chugoku wa kyoi ka* [Is China Threat?]. ed. Amako Satoshi. Tokyo: Keiso Shobo, 1997.

Nakamura, Akira. *Sengo seiji ni yureta kenpo 9 jo* [The Ups and Downs of Article 9 of the Constitution in Postwar Politics]. Tokyo: Chuo Keizai Sha, 1996.

Nakamura, Hisashi, and Malcolm Dando. Japan's Military Research and Development: A High Technology Deterrent. *Pacific Review* 6 (1993): 177–90.

Nakanishi, Hiroshi. Jiritsu-teki kyocho no mosaku: 1970–nendai no Nihon gaiko [Groping for Self-sufficient Cooperation: Japan's Diplomacy in the 1970s] in *Sengo Nihon gaiko-shi* [The Postwar History of Japanese Diplomacy] ed. Iokibe Makoto. Tokyo: Yuhikaku, 1999.

Nakasone, Yasuhiro. Rethinking the Constitution—Make It a Japanese Document. *Japan Quarterly* 44:3 (July-September 1997).

Nakasone, Yasuhiro. Yomiuri Shimbun Constitutional Studies Group, A Proposal for a Sweeping Revision of the Constitution. *Japan Echo* 22:1 (1995).

Nakata, Toyokazu. Budding Volunteerism. *Japan Quarterly* (January–March 1996); Umahashi Norio, "Gendai kokusai kankei ni okeru NGO: Kokuren o chushin ni" [NGOs in Contemporary International Relations: Focusing on the UN]. *Kokusai mondai* (December 1996): 2–16.

Nani ga Nihon no kokueki nano ka [Symposium: What Is the Japanese National Interest?], *Chuo Koron* (February 1996).

National Institute for Research Advancement. *Jiten 1990 nendai: Nihon no kadai* [The Era of the 1990s: Tasks for Japan]. Tokyo: Sanseido, 1987.

Neilan, Edward. Blame Japan for Much of the Asian Crisis. *Japan Times,* 18 January 1998.

Newhouse, John. The Diplomatic Round: Earth Summit. *The New Yorker,* 1 June 1992.

Newhouse, John. Europe's Rising Regionalism. *Foreign Affairs* 76:1 (January–February 1997): 67–84.

Nihon Kokusai Koryu Senta (Japan Center for International Exchange), ed. *Ajia Taiheiyo no NGO* [NGOs in Asia Pacific]. Tokyo: Aruku, 1998.

Nihon Kokusai Koryu Senta [Japan Center for International Exchange] and Jichitai Kokusaika Kyokai [Council of Local Authorities for International Relations]. *Chiho jichitai no kokusai kyoryoku katsudo no genjo to kadai* [The Status and Problems of International Exchange and Activities of Local Governments]. Tokyo: 1997.

Nihon Kokusai Seiji Gakkai, eds. *21–seiki no Nihon, Ajia, sekai* [Japan, Asia, and the Global System: Toward the Twenty-First Century]. Tokyo: Kokusai Shobo, 1998.

Nihon seiji gakkai nenpo (Annals of the Japanese Political Science Association).*Niju-isseiki ni mukete no ODA kaikaku kondankai hokokusho* [Report of the Council on ODA Reform for the Twenty-first Century]. Tokyo, January 1998.

Nimmo, William F. *Japan and Russia: A Reevaluation in the Post-Soviet Era*. Westport, CT: Greenwood Press, 1994.

Nishimura, Kumao. *Kaitei shinban, Anzenhosho joyaku-ron* [Revised Edition, On the Security Treaty]. Tokyo: Jiji Press, 1967.

———. *Sanfuranshisuko Heiwa Joyaku* [The San Francisco Peace Treaty]. Tokyo: Kajima Kenkyujo Shuppankai, 1971.

Nolan, Cathal J., ed. *The Longman Guide to World Affairs*. London: Longman, 1995.

Nuttall, Simon. Japan and the European Union: Reluctant Partners. *Survival* 38:2 (Summer 1996): 104–20.

Nye, Joseph S., Jr. and William A. Owens. America's Information Edge. *Foreign Affairs* 75:2 (1996).

Nye, Joseph. Coping with Japan. *Foreign Policy* 89 (1992): 96–115.

ODA. Summary 1997, Ministry of Foreign Affairs Internet website, September 1998.

OECD. *Environmental Policies in Japan*. Paris: OECD, 1977.

OECF. *What's the OECF.* Tokyo: OECF, 1990.

———. Operations in FY 1997," OECF Press Release http://www.oecf.go.jp/press/press98/1998/0428–e.htm> (28 April 1998)

Ogata, Sadako. *Sengo Nit-Chu, Bei-Chu kankei* [Japan-China and U.S.-China Relations in the Postwar Era], trans. Soeya Yoshihide. Tokyo: University of Tokyo Press, 1992.

Ogura, Kazuo. Japan's Asia Policy, Past and Future. *Japan Review of International Affairs* 10:1 (Winter 1996): 3–15.

Ohta, Hiroshi. *Japan's Politics and Diplomacy of Climate Change,* doctoral dissertation, Columbia University, New York, 1995.

Okabe, Tatsumi, ed. *Chugoku o meguru kokusai kankyo* [The International Environment Surrounding China]. Tokyo: Iwanami Shoten, 1990.

———. *Ajia seiji no mirai to Nippon* [The Future of Asian Politics and Japan]. Tokyo: Keiso Shobo, 1995.

Okazaki, Hisahiko. *Kokusai josei handan: Rekishi no kyokun, senryaku no tetsugaku* [Judging the International Situation: The Lessons of History, Strategic Philosophy]. Tokyo: PHP Kenkyujo, 1996.

Okonogi, Masao. Masatsu to kyocho no Nik-Kan kankei: Kanjo-teki giron o haise [Friction and Harmony in Japan-Korea Relations: Let's Get Rid of Emotional Arguments]. *Gaiko forum* (December 1995).

Omae, Kenichi. *The Borderless World.* London: Collins, 1990.

Orr, Robert M. *The Emergence of Japan's Foreign Air Power.* NY: Columbia University Press, 1990.

Otake, Hideo. Nihon no boei to kokunai seiji [Japan's Defense Policy and Domestic Politics]. Tokyo: San-ichi Shobo, 1983.

———. *Zoho kaiteiban gendai Nihon no seiji kenryoku keizai kenryoku* [Political and Economic Powers in Contemporary Japan, Expanded and Revised]. Tokyo: San-ichi Shobo, 1996.

Ott, Marvin C. Cambodia: Between Hope and Despair. *Current History* (December 1997).

Overby, Charles. A Quest for Peace with Article 9. *Japan Quarterly* 41:2 (1994).

Owada, Hisashi. "Statement at the Special Committee on Peace-keeping Operations." <http://www.mofa.go.jn/policy/un/pko> (1997).

Ozawa, Ichiro. *Nihon kaizo keikaku* [Plan for restructuring Japan]. Tokyo: Kodansha, 1993.

———. *Blueprint for a New Japan: The Rethinking of a Nation.* Tokyo: Kodansha International, 1994.

Park, Megan. The Growing Role of Non-Governmental Organizations in Global Politics. *Swords and Poughshares: A Journal of International Affairs* 7:1 (1997): 47–62.

Paul, Erik. Japan in Southeast Asia: A Geopolitical Perspective. *Journal of the Asia Pacific Economy* 1:3 (1996): 392–94.

Peek, John M. Japan, the United Nations, and Human Rights. *Asian Survey* 32:2, (February 1992).

Piesse, E. L. Japan and Australia. *Foreign Affairs* IV:3 (1926): 476.

Prestowitz, Clyde V. Jr. *Trading Places: How We Allowed Japan to Take the Lead.* NY: Basic Books, 1988.

Prime Minister's Office. *Heisei 4–nen ban seron chosa nenkan—Zenkoku seron chosa no genkyo* [Public Opinion Polls Yearbook 1992: The Current Situation in National Public Opinion Polls]. Tokyo: Ministry of Finance Printing Bureau, 1993.

Prime Minister's Office. *Monthly Public Opinion Poll,* 1988–93.

Prime Minister's Office, Office of Public Relations, ed. *Seron chosa* [Public Opinion Polls]. Tokyo: Ministry of Finance Printing Bureau, 1998.

Princen, Thomas, and Matthias Finger. *Environmental NGOs in World Politics: Linking the Local and the Global.* London and NY: Routledge, 1994.

Putnam, Robert D. Diplomacy and Domestic Politics: The Logic of Two-level Games. *International Organization* 42:3 (1988): 427–60.

Pyle, Kenneth B. *The Japanese Question: Power and Purpose in a New Era.* Washington, DC: The AEI Press, 1996.

Ranshofen-Wertheimer, E. F. *The International Secretariat: A Great Experiment in International Administration.* Washington, DC: Carnegie Endowment for International Peace, 1945.

Reinicke, Wolfgang H. Global Public Policy. *Foreign Affairs* 76:6 (1997).

Research Institute for Peace and Security (RIPS), ed. *Asian Security 1983.* Tokyo: RIPS, 1983.

———. *Asian Security 1990–91.* London: Brassey's, 1990.

———. *Asian Security 1994–95.* London: Brassey's, 1994.

Rix, Alan. *Japan's Economic Aid: Policy-making and Politics.* London: Croom Helm, 1980.

———. *Coming to Terms.* Sydney: Allen and Unwin, 1986.

———. *Japan's Foreign Aid Challenge: Policy Reform and Aid Leadership* . London and NY: Routledge, 1993.

———. *The Australia-Japan Political Alignment.* London: Routledge, 1999.

Robertson, Myles C. *Soviet Policy Towards Japan.* Cambridge: Cambridge University Press, 1988.

Rodrik, Dani. Sense and Nonsense in the Globalization Debate. *Foreign Policy* 107 (1997): 19–36.

Rosecrance, R. N. *Australian Diplomacy and Japan 1945–1951.* London: Melbourne University Press, 1962.

Ross, Robert S. *Managing a Changing Relationship: China's Japan Policy in the 1990s.* Strategic Studies Institute, U.S. Army War College, 1996.

Rozman, Gilbert. *Japan's Response to the Gorbachev Era, 1985: A Rising Superpower Views a Declining One.* Princeton, New Jersey: Princeton University Press, 1992.

———. Backdoor Japan: The Search for a Way Out Via Regionalism and Decentralization. *Journal of Japanese Studies* 25:1 (1999): 3–31.

Sachs, Wolfgang. Environment. In *The Development Dictionary,* ed. Wolfgang Sachs. London: Zed Books, 1992.

Sakai, Tetsuya. Kyujo-Anpotaisei no shuen [The End of the Article 9/Security Treaty System]. *Kokusai mondai* (March 1993): 32–45.

Salamon, Lester M. The Rise of the Nonprofit Sector. *Foreign Affairs* 73:4 (1994): 109.

Sandholtz, Wayne, Michael Borrus, John Zysman, Ken Conca, Jay Stowsky, Steven Vogel, and Steve Weber. *The Highest Stakes: The Economic Foundations of the Next Security System.* A BRIE Project. NY: Oxford University Press, 1992.

Sasaki, Yoshitaka. Japan's Undue International Contribution. *Japan Quarterly* 40:3 (July–September 1993).

Sase, Masamori. "Shudanteki jieiken" kaishaku no kai [Association for Interpretation of the "Right to Collective Defense"]. *Voice* 223 (July 1996): 128–49.

Sassa, Atsuyuki, Taoka Shunji, and Higaki Takashi, Roundtable discussion. *Ronza* (August 1996), pp. 10–19; reported in FBIS-EAS-96-138.

Sato, Seizaburo. Clarifying the Right of Collective Self-Defense. *Asia-Pacific Review* 3 (Fall–Winter 1996): 91–105.

Scalapino, Robert A., ed. *The Foreign Policy of Modern Japan.* Berkeley: University of California Press, 1977.

Schweller, Randall L. Bandwagoning for Profit: Bringing the Revisionist State Back In. *International Security* 19:1 (1994): 72–107.

Schoppa, Leonard. *Bargaining With Japan: What American Pressure Can and Cannot Do.* NY: Columbia University Press, 1997.

Sekai, Heiwa Kenkyujo, ed. *Nakasone naikakushi: Shiryo-hen* [History of the Nakasone Cabinet: Documents and Materials]. Tokyo: Sekai Heiwa Kenkyujo, 1995.

Sekimoto, Tadahiro. Manufacturing: Japan's Key to the Twenty-first Century. *Japan Echo* 23:4 (1997).

Shinoda, Tomohito. *Soridaijin no kenryoku to shidoryoku* [The Power and Leadership of Prime Ministers]. Tokyo: Toyo Keizai Shimposha, 1994.

Shiroyama, Hideaki, Suzuki Hiroshi, and Hosono Sukehiro, eds. *Chuo shocho no seisaku kettei katei—Nihon kanryosei no kaibo* [The Decision-making Processes of Central Ministries and Agencies: The Anatomy of the Japanese Bureaucracy]. Tokyo: Chuo University Shuppankai, 1999.

Shuman, Michael H. Dateline Main Street: Local Foreign Policies. *Foreign Policy* 65 (1986–87): 154–74.

Silliman, G., and Lela Garner Noble, eds. *Organizing for Democracy, NGOs, Civil Society and the Philippine State.* Honolulu: University of Hawaii Press, 1998.

Smith, Charles. Loyalties under Fire. *Far Eastern Economic Review,* 24 January 1991: 10–12.

Soejima, Takahiko. *Zokkoku Nipponron* [Japan, a Tributary State]. Tokyo: Satsuki Shobo, 1997.

Soeya, Yoshihide. *Nihon gaiko to Chugoku 1945–1972* [Japanese Diplomacy and China 1945–1972]. Tokyo: Keio Tsushin, 1995.

Bibliography

———. Ajia no chitsujo hendo to Nihon gaiko [The Changing Order in Asia and Japanese Diplomacy]. *Kokusai mondai* 444 (March 1997).

———. A Presidential Overflight Rattles Japan. *Wall Street Journal*, 7 July 1998.

Song, Young-sun. Japanese Peacekeeping Operations: Yesterday, Today and Tomorrow. *Asian Perspective* 20:1 (1996).

Stephan, John J. *The Kuril Islands*. Oxford: Clarendon Press, 1974.

Stockwin, J. A. A. *Governing Japan*. Oxford: Blackwell, 1999.

Stockwin, J. A. A., et al. *Dynamic and Immobilist Politics in Japan*. Honolulu: University of Hawaii Press, 1988.

Stokes, B. Divergent Paths—US–Japan Relations Towards the 21st Century. *International Affairs* 72:2 (1996).

Sudo, Sueo. *The Fukuda Doctrine and ASEAN: New Dimensions in Japanese Foreign Policy*. Singapore: Institute of Southeast Asian Studies, 1992.

Sumi, Kazuo. *ODA enjo no genjitsu* [The Realities of ODA]. Tokyo: Iwanami Shinsho, 1989.

Suzuki, Yoji. Kanbojia no kyokun [The Lessons of Cambodia]. *Sekai* 584 (July 1993): 22–30. Takabatake, Michitoshi. Keizai no teitai, Nihon no kosei ni kikikan [Economic Stagnation, Feeling Threatened by Japan's Aggression]. *Ushio* 352 (August 1988).

Takabatake, Michitoshi. Nihon e no keikaishin to hankan no haikei [The Background to Feelings of Foreboding and Prejudice against Japan]. *Ushio* 359 (March 1989): 370–78.

Takeda, Isami. Hakugo seisaku no seiritsu to Nihon no taio [The Establishment of the White Australia Policy and Japan's Response]. *Kokusai seiji* 62:2 (1981).

———. Aratana chiiki kyoryoku to kaihatsu sekinin o motomete [Demanding Responsibility for New Regional Cooperation and Development]. *Sekai rinji zokan* 553 (April 1991).

Tanaka, Akihiko. *Nit–Chu kankei 1945–1990* [Japan–China Relations 1945–1990]. Tokyo: University of Tokyo Press, 1991.

———. *Anzen hosho: Sengo 50 nen no mosaku* [National Security: Postwar Japan's Fifty Years of Groping]. Tokyo: Yomiuri Shimbunsha, 1997.

Tanaka, Takahiko. *Nis-So kokko kaifuku no shiteki kenkyu* [A Historical Study of the Restoration of Japan-Soviet Relations]. Tokyo: Yuhikaku, 1993.

Tanaka, Tsutomu. Chikyuyteki kibo no kankyo mondai ni taisuru waga kuni no taio [Japan's Response to Global Environmental Problems]. *Kikan kankyo kenkyu*. Tokyo: Environmental Research Center. 33 (1981). Taniguchi, Masaki. *Nihon no taibei boeki kosho* [Japan's Trade Negotiations with the United States]. Tokyo: University of Tokyo Press, 1997.

Taylor, Mark Z. Dominance through Technology. *Foreign Affairs* 74:6 (1995).

Taylor, P., and A. J. R. Groom, ed. Introduction to *International Organization. A Conceptual Approach*. London: Frances Pinter Ltd., 1978.

Taylor, P. and A. J. R. Groom. *The United Nations and the Gulf War, 1990–91: Back to the Future?* The Royal Institute of International Affairs Discussion Paper 38. London, 1992.

Tenno, Heika. no Yo Shokon kokka shuseki shusai bansan-kai ni okeru toji [The Emperor's Address in Reply at the Farewell Banquet Sponsored by Yang Shangkun]. In *Nit–Chu kankei kihon shiryo-shu 1970–1992* [A Collection of Basic Documents on Japan-China Relations 970–1992]. Tokyo: Kazankai, 1994.

Terry, Edith. Crisis? What Crisis? Japan Policy Research Institute Working Paper, 50 (1998).

The Australia-Japan Relationship: Towards the Year 2000. Canberra and Tokyo: Australia-Japan Research Centre and Japan Center for Economic Research, 1989.

The Executive Committee of People's Forum for the Global Environment. *Proceedings*. Tokyo, November 1989.

The World Conservation Strategy, compiled and published in 1980 by the International Union for the Conservation of Nature and Natural Resources (IUCN) and the United Nations Environment Programme (UNEP).

This is Yomiuri: Nihonkoku kenpo no subete [Everything You Need to Know about the Japanese Constitution]. Tokyo: Yomiuri Shimbun, May 1997.

Tomita, Nobuo, and Sone Yasunori, eds. *Sekai seiji no naka no Nihon seiji* [Japanese Politics in World Politics]. Tokyo: Yuhikaku, 1983.

Tsuchiyama, Jitsuo. Nichi-Bei domei no kokusai seijiron: Riarizumu, riberaru seidoron, konsutorakutibizumu [International Relations Theories of the U.S.-Japan Alliance: Realism, Liberal-Institutionalism, and Constructivism]. *Kokusai seiji* 115 (1997): 161–79.

Tsuchiyama, Jitsuo. The End of the Alliance?: Dilemmas in the U.S.-Japan Relations. In *United States-Japan Relations and International Institutions after the Cold War*, eds. by Peter Gourevitch, Takashi Ino-guchi, and Courtney Purrington. San Diego: University of California, 1995.

Tsujinaka, Yutaka. *Rieki shudan* [Interest Groups]. Tokyo: Tokyo Daigaku Shuppankai, 1988.

Tsuru, Shigeto. *Nichi-Bei ampo kaisho e no michi* [Pathway to the Dissolution of the U.S.-Japan Security Alliance]. Tokyo: Iwanami Shoten, 1996.

Tsuru, Shigeto, and Helmut Weidner, eds. *Environmental Policy in Japan*. Berlin: Edition Sigma, 1989.

Tweedie, Sandra. *Trading Partners: Australia and Asia 1790–1993*. Sydney: University of New South Wales Press, 1994.

Ueki, Yasuhiro. Japan's UN Diplomacy: Sources of Passivism and Activism. In *Japan's Foreign Policy*, ed. Gerald L. Curtis. New York & London: M.E. Sharpe, 1993.

United States Department of Defense. *A Strategic Framework for the Asian Pacific Rim: Report to Congress*. Washington, DC: Department of Defense, 1992.

United States Department of Defense, Office of International Security Affairs. *United States Security Strategy for the East Asia-Pacific Region*. Washington, DC: Department of Defense, 1995.

United States Department of State. *Foreign Relations of the United States, 1950, VI, East Asia and the Pacific*. Washington, DC: U.S. Government Printing Office, 1976.

Van Wolferen, Karel. *The Enigma of Japanese Power*. Tokyo: Charles E. Tuttle Company, 1993.

Vogel, Ezra F. *Japan as Number 1: Lessons for America*. NY: Harper Colophon Books, 1979.

———. Pax Nipponica. *Foreign Affairs* 64:4 (1986).

Wade, Robert. Japan, the World Bank, and the Art of Paradigm Maintenance: The East Asian Miracle in Political Perspective. *New Left Review* 217 (May–June 1996).

Wakaizumi, Kei. *Tasaku nakarishi o shinzemu to hossu* [I Want to Believe We Had No Alternatives]. Tokyo: Bungei Shunju, 1994.

Walt, Stephen M. *The Origins of Alliances*. Ithaca: Cornell University, 1987.

Walters, F. P. *A History of the League of Nations*. London: Oxford University Press, 1960.

Waltz, Kenneth N. The Emerging Structure of International Politics. *International Security* 18:2 (Fall 1993).

Wan, Ming. Japan and the Asian Development Bank. *Pacific Affairs* 68:4 (Winter 1995–96).

Watanabe, Akio. Nichi-Go kankeishi no shomondai [Some Problems in the History of the Japan–Australia Relationship]. *Kokusai seiji* 68:2 (1981).

———. *Ajia Taiheiyo no kokusai kankei to Nihon* [The International Relations of the Asia–Pacific Region and Japan]. Tokyo: University of Tokyo Press, 1997.

Watanabe, Toshio, and Kusano Atsushi. *Nihon no ODA o dosuruka* [What Should We Do About Japan's ODA?]. Tokyo: NHK Books, 1991.

Watanabe, Toshio. *Nishi-taiheiyou no jidai: Ajia shinsangyo kokka no seiji-keizaigaku* [The Era of the Western Pacific: The Political Economy of Asian Newly Industrializing Countries]. Tokyo: Bungei Shunju, 1989.

Watt, Alan. *The Evolution of Australian Foreign Policy 1938–1965*. Cambridge: Cambridge University Press, 1967.

Weidner, Helmut. Japanese Environmental Policy in an International Perspective: Lessons for a Preventive Approach. In *Environmental Policy in Japan*, eds. Shigeto Tsuru and Helmut Weidner. Berlin: Edition Sigma, 1989.

Weinstein, Martin E. Strategic Thought and the US-Japan Alliance. In *Forecast for Japan: Security in the 1970s*. ed. James William Morley. Princeton: Princeton University Press, 1972.

Weinstein, Martin E. *Japan's Postwar Defense Policy.* NY: Columbia University Press, 1969.
What Has Become of WHO? *Wall Street Journal,* 5 May 1993.
White, James W., Michio Umegaki, and Thomas R. H. Havens, eds. *The Ambivalence of Nationalism: Modern Japan between East and West.* Lanham, MD: University Press of America, 1990.
Willetts, Peter, ed. *"The Conscience of the World": The Influence of Non-governmental Organisations in the UN System.* London: Hurst & Company, 1996.
Winston, Walter B. Bits, Bytes, and Diplomacy. *Foreign Affairs* 76:5 (1997).
Wolfers, Arnold. *Discord and Collaboration.* Baltimore: The Johns Hopkins University Press, 1962.
Woods, Lawrence T. *Asia-Pacific Diplomacy, Non Governmental Organisations and International Relations.* Vancouver: University of British Columbia Press, 1993.
World Commission on Environment and Development (WCED). *Our Common Future.* Oxford: Oxford University Press, 1987.
Yamaguchi, Jiro. *Igirisu no seiji Nihon no seiji* [British and Japanese Politics]. Tokyo: Chikuma Shobo, 1998.
Yamamoto, Tadashi and Yoichi Funabashi. *The Role of Non-State Actors in International Affairs: A Japanese Perspective.* Tokyo: Japan Center for International Exchange, 1995.
Yamamoto, Tadashi, ed. *Emerging Civil Society in the Asia Pacific Community.* Singapore: Institute of Southeast Asian Studies and the Japan Center for International Exchange, 1996.
Yamauchi, Naoto, ed. *NPO detabukku* (Yuhikaku, 1999).
Yanagida, Kunio. *Nihon wa moeteiruka* [Is Japan in Flames?]. Tokyo: Kodansha, 1983.
Yanagitsudo, Hiroyuki. Japan's Economic Assistance after the Cold War. *Japan Times Weekly,* 4–10 December 1995.
Yasutomo, Dennis T. *The Manner of Giving: Strategic Aid and Japanese Foreign Policy.* Lexington, MA: Lexington Books, 1986.
———. T. *The New Multilateralism in Japan's Foreign Policy.* London: Macmillan, 1995.
Yomiuri nenkan [Yomiuri Yearbook] *1999 Data File.* Tokyo: Yomiuri Shimbunsha, 1999.
Yong, Deng. Japan in APEC: The Problematic Leadership Role. *Asian Survey* 37 (1997): 355.
Yoran chosa nenkan [Annual Surveys]. Tokyo: Chuo Chosasha, individual years.
Yoshida, Shigeru. *Kaiso junen* [Reminiscences of Ten Years]. 2 Vols. Tokyo: Shinchosha, 1957.
Young, Oran R. *International Cooperation.* Ithaca: Cornell University Press, 1989.

INDEX

Afghanistan 54, 124, 163, 214, 215
Africa 54, 60, 128-129, 130
   ODA 60, 110, 112, Figure 9.1, 155, 164-165, 168
   Tokyo International Conference on African Development (TICAD) 165
   UN 55, 56, 58, 86, 125, 128, 130
AIDS/HIV 166, 257-258
Akao Nobutoshi 102, 103
Akihito Emperor 235, 237, 245
Article 9 50-51, 96, 105, 124-125, 131, 136-139, 142, 163, 186
   see also Constitution, disarmament
Ashida Hitoshi 138, 139, 140
Asian Development Bank 46, 50, 60, 61, 72, 79, 153
Asian Monetary Fund (AMF) 78, 80, 252, 253, 260, 261
   see also IMF World Bank
Asian Pacific Economic Cooperation (APEC) 13, 50, 62, 78, 206
   Australia 290, 292, 293, 295
   Japanese views 181, 182
Association of South-East Asian Nations (ASEAN) 56, 76, 206, 251, 260, 263, 271, 276
   Asian Regional Forum (ARF) 183, 206, 217, 252, 257, 268, 269, 292
   August 1997 meeting 160-161
   Cambodia 251, 254-256
   Post-Ministerial Conference (PMC) 257

Bangladesh 77, 271, 274-275, 279
Basic Treaty of Friendship and Cooperation of 1976 290, 294
big business (*zaikai*) 13-14, 213
   see also Doyukai, gyokai
Brazil 24, 113, 168
   Rio de Janeiro Earth Summit of 1992 (UNCED) 106, 108, 109
Brezhnev, Leonid 179, 211
Britain *see* United Kingdom
Brunei 154, 256, 258
Bruntland Commission 98-99
bubble economy 102, 146, 170, 260
bureaucracy 7-11, 218, 264
   see also Diet, LDP, prime ministers

Burma *see* Myanmar
Bush, George H. 69, 220

Cabinet 6, 7
   see also Diet
Cambodia 128-130, 155, 251, 252, 254-255, 258
Carter, Jimmy 88, 179, 242
China (PRK) 226-240, 246-248, 251, 254
   aid 26, 77, 205, 271
   Cambodian civil war 254-255
   defense 183, 187
   diplomacy 178, 179, 187, 214, 215
   fears of Japan 125, 129, 132
   'Hozan (Baoshan) shock' 232, 233
   human rights 26, 85, 90, 181
   nuclear capability 186, 235-236, 239-240, 269-270
   territorial disputes 186, 190, 236-237, 256-257
   trade 70, 204, 227-228
   Treaty of Peace and Friendship (1978) 215, 230, 231, 237
Chun Doo-hwan, 242, 243, 245
Clean Government Party (*Komeito*) 12-13, 106, 127, 131
Clinton administration 186
Clinton, Bill 79, 185, 269
   and Hashimoto joint declaration 147, 148, 186-187, 236, 246
Cold War 253, 267
   end 14, 49, 52, 96, 105, 145, 147, 180
   Japan-Soviet ties 210, 214-215, 222-223
Colombo Plan 50, 155-156
Common Foreign and Security Policy (CFSP) 194, 203, 207
Comprehensive Test Ban Treaty (CTBT) 54, 167, 270
Constitution 4, 25, 46, 137, 162, 178, 237
   Article 9 50-51, 96, 105, 124-125, 131, 136-139, 142, 163, 186
   proposed revisions 14, 131, 132
Convention Against Torture (CAT) 90, 94
Convention on the Elimination of All Forms of Racial Discrimination (CERD) 86, 87
CLAIR (Council of Local Authorities for International Relations) 24, 30- 31, 262, 278
   see also MOHA

Index

currency crisis 78-80, 203-204, 251
   Indonesia 78, 252, 260, 261
   see also AMF

Defense Agency (*Boeicho*) 215-217, 258
Defense Outline *see* National Defense Program Outline
defense policy 136-149
   see also Article 9, disarmament, U.S.-Japan security treaty
Democratic Party of Japan (DPJ-*Minshuto*) 11-12
Democratic Socialist Party of Japan (DSP-*Minshato*) 106, 127
Deng Xiaoping 231, 232
DAC (Development Assistance Committee) 156-158, 160, 163, 171
   see also ODA
Diet 4-7, 11-13, 92, 127, 129, 264
   budgets 262
   EU 197
   nuclear nonproliferation 139, 143, 144, 267-268
   ODA 170
   see also bureaucracy, LDP, prime ministers
diplomacy 132, 231, 242
   Asia 226-248, 255-256, 270
   'bandwagoning'/'balancing' 140-141
   'checkbook' 33, 34, 126, 180, 255
   Russia ('smile') 211, 212, 219-222
disarmament 136-149
   see also Article 9, nuclear disarmament
Discussion Group on Global-scale Environmental Problems 98-99
   see also WCED
domestic politics 3-15
   see also Cabinet, Diet, *and under* specific political parties
Doyukai (Japan Committee for Economic Development) 13, 14 *see also gyokai, zaikai*

Earth Summit of 1992 in Rio de Janeiro 104, 106, 107, 108, 109
Eastern Europe 56, 130, 214
   ODA 110, 112, 113, Figure 9.1, 155
EMU (Economic and Monetary Union) 203-204, 207
   see also EU
EPA (Economic Planning Agency) 4, 8, 167, 170
EROA (Economic Rehabilitation in Occupied Areas) 100-101
   see also GAROIA
environment 96-117, 169, 217, 258-259, 261
   NGOs 28
   SNGs 24, 25
EU (European Union) 22, 75, 194-207
   political relations 177, 202-203, 204-206
   trade 195, 197-202, Table 11.1, 199

FDI (foreign direct investment) 70-71
foreign pressure (*gaiatsu*) 3, 182
Fourth Japan-China Agreement on Nongovernmental Trade 228, 229
Fukuda Doctrine 160-161, 254, 263

gaimusho see MOFA
GATT (General Agreement on Tariffs and Trade) 67, 69, 140, 195, 197, 198, 288
   Kennedy round 157
   Uruguay round 69
globalism 180-181
globalization 66-67, 70-75, 217-218
   business interests 14, 18, 65, 80

Gorbachev, Mikhail 146, 214-216, 219, 220
GARIOA (Government and Relief in Occupied Areas) 100-101, 153
   see also EROA
GNP (Gross National Product) 157, 195
   defense budgets 144, 145
   Japan's global share Figure 4.1, 70
   ODA 101, Figure 9.2, 157, Figure 9.3, 158
Group of Eight Industrialized Nations (G8) 255, 268
Group of High Level Intergovernmental Experts (G18) 52
Group of Seven Industrialized Nations (G7) 219, 220, 234-235, 259, 261
   summits 100, 216, 220, 234
Guidelines for U.S.-Japan Defense Cooperation of 1978 6, 9, 144, 145, 186
   revised 1997 26, 147, 148, 258
Gulf War 33, 73, 96, 197
   human rights 89-90
   Japan's role 126-127, 146, 180, 185
gyokai (sectoral world) 13 *see also Doyukai, zaikai*

Habomai islands *see* Northern Territories
The Hague Declaration of 1991 (Joint Declaration between the EC and Japan) 202-203
Hashimoto administration 5, 6, 10, 92, 170, 189
Hashimoto Discussion Group for Fundamental Environmental Issues, 104-105, 106
Hashimoto Ryutaro 268-269, 280
   ASEAN 239, 252, 257-258, 261, 268-270, 280
   and Clinton Joint Declaration 147, 148, 186-187, 236, 246
   environment policy 103
   ODA 165, 261
   and Yeltsin plan 217-219, 221
Hatoyama administration 11, 138
Hatoyama Ichiro 138-139, 210
Hirohito, Emperor 245
Hosokawa administration 146
Hosokawa Morihiro 11, 73, 237, 245
humanitarian aid 33, 61, 73, 122-134, 217, 218
human rights 26, 83-94, 181, 242
   ODA 167-168

Ikeda Hayato 228-229
India 274-275, 277-279
   anti-Japanese feeling 132, 161, 254
   currency crisis 78, 252, 260-261
   environment 110, 112, 258
   Indonesia 85, 129, 251-252, 256, 278
   nuclear testing 26, 54, 60, 266-270, 275-276, 279-280
   ODA 77, 79, 110, 113, 155, 156, 165, 167, 169, 271-272
International Convention on Civil and Politics Rights (ICCPR) 86-89
International Convention on Economic, Social and Cultural Rights (ICESCR) 86-88
internationalism 53, 57
internationalization 48-49, 68-69, 101-103, 104
IMF (International Monetary Fund) 69, 74, 140, 165, 217, 259, 261, 263
   see also AMF, World Bank
International Peace Cooperation Law (IPCL) 122, 127-128, 129, 134
investments 198-199, Table 11.2, 201, 204
   in Asia 274-275, 279
   see also ODA, trade
Iraq 54, 57, 124, 126
Ishihara Shintaro 26, 65, 75

Japan Chamber of Commerce and Industry (*Nissho*) 13
Japan Committee for Economic Development (*Doyukai*) 13, 14
Japan Communist Party (JCP) 11, 12, 106
Japan Exchange Teaching (JET) Program 24, 30-31
Japan Federation of Economic Organizations (*Keidanren*) 13, 171, 213, 262, 275
   Doko Mission 197
   environment Charter 107-108
Japan Federation of Employers' Associations (*Nikkeiren*) 13
The Japan Foundation 277-278
Japan International Cooperation Agency (JICA) 111-112, 153, 165-166, 168, 278
Japan New Party (JNP/*Nihon Shinto*) 11, 131
Japan Socialist Party (JSP) 11,12, 92, 127
   see also Social Democratic Party of Japan
JANIC (Japanese NGO Center for International Cooperation) 19
Japanese studies 200, 207
Joint Declaration of 1956 (Japan and the Soviet Union) 210, 221
Joint Declaration between the EC and Japan (The Hague Declaration of 1991) 202-203
Joint Declaration between Hashimoto and Clinton 147, 148, 186-187, 236, 246

Kaifu Toshiki 100, 104, 245, 271
   Gulf War 126, 127
   ODA policy 92, 93, 163-164, 216, 234-235, 276
Keidanren see Japan Federation of Economic Organizations
Kim Dae-jung 237, 245-246
Kishi Nobusuke 122, 139, 156
   foreign policy 210-211, 228, 229
Komei/Komeito see Clean Government Party
Korean Peninsula 3, 7, 243, 254, 257
   invasions 68, 177
   Korean Peninsula Energy Development Organization (KEDO) 183, 205, 244
   'Rhee Line' 240-241
   security 186, 241-242, 244
   see also Korean War, South Korea, North Korea
Korean War 138, 140-141, 178, 240, 246
Kuril Islands 211
   see also Northern Territories

landmines, efforts to eliminate 28-29, 54, 183, 206
Laos 155, 166
Latin America 24, 58, 106, 124, 128
   ODA 111, 112, 113, Figure 9.1, 155, 163, 168
less developed countries (LDCs) 159, 168, 169
   see also newly industrialized economies
Liberal Democratic Party (LDP) 4, 11, 12, 146, 178
   business interests 13-14
   coalition politics 11, 12, 46, 56, 92, 106
   Cold War politics 212
   Constitution 131
   criticism of 14
   Diet 11, 221
   diplomacy 133, 187
   economic reforms 262
   environmental policy 103-107
   human rights policy 88-89
   NGOs 28
   peacekeeping 46
   Russia policy 212, 213, 219, 221
   security policy 106
   support of U.S.-Japan security alliance, 13, 144

   UN 133
   Yoshida faction 212
   see also bureaucracy, Diet, prime ministers
Liberal Party (*Jiyuto*) 12, 13, 46, 56, 106
   see also Ozawa Ichiro

Mahathir bin Mohammed 82, 85, 182, 261
Malaysia 85, 251, 258, 278, 292
   currency crisis 78, 260, 261
   ODA 169
   Spratlys dispute 256
Maldives 266, 278
Maritime Self-Defense Force (MSDF) 126-127, 244
   see also Self-Defense Force
media 8, 14-15, 19, 27, 132, 232-233, 242
Mexico 111, 112
Middle East 54, 57, 102, 124, 197, 202, 267, 277
   ODA 110, 112, 154, Figure 9.1, 155, 162
   Palestine 205
   PKO 126, 128
Miki administration 143, 144
Miki Takeo 144, 145
minimalism 226, 234
Ministry of Foreign Affairs (MOFA) (*Gaimusho*) 6-10, 18, 31, 53, 102
   human rights 89-90, 91
   NGOs 28-29, 30
   ODA 92-94, 167, 171, 261
   Russia 212, 213
   UN 90-91
   U.S.-Japan security treaty 141
Ministry of Home Affairs (MOHA) 24, 31
   see also CLAIR
Ministry of International Trade and Industry (MITI) 8, 10, 31, 213, 214
   environmental projects 113-114
   Multifunction Polis 293-294
   ODA 31, 159, 160, 167, 171
Miyazawa Kiichi 74, 79, 106, 133, 261
Multifunction Polis (MFP) project 284, 293-294
multilateralism 43-48, 55, 61, 67, 74-75
   Australia 292, 294
Murayama administration 12
Murayama Tomiichi 92, 235, 237, 256
Myanmar (Burma)78, 155
   Aung San Suu Kyi 256
   ODA 164, 167-168, 169, 251, 252, 256

Nakasone administration 73, 145, 148
Nakasone Yasuhiro 7, 65, 89, 101, 126
   'autonomous defense' plan 144
   China 73, 233
   Korea 242-243
   Russia 221-222
National Defense Program Outline of 1976 (NDPO) 6, 144, 146, 238, 246
National Police Agency 5, 6
National Police Reserve 138
   see also Self-Defense Force
National Safety Force 138
   see also Self-Defense Force
nationalism 180, 182-183
   Chinese 215
NATO (North Atlantic Treaty Organization) 33, 148, 207
Nepal 27, 89, 266, 278
newly industrialized economies (NIEs) 70, 76, 78, 259
   see also less developed countries
New Frontier Party (NFP-*Shinshinto*) 11-12, 106
   see also Ozawa Ichiro

Index

New Japan Party (*Nihon Shinto*) 11, 106
Nikkeiren see Japan Federation of Employers' Associations
Nissho see Japan Chamber of Commerce and Industry
Nixon, Richard 51, 142-144, 179, 230
   and Sato joint communiqué of 1969 242, 243
nongovernmental organizations (NGOs) 18-37, 58, 171, 278
   see also SNGs
nonprofit organizations (NPOs) 19
North Korea (DPRK) 25, 67, 148, 240-248
   fears of Japan 132, 133, 242
   humanitarian aid 205
   nuclear development 117, 147, 148, 244, 267
   threats 187, 188
   see also Korean Peninsula, Korean War, South Korea
Northern Territories (Habomai islands) 178, 190, 210-213, 215, 223
   Day of 1981 212
   demilitarization 216
   economic cooperation 217, 218
   peace treaty 209, 210, 219, 220-221
   public opinion 211, 215, 219, 220, 221, 222
   residents 220
   'two island' offer 210, 211
   'syndrome' 211
   see also territorial disputes
nuclear development, 244, 266
nuclear disarmament 25-26, 54-55
   Diet 139, 143, 144, 267-268
   foreign policy 11, 139, 167, 216, 267-271, 276-277
Nuclear Non-Proliferation Treaty (NPT) 54, 143-144, 183, 235-236, 267-268

Obuchi administration 4, 5, 6, 10
Obuchi Keizo 28, 33, 104, 165
   currency crisis 79, 80
   diplomacy 216-220, 221, 237, 245
   environment 258-259, 261
ODA (Official Development Assistance) 54, 61, 62, 90, 152-172
   in 1996 93-94, Table 9.1, 154
   Asia 77, 79, 80, 155, 160, 165-166
   Charter 164, 271-272
   China 26, 167, 231
   currency crisis relief Table 4.1, 79
   doubling plan 160-161, Figure 9.5, 161
   environmental 109-115, Table 6.1, 110, Table 6.2, 113, Table 6.3, 115-116
   four principles 92-93
   global 71-72, Figure 4.3, 72, 160-162, 185
   nuclear disarmament policy 164, 167, 270-271, 277
   peace efforts 55, 165
   SNGs 24
   South Asia 271, 272, 280
   Southeast Asia 168, 252, 255, 261, 271-273
   see also DAC, OECD
Ohira administration 73
Ohira Masayoshi 101, 162, 232
Okinawa 6, 143, 236
   rape incident of 1995 14-15, 147, 185
   reversion 143, 144, 185, 211, 242
Organization for Economic Cooperation and Development (OECD) 50, 62, 69, 140, 156-157
   DAC 160, 163
   energy cooperation 204-205
   environmental policy 97, 169
   nuclear disarmament policy 268
   see also DAC, ODA

Organisation for Security and Cooperation in Europe (OSCE) 149, 207
Overseas Economic Cooperation Fund (OECF) 167
Ozawa Ichiro 5, 73, 127, 130, 131, 133
   Liberal Party (*Jiyuto*) 12, 13, 46, 56, 106
   New Frontier Party (*Shinshinto*) 11-12, 106

Pakistan 124, 274-275
   nuclear development 26, 54, 266-270, 275, 276, 279-280
   ODA 77, 162, 167, 271-272
Peace and Reform Network 13
   see also Komeito
peacekeeping efforts 33, 34, 46, 54, 55-57, 122-134, 180
Philippines 78, 89, 125, 132, 256
   ODA 77, 113, 155, 166
PKOs (UN Peacekeeping Operations) 56, 122, 123-124, 127-128, 181, 255-256
   see also peacekeeping efforts
Plaza Accord 71, 101, 259
pluralism 19-20, 32-33
political parties 11-13, Table 1.1, 12
   see also under specific party names
prime ministers 4-7, 9, 15
   see also bureaucracy, Diet, LDP

racism 89, 92
   Australia 283-284, 286-287, 289
Reagan, Ronald 145, 163, 179, 184, 242
regionalism 180-182, 218
regionalization 65-81
Rengo (Japanese Trade Union Council) 131
Rhee Syngman ('Rhee Line') 240-241
Russia 57, 148, 183, 190, 209-223, 242
   China 227, 230-231, 237, 246
   nuclear capability 186, 216
   see also Northern Territories

San Francisco Peace Treaty 154, 277
   Korea 141, 240, 246
   Russia 178, 210, 211, 226-227
   Taiwan 226-227
   see also United Nations
Sato Eisaku 230
   and Nixon joint communiqué of 1969 142-144, 242-243
security 13, 55-57
   economics-driven 184, 186
   US-guaranteed 139, 143, 238
   see also U.S.-Japan security treaty
Self-Defense Force (SDF) 5, 138, 188, 277
   1957 law 124, 141, 189
   overseas deployment 73, 102, 122, 127-128, 129
   see also Maritime Self-Defense Force
Senkaku (Tiaoyu) islands 186, 190, 236, 237, 247
Shinshinto see New Frontier Party
Singapore 85, 90, 154, 258, 262, 278
   fears of Japan 125, 129
sister cities 21, 22, 24, 25, 36
Social Democratic Party of Japan (SDPJ) 4-5, 11, 12, 106, 133
   see also Japan Socialist Party
South Asia 266-280
   see also specific countries
South Asia Association for Regional Cooperation (SAARC) 276
   see also ASEAN
Southeast Asia 251-264
   see also currency crisis

Index

South Korea (ROK) 25, 89, 165, 237, 240-248, 251, 267
  currency crisis 78, 80, 260
  fears of Japan 125, 129, 132, 240-241
  Russia 213, 215, 220
  see also Korean Peninsula, Korean War, North Korea
Spratly Islands 236, 252, 256-257
Sri Lanka (Ceylon) 266, 273, 274, 277, 278
  Colombo Plan 50, 155-156
  ODA 77, 113, 271
Strategic Defense Initiative (SDI) 145, 148
Structural Impediment Initiatives (SII) 69, 74
subnational governments (SNGs) 18-37
  see also NGOs
Suharto, General 252, 258, 260, 261
  see also Indonesia
Suzuki administration 145, 163
Suzuki Zenko 7, 97, 105, 242

Taiwan 26, 148, 177, 239, 251, 254, 278
  China 186, 187, 228, 233, 235, 236, 247
  San Francisco peace treaty 226-227
  Senkaku (Tiaoyu) islands 236
Taiwan Straits 142, 228, 236, 239
Takeshima islands 241, 247
Takeshita Noboru 100-101, 103-104, 125-126, 161
  UNCED 108, 220
Tanaka Kakuei 3, 161, 254, 290
  diplomacy 213, 222, 226, 230, 242
territorial disputes
  Habomai islands *see* Northern Territories
  Senkaku (Tiaoyu) islands 186, 190, 236
  Spratly islands 236, 252, 256-257
  Takeshima islands 241, 247
Thailand 111, 251, 258, 278
  anti-Japanese feelings 161, 254
  currency crisis 78, 260
  ODA 77, 79, 113, 165
Theater Missile Defense (TMD) 148-149
Tiananmen Square incident 93, 234, 239, 240
Tiaoyu islands *see* Senkaku islands, territorial disputes
trade 3, 162, 195, 197-205
  Australia 286, 288, 289, 290
  China 70, 204, 227-228
  Russia 212-214, 218
  South Asia 273-275
Treaty of Friendship and Cooperation of 1976 284, 289, 290
Treaty of Peace and Friendship of 1978 215, 230, 231, 237
Treaty of Rome 194, 195, 196
Tumen project 213, 214

United Kingdom (UK) 140, 143, 156, 207
  Australia 285-287
  trade 198, 199, 200, 201, 203-204
United Nations (UN) 43-48, 50-60, 90-91, 153, 212, 230
  centrism 122-123, 130
  Charter 60, 85, 93, 96, 125
  CTAD (Conference on Trade and Development/UNCTAD) 157
  HCR (UN High Commissioner for Refugees) 55, 85, 86
  HRC (UN Human Rights Committee) 86, 88, 89, 91
  Japan's membership 50, 69, 122
  reforms 52, 58, 60

TAC (Transitional Authority in Cambodia/UNTAC) 255
  see also San Francisco Peace Treaty
UNCED (UN Conference on Environment and Development) 102, 166
  Rio de Janeiro Earth Summit of 1992 104, 106, 107, 108, 109
UN PKOs (UN Peacekeeping Operations) 56, 122, 123-124, 127-128, 181, 255-256
  see also peacekeeping efforts
UN Security Council 50, 52, 57, 123, 132, 188 206, 254, 270
  divisions in 269-270
  Japan's bid for permanent seat 47, 51, 58-59, 130, 132-133, 203, 216
  reforms 58, 59-60
United States (US) 49, 79, 177-191, 184-189
  diplomacy 44, 75, 210
  human rights 83, 88, 89, 94
  kenbei (dislike of USA) 182, 183
  SDI 145, 148
  SII 69, 74
  trade with 66, 76-77, 195
  UN 51, 188
U.S.-Japan security treaty 12, 96, 142, 178-179, 185, 188
  ASEAN 257, 258
  China policy 237-240
  Cold War 214, 215
  criticisms 182, 186
  interpretations 141
  Joint Security Declaration of 1996 238, 246
  revisions 211, 229
  South Asia 277, 279
  support for 184, 217
  see also Article 9

Vietnam 142, 242, 254-255, 274
  investments in 275-276
  Spratlys dispute 256
  war 27, 179

Whitlam, Gough 289-290
World Bank 60, 61, 72, 79, 109, 153
  repayment of funds 154, 166, 259
  see also AMF, IMF
WCED (World Commission on Environment and Development/Brundtland Commission) 98, 99
  see also Discussion Group on Global-scale Environmental Problems
WHO (World Health Organisation) 50, 59, 123
WTO (World Trade Organization) 22, 50, 74, 181, 203
World War II 232-233, 253, 254, 276-277
  Australia 283, 287, 291
  reparations 154-155, 178

Yeltsin, Boris 216, 217, 219, 220
Yoshida administration 138, 210
Yoshida Doctrine 44, 69, 73, 77, 141-142
Yoshida Shigeru 125, 137, 140, 154-155
  China relations 227, 247
  LDP faction 212
  US security treaty 138, 227
Yugoslavia 33-34, 197, 205, 206

zaibatsu (business cliques) 137, 138, 178
zaikai (big business) 13-14, 213 *see also* Doyukai, gyokai

Printed in the United States
86525LV00002B/160-189/A